The Single Woman in Medieval and Early Modern England:

Her Life and Representation

Medieval and Renaissance
Texts and Studies

Volume 263

The Single Woman in Medieval and Early Modern England:

HER LIFE AND REPRESENTATION

by

Laurel Amtower

&

Dorothea Kehler

Arizona Center for Medieval and Renaissance Studies
Tempe, Arizona
2003

Dust jacket design by Dorothea Kehler.

© Copyright 2003
Arizona Board of Regents for Arizona State University

Library of Congress Cataloging-in-Publication Data
Amtower, Laurel.
  The single woman in medieval and early modern England : her life and representation / by Laurel Amtower & Dorothea Kehler.
    p. cm. — (Medieval and Renaissance texts and studies / v. 263)
  Includes bibliographical references and index.
  ISBN 0-86698-306-6 (alk. paper)
  1. English literature — Early modern, 1500–1700 — History and criticism. 2. Women in literature. 3. English literature — Middle English, 100–1500 — History and criticism. 4. Women and literature — England — History — 16th century. 5. Women and literature — England — History — To 1500. 6. Women — England — History — Renaissance, 1450–1600. 7. Women — England — History — Middle Ages, 500–1500. 8. Single women — England — History — 16th century. 9. Single women — England — History — To 1500. 10. Single women in literature. I. Kehler, Dorothea, 1936- . II. Title. III. Medieval & Renaissance Texts & Studies (Series) ; v. 263.

PR151.W6A76 2003
420.9'3522--dc22   2003059605

This book is made to last.
It is set in Bembo,
smythe-sewn and printed on acid-free paper
to library specifications.

Printed in the United States of America

For Teddy —

"A son who is the theme of honor's tongue …"

Contents

Introduction   ix
    Laurel Amtower and Dorothea Kehler

Part I: Celebrating Celibacy

1   The Single Woman as Saint: Three Anglo-Norman Success Stories   1
    Jane Zatta

2   I Want to Be Alone: The Single Woman in Fifteenth-Century Legends of St. Katherine of Alexandria   21
    Paul Price

3   Gender, Marriage, and Knighthood: Single Ladies in Malory   41
    Dorsey Armstrong

Part II: Repudiating Marriage

4   To Be or Not to Be Married: Single Women, Money-lending, and the Question of Choice in Late Tudor and Stuart England   65
    Judith M. Spicksley

5   A Strange Hatred of Marriage: John Lyly, Elizabeth I, and the Ends of Comedy   97
    Jacqueline Vanhoutte

Part III: Imaginary Widowhood

6   Chaucer's Sely Widows   119
    Laurel Amtower

7	(Re)creations of a Single Woman: Discursive Realms of the Wife of Bath Jeanie Grant Moore	133
8	Good Grief: Widow Portraiture and Masculine Anxiety in Early Modern England Allison Levy	147

Part IV: Sexuality and Revirgination

9	Working Girls: Status, Sexual Difference, and Disguise in Ariosto, Spenser, and Shakespeare Tracey Sedinger	167
10	"News from the Dead": The Strange Story of a Woman Who Gave Birth, Was Executed, and Was Resurrected as a Virgin Susan C. Staub	193
11	Frances Howard and Middleton and Rowley's *The Changeling*: Trials, Tests, and the Legibility of the Virgin Body Mara Amster	211

Index 233

INTRODUCTION

During the Middle Ages and the Renaissance, women in England might occupy several different social categories in accordance with their life stages, lifestyles, and economic status. Among these, the category of "single woman" is surely the largest and most complex, including not only "life-cycle" single women[1] — widows or young women who might eventually marry — but also women who never married: well-born "spinsters" provided for by their families, entrepreneurs, wage earners — many of whom were servants or farm workers — nuns and the handicapped (the latter also often sheltered by the church), unwed mothers, crossdressers, some of whom may have been lesbians, kept women, and prostitutes.[2] The exaggerated range of experiences to which each of these lifestyles and professions is open leads to a dizzying picture of the category of unmarried women in the Middle Ages and early modern period. That is to say, since at some stage in her life, if only the earliest, every female is single, every woman is a life-cycle single woman and grist for our mill.

There is no shortage of grist. As Maryanne Kowaleski's recent study of single women observes, some thirty percent of all women were single in the late fourteenth century.[3] And yet single women play only a peripheral role in the official

---

[1] Judith M. Bennett and Amy M. Froide, eds., *Singlewomen in the European Past, 1250–1800* (Philadelphia, 1999), 2.

[2] See Olwen Hufton's superb historical account, *The Prospect Before Her: A History of Women in Western Europe 1500–1800* (New York, 1998).

[3] Maryanne Kowaleski, "Singlewomen in Medieval and Early Modern Europe: The Demographic Perspective," in *Singlewomen in the European Past*, 46, 326. The mid-seventeenth century was another demographic high water mark for single women. Note that Kowaleski's seventeenth-century statistics are only for lifelong single women: see "Singlewomen," 53. For other studies on the demographics of single women, see Vivien Brodsky Elliott, "Single Women in the London Marriage Market: Age, Status and Mobility, 1598–1619," in *Marriage and Society: Studies in the Social History of Marriage*, ed. R. B. Outhwaite (New York, 1981), 81–100; David R. Weir, "Rather Never Than Late: Celibacy and Age at Marriage in English Cohort Fertility, 1541–1871," *Journal of Family History* 9 (1984): 340–54; Roger Schofield, "English Marriage Patterns Revisited," *Journal of Family History* 10 (1985): 2–20; L. R. Poos, *A Rural Society After the Black Death: Essex 1350–1525* (Cambridge, 1991), esp. 148–58 and the chapter on servants, 183–206; and P. J. P.

and literary discourse of the Middle Ages. Though single women appear everywhere in the literary landscape, they appear only rarely as major protagonists; they are allotted only infrequent speaking roles, and are seldom treated as members of a broader class sharing specific economic and social interests. Not until the sixteenth century do single women begin to take their place in literature as individuals whose interest and philosophy derive at least in part from their single status and its concerns.

Insofar as single women are not so much nonexistent as they are simply omitted from discourse or elided into the more general concept of "everyman," the problem for scholars of women's history is to recover their various voices from the "white spaces" of the text. Yet the discourse of representation — whether expressed in the literary text, the portrait, or the performance — has ineluctable deficiencies when used as an instrument for recovering the absent or marginalized voice. We can, if not recover, approximate recovery by assuming that the subject represented is always accompanied by what is *not* represented or what is not said, insofar as the dominant voice or image emerges only at the cost of suppressing or even erasing subordinated elements. There is no such entity as the eponymous "everyman" that so glibly presents himself as the homologous median of medieval and early modern culture. Nor can a discourse of representation itself exist without a silencing or erasure of the assumptions upon which its illusion of verisimilitude is based. The task of analysis is to identify what is absent in representational discourse: to make the silence speak, to decode the unspoken, and to translate the dissimulation.

Yet how to accomplish this? If we understand the representation of reality in Baudrillard's sense as the endless reproduction of "simulacra" whose original model never existed, then ideology and its authorized discourses merely project an illusion of essentiality that not only distorts reality but also conceals the utter absence of the real. Certainly the representation of women in both official and popular discourse is itself fictive, insofar as women are stylized according to a framework that replicates the values of the controlling ideology. Mary Douglas writes that the body, and particularly the female body, is less physical than symbolic in construct: situated and situational, it becomes for most societies the central locus for a series of coded relations to authority and traditional belief.[4] When this symbolic body is invoked as literary representation, it is even further from a reality that never was. The essence of women themselves is presented as only the "shadow" in a discourse that "distorts rather than imitates" historical actuality.[5] Nevertheless, if literature seems doubly illusionary insofar as it exists at the "shadow limits" of a reality forever absent to discourse, it still allows us a medium through which an author can both unravel

---

Goldberg, *Women, Work, and Life Cycle in a Medieval Economy: Women in York and Yorkshire, c. 1300–1520* (Oxford, 1992).

[4] Mary Douglas, *Natural Symbols: Explorations in Cosmology*, 2nd ed. (New York, 1982), xxii.

[5] We borrow the metaphor from Pierre Macherey, *A Theory of Literary Production*, trans. Geoffrey Wall (London, 1978), 61.

illusion and transform a reader's relationship to ideology.[6] If we cannot entirely recoup the experiences of single women, we can at least trace the presence of those experiences by exposing the various mechanisms of their erasure.

Happily, several excellent studies of single women have recently appeared that begin to undertake this work. Most notably, Judith M. Bennett and Amy M. Froide's anthology, *Singlewomen in the European Past*, spans the Middle Ages through the eighteenth century, and treats never-married women as occupying not only such traditional categories as lawful workers and dependents but also as epitomes of courtly behavior and, in contrast, as prostitutes and lesbians. Another recent collection, *Young Medieval Women,* edited by Katherine J. Lewis, Noël James Menuge, and Kim M. Phillips, touches upon the issue of singleness by defining gendered identity through life-cycle experience. Olwen Hufton's monumental social history, *The Prospect Before Her*, while limited neither to single women nor to England, includes important chapters on widows, kept women, and prostitutes. Various other studies are relevant to particular categories of single women or to aspects of their lives.[7]

What this research shares is an approach to the study of women that insists upon their irreducibility to a single general category or experience. If each stage of the woman's life and each occupational status is organized around a theoretical principle of femininity, or a feminine body, it is not because the female body contains an essential nature or gendered being. By emphasizing the importance of the many variables that affect the female's experience and self-identification — her nationality, her stage in the life-cycle, her occupation, familial or marital status, and the like — the female body may be decoded according to the defined contexts that represent or encode it in historically specific ways. Thus, women's history may be approached not merely as an attempt to unmask supposed suppression by the patriarchy, but as

---

[6] Macherey, *Theory of Literary Production*, 64.

[7] See especially *Maids and Mistresses, Cousins and Queens: Women's Alliances in Early Modern England*, ed. Susan Frye and Karen Robertson (New York and Oxford, 1999); Mark Thornton Burnett, *Masters and Servants in English Renaissance Drama and Culture: Authority and Obedience* (New York, 1997); Vern L. Bullough and James A. Brundage, *Handbook of Medieval Sexuality* (New York, 1996); Ruth Mazo Karras, *Common Women: Prostitution and Sexuality in Medieval England* (Oxford, 1996); Judith M. Bennett, *Ale, Beer and Brewsters in England: Women's Work in a Changing World 1300–1600* (Oxford, 1996), and P. J. P. Goldberg, ed., *Woman is a Worthy Wight: Women in English Society c. 1200–1500* (Wolfeboro Falls, NH, 1992). Several collections on widows have also appeared recently: see especially Sue Sheridan Walker, ed., *Wife and Widow in Medieval England* (Ann Arbor, 1993); Caroline M. Barron and Anne F. Sutton, eds., *Medieval London Widows 1300–1500* (London, 1994); Sandra Cavallo and Lyndan Warner, eds., *Widowhood in Medieval and Early Modern Europe* (London, 1999); and Cindy L. Carlson and Angela Jane Weisl, eds., *Constructions of Widowhood and Virginity in the Middle Ages* (New York, 1999). Other recent works on women in early modern England with sections on single women include Amy Louise Erickson, *Women and Property in Early Modern England* (London, 1993); Kate Aughterson, ed., *Renaissance Woman: A Sourcebook: Constructions of Femininity in England* (New York, 1995); Margaret R. Sommerville, *Sex and Subjection: Attitudes to Women in Early Modern Society* (London, 1995); and Joan Larsen Klein, ed., *Daughters, Wives and Widows: Writings by Men About Women and Marriage in England, 1500–1640* (Urbana, 1992).

a chance to understand the female body in its various manifestations as a site upon which a very particular symbolic load is invested and exercised.

Groundbreaking as is the past decade's work on women's history, books that deal with ideological representations of single women in the literary or visual media are rare.[8] We seek to remedy this situation. While the essays in this anthology are culturally sensitive, all but one — Judith Spicksley's crucial research on money-lending by single women — have to do with representation. Aside from Spicksley's study and Allison Levy's on widow portraiture, this anthology is comprised of literary essays. Analyzing male-authored texts, our critics uncover how the practice and business of art was shaped by patriarchal ideology and institutions. But whether or not particular texts served as deliberate strategies for playing the system, expressed fear of women or sympathy for them, were penned skillfully or dimly, the very nature of language and literature dictates that they exceed authorial intention, and not least when seen from the perspective of a twenty-first-century feminist critic.[9] Such theorists as Pierre Macherey and Roland Barthes have taught us to read between the lines in order to recover the absent voice, so that the cohesiveness and unity of traditional narrative might not occlude the (patriarchal) text's fissures and contradictions. Moreover, Jurij Lotman's dictum of the "minus device," asserting that a conspicuous omission, or "meaningful absence" of the expected, is in itself a statement, can be extended to characterization and action as well as to discrete semiotic codes and devices.[10] The sheer magnitude of single women as a category — a potentially threatening bit of information — is such an omission, concealed through the balkanization of the unmarried into sub-classes, by discounting the exigencies of poverty, illness, and powerlessness; negating the possibility of choice by the financially fortunate; and ignoring sexual preference and family commitments. These convenient elisions were substantiated through an institutionalized discourse of representation that suspended not only the material conditions at stake but also women's very human desire for control over their lives.

Within the institutionalized framework a maid or virgin occupied a chaste transitional space between childhood and wifehood, though exceptions were made for saints, Arthurian ladies, goddesses, and Queen Elizabeth. Thus, a woman who never married was a spinster; at various times she might be mocked as comical or harangued as sinful, having failed in her duty to reproduce.[11] The unwed but sexually experienced were whores, unruly women. "Singlewoman" was used synonymously with "prostitute" in sixteenth-century England.[12] A "widow indeed," to use St. Paul's phrase, did not remarry.[13] Proverbial wisdom taught that most widows were

---

[8] Frye and Robertson's *Maids and Mistresses, Cousins and Queens* is a significant exception.

[9] See Hans-Georg Gadamer, *Truth and Method*, orig. *Wahrheit und Methode* (Tübingen, 1960), trans. G. Barden and J. Cumming (New York, 1975), 336.

[10] Jurij Lotman, *The Structure of the Artistic Text*, trans. Ronald Vroon, Michigan Slavic Contributions 7 (Ann Arbor, 1977), 51.

[11] Bennett and Froide, *Singlewomen*, 19–20.

[12] Ruth Mazo Karras in Bennett and Froide, *Singlewomen*, 128; see her important chapter, "Sex and the Singlewoman," 127–45.

[13] 1 Timothy 5:3, 5.

wealthy or lusty or, like the widow Hortensio marries in Shakespeare's *Taming of the Shrew*, both.[14]

Outside this construal stood the one-fifth of sixteenth-century rural English brides who came to the altar pregnant,[15] having won husbands by proving their fertility. There, too, could be found the spinsters who lacked a dowry, good health, or interest in men.[16] Also unspoken for were defenseless servant girls (and girls could be placed in service as early as seven years of age), raped or seduced by their employers or fellow servants, and dismissed lest they turn informer or ask for child support. Such women, unable to find lawful employment, might turn to prostitution for survival.[17] Many widows survived on parish charity; in fact, widows were the chief beneficiaries of community relief programs. Most widows were not wealthy because their husbands had not been wealthy, riches being reserved for the privileged few in a hierarchical society. Remarriage, when a possibility, was often an economic necessity; widows who were better off might choose independence. Sadly, elderly, impoverished widows could easily be taken for witches,[18] and madness, senility, and demonism were fungible.

In every society and every key area of experience we may expect to find an official ideology or party line. Such an ideology gives rise to the stereotypes generated from inconsistencies, conspicuous omissions, and distortions of fact that are expressed in the arts but are also subverted, either intentionally or unconsciously. It is the disparity between ideology and practice that our contributors address, continuing and extending recent social histories of the multivalent experiences of single women, especially as constituted through popular and fictive discourses. Although all of our contributors locate their findings historically, the essays in this volume stress the visual and literary representation of single women, foregrounding singleness as a cultural concern. Supplementing historiography or demographics, the fictions traced here expose the operations of ideology in ways not necessarily accessible through other modes of inquiry.

The eleven essays that comprise the collection discuss idealizing virginity, deferring marriage, making a living, and anticipating widowhood. The anthology mirrors the negotiations between the actual life circumstances of women and their ideological constructions on the page and stage. The multivalent interpretations that result in some ways sustain, in others contradict, the received notion of an increasingly

---

[14] Thus, "The rich Widow weeps with one eye and casts glances with the other," in Morris Palmer Tilley, *A Dictionary of the Proverbs in England in the Sixteenth and Seventeenth Centuries: A Collection of the Proverbs Found in English Literature and the Dictionaries of the Period* (Ann Arbor, 1950), 722; also see *The Taming of the Shrew*, 4.2.37, 50 in G. Blakemore Evans, gen. ed., *The Riverside Shakespeare*, 2nd ed. (Boston and New York, 1997).

[15] Hufton, *Prospect Before Her*, 134.

[16] See Bennett and Froide, *Singlewomen*, 6; Sara Mendelson and Patricia Crawford, *Women in Early Modern England, 1550–1720* (Oxford, 1998), 168; and Hufton, *Prospect Before Her*, 258–59.

[17] See Jodi Mikalachki, "Women's Networks and the Female Vagrant: A Hard Case," in Frye and Robertson, *Maids and Mistresses*, 52–69, esp. 57–58; Hufton, *Prospect Before Her*, 335; and Mendelson and Crawford, *Women*, 107.

[18] See Hufton, *Prospect Before Her*, 351–52, 362.

vehement patriarchalism limiting opportunities for women's independence and offering few fictional models of women who found happiness outside of marriage.

Our contributors are divided between those who discuss the stifling effects of misogyny and those who uncover not only significant pockets of resistance to inequality but also a blithe disregard of misogynous traditions on the part of English institutions as well as individuals. In toto, their essays build a picture of an early society for which the struggle to regulate the unmarried female body was tantamount to controlling the otherwise unknowable private domain.

And yet single women ever found creative means to evade total regulation and sustain their singleness. Contrary to received scholarly opinion, opportunities for single women did not necessarily shut down with the close of the monasteries and the advent of industrialization. These women remained marginalized, but were never entirely excluded. For example, though some opportunities, such as guild membership, closed down, others, such as money-lending, opened up. As the more conservative ideologues continued their misogynous harangues, women came to play important roles within the dissenting religions. Harassed by common law as servants and unwed mothers, women were protected by ecclesiastical and equity law as widows. Similarly, in literary and dramatic texts, the servant girl's absent subjectivity highlights the sophisticated subjectivity granted her "gentle" mistress. So, too, despite the legal force of virginity tests, the dramatization of their failure demonstrated the precariousness of a patriarchal property system based on female chastity. And the courtly comedies in which marriage is sidestepped — as it was by Queen Elizabeth and, in the seventeenth century, by fifteen percent of aristocratic women — remind us that more than one code of behavior was viable for some, if not for all.

The anthology's first section, "Celebrating Celibacy," explores how virginity and the single state functioned as an idealized model inspiring both male and female readers. Though on their surface the literary representations analyzed here affirm an official discourse of female chastity, they also suggest surprisingly powerful possibilities for women who successfully transform the official doctrine into a private one. Jane Zatta, in "The Single Woman as Saint: Three Anglo-Norman Success Stories," examines ways in which depictions of virginal women might be used as models for sanctioned rebellion among the monastic institutions of Anglo-Norman England. Contextualizing three Anglo-Norman saints' lives against a political backdrop in which Norman abbots found their monastic houses encroached upon by competing Norman institutions, both royal and episcopal, Zatta observes that Anglo-Norman lives of English virgin saints provided examples of women who could be both independent of male authority and yet socially as well as morally victorious. Each of the lives adapts the biography of the virgin martyr to the predicament of an English abbess, so that the woman's struggle to defend her virginity — itself a metaphor for property rights — against encroachment is defended by God. In such a way the virgin saint provided monastic institutions with a model for rebellion against political coercion that was not necessarily incompatible with respect for social hierarchy. By imposing the struggles of the largely male aristocracy onto the lives of medieval virginal women, however, the lives also offer surprisingly independent and openly rebellious models for women who might, through the sexual manipulation and civil disobedience depicted in the text, also gain a measure of autonomy.

Late medieval texts continue to find models for women's singleness, albeit by expressing singleness with an increasing insistence on inward rather than public action. Paul Price's essay, "I Want to Be Alone: The Single Woman in Fifteenth-Century Legends of St Katherine," illustrates how the single woman becomes a thinkable concept within the fifteenth-century middle-English tradition of the virgin martyr, St. Katherine of Alexandria. Although earlier treatments of various female martyr figures foreclose on any notion of feminine singleness, defining the female martyr entirely by her *sponsa Christi* (bride of Christ) office, formal developments in the fifteenth-century tradition of Katherine produce a more nuanced figure whose virginity emanates from a powerful private desire to devote the self to Christianity. This tradition culminates in the text of John Capgrave, whose heroine resists the prospect of a husband not as an implicit testimony to an already formed supernatural attachment, but out of an explicit desire for singleness. Placed within the context of a growing constituency of female lay readers who are not the sum of either religious or secular married lifestyles, these late developments in the St. Katherine legends reveal a growing acknowledgment of the will and desires of women who actively choose the deployment of their own bodies.

In contrast to these examinations of hagiographical models for singleness, Dorsey Armstrong's essay, "Gender, Marriage, and Knighthood: Single Ladies in Malory," examines the interest in maidenhood from a secular and popular perspective. The foundation of chivalry is the relationship between a knight and the lady who inspires and motivates chivalric acts. In Malory, as Armstrong observes, the construction becomes even more rigid, with single women playing a crucial role, mediating and confirming knightly identity only insofar as they retain their autonomous status. Once married and potential mothers, Malory's women lose their power to facilitate the construction of knightly identity. Their importance having been diminished to what Luce Irigaray calls "use value," they no longer figure in the patriarchal marketplace. Examining the "Tale of Sir Gareth of Orkney" and the adventures of the tragically misguided Lancelot, Armstrong traces the power and function of the single woman, who, frequently through negative and denigrating forms of motivation, impels her knight to continued service until he fulfils the chivalric ideal. Even Lancelot must channel his service to the queen through public displays of dedication to single women, who both mask the real object of his devotions and at the same time provide him the vehicle for continued public service. By renouncing his commitment to the ideal of singleness and making his devotion to the married queen public, he heralds the end of the magnificent Arthurian chivalric project.

As these essays show, representations of virginity offered single women a strategy of resistance against official institutions inclined to appropriate the female body. Such representations, however, were accessible almost exclusively to the comparative few who could read. Section Two, "Repudiating Marriage," deals with a much larger population. Judith Spicksley explains how celibacy could be and in fact was made affordable for all but the poorest women in early modern England, and Jacqueline Vanhoutte explores how and why (comedy's obligatory marriage notwithstanding) celibacy was made appealing to substantial numbers of Elizabethan playgoers. These essayists map socio-economic and literary transitions from the Middle Ages to the sixteenth and seventeenth centuries.

In earlier demographic studies, women's falling marriage rates from the late sixteenth through the eighteenth centuries have been explained as the result of economic inadequacy, poor health, or sheer inability to find a suitable husband. Largely neglected is the possibility that women may have, for any number of reasons, deliberately chosen to remain single. Such a choice, of course, was surely enabled by financial solvency, and since employment opportunities for women shrank in early modern England, solvency is thought to have been in short supply. However, one burgeoning area of the service sector (though one would never know it from *The Merchant of Venice*) was money-lending. Legalized in 1571 as an acceptable practice on the part of Christians in England (and who was not?), money-lending guaranteed a return of ten percent, although some fluctuation followed in the next century. By charting references to formal and informal lending practices in the wills and inventories of single women in Lincolnshire and Cheshire, Judith M. Spicksley has found that some sixty percent of single women were money-lenders, and that women with less than five pounds to lend could supplement their income from labor and thus remain independent. Others, such as the daughters of husbandmen, who had received bequests of twenty pounds yielding interest of two pounds a year, could live at least as well as a servant without working. Those with more money to lend — one single woman lent more than two thousand pounds — could live comfortably or lavishly. Spicksley concludes "To Be or Not to Be Married: Single Women, Money-lending, and the Question of Choice in Late Tudor and Stuart England" by insisting that however much or little they lent, all such self-supporting single women were a communal resource, and not the pitiful, dependent spinsters of patriarchal ideology.

While women were finding an economically viable option to marriage, a handful of playwrights were staging that option and not losing any money by it. Arguably, the lack of verbal commitment that marks Luciana of *The Comedy of Errors*, the princess and her ladies (as well as pregnant and single Jaquenetta!) of *Love's Labor's Lost*, Diana of *All's Well That Ends Well*, and Isabella of *Measure for Measure* has its source in Shakespeare's acquaintance with the plays of John Lyly. Lyly also provides a precedent for sexually ambiguous attractions. In "A Strange Hatred of Marriage: John Lyly, Elizabeth I, and the Ends of Comedy," Jacqueline Vanhoutte argues that Lyly regularly subverts the "compulsory heterosexuality" we expect from comedy, answering two key questions negatively: Must women always marry *men*? Must women always *marry*? Lyly's plays obsessively catalogue different types of unmanned women, from chaste goddesses and queens (Cynthia in *Endymion*, Sappho in *Sappho and Phao*) to unmarried virgins (Haebe, Phyllida, and Gallathea in *Gallathea* and Campaspe in *Campaspe*) to old hags (Sibylla in *Sappho and Phao*, Dipsas and Bagoa in *Endymion*). All of these were court dramas, performed by young boys before Elizabeth I. As England's most famous single woman, she would doubtless have been interested in plays that reflected the ongoing debate regarding the desirability of her marriage, especially insofar as they testify to women's marital subordination — a condition she found wholly unwelcome.

Single women were not comprised entirely of maidens and the religious, however. The third section of our book, "Imaginary Widowhood," explores the dynamic of widowhood, examining not only how widows are conceptualized by the literature of their periods but also how they imagine their own possibilities for action and interaction. Both medieval and early modern literature typically depict widows as sexually aggressive, overtly knowledgeable both about the marriage bed and the marriage dowry, and always on the prowl for the next hapless male, as Laurel Amtower's essay "Chaucer's Sely Widows" observes. Chaucer, however, portrays his widows with considerably more sympathy than stereotypical depictions might allow. Chaucer's interest in these liminal figures is directly linked, Amtower argues, to his interrogation of the rules of discourse. Insofar as "unheaded" women are essentially deprived of their right to speak upon the death of their marriage partner, they become ideal vehicles upon which to invest the largely unspoken desires of unmaturated or otherwise predatory males. Even the good widow of the Friar's Tale is accused of adultery by the hell-bent summoner, while the younger Dido and Criseyde, Cleopatra and the Wife of Bath become outright targets for lascivious imaginations or the butts of bawdy jokes. Thus the concept of widowhood remains sexually charged despite institutional exhorations to adopt lives of humility and abstinence. The widow's metaphoric "unheadedness" combined with her physically marginalized position ensure that she will be unable to repudiate her new status as fantasy object.

Though much of this metaphoric refiguring of the widow's condition occurs through language, language also provides a means through which widows may at least imaginatively create a viable social stake for themselves. Jeanie Grant Moore's essay, "(Re)creations of a Single Woman: Discursive Realms of the Wife of Bath," begins with the observation that despite being designated "Wife," Alison's self-narrative issues from outside her marriages, as if the unmarried state is the only position from which women can give shape and meaning to their various roles as wives. As a single woman who discursively produces both her own identity and the identities of her various husbands, Alison establishes the significance of her own voice by neutralizing the gendered force of the various medieval roles that intervene in women's lives: the *auctor*, the husband, the hero-knight, the king. By imagining both male and female roles androgynously, Alison constructs a new world in which single women are heard and their advice taken. Ironically, however, as the hag's problematic marriage to the rapist-knight of the tale shows, once the single woman dwindles into marriage, her voice and identity again submerge into the patriarchy.

Yet for the most part, the status of "widow" tells us more about men than their wives. In her study of mourning ritual and representation, "Good Grief: Widow Portraiture and Masculine Anxiety in Early Modern England," Allison Levy notes that concepts of widowhood were frequently shaped by the husband's anxiety. As if temporal extinction were not a sufficient cause for grief, a man's death ineluctably signified male vulnerability that fissured a system supporting male superiority and importance. Widow portraiture, Levy argues, was a memorial strategy, a way of conferring permanence upon the deceased husband. But why wait for death before invoking the strategy? In an attempt to quell anxiety, some Englishmen commissioned portraits of their wives dressed as widows, mourning deaths that had not yet occurred. One such portrait is that of the seventeenth-century wife Jane Hodgson Cartwright. She was one of the actor's three wives, all of whom actually predeceased him, leaving him without the inconsolable mourner he had been so eager to assure himself of. Examining this portrait among others, Levy calls attention to Jane, the model, as an actor, her pre-posthumous (and preposterous) mourning an unconvincing performance that challenges her husband's strategy through the discrepancy between the static, often monotonous and predictable representation of the "widow" and her unstable, now uncertain, social status.

Clearly running through the last section of our book, "Sexuality and Revirgination," is a concern with class no less than with physical desire and its consequences. Despite the question of whether class membership can exist without class consciousness, i.e., without solidarity in the face of exploitation, class status did exist in the early modern period. The distinction between social classes (or estates) and the role of female sexuality as a marker is explicit in Tracey Sedinger's analysis of *Much Ado About Nothing* and its sources. No less class-marked is the punishment of Anne Green, an unwed mother, who would have been treated quite differently had she been an aristocrat and not a servant. Similarly, while married to her first husband Frances Howard had an affair with her second, but because of her membership in one of the most important English families she was allowed to pass for a virgin. Our final three essayists delineate ideology both endorsed and challenged in the literary works they analyze.

By comparing Margaret in *Much Ado About Nothing* with her counterparts in Shakespeare's source texts, *Orlando Furioso* and Book 2 of *The Faerie Queene*, Tracey Sedinger interrogates recent feminist criticism insufficiently aware of, or too quick to erase, economic difference between women. Sedinger's "Working Girls: Status, Sexual Difference, and Disguise in Ariosto, Spenser, and Shakespeare" asserts the importance of economic difference as a barrier to alliances based on a common gender. In these texts a single woman lacking money and status is represented as lacking agency. For the maidservant but not for her mistress, marriage is an inaccessible goal — a situation generating the maid's envy, and destroying the possibility of genuine friendship between them. Sedinger also traces the truncated representation of the maidservant. Renouncing desire, Ariosto's Dalinda enters a convent, Spenser's Pyrene disappears from the narrative, and Shakespeare's Margaret is left without a suitor. The authors do not allow the servants to explain their motives for agreeing to the masquerade, for these works are not about them but about marriages among the elite. Nevertheless, for the sympathetic reader, the maid's disguise intimates her sacrificed subjectivity.

Not by chance, Anne Green, an unwed mother who was hanged for supposedly murdering her baby, was a servant. What is serendipitous is that Anne survived her hanging, whereupon she was exonerated and became the subject of at least five popular publications. In " 'News from the Dead': The Strange Story of a Woman Who Gave Birth, Was Executed, and Was Resurrected as a Virgin," Susan Staub explains Anne's sentence as exemplifying attempts to regulate female sexuality (rather than save the lives of "bastards") through onerous legislation. Although infanticide was rare, laws became increasingly harsh between the sixteenth and seventeenth centuries. Anne was convicted under a 1624 law, not repealed until 1803, that presumed the guilt of an unwed mother whose baby had died, unless she could prove the contrary. Just as the maidservants are silenced in *Much Ado* and its predecessors, so in the publications evoked by the resurrection of Anne Green, her voice disappears, and is replaced by those of male providentialist authors. Whereas the journalists among them adopt a medical approach to her body, the literati reconstruct her as a holy maid: "All's purg'd by Sacrifice: / The Parent slain, doth not a Virgin Rise?" Staub points out that by mystifying Anne's experience, the writers in effect justify unjust persecutory laws, since God can be counted upon to protect the innocent.

"Frances Howard and *The Changeling*: Trials, Tests, and the Legibility of the Virgin Body," by Mara Amster, is concerned with quite a different failure of law. How could the marriage of Frances Howard be annulled on the grounds of her husband's impotence, so that she could wed King James' favorite, Robert Carr? If only Frances, known for her affairs, were a virgin! And remarkably, she was. Because Frances requested that her face be veiled during her physical examination, contemporary writers assumed she had made use of a sexually uninitiated surrogate — a situation evoked by Thomas Middleton and William Rowley in *The Changeling*'s comic virginity test. The playwrights avoided the ideological challenge implicit in the contrast between a licentious noblewoman and her chaste servant by depicting Beatrice as a "white devil" and Diaphanta as sexually eager. Even so, the play, like Frances Howard's examination, exposes hegemonic weakness. In a patriarchal economy chastity is a woman's supreme virtue, and virginity the hallmark of the single woman's chastity. Yet if virginity is not essential but performative, discernment becomes wholly unreliable, and its economy is inevitably destabilized.

The essays in this collection approach aesthetic space — writing, portraiture, and the like — not merely as the creation of illusion, but as more than that: as a means through which cultural mystifications of class, sex, economics, politics, and religion are revealed and concealed. Not that literary or aesthetic production is more authentic or "truer" than the discourses, illusions, and stereotypes they invoke. Yet such aesthetic works can nonetheless function as a path to knowledge by illuminating the kinds of illusions that obstruct our understanding of single women. Widow caricatures veil very real anxieties regarding patrilineage and a man's social and even eternal succession. Hagiography reimagines individual control over the body for institutional agendas. At the same time, poetic and dramatic representations that give voice to single women imagine a different range of possibilities for single life. In such a way, writes Macherey, fiction breaches the "insufficiency" of illusion and "transform[s] our relationship to ideology."[19] Yet such aesthetic productions cannot perform the work of analysis; it is the task of theory, in Macherey's view, to fix and determine the kind of language that describes otherwise only hollow forms, or, in other words, to show not only "what the text 'knows,'" but "how it 'knows.'"[20] We hope that these essays, examining representations of single women against an entire nexus of texts, traditions, and institutional conditions that inform

---

[19] Macherey, *Theory of Literary Production*, 64.
[20] Macherey, *Theory of Literary Production*, 64.

and are transformed by the aesthetic production at hand, will contribute to the growing body of scholarship by illuminating the ideological mystification of single women.

This volume has greatly benefited from the kind efforts and support of many individuals and institutions. We would especially like to express our gratitude to the general editor of MRTS, Robert Bjork, whose encouragement and vision guided this project from its inception to its end, and each of our insightful and conscientious contributors, whose stimulating and careful work made this volume a pleasure to put together. Thanks, too, go to the College of Arts and Letters at San Diego State University, which provided three generous grants that helped us complete this work; Kimberly Norlund for her technological savvy; and Jason Dunn and Tawnya Richardson, who compiled our index for us. Finally, we would like to thank our research assistant Raymond Salcedo. His diligence and impeccable research could not have been better — we were lucky to have him.

Laurel Amtower and Dorothea Kehler
San Diego State University

PART I:

CELEBRATING CELIBACY

1

THE SINGLE WOMAN AS SAINT:
Three Anglo-Norman Success Stories

A little-appreciated fact is the existence among the corpus of Anglo-Norman saints' lives of three lives of Anglo-Saxon women saints — Osith, Etheldreda, and Modwenna — which locate a juncture of numerous inscriptions of gender and ethnicity. The women in these stories are doubly other: they are pre-Conquest Saxon women portrayed for Norman ecclesiastics. Yet despite their double remove, the significance of the lives of the English virgin saints is not their distance but their proximity. Whereas defiant career virgins like Catherine and Margaret supposedly lived in cultures safely remote in time and place from the present, the point of the Anglo-Saxon lives is their "here and nowness," the deep connection between their lives, cults, and relics and the monastic traditions and political landscape of twelfth- and thirteenth-century Norman England. They show us not so much how Normans saw English ethnicity, nor how they saw women, but how these two alterities could be triangulated to protect the claims of individual monastic houses against the encroachments of the highest levels of Norman royal or episcopal ambitions.

It could be said that Anglo-Norman lives of English saints trojanized Anglo-Saxon Christianity by portraying the Norman succession to the government of English religious houses as a kind of *translatio ecclesiae*, in much the same way as the royal historians had portrayed the Norman Conquest of England as an ongoing project of political perfection progressing from pagan Troy to transitional Rome to Christian Europe. Norman lives of Anglo-Saxon saints highlight their role as the founders of English Christianity, the transition point between the Danish pagan past and the Christian future destined to culminate in the supercession of the Normans. Not only were English founding saints not rejected by the Normans; they were embraced, as S. J. Ridyard has shown, and claimed as the *antecessores* of the Norman abbots, whose cults they perpetuated by commissioning new *vitae*.[1] The production

---

[1] S. J. Ridyard, "*Condigna Veneratio*: Post-Conquest Attitudes to the Saints of the Anglo-

of *vitae*, like that of false charters, was one method used by Norman abbots to justify their claims to special exemptions and privileges deriving from rights supposedly given by ancient English kings, whose heirs the Normans claimed to be and whose laws the Normans kings swore to respect. Houses founded by royal saints had a particular claim to independence from both royal and episcopal interference. Thus Osbert of Clare's *Vita beati Eadwardi* features a legend according to which Westminster had first been consecrated by St. Peter himself, and then uses the tradition to claim independence from the see of London.[2]

After the Norman Conquest, English religious houses faced a number of threats to their economic survival, which included despoliation by the Conqueror in 1070, the usurpation of their lands by Norman invaders, the imposition of gelds and taxes, including the Norman innovation of requiring religious houses to enfeoff knights, and even the raiding of their treasures to furnish churches and abbeys in Normandy.[3] Another threat to monastic houses was episcopal encroachment. Tension between religious houses and bishops was a prominent feature of post-Conquest ecclesiastical history. Episcopal sees were largely small and poor, and a bishop could greatly increase his power and influence by taking over one of the large Benedictine houses established in the tenth century.[4] By the early twelfth century, the number of monastic cathedrals had more than doubled, increasing from the pre-Conquest number of four to nine out of a total of seventeen.[5] The establishment of an episcopal see in an abbey threatened not only the wealth of the community, which had to be divided between the convent and the bishop and his *familia*, but also the independence and the status of its head,[6] and it is not surprising that

---

Saxons," *Anglo-Norman Studies IX*, ed. R. Allen Brown (Woodbridge, Suffolk; Wolfeboro, NH, 1987), 179–206. Ridyard says (184): "The Norman abbots, it seems, regarded themselves primarily as abbots of Ely, only secondarily as Norman conquerors. Their reputations depended upon their effectiveness in defending and enhancing the position of the church committed to their care; and in pursuit of that priority they were prepared to utilise any tool which came to hand."

[2] Osbert of Clare, Prior at Westminster under the abbacy of Gervase of Blois, helped to defend the independence of Westminster Abbey from the see of London by forging charters supposedly issued by the chancery of Edward I and by composing a *Vita beati Eadwardi*; the latter prominently featured a legend according to which Westminster had first been consecrated by St. Peter himself in the days when Mellitis was Bishop of London. See Kathryn Young Wallace, "Introduction," Matthew Paris, *La Estoire de Seint Aedward le Rei* (London, 1983), x–xii.

[3] The *servitium debitum* imposed on Ely was forty knights. See Edward Miller, *The Abbey and Bishopric of Ely: The Social History of an Ecclesiastical Estate from the Tenth Century to the Early Fourteenth Century* (Cambridge, 1951, repr. 1969), 67–68.

[4] See Ann Williams, *The English and the Norman Conquest* (Woodbridge, 1995), 45. In 1070 William had all the monasteries in England plundered to seize the money which the wealthy English had deposited in them. However the monks of Abingdon claimed that the king's officers carried away the church's treasures as well.

[5] Williams, *Conquest*, 136.

[6] Lanfranc's account of the complaints against Peter, bishop of Lichfield, who attempted to remove the see of Chester to Coventry, describes what the community endured at Peter's hands. The bishop's men forced entry into their dormitory, broke into their strongboxes, robbed them

communities so threatened resisted vigorously. Norman abbots found themselves at odds not with the English monks under their guidance, but with Norman sheriffs, nobles, and bishops as well as with the king himself at times. William's insistence that the Normans were the legitimate heirs to the English throne rather than invaders, as well as his claim to respect the laws and customs that had prevailed under Edward I, spurred a flurry of interest in the English past as threatened landholders sought to produce charters and chronicles proving the antiquity of their claims to disputed lands.[7] Thus Norman abbots whose own fates were attached to the English houses that had fallen to their charge found that when chronicles and charters failed, their best defense was an alliance with the institution's English patron saint.

Within this socio-saintly economy, Anglo-Saxon virgin saints had a particular role, because their divinely conceded exemption from a woman's normal social subordination provided another precedent for justifying the rebellion of a monastic house against political coercion. From a political point of view, these lives show that insubordination to lawful authority when directed by God constitutes obedience rather than rebellion and is not incompatible with respect for social hierarchy. The three Anglo-Norman women that concern this essay, Osith, Etheldreda, and Modwenna, enjoy successful and independent careers, thanks to the divine favor that allows them to negotiate a compromise between the demands of social hierarchy and moral independence. Two marry — one of them multiple times — and the third is a successful career virgin, who founds numerous houses and is deferred to by both the ecclesiastical and royal rulers. Both of the saints who marry do so in obedience to their families, but then resist their husbands and eventually free themselves in deference to their duty to God. Whereas the classical virgin martyrs provide powerful images of women who successfully defy male authority, their defiance does not result in success on earth. Although these stories show the woman to be the moral, intellectual and physical superior of her male tormentor, the cost of this superiority is utter destruction, both of the corrupt political order and the virgin herself. Whereas the girl may be morally victorious, her triumph is incompatible with life on earth. In dramatic contrast to the classical virgin martyr stories and no doubt as an unexpected consequence of other political purposes, the Anglo-Norman lives of English virgin saints provided women with the models of saints who could be both independent of male authority and socially as well as morally victorious.

All three of the vernacular lives of early English virgin saints were based on Lat-

---

of their horses and goods, pulled down their houses and had the building materials taken to his own residences, and remained in the monastery with his retinue for eight days, consuming all the monks' provisions: Williams, *Conquest*, 136.

[7] From the time of William, all Norman rulers claimed to uphold the laws of Edward the Confessor. See Williams, *Conquest*, 155–58. Thus the abbot of Battle appealed to Henry II to enforce the supposed indemnities and exemptions of Battle Abbey against the pretenses of Hilary, bishop of Chichester by presenting forged royal charters in the king's court. See Marjorie Chibnall, *Anglo-Norman England: 1066–1166* (Oxford, repr. 1995), 203.

in lives begun in the first half of the twelfth century for the purpose of defending the property rights and independence of the institutions on which their cults centered. The *Liber Eliensis*, which is the source of the *Vie Ste. Audree*, was written by an unknown monk at Ely in the years between 1131 and 1174 and was a compilation from various sources, including cartularies and chronicles as well as Bede's life of St. Aethelthryth. In part as a result of William's anger because of its association with the Hereward rebellion, Ely suffered particularly after the Conquest, losing almost three quarters of its dependents between 1065 and 1082.[8] In addition, Ely was an early target of the Lincoln diocesan, which established an episcopal see there in 1109. The hagiographic tradition of Etheldreda shows that both the abbots and later the bishops found it convenient to ally themselves with the Anglo-Saxon saint against Norman despoilers.[9] As the vengeance miracles of the *Liber Eliensis* show, Norman abbots portrayed aggressions against their own tenurial situations as aggressions against Etheldreda and God and promoted the tradition of divine retribution that would strike the offenders.[10] Other miracles from later periods, such as the liberation of Brihstan, who had been imprisoned by Henry I for treason, imply breathtaking assertions of autonomy for the Ely community. The *Vie Ste. Osith* has a similar background.[11] The Anglo-Norman life is a translation of an earlier Latin life that was probably written to emphasize the role of the Norman bishops as the heirs to the early English Christian tradition. Since the *Vie Ste. Osith* culminates with the exemplary punishment by the saint of Bishop Richard of London, it is likely that the Anglo-Norman life represents an updating of the Latin *vita* in response to a series of disputes between St. Osith's and the see of London in the mid-twelfth century.[12] The *Vie St. Modwenna*, the latest of the three vernacular lives of

---

[8] Susan J. Ridyard, *The Royal Saints of Anglo-Saxon England* (Cambridge, 1988), 199.

[9] The first account of St. Etheldreda is that by Bede in the *Historia ecclesiastica*. In the tenth century, Aelfric gave an account of her life in his collection of saints' lives. After the Norman Conquest the program of hagiographic promotion of Ethelthreda increased. The most important twelfth-century life is that contained in the *Liber Eliensis*, which was the source for the Anglo-Norman poem. For a complete discussion of post-Conquest lives of Etheldreda, see Ridyard, *Royal Saints*, 53–55.

[10] As Ridyard notes: *Royal Saints*, 205.

[11] Osith is a pseudo-historical seventh-century composite connected to other holy women of the ninth and tenth centuries. Osgytha was the granddaughter of Penda and wife of Sighere, King of Essex, a seventh-century king mentioned by Bede; Edith was a composite figure but connected in the Anglo-Norman *Vie Ste. Osith* to a sister of Athelstan of the late tenth century; Osith is also connected to St. Monenna, foundress of Killevy d. 517, and Modwenna of the mid-seventh century. For the genealogy of Osgytha, see Keith Bailey, "Osyth, Frithuwold and Aylesbury," *Records of Buckinghamshire* 32 (1990): 37–48. For the relationship of Osyth, Edith, and Modwenna, see Christopher Hohler, "St. Osyth and Aylesbury," *Records of Buckinghamshire* 18 (1966): 61–72 and A. T. Baker, "An Anglo-French Life of St. Osith," *Modern Language Review* 6 (1911): 476–502; 7 (1912): 74–93; 157–92.

[12] The dispute centered on certain churches originally given to St. Osith's by Bishop Richard I but re-appropriated for the treasurership of St. Paul's by his successors Robert and Richard II. John of Salisbury interceded with the Pope on the side of St. Osith's. See Denis Bethell, "Richard

early English royal abbesses, was also the translation of a twelfth-century Latin life: that of Geoffrey of Burton, which had in turn been based on a prior life by the Irish hagiographer Conchubranus. Writing in the first half of the twelfth century, Geoffrey added to Conchubranus's life a series of vengeance miracles that emphasize Modwenna's role in protecting the property rights of the house at Burton.[13]

It is clear, then, that the interest of the hagiographers did not center on providing biographies of holy women, nor even primarily on inspiring piety, but rather on using the ideological paradigms offered by virgin saints for local political interests. For Anglo-Saxon hagiographers such as Bede, the primary significance of the saintly queen who rejected rank, status, marriage, and children in exchange for a religious life was to make religious life and secular life absolutely incompatible for women.[14] Far from being a prerogative of royalty, in Anglo-Saxon hagiography queens who attained sanctity did so by the explicit renunciation of the power and privileges of rank — a sign of the preferability in God's eyes of the religious over the worldly life. In the twelfth century, however, the stories of classical virgin mar-

---

of Belmeis and the Foundation of St. Osyth's," *Transactions of the Essex Archaeological Society* 2 (1970): 299–328.

The Anglo-Norman life may have been based on the now-lost text written by William de Vere who grew up in the court of Henry I. In any event the story of the source of the *Vie Ste. Osith* is probably represented by the text preserved in another twelfth-century life, that of MS. Bodley 285. Both the textual and cultic tradition of this saint are complex. The extant medieval lives are the following.

1) MS. Bodley 285, a Latin life surviving in a manuscript of the mid- to late twelfth century, probably from Ramsey abbey, written certainly after 1107 and probably after 1127.
2) MS. Landsdowne 436, a Latin life surviving in a fourteenth-century manuscript from Romsey nunnery in Hampshire. Bethell considers this an abbreviation of Bodley 285, as does A. T. Baker. But Morgan J. Desmond considers Landsdowne to be the earlier.
3) the Anglo-Norman life, surviving in a single manuscript, Welbeck Abbey MS. I C. I which, in the fourteenth century, belonged to the nunnery at Campsey in Suffolk, where it was used for readings at mealtimes.
4) a life embedded in a series of Lessons for St. Osyth's feast day, Oct. 7, surviving in a fourteenth-century compilation of saints' lives, made at Bury St. Edmund's abbey in Suffolk, now MS. Bodley 240.
5) a series of notes composed by the sixteenth-century antiquarian Leland, taken from the lost Life composed by William DeVere in the late twelfth century.

For one reconstruction of the relationships among the Lives, see Denis Bethell, "The Lives of St. Osyth of Essex and St. Osyth of Aylesbury," *Analecta Bollandiana* 88 (1970): 75–127. For a discussion of the relationship between the Aylesbury and Essex traditions, see Hohler, "St. Osyth and Aylesbury"; R. P. Hagerty, "The Buckinghamshire Saints Reconsidered 2: St. Osyth & St. Edith of Aylesbury," *Records of Buckinghamshire* 29 (1987): 125–32; Keith Bailey, "Osyth, Frithuwold, and Aylesbury," *Records of Buckinghamshire* 32 (1990): 37–48.

[13] A. T. Baker and Alexander Bell, *St. Modwenna* (Oxford, 1947; repr. New York, 1967), xxiii.

[14] Ridyard, *Royal Saints*, 82–92.

tyrs, which became the most popular form of female hagiography,[15] began to take on a new political tinge. It is not hard to see in these stories, which pit a spotless virgin against a ruthless tyrant, the subtext of an ecclesiastical polemic against secular government. These stories, in which a secular ruler who is obtuse, brutal, and lustful is successfully challenged by a weak and defenseless young girl, not only question the authority of the secular ruler, potentially they question all hierarchical social ordering.[16] All three of these lives attempt to some degree to adapt the biography of an English abbess to the profile of the virgin martyr, especially to show how God defended the virginity of a helpless woman against aggression and depredation, as well as her property rights of which her virginity is a homologue. But in mapping an essentially male power struggle onto the biographies of women, these lives create startling portrayals of recognizably contemporary women, who are praised for achieving independence from male authority and, moreover, who do so by such means as sexual manipulation, disobedience, and open rebellion.

The political exploitation of the subversive potential of the virgin martyr story by the Anglo-Norman redactor of the *Vie Seinte Osith* is easily seen by comparing the Anglo-Norman life to its Latin source.[17] The Latin life tells the story of the career of Osith, the Christian daughter of the virtuous king Penda, who, although a pagan himself, allowed his relatives to receive Christianity. After marriage to Siher, king of the East Saxons, Osith avoids sexual relations with her husband and ultimately decides to pursue a religious career, taking advantage of her husband's momentary absence in pursuit of a mysterious white deer to receive the veil from her priests Ecca and Bedewin. On his return, her husband, though saddened, accepts her decision and endows her with his vill of Chich for a monastery, which Osith governs until her death. After her murder at the hands of Danish pirates, who kill her because she refuses to renounce her faith, she carries her severed head into the church — dedicated to saints Peter and Paul — thereby symbolizing the triumph of English Christianity over Danish paganism. The life next records the translation of her relics by bishop Maurice, the founding of the monastery by bishop Richard, several miracles that took place near her tomb, and one conventional miracle regarding the saint's revenge for the theft of a small piece of marble. The

---

[15] Jocelyn Wogan-Browne, "Rerouting the Dower: The Anglo-Norman Life of St. Audrey by Marie (of Chatteris?)," in *The Power of the Weak: Studies on Medieval Women*, ed. Jennifer Carpenter and Sally-Beth MacLean (Urbana and Chicago, 1995), 27.

[16] See for example Thomas J. Heffernan (*Sacred Biography: Saints and Their Biographers in the Middle Ages* [New York, 1988], 299) who notes the potentially provocative nature of the virgin martyr lives that exalt a young girl who successfully defies the authority structures of the secular state, and concludes that "The liturgical context supplied by the church makes it easier to see how these lives might also allow women and men to indulge in a type of ritualized emancipation from their rigidly appointed roles, free from the personal stigma of sin and guilt."

[17] For a description of the account in MS. Bodley 285, see Morgan J. Desmond, "The Concept of Narrative among Twelfth-Century Vernacular Hagiographers: A Comparison of the *Vie de Sainte Marguerite*, the *Vie de Saint Gilles*, and the *Vie de Sainte Osith* with Their Latin Sources," Ph.D diss., University of Wisconsin-Madison, 1978.

purpose of this life is clearly to link the see of London to the promotion of the cult of Osith, a symbol of the venerability of English Christianity of which the Normans claimed to be the continuators.

The purpose of the Anglo-Norman text, written probably in the context of a dispute between the monastery of St. Osith's and the London see on which it depended, is to show that an act of disobedience to lawful superiors can sometimes constitute obedience when performed in accordance with God's will.[18] The poet therefore makes several striking changes to the plot, designed to place Osith in conflict with representatives of every recognized authority of her day, familial, political, and ecclesiastical — all of whom, the poet is careful to point out, are behaving according to law and custom. The result is to transform a stylized tale of hagiographic renunciation into a psychologically complex and realistic portrayal of a clever, determined, and manipulative woman, who outwits her family, husband, and religious advisers to attain freedom and independence. The poet begins by inserting a layer of conflict between Osith and her parents that is absent in the Latin life. While still a child, Osith vows her virginity to God and earns divine favor, which is demonstrated by her miraculous preservation from an accidental drowning while under the care of the holy woman Modwenna, to whom she had been sent to be raised. After Modwenna dies, Osith is recalled by her father, who arranges a suitably prestigious marriage for his daughter to the "poestif homme le rey Syer" (386) in accordance with the advice of his noblemen. He is unaware of his daughter's objections to the marriage, since she keeps her vow of virginity and desire for a religious career to herself.

Siher likewise is unaware of his wife's vow. One of the many attractions of this remarkable poem is the extreme psychological realism that characterizes the poet's portrayal of Siher's struggle to come to terms with the unexpected behavior of his wife. Instead of the murderous villains confronted by a Catherine or a Cecilia, Siher behaves like any newly married man: "as soon as he saw her he greatly desired her and lusted after her." Nevertheless, he grudgingly consents to his wife's request to delay the consummation of their marriage, perhaps swayed by her promise of an ultimate fulfillment of his wishes that, she implies, will make his wait worthwhile:

> Pur Deu merci, kar m'entendez,
> Et aukes de respit me donez;

---

[18] The editor of the *Vie Ste. Osith*, A. T. Baker, believed that the poem was actually a composite consisting of a base text written at the end of the twelfth century to which two successive poets added interpolations, the last dating from the second half of the twelfth century. In my essay, "The *Vie Seinte Osith*: Hagiography and Politics in Anglo-Norman England" [*Studies in Philology* 96 (1999): 367–93], I explained why I believe Baker's theory of a composite poem cannot be accepted. If the poem was composed in the second half of the twelfth century, as I believe, then an obvious impetus to its composition would be furnished by the territorial disputes which embroiled St. Osith's and the see of London for much of the middle of the century.

> De ceste assemblée entre nus
> Dunt vus estes tant desirus,
> Respit vus requer sire rey,
> Si ja voilliez joir de mey. (ll. 447–452)[19]

[For the love of God, listen to me and give me some respite from this union between us which you so ardently desire. I ask you for a small delay, sire King, if you ever wish to enjoy me.]

For three and a half years, Siher attempts to break down her resistance, while Osith teasingly puts him off with one excuse after another:

> Cil la ne vout pur rien oir
> Mes tut dis tire a son desir.
> Cele pur rien ke sace dire,
> Par boneirté plus ke pur ire,
> Ne vout faire ne consentir
> A son talent n'a son pleisir. (ll. 453–458)

[He did not want to listen to her but always tries to achieve his own desire. She, by anything she could think of to say, but more amiably than in anger, does not wish to consent to his desire or pleasure.]

Siher is understandably frustrated by his wife's contradictory behavior. As time goes on, he reacts with a mixture of exasperation, anger, and hope:

> Li reis comence a losenger,
> E tel oure est, a coroucer (ll. 475–476)

[The king first begins to flatter, and then to become angry].

His masculine simplicity and directness are, however, no match for the wiles of his wife. Osith never tells him her true intentions, but puts him off by implying that she will eventually give in to him. She deceives him with behavior that is teasing, playful, flirtatious:

> Mes tant a purchasé e quis
> E tant feit entre giu e ris,
> De jur en jur est purloinié. (ll. 477–479)

---

[19] Citations are to A. T. Baker, "An Anglo-French Life of St Osith," *Modern Language Review* 6 (1911): 476–502; 7 (1912): 74–93; 157–92. Translations are my own.

[But she begged and pleaded so much, and did so much between game and laughter, that day after day he was put off.]

Things come to a head three and a half years after their marriage, following an elaborate birthday party during which Siher has drunk too much. He summons her to his bed, resolved to rape her if necessary, but then postpones his decision upon the appearance of a mysterious white deer, which lures Siher and all the men of his court off on a fruitless hunt.

After having portrayed Osith's religious vocation as a defiance of both her father and husband, the poet next places Osith in conflict with episcopal authority. Realizing that she can deceive her husband no longer, Osith requests the bishops Ecca and Bedewin to veil her. In contrast to the Latin version of the life, in which they gladly accept Osith's request, Bedewin and Ecca refuse, citing her marriage and advising her to wait.[20] Osith persists in her demands, imploring them in God's name to grant her wish. Their further refusal sets the stage for a dramatic act of defiance. Osith pulls a veil out of her bosom, offers it on the altar, then places it on her own head, commending herself to God, who rewards her resolution and determination with his protection:

> Plus en apres leva sa main
> E treit le veil hors de son sein,
> E sur l'auter offrir le vait,
> Puis de sa main vers li le trait,
> E sur son chief le veil ad mis,
> E ataché e bien asis;
> E dit: 'Dampnedeu tut puissant,
> Cors e alme ci vus comant,
> Si me gardez pur vostre nun,
> Car ne ay d'autre guarisun.'
> Seinte Osith ad cest oure en pris
> Ke sur son chief le veil ad mis. (ll. 667–678)

[Then she raised her hand and drew the veil out of her bosom and went to offer it on the altar. Then with her hand, she draws it towards herself and placed the veil on her own head, and attached it and fixed it well and said: "God the almighty, I commend to you my body and soul. Protect me in your name, be-

---

[20] Canon law also forbade that a virgin who had previously taken a vow of chastity should be forced by her parents to marry, but, as Jocelyn Wogan-Browne pointed out, Osith's was not the formal and public vow which would have exempted her. See Jocelyn Wogan-Browne, " 'Clerc u lai, muïne u dame': Women and Anglo-Norman Hagiography in the Twelfth and Thirteenth Centuries," in *Women and Literature in Britain 1150–1500*, ed. Carol M. Meale, 2nd ed. (Cambridge, 1996), 61–85.

cause I have no other surety." He took St. Osith at that hour because she had placed the veil on her head.]

The poet's portrayal of the conflict that sometimes exists between commitment to God and the normally constituted authorities opens the space for an unusually complex portrayal of Siher. It is impossible not to sympathize with the duped king when he returns from the failed hunt to find his wife in her cowl. His first reaction is sheer horror:

> La reine a tost demandé,
> E ele vient en son neir veil,
> Al rei en fremist chacun peil. (ll. 688–690)

[He immediately sent for the queen who comes to him in her black veil. The king's every hair stood on end.]

Next come rage, frustration, despair, and finally resignation. Siher first becomes angry, shouting, cursing, threatening, and finally begging his wife to change her mind. When he realizes that he can neither bully nor wheedle her into submission, he falls into despair. He shuts himself up in his room, stops eating and drinking, and refuses to speak to anyone. Finally, grief also runs its course, and he resigns himself to his wife's decision:

> Kant sa dolur a fet asez
> Ke tut put estre alessez,
> Purpense sey a chef de tur
> Ke rien ne vaut sa dolur,
> Kant veit ne puet estre muée
> A seinte Osith a gr[a]antée,
> Ke remaine tut autresi
> En cel abit k'ele ad choisi. (ll. 719–726)

[When he had mourned enough, so that everything was relieved, he thought at last that his grief was useless. When he sees that she cannot be changed, he gave his permission to St. Osith to remain as she was, in the habit which she had chosen.]

Osith's single-minded and cagey pursuit of the career goal she had secretly cherished since childhood is finally rewarded as Siher ultimately not only accepts his wife's decision, but endows her with land and buildings for a monastery and grants the second daughter of each of his counts and barons for her convent. In arguing that Osith's devotion to God justified her rebellion against both secular and religious authorities, the poet has created a saint who attains not just the rewards of a mystic marriage with the heavenly bridegroom, but independence and self-determination on earth, and who does so not by ascetic renunciation, deprivation, or bodily suffering, but by deceit, cajolery, manipulation, and disobedience.

More medieval vernacular lives were composed about Aethelthryth (Latin: Etheldreda) of Ely than any other native female saint.[21] *The Vie Seinte Audree* is an Anglo-Norman reworking of the Latin life of St. Etheldreda, composed by a monk of Ely in the mid-twelfth century and included in the *Liber Eliensis*, a chronicle and cartulary compiled largely to assert the continuity of the monastic tradition at Ely. Like other religious houses, the monks at Ely took advantage of the professed Norman reverence for the rights and customs of the English past to seek to restore their losses. The Norman hagiographical interest in Etheldreda seems to have initiated under Bishop Hervey, who sponsored the Corpus/Dublin Life completed prior to the death of Henry I. This was followed by the *Liber Eliensis*, composed between 1133–69, and the Anglo-Norman life, composed probably around 1200.[22] The author, a woman named Marie, was most likely a member of a female religious house dedicated to Saint Etheldreda — perhaps the Benedictine abbey of St. Mary at Chatteris, which was given to Ely by Henry I in the early twelfth century.[23]

Briefly, the *Vie Seinte Audree* relates the following story. Audree was the daughter of King Anna of the East Angles. After an exemplary childhood, characterized by piety, goodness, wisdom, charity, and rigorous asceticism, she was married unwillingly to Tonberht, an aldorman of the South Gyrwas, with whom she lived in a mutually accepted chaste union for three years before Tonberht died. After Tonberht's death, Audree retired with a company of holy women to her dower island of Ely, where they lived in solitude and silence. However, five years later, after the death of her father Anna, Audree was given in marriage by her uncle to Ecgfrith, son of King Oswy of Northumbria. For several years, Audree preserved her virginity in her marriage to Ecgfrith, during which time they formed a close friendship with Bishop Wilfrid of Northumbria. Ecgfrith eventually lost patience and attempted unsuccessfully to seduce her, rape her with the aid of his servants, and bribe Wilfrid to convince his wife to fulfill her marital obligations — aggressions which Audree steadfastly repelled. After twelve years of importuning her husband to release her from her marriage vows, Ecgfrith finally relented and Audree, with Wilfrid's assistance, entered into the religious life at the monastery at Coldingham, presided over by Ecgfrith's aunt, Aebbe, another patron of Wilfrid. Ecgfrith then changed his mind and pursued his wife to Goldburch peak, where she had fled to escape him. God performed a miracle to protect her by making the sea rise up and surround the peak. A year after receiving the veil at Coldingham, Audree returned to Ely, where Wilfrid made her abbess of a newly-founded monastery, over which she ruled in an exemplary manner until her death from the plague seven years later. The abbey continued to exist, first under her sister and other female relatives, until it was destroyed in the ninth century by Danish raiders. Following a period in which the relics were poorly guarded by priests, it was refounded by St. Aethelwold in the tenth century as a male house, for which King Edgar made generous

---

[21] Wogan-Browne, "Rerouting the Dower," 28.
[22] See Ridyard, *Royal Saints*, 53–55, 200–10.
[23] Wogan-Browne, "Rerouting the Dower," 47.

provisions. The narrative continues with miracles of healing and of vengeance that took place during the Norman rule, ending with an episode of 1169.

The picture that emerges from this *vita* is that of an embattled woman, fiercely protecting herself from the sexual aggression of her husband, attacks by the ecclesiastical establishment who fail to respect her, and attempts by both her lay tenants as well as royal agents to defraud, cheat, and rob her of her possessions and rights. The *Liber Eliensis* had purposely heightened the aggression of Ecgfrith over his portrayal in Bede's life in which, while unhappy over Audree's choice, he did not oppose her. The reason for the increased threat from Ecgfrith in the twelfth-century life was to recast Audree in the mode of the classical virgin martyrs, presenting her as a representative of the cause of Ely who had triumphed over formidable attacks against her. The vernacular life goes even further, presenting not just Audree's defense against Ecgfrith, but virginity itself as a war waged against the flesh. Described unrelentingly in martial terms of "defense," "conquest," and "victory," virginity here is not a state but a process, an ongoing spiritual war against the flesh, which Audree wages by disciplining and subduing her body.

> Par les travaus ke ele suffri
> Tut charneus desirs venqui.
> La victoire de sa bounté
> Et de sa grant virginité
> Fu par tut le regne espandue
> Et entre le poeple sue.[24] (ll. 772–776)

[By the travails which she suffered she vanquished all carnal desire. The victory of her goodness and virginity spread throughout the kingdom and was known by all the people.]

One of the main changes to the Latin source text is the way this life militarizes Audree's virginity. Virginity is synonymous with strength and power, the qualities necessary for its attainment:

> Nul ne doit aveir mescreance
> Ke grant vertu et grant poissance
> N'eust la virge en honesteté
> De guarder sa virginité. (ll. 981–984)

[No one should doubt that the virgin had great strength and power to guard her virginity honestly.]

---

[24] Citations are to Östen Södergård, ed., *La Vie Seinte Audree: Poème Anglo-Normand du XIIIe Siècle* (Uppsala, 1955). Translations are my own.

Whereas in the Latin Audree's virginity was largely a passive resistance, the vernacular life makes it a conquest. Her resistance to Ecgfrith is described almost as a cosmic battle between good and evil: Ecgfrith is the "enemi malingne" whom Audree manages to defeat, thanks to the aid of God in his "gloire benigne."

Virginity in this life, far from being a posture of humility, submission, and renunciation, is a militant position of war and combat. Audree "venqui bien son premer mary / Et l'autre aprés dont ge vous cont" [vanquished her first husband and then the other that I have told you about (ll. 978–979)]. The portrayal of the saint that emerges from this *vita* is that of a fierce, even harsh defender of her own rights and interests, a saint who enjoys what amounts to a military alliance with God, who works to enforce her proprietary rights over her body and over the lands and wealth with which her body is homologous.

> Grant grace out de Deu receue,
> Kant ne pooit estre venceue,
> Kar issi come ele venqui
> Le quer de son primer ami
> Par la force Jhesu Crist
> Venquie ele l'autre, ceo dist. (ll. 1039–1044)

[She received a great grace from God since she could not be defeated. Because just as she had vanquished the heart of her first lover, by the strength of Jesus Christ it is written that she vanquished the other also.]

The reinscription of virginity as the locus of a conflict between a diabolically inspired aggressor and God's faithful is particularly evident in the posthumous miracles relating to Audree's burial and translations. While the miracles of the Norman period are primarily either cures meted out by Audree as a reward for faithful service or punishments for various kinds of offenses against her monastery, the period from the time of Audree's burial to the refounding by Aethelwold are dominated by corpse miracles, of which there are no fewer than four. These concern Audree's miraculously intact corpse and her efforts to protect it from violation, first by invading Danes and later by faithless priests. The purpose of these miracles is on the one hand to establish the fact of Audree's virginity witnessed by her incorrupt body, which preserves her property rights to her dower island of Ely (and thus those of the monks as guardians of her relics), and on the other to show Audree's defense of her body even in death. The first miracles, those surrounding Audree's burial and translation sixteen years after her death by her sister Sexburgh, serve to establish the miraculous incorruption of Audree's body and to draw a divine line in the sand warning against further attempts to violate her corpse. After having decided to translate her sister's body from the churchyard where it was buried to a more honorable situation inside the church, Sexburgh's men, sent in search of a suitable tomb, find a marvelous marble sarcophagus beside the city wall at Armesworde; it turns out to be an exact fit for Audree's body. Moreover, when Audree is installed in her new resting place, the lid forms a perfect seal, creating an indivisible enclosure — an obvious symbol of Audree's intact virginity as well as a sign that her tomb should be no more disturbed. During the ceremony — witnessed by many who had been present at her burial, including Bishop Wilfrid and Kinefrid, the physician who had attended Audree during her last illness — Audree's body is observed to be perfectly incorrupt. Moreover, a surgical wound in her neck, made by Kinefrid, who had lanced the swelling three days before her death, was observed to have healed in the tomb. In addition, all of those who participated in the ceremony and who came into contact with her clothing or tomb receive miraculous blessings of healing. Finally, a health-giving spring bubbles forth from the site where her body had been buried in the ground.

In the post-burial miracles, aggression against Audree's lands and privileges is synonymous with aggression against her body, and her self-defense is reinforced by divine vengeance. Given the miracle of the indivisible sarcophagus, which clearly showed God's will that Audree's body be left undisturbed, it is no surprise that Audree's tomb should locate a symbolic struggle between God's faithful and the devil's agents. The first attack comes from pagan Danish raiders of the ninth century, who destroyed the convent and killed the nuns. Inspired by the devil, one of the Danes brutally attacks Audree's sarcophagus, hacking a hole through the stone in hopes of finding treasure inside; he is punished by losing his eyes and dying. This conflict sets the stage for an elaborate and scathing denunciation of the role of seculars at Ely. The next assault on Audree comes not from alien pagans, but from those whom the text paints as their moral equivalents: the priests, who had replaced the monks as guardians of Audree's relics after the destruction of the monastery. The negative portrayal of the priests here is part of a narrative thread of competition between seculars and monastics for control of Ely; the contest culminates when King Edgar, under the instructions of a divine voice, expels the seculars and installs monks. But what is interesting for our purposes is the way in which this episode portrays virginity as an act of conquest, a military victory that can only be attained by a continual process of defense against aggression, even after death.

In what is a thinly veiled symbolic rape, the head priest, having often proclaimed his disbelief in the "old stories" told about Audree, decides to inspect the body for himself. Undissuaded by one of his fellows, who relates in vain several miracles to prove Audree's sanctity, he attempts to view the body by holding a candle to the hole that had been made by the Danish grave robber. To the great horror of the people, the candle falls inside, but even though it continues to flame within the tomb, it miraculously does no damage either to Audree's coverings or to her corpse. Despite the warnings shouted out to him by the crowd, he summons four young men and attempts to penetrate the hole in her sarcophagus with rods equipped with iron hooks — "which travel in and out eight times" — in order to pull the clothing off the body and view its state. When she feels that someone is trying to remove her clothing, Audree reacts by pulling her clothing back through the hole "with such force, in their opinion, as if the hand of a man were pulling," and by issuing a warning that they will suffer dire consequences, since they do not have permission either from herself or from God to displace her shroud. In an echo of the punishment of the Danish pagan, the chief priest is punished by the destruction of his house, property, and family, while the devil drags his soul off to hell.

The *Vie Ste. Modwenna* is a thirteenth-century reworking of an earlier Latin life of Modwenna, most likely that of Geoffrey, abbot of Burton (1114–51). This life was itself a reworking of an eleventh-century *vita* by the Irish hagiographer, Conchubranus. The cult of Modwenna was most closely associated with Burton. Modwenna is a composite saint, a conflation of the fifth-century St. Darerca, also known as Moninne, who was the foundress of Killevy, and St. Monenna, also known as Modwenna, who flourished in the mid-seventh century, founding many churches in England and Scotland. The Anglo-Norman life, at more than eight thousand lines, is one of the longest texts of thirteenth-century insular hagiography. Particularly interesting is the way it portrays female religious authority within a male ecclesiastical hierarchy. The *Vie Ste. Modwenna* conforms to a familiar hagiographical tradition of positing a parallel between the flesh and femininity, yet within this tradition the *Vie Ste. Modwenna* describes a more positive role for the flesh (and thus for female identity) insofar as it offers the means to redemption through subordination and control. Reflecting thirteenth-century concerns about the role of pastoral care in salvation, a central theme of this "romanz," as it is called in MS. Digby 34, is the "nature" of nature, and in particular the significance of the incarnation. Over and over the stories stress the analogy between miraculous reversals of the course of physical nature and the reversal of the fallen state of human nature through the supervention of grace. A miracle in which Modwenna transforms water into wine is followed by one in which she reforms the conscience of a wayward nun, the transformation of physical nature providing a type for the greater miracle of spiritual transformation. Nature is not fixed and immutable, but constantly slipping between perdition and the redemption that can come about through pastoral education or supervenient grace. An episode in which Modwenna converts a wolf from his predatory ways into the guardian of cattle shows pastoral chastisement to be redemptive and decisive. The cultural transformation becomes a transformation of the bodily nature itself, when not only the wolf but its offspring refrain from harming domestic animals and develop a white mark to indicate their transformed nature. The miracle that follows describes a cattle thief, who is confounded by a miraculously changing landscape; it confines him within boiling streams and drives him to repentance, emphasizing that Modwenna's miracles' "encontre nature" echo the miracle of spiritual transformation brought about through preaching. Likewise Modwenna, by renouncing the claims of nature, including "cunfort d'ami e de parent," can transcend the limits of her feminine corporality and actually exceed her male counterparts in virtue without disrupting the social hierarchy necessary in the post-lapsarian world. As a result, she exercises what is in effect a masculine moral authority, thanks to her constantly reiterated ability to dominate nature — most importantly her own nature. Her miracles, overturning the laws of physical nature, are a metaphor for this ability.

Man's sinful nature is therefore not only not an impediment to salvation and grace, but actually the means whereby salvation may be achieved. This *vita* emphasizes the fundamental role that the body plays in restoring the original state of perfection that was the original "nature" of God's created world. Ascesis and physical domination of the body are a means to self-regeneration: by punishing the body, the cause of original sin is overcome. Thus when, by means of the gift of Modwenna's girdle, Columkille (St. Columba) manages to overcome the lust that had tormented him all his life, he finds that the relief leads to spiritual laxness. Now the angels who had previously helped him in his combat against lust refrain from visiting him. Once Columkille absorbs the message — that his struggle against lust had served as a spiritual training field and gymnasium — he returns Modwenna's girdle so that the temptation will return. When that happens, the angels resume their visits.

In this view, the weak and defective body of a woman actually offers more opportunities for spiritual exercise and the attainment of spiritual perfection than that of a man. The spiritually perfected body of Modwenna is even physically stronger than a man's. When Modwenna's friend, the nobleman Erdulf, visits her and forgets to bring a book he had wanted to read to her, Modwenna sends two girls from her convent to travel to Erdulf's home by boat to fetch it. During the course of their journey the boat is overturned, but God miraculously saves them by making the water withdraw into two solid walls, leaving the river bed dry and the girls huddled underneath the overturned boat. When Modwenna and Erdulf arrive and witness the miracle, Erdulf attempts to raise the boat and release the girls; lacking the strength to do so, he turns to Modwenna and says, "If you want it lifted, lend your hand; it is stronger, as you know, than mine, because of your goodness."[25]

Yet while the flesh is something that must be mastered and controlled, it cannot be denied, since bodily identity — the payment of the debt of nature — is essential to salvation. Just as negotiating the proper relationship between body and spirit requires recognizing the needs of the body, so also must the emotional needs of human nature be acknowledged. This text is notable for its nuanced, layered, and complex treatment of such human needs as the desire for affection. In one episode, Modwenna's spiritual daughter, St. Bride (St. Brigid), offers Modwenna a silver cup, which she begs her to accept as a sign of her love. Modwenna, for virtually the only time, "ne se set si cunseiller," and even more surprisingly, resorts to a deception. Torn between the claims of Bride's sincere devotion and her own desire to avoid pride and inspire love for God rather than love for herself, she pretends to accept the cup and then hides it where she thinks it will never be found. Some time after Modwenna has left and returned to Killevy, a nun finds the cup and takes it to St. Bride, who exclaims bitterly that Modwenna must surely have set little store by her love if she so carelessly abandoned the cup. While Modwenna

---

[25] Se vus pleist qu'il seit levez
La vostre main i metez;
Ele est plus forte, ço sachiez,
Ke la meie pur vos buntez. (ll. 6085–6088)

Citations are to *St. Modwenna*, ed. Baker and Bell. Translations are my own.

wishes to avoid earthly encumbrances, at the same time the human need to feel love is a condition of mortality. In this episode, Bride reacts with very human feelings of betrayal and hurt before she is led to a true understanding of the cup's meaning, tossing it into a river where it miraculously navigates against the current, finally reaching its intended recipient.

At the same time that the text affirms that Modwenna's goodness comes not just from her renunciation of physical comforts and material goods but from her renunciation of all worldly attachments, including affection and the "comfort of relatives and friends," it does not condemn these human needs. Rather the text acknowledges them and by doing so incorporates and rehabilitates the values of affection and friendship into the redemptive message. Just as the privations imposed on the body, with its natural desires for comfort, ease, and pleasure, should not aim at mutilating or destroying that body, the value of disciplining normal human desires for emotional bonds lies in directing them towards God's love rather than human love. Although the story confirms the incompatibility of placing human desires before holiness, it problematizes the issue by legitimizing Bride's sentiments, which are also acknowledged by Modwenna. Tender human sentiments, like the tender flesh of woman, paradoxically offer the means for the exercise of superior spiritual power that comes from disciplining this human need towards fulfillment in God. In a hagiographical culture inclined to see female sanctity in terms of a radical de-feminizing of the protagonists, the *Vie Ste. Modwenna* offers a subtle reinscription of feminine religious authority — authority proceeding not from the negation of the flesh, but by virtue of its incorporation and subjection in a redemptive transformation.

The hierarchical structure of society is the social analogue of the relationship between fallen nature and the perfected nature that represents both God's original creation as well as the reward of the faithful (those who accept the consequences of the fall — which are sin and death — and who express their faith by confession and repentance). Whereas the social hierarchy does not reflect divine favor or moral status, it is the necessary condition of life on earth and must be respected, even though the relations that it instantiates may be the exact opposite of the divine order. Thus while Modwenna is the acknowledged moral superior of both the secular and religious authorities she meets, she not only accepts but insists on her "natural" subservience to her institutional superiors. When Bishop Ibar asks Modwenna as a favor to accept his relative into her convent, Modwenna tells him "You should not ask me to do this . . . but rather command me, sir. It is yours to command, and mine to obey; mine to ask, yours to consent. Thus we must play our parts, if it pleases you" (ll. 3091–3096).[26]

---

[26] 'Ne m'en devez de ço preer,'
   Fait ele, 'sire, mais comander.
   Vus comander, jo obeir;
   Jo requere, vus cunsentir;
   Isci devum le giu partir,
   S'il vus vient bien a pleisir.'

Just like fallen nature, which by its very defects points to its perfected opposite, institutional authority points to the gap between human social organization and the divine hierarchy. The episode in which Modwenna resurrects a pig shows that whereas man can order and "civilize" the fallen natural world through the imposition of ceremony and structure, only divine power can regenerate the natural world. In this story, a reformed swineherd expresses his gratitude to Modwenna by killing a pig and bringing the prepared meat to her convent as a gift, whereupon he is distressed to learn that he has killed his pig for naught since Modwenna and the members of her convent have given up eating meat. Modwenna consoles him by praying over the sliced meat, which miraculously gathers and reassembles itself into a living pig. Modwenna next expresses her willingness to accept a wild beast as a gift and tells him that he will find one waiting. In an obvious allusion to Abraham, the rustic finds a wild deer hung by the horns in a thicket; he manages to kill the deer and bring it back "without a hound, without a dog, without a bow, without an arrow, to Modwenna." The true miracle at the heart of this story is the spiritual renewal of the sinner, which is brought about through Modwenna's pastoral teaching. Hunting, characterized by the structuring and ceremony reserved for the upper classes and typical of the human social order, is placed in stark contrast to the regenerative power of Christian faith and charity symbolized by the episode of Abraham and Isaac. Human hierarchy requires the socially mediated knowledge of the ceremonies of the hunt, such as forking the deer or raising the haunch, which contrast with the charity and love represented by Abraham's willingness to sacrifice his own son, and which is symbolized by the offering of the ram caught in the brambles. Just as the defects of man's fleshly nature point to the perfection of God's original creation, so the social hierarchy which serves to order and contain fallen nature also points to its biggest failure: the inability to regenerate nature.

Like her saintly sisters, Osith and Audree, it is undoubtedly true that Modwenna represents not a biography but an idea: the triumph of the weak and the fallen through God's grace. As a woman, Modwenna symbolizes God's ability to redeem fallen human nature through repentance leading to forgiveness. Yet it would be a mistake to discount the real-life influence of hagiographic models simply because hagiography is primarily concerned with abstract ideas. In the Middle Ages, hagiography was the primary literary genre that treated women as protagonists. Moreover, hagiography is the literary genre in which women are treated as independent, authoritative, and equal to men in moral stature and social influence. Even though the social status of the women depicted in these texts was a fiction created by a complex intersection of colliding political and religious constructs, the literary characters that live in these works may have had an important role in mapping a feminine ideal of equality, power, and independence.[27] This is especially true if

---

[27] See Jocelyn Wogan-Browne's discussions of the possible reception and impact of the *Vie Ste. Modwenna* in "Rerouting the Dower" and in Jocelyn Price, "*La Vie de Sainte Modwenne*: A Neglected Anglo-Norman Hagiographic Text, and Some Implications for English Secular Literature," *Medium Aevum* 57 (1988): 172–89.

one considers that the Anglo-Norman translations, which date from the end of the twelfth century and remained popular into the fourteenth, bring these saints to a new and socially different audience, removed from the political conditions that created the originals. All three of the lives discussed here are found in the famous manuscript known as Welbeck I C. I, which, in the fourteenth century, was owned by the nunnery of Campsey Ash, Suffolk, where it was used for mealtime readings.[28] Although created for other purposes, the positive literary representation of saints as self-affirming single women must surely have offered inspiring models for the real women who read them.[29]

Jane Zatta
Southern Illinois University

---

[28] All three of these lives are found in one manuscript, which in the fourteenth century was owned by the nunnery of Campsey Ash in Suffolk, where, according to an annotation on one folio, it was used for mealtime readings. See Wogan-Browne, " 'Clerc u lai,' " 79 n. 12. One can only imagine how such lives would have resonated for women of the fourteenth century, many coming from aristocratic backgrounds similar to the heroines. Formerly known as Welbeck Abbey MS. I C. I, it is now on permanent loan to the British Library as British Library MS. Additional 70531. It has been described by Louis Karl, "Notice sur l'unique manuscrit français de la bibliothèque du duc de Portland a Welbeck," *Revue des Langues Romanes* 54 (1911): 210–29.

[29] For example, the psalter produced by the monks of St. Albans for Christina of Markyate contained the earliest extant text of the Alexis legend. This figure, who began his saintly career by rejecting a marriage arranged by his wealthy parents, recalls the life of Christina, who also rebelled against her father's wishes and refused the marriage chosen for her by him in preference for a religious career. See Wogan-Browne, " 'Clerc u lai,' " 71.

2

I Want to Be Alone:

The Single Woman in Fifteenth-Century Legends of St. Katherine of Alexandria

In terms of extant Middle English texts, there are more versions of the story of the virgin martyr Katherine of Alexandria than there are of any other saint.[1] This is largely due to its popularity in the latter part of the fourteenth and fifteenth centuries, in which the legend enjoyed a pronounced dynamism. More than half of the thirteen legends listed in *Writings in Middle English* by D'Evelyn and Foster were produced in this period. In particular, the *Late Middle English Prose Katherine* (hereafter *LMEPK*), first developed around 1420, branched out immediately into five different versions and now survives in twenty-three manuscripts.[2] The *LMEPK* is indicative of a new interest in a life-story of Katherine as opposed to a *passio*, two terms which will be explained via a quick summary of the legend's traditional narrative.

A remarkable fact about Katherine is that there is no evidence that she ever

---

[1] See Charlotte D'Evelyn and Frances A. Foster, "Saints' Legends," in *A Manual of the Writings in Middle English*, gen. ed. J. Burke Severs, 9 vols. (New Haven, 1970), 2: 599–602. This bibliography lists thirteen Middle English versions of the legend. Moreover, this number excludes other versions listed by Jacqueline Jenkins, " 'Such peple as be not letterd in scripture': Popular Devotion and the Legend of St. Katherine of Alexandria in Late Medieval England," Ph.D. diss., University of Western Ontario, 1996.

[2] Auvo Kurvinen, "The Life of St. Catharine of Alexandria in Middle English Prose" (Ph.D. diss., Oxford University, 1960), divided twenty-two of these manuscripts into four versions. The fifth, Southwell Minster MS. 7, has been edited: *St. Katherine of Alexandria: The Late Middle English Prose Legend in Southwell Minster MS. 7*, ed. Saara Nevanlinna and Irma Taavitsainen (Cambridge, 1993).

existed.[3] Nevertheless, while specific dates vary across her tradition, Katherine was reputedly martyred in Alexandria in the early fourth century under the persecutions of Maximian. According to her legend, Katherine is the only and long-awaited child of the rich and noble king of Alexandria, Costus. She is remarkably well educated and of formidable intellect. When her father dies she is urged to marry in order to provide the realm with a male ruler who will continue the family dynasty. She resists this pressure because she would prefer to remain single. Instructed in the Christian faith by an eremitic monk, she undergoes a heavenly marriage to Christ. It is only the tradition of her life-story that gives substantial consideration to these early stages of Katherine's life before it then moves on to the subject of her martyrdom. By contrast, *passio* narratives of Katherine — shorter narratives attending to the saint's passion — begin at the following point of her life-story. When Maxentius, the Roman prefect, instigates pagan worship and animal sacrifice in Alexandria, Katherine protests and is thrown in jail, but not before she has impressed Maxentius with her ability to reason and argue. He summons fifty scholars to Alexandria in the hope that they will publicly put down Katherine and her creed in an intellectual contest. Instead she refutes the arguments of the pagan scholars and converts them. The fifty scholars are burned as martyrs and Katherine is thrown back into prison, where she also manages to convert Maxentius's wife and the head of his guard. Both are martyred, the former having been brutally tortured. Because Katherine consistently refuses to renounce her faith, a devilish instrument of torture is designed to try and overcome her will: the "Katherine Wheel." Before it can harm her, the wheel miraculously shatters into pieces and kills thousands of pagans. Exasperated by her intellect and obdurate faith, Maxentius has Katherine beheaded.

The later medieval enthusiasm for Katherine is reflected both in the amount of narratives produced and in changes in narrative form. The dynamic *LMEPK* is testimony to a growing fifteenth-century English interest in a version of Katherine telling her complete story, rather than only the latter part. This interest can be observed in the formal composition decisions of the century's two translations of that *locus classicus* of medieval hagiography, Jacobus de Voragine's *Legenda aurea* (c. 1260;

---

[3] Scholars have tried to find such evidence. It is, for instance, a thesis put forward by Einenkel that Katherine is a version of the pagan female philosopher Hypatia, "so striking are the similarities of the life of our saint with that of her pagan paragon": *The Life of Saint Katherine*, ed. Eugen Einenkel, EETS 80 (London, 1884), xi. See also *St. Katherine of Alexandria*, ed. Nevanlinna and Taavitsainen, 4; Jenkins, "'Such peple,'" 32; Jennifer Relwyn Bray, "The Legend of St. Katherine in Later Middle English Literature" (Ph.D. diss., University of London, 1984), 17. Bray makes the best that can be made of the Hypatia analogue. She regards it as, perhaps, "part of a background of credibility against which the Katherine legend developed." Katherine has also been associated with another figure persecuted by Maximian and described by Eusebius (A.D. 260–340) in his *Historia Ecclesiastica*, "a noblewoman renowned for wealth, birth and education": Eusebius, *The Ecclesiastical History*, trans. J. E. L. Oulton (London, 1932), 2.8.14. However, this figure has been associated with the tradition of Dorothy: see Bray, "Legend," 84–85; Jenkins, "'Such peple,'" 9; and Manfred Görlach, *The South English Legendary, the Gilte Legende and the Golden Legend* (Braunschweig, 1972), 13.

hereafter *La*). In the thirteenth-century Latin text, Katherine, like all other female and most male martyrs, is represented by a *passio* narrative.[4] However, the two fifteenth-century English versions of this Latin collection — the *Gilte Legende* of 1438 and Caxton's *Golden Legend* (1483) — graft Version B of the *LMEPK* onto Jacobus's *passio* to complete a consideration of Katherine which, in terms of the *La*'s tendency towards abbreviated treatments of saints, is unique in its comprehensiveness.[5] Finally, the exhaustive *Katharine*, produced between 1438 and 1445 by John Capgrave, an Augustinian prior at the convent in Lynn (East Anglia), is over eight thousand lines long.[6] The fifteenth-century enthusiasm for a fuller account of Katherine is an important entry in an account of the single woman in Western culture. The longer narrative form embraces the development of feminine singleness as a thinkable concept within a context where only relational constructs of the female seem previously to have prevailed.

The *passio* form of narrative is sympathetic to the priorities of the martyr it celebrates. Christian martyrs evidently regard their life as something of no importance in respect of the faith they hold. Medieval hagiography often celebrates the ostensibly destructive process of martyrdom as a positive form of creation or refinement. Thus Jacobus de Voragine concludes his version of Vincent with Augustine's exegesis: "He was stretched and twisted to make him suppler, scourged to make him learn better, pummeled to make him more robust, burned to make him cleaner" (*GL*, 1: 107).[7] Notions of victimization as shaping, making, purging, purifying,

---

[4] See Jacobus a Voragine, *Legenda aurea*, ed. T. Graesse, 3rd ed. (Vratislava, 1890; repr. Osnabrück, 1965). The term "life-story" here is a working term, the Middle English generic terms within hagiography being a complex business: see Paul Strohm, "*Passioun, Lyf, Miracle, Legende*: Some Generic Terms In Middle English Hagiographical Narrative," *The Chaucer Review* 10 (1975): 62–75, 154–71. *Passio*, by contrast, designates a quite distinct matter in a medieval context, as Strohm shows: a "passio [is] for the events associated with the trial, suffering, and death of a martyr" (67). We see the distinction between a *passio* and a fuller treatment working in the Katherine narrative of one medieval hagiographer, Osbern Bokenham, who is contemporaneous with the substance of much of this discussion and who is discussed below. He declares that he will not "telle hou she fyrst began/ To be crystyne, & howe oon clepyd Adryan / Hyr conuertyd & crystnyd in hyr youthe." Rather he will tell "No more but oonly þe passyoun": see Osbern Bokenham, *Legendys of Hooly Wummen*, ed. Mary S. Serjeantson, EETS 206 (London, 1938), 6350–64.

[5] A transcription of Version B of the *LMEPK*, taken from Stonyhurst Archives, MS. XLIII, fols. 1–19[v], can be found in Kurvinen, "The Life of St. Catharine of Alexandria." There is as yet no complete edition of the *Gilte Legende*, but see *Three Lives from The Gilte Legende*, ed. R. Hamer (Heidelberg, 1978), 11 for this inclusion. For the inclusion of Version B in Caxton's *Golden Legend* see *The Golden Legend or Lives of the Saints as Englished By William Caxton*, ed. F. S. Ellis, 7 vols. (London, 1900), 7: 1–30.

[6] John Capgrave, *The Life of St. Katharine of Alexandria*, ed. Carl Horstmann, EETS 100 (London, 1893; repr. New York, 1973). This text is discussed later. All references are to this edition.

[7] *La*, 120. All quotations of the *La* are taken from the translation, Jacobus de Voragine, *The Golden Legend: Readings on the Saints*, trans. William Granger Ryan, 2 vols. (Princeton, 1993), hereafter *GL*. References to the original Latin *La* (ed. Graesse) are given in the notes. I am here using the *La* as a text representative of the medieval *passio* narrative. This is a legitimate reflection of the *La*'s importance. Almost all post-*La* English hagiographers had read Jacobus de Voragine's

dressing, and baptism are common. The martyr Ignatius provides a good male example; before he is thrown to the lions he prays, "I am the wheat of Christ! May I be ground fine by the teeth of the beasts, that I may be made a clean bread!" (*GL*, 1: 142).[8] Agatha offers a good female example: during her own torture she declares that, "The wheat cannot be stored in the barn unless it has been thoroughly threshed and separated from the chaff: so my soul cannot enter paradise unless you make the headsman give my body harsh treatment" (*GL*, 1: 155).[9] Martyrdom, then, is a kind of alchemy, where raw materials are transformed into their quintessence. It is not so much a defining act as a re-defining act. It is of such a transcendent nature in this regard that it obviates any detailed consideration of the personal, character-defining history of the martyr who undergoes it. Why write about raw materials or chaff when it is the product, the wheat, that matters? There is, therefore, something highly appropriate about a narrative form which disregards biographical features and only concentrates on the martyr's self-sacrificial performance.

In keeping with such priorities, biographical features within *passio* narratives are both kept to a minimum and are fore-destined. The opening of the *La* Agatha *passio* illustrates this:

> The virgin Agatha was highborn and a great beauty, living in the city of Catania, where she worshipped God at all times and in all holiness. Quintianus, the consular official in Sicily, who was baseborn, libidinous, greedy, and a worshipper of idols, was determined to get her in his grasp. Being of low degree he would gain respect by lording it over a noble, her beauty would satisfy his libido, he would steal her riches to feed his avarice, and, being a pagan, he would force her to sacrifice to the gods.
> So he had her brought before him. . . . (*GL*, 1: 154)[10]

The minimalism of biographical detail scarcely needs elaborating: prior to Agatha's summons to the stage of martyrdom, all that it is necessary for us to know is that she was a noble, beautiful and pious virgin from Catania. The geographical detail apart, such characteristics render her pretty much indistinct from many female martyrs. The fore-destination of biographical detail, however, requires explanation. Fore-destination describes a mode of characterization that imagines the martyr-to-be as utterly incapable of any other destiny but martyrdom. Thus Agatha is totalized by her destiny before it comes about insofar as her life is dedicated to God — "she

---

extensive collection in some form; it is a source for all Middle English hagiographic collections. It survives in over one thousand manuscripts, and with the development of printing in the 1450s it appears to have been translated into every Western European language.

[8] *La*, 157.

[9] *La*, 171. The tradition of the Holy Innocents is, perhaps, the founding example of the theological principle of martyrdom as baptism: "And by their martyrdom they attained baptismal innocence, being cleansed of original sin" (*La*, 63/*GL*, 1: 56).

[10] *La*, 170.

worshipped God at *all* times and in *all* holiness" (my emphasis) — *before* that dedication is physically enacted as self-immolation. Thus we have something of a paradox. Martyrdom is a great changing process wherein raw materials are refined. However, when it figures as the subject-matter of a narrative, martyrdom has an impact upon narrative style such that martyrs-to-be are refined of qualities superfluous to their future destiny. *Passio* narratives tend to show martyrs-in-waiting, rather than raw materials becoming martyrs. The great change that the narrative form celebrates almost occurs *avant la lettre* of its narratives.

For female martyrs, this means that the form forecloses upon the question of feminine singleness. The fore-destination of martyrological qualities requires that a conflicting human relationship be co-extensive with the female martyr. The female martyrological text's preoccupation with virginity or chastity (in line with a patristic and medieval theologizing of female religiosity) is crucial in this regard: female martyrological sanctity is always dependent upon what the female does — or does not do — with her body.[11] Pagan opponents testify to the peculiarly carnal location of female sanctity in the numerous legends where they attempt to counter the female martyr's faith with sexual corruption or rape.[12] The bodily nature of female faith is more generally implicit in the many legends where the female martyr does not so much die for the Christian faith she believes in, but dies, rather, because this faith takes a form (i.e., virginity) that fatally collides with a prospective earthly relationship.[13] In both cases, female sanctity is characterized as a relational state insofar

---

[11] For discussions of virginity theology which illustrate the centrality of virginity to female religiosity, see John Bugge, *Virginitas: An Essay in the History of a Medieval Ideal* (The Hague, 1975), 59–110; Peter Brown, *The Body and Society: Men, Women, and Sexual Renunciation in Early Christianity* (New York, 1988), 259–84; Rosemary Radford Reuther, *Religion and Sexism* (New York, 1974), 150–83; Clarissa W. Atkinson, " 'Precious Balsam in a Fragile Glass': The Ideology of Virginity in the Later Middle Ages," *Journal of Family History* 8 (1983): 131–43; Barbara Newman, "Flaws in the Golden Bowl: Gender and Spiritual Formation in the Twelfth Century," *Traditio* 45 (1989–1990): 111–46; Marina Warner, *Alone of All Her Sex: The Myth and the Cult of the Virgin Mary* (London, 1976), 65–81; and R. Howard Bloch, *Medieval Misogyny and the Invention of Western Romantic Love* (Chicago, 1991), 93–112. For discussions specifically detailing the significance of virginity for the female martyrological text, see the introduction to *The Lady as Saint: A Collection of French Hagiographic Romances of the Thirteenth Century*, ed. Brigitte Cazelles (Philadelphia, 1991), 3–12; and Joyce E. Salisbury, *Church Fathers, Independent Virgins* (London, 1991), 26–39.

[12] See the legends of Lucy (*La*, 31/*GL*, 1: 27–29), Agnes (*La*, 116/*GL*, 1: 101–4), Agatha (*La*, 170/*GL*, 1: 154–56), The Virgin of Antioch (*La*, 274/*GL*, 1: 250–54), and Euphemia (*La*, 621/ *GL*, 2: 181).

[13] See the legends of Margaret (*La*, 400–3/*GL*, 2: 232–33), Agnes, and Agatha. Ursula and the Eleven Thousand Virgins (*La*, 701–5/*GL*, 2: 256–60), Cecilia (*La*, 771–77/*GL*, 2: 318–23) and Juliana (*La*, 177–78/*GL*, 1: 160–61), are martyred because they represent an ideological danger in a pagan society. However, their course towards martyrdom is activated by the prospect of an earthly sexual relationship. Thus, even though it is meaningless, in terms of what they are martyred for, they are still dramatized as figures whose faith makes them incompatible with an earthly relationship. Such narratives could almost be said to go out of their way to make this point.

as it appears to be a transcendent bond that earthly sexual relations would ruin. The tormentor who would have Lucy raped, for instance, intends thereby to violate her relationship with the Holy Spirit: "Your body will be defiled and you will lose the holy spirit" (GL, 1: 28).[14] Agnes, executed because she will not requite a pagan's love, articulates this transcendent bond explicitly:

> I am already pledged to another lover ... The one I love is far nobler than you, of more eminent descent. His mother is a virgin, his father knows no woman, he is served by angels ...
>
> He has placed a wedding ring on my right hand, and a necklace of precious stones around my neck, gowned me with a robe woven with gold and jewels, placed a mark on my forehead to keep me from taking any lover but himself, and his blood has tinted my cheeks. Already his chaste embraces hold me close, he has united his body to mine, and he has shown me incomparable treasures, and promised to give them to me if I remain true to him. (GL, 1: 102)[15]

This is the *Sponsa Christi* or Bride of Christ trope: the interpretation of virginity as an intimate partnership between virgin and saviour. Further, to quote Ambrose (c. A.D. 339–397), who demonstrates the antique nature of the topic, "a virgin is one who gives her hand to God."[16]

The history of this complex trope makes it clear that the Bride of Christ is not always a female office.[17] However, the martyrological corpus is a reflection of the degree to which the trope has a ready application to the female religious. Not all female martyrs are explicitly labeled *Sponsa Christi*, but the overwhelming majority of them are represented by dramas which, in varying ways, observe that their sanctity is dependent on the exclusively heavenward orientation of their sexuality. This is the reason why the *passio* form tends to foreclose on any question of the female martyr's singleness. For, in the typical structure of female martyr *passio* narratives, a *Sponsa Christi* destiny means that the ostensibly single female martyr is totalized as a *Sponsa Christi* in waiting. This varies in form: either the martyr's faithful virginity is stated positively as a marital-type bond with a heavenly bridegroom, *à la* Agnes, or it is dramatized negatively through resistance to (another) relationship. But what does not vary is the way that this faithful, *attached* virginity is something of a naturalized assumption within the narrative. The notion that a female may wish to avoid union with men simply out of a subjective preference for a single, independent life is not so much denied as it is unthinkable.

---

[14] *La*, 31.

[15] *La*, 114.

[16] Ambrose, *De Virginibus* 8.52, PL 16. 203: "Virgo est, quae Deo nubit."

[17] Bugge, *Virginitas*, 60, quotes an instance from the apocryphal *Acts of the Apostle Thomas* where Christ urges the virginal life upon a newly married couple: "Receive that marriage incorruptible and true; and you will be in it companions of the bridegroom, going in along with Him into that bridal chamber full of immortality and light."

A few brief illustrations will clarify, one of which has been cited already, the opening of the Agatha legend. What is telling is the blithe way that this opening moves from minimal biographical details to the desire of Agatha's suitor, Quintianus. At the end of her legend when she is martyred, Jacobus (quoting Ambrose) describes Agatha as a "bride [borne] heavenward to Christ" (*GL*, 1: 157).[18] This ultimate destiny is the reason why Quintianus's desire for Agatha at the outset of the legend seems to have an almost *a priori* status. For the adamantine nature of Agatha's faithful commitment to her future bridegroom is defined by her defense of it in the face of the threatening desire of Quintianus. Thus Quintianus' entrance in the narrative —

> she worshipped God at all times and in all holiness. Quintianus, the consular official in Sicily, who was baseborn, libidinous, greedy, and a worshipper of idols, was determined to get her in his grasp

— which seems almost to proceed on the basis that it has been *implied*, is, in this respect, an example of how the narrative encodes the assumption that Agatha's vocation is a religious office that is above all resistant to sexual relations. To put it another way, Quintianus's entrance only *relevantly* follows Agatha's holiness according to an encoded assumption that her holiness is incompatible with a sexual attachment (cue Quintianus). Therefore, at a level that structures narrative, her holiness is being felt as the exclusive *Sponsa Christi* attachment it is destined to become.

What is significant about this example is that it shows feminine singleness to be something of a blind spot. As a vocational virgin, Agnes is ostensibly a single woman, yet the terms in which her narrative naturally proceeds sublimate an inability to think of her in this way: according to this sublimation, it is implicitly seamless, rather than tangential, that her narrative should move from her faith to the *other* carnal attachment that threatens it. In the martyrological corpus, that virginal women are not single women, but are attached, is not so much something written of women as much as it is *the* way of writing *about* them. A general illustration of this is the generic predilection for young female martyrs on the threshold of a sexual life: in the *La*, and at the outset of their *passio* narratives, Lucy and Juliana are betrothed, Agnes and Katherine are betrothed to God, Ursula is of betrothal age, Anastasia and Cecilia are newly married, the Virgin of Antioch is described as *puella*, and Margaret is fifteen.[19] Jacobus de Voragine does not give the age of Christine, but in the *South English Legendary*, an English collection of the late thirteenth century, we are told that her martyrological ordeal lasted two years, beginning at the age of twelve and ending with her death at fourteen.[20] In the legends

---

[18] *La*, 174.

[19] One need only consider how rare it is for a female martyr to be advanced in years. Jacobus de Voragine would appear to offer us only one example amongst the 263 saints included in the Graesse edition, that of Apollonia (*La*, 293–95/ *GL*, 1: 268–69).

[20] The *South English Legendary* is the first major collection of saints' lives in the vernacular. It

of Euphemia, Justina, and Agatha, the saint's age is not specified, but she is introduced to us as a beautiful, virginal daughter. With the female martyr's adolescence, or a very specific threshold of sexuality, as their point of departure, these narratives presuppose that the meaningfulness of the martyr's fundamentally relational faith coincides with the meaningfulness of her sexuality. Her transcendent attachment as a Christian virgin is coincident with the sexual maturation that makes being a virgin significant and contestable. Thus the genre does not conceive of feminine singleness *because* it is concerned with female faith. The logic of this occlusion is that female faith is a matter of a virginal and relational vocation held in respect of Christ. Such a vocation is coextensive with a sexual life even to the extent that martyrs are betrothed to Christ as schoolgirls (as, for example, in the case of Agnes). The genre conceives only of brides and children.

This should, I hope, begin to suggest the significance of the fifteenth-century popular English development of a life-story of Katherine. Before Katherine is a Christian virgin, martyr, and *Sponsa Christi* contesting on behalf of the faith with pagan authorities, she is an unmarried woman of eighteen. She has the female martyr's typical resistance to sexual relations or marital prospects. However, as a pagan, she does not have a *Sponsa Christi* orientation to her virginity. An increasing interest in her full life-story is at least, in part, an interest in how someone who is not yet a martyr *becomes* a martyr, including, specifically, the progress of a single woman with an undisclosed future, who then becomes Bride and martyr of Christ in what is, therefore, an expression of choice and subjectivity. Such becoming and subjectivity is precluded by the one-dimensional personas and narratives of the *passio* form. The two texts in question here are those mentioned at the outset, the *LMEPK* (more specifically, the Version B of particular popularity) and John Capgrave's *Katharine*. The form of these two texts gradually allows for the progressive conception of feminine singleness in one key scene, the parliamentary marriage debate, where the as yet un-Christian Queen Katherine is put under considerable pressure to marry in order to provide her realm with a ruler.

I shall begin with the *LMEPK*. The debate begins with Katherine's initial objection to marriage. She argues that she has loyal servants enough to guarantee law and order without the imposition of a "straunge lord" on her and the country.[21] Her uncle then stands up and points out that Katherine is, by nature, in possession of a four-fold excellence: royal blood, most noble womanhood, pre-eminent intelligence, and physical beauty (168–75). The thrust of his argument is that Katherine has been superbly designed for marriage. Katherine is grateful for this praise but ingeniously trumps it: "lyk as ȝe have dyscryved us, we wyl discryve hym þat we

---

is written in verse. Still extant in fifty-one manuscripts, it was the most widely circulated and popularly available representation of sanctity from the end of the thirteenth century to the middle of the fifteenth. For this detail about Christine see *The South English Legendary*, ed. Charlotte D'Evelyn and Anna J. Mill, 3 vols., EETS 235, 236, 244 (London, 1956, 1959), 1: 327, 362–63.

[21] All references to Version B of the *LMEPK* are taken from the line numbers of Kurvinen's transcription in "The Life of St. Catharine of Alexandria."

wyl have to oure lord and husbond" (181–82). The only man she will marry will also be in possession of "iiij notable thyngys." He shall be so noble that all kings must worship him, so great that she would never dare to think she made him king, surpassing all others in riches, so beautiful as to transfix angels, so pure that his mother is a virgin, and so benign as to forgive all (184–92; this would appear to be more than four points, but the important point is her rhetorical *touché*). Her response angers her mother, who asks, "Qwo saw ever ony woman forge here an husbond wyth wurdys? seche oon as 3e have devysed was never noon, ne never shal be" (203–5). With a "pytows syhynge voys" Katherine responds:

> Madame, I wot be very reson þat þer is oon meche better þan I can devyse hym, who so had grace to fynde hym. And but he be hys grace fynde me, trostyth fully þat I xel never have joye; for I fele wyth gret reson þat þer is a trew wey that we be clene out of, overfore we be in derknesse, and tyl þe light of grace come, we mow not see þe cler wey. And qwan hym list to come, he xal voyde alle þe derk clowdes of ignoraunces and schewe hym clerly to me, that myn hert so fervently desyryth and lovyth. And if so be that hym list not þat I fynde hym, 3et reson comaundyth to kepe hool þat is onhurte; wherfore I beseche yow umbly, my lady my modyr, þat ye ne noon othir never meve me of þis matere, for I behyght 3ow pleynly þat for to dey þerfor I schal never have othir but only hym þat I have discryved, to whom I xal truly kepe alle the pure love of my hert. (208–20)

This is the last word on the subject. Katherine returns to the solitude of books and contemplates how she might find the pre-eminent lord she has described. The narrator tells us, however, that he was "ful ny3e here hert" and had "kyndalyd in here hert & brennyng fyre of love" (222–32).

In terms of the martyrological corpus's development of the very idea of a single woman, the *LMEPK* is something of a transitional text. As Katherine is essentially a convert, the longer form of Katherine, which deals with her pre-Christian history, necessarily envisages a point where she is what we would call a single woman. According to one interpretation, the *LMEPK* would appear to struggle with this idea. While it represents a progression away from a naturalized notion that the female martyr is attached *per se*, it possibly shows how embedded such thinking is. In the above, Katherine is imagined to be single because she exclusively desires attachment to the one whom she will eventually marry, *even though she has no knowledge of him.* The hagiographer will not conceive of a singleness that is not actually attachment-in-waiting, even though this requires Katherine to transcend her pagan state of mind and to have a miraculous and accurate premonition of whom she is waiting to marry. Thus, in a speech very similar to the description of the bridegroom given by Agnes, a single Katherine speaks like a *Sponsa Christi* even though she cannot be one.

However, an alternative reading is available. Key aspects of the excerpt above are notions of intelligence and ignorance. Katherine's intuition that there is a Christ to be a bride of is borne of "very reson." She describes herself and her people as being in the darkness of ignorance, waiting for the illuminating light of Christ. Her premonitory hunch about a Christ bridegroom is thus couched in characteristics that are veritably her own. She is, after all, the intellectual female martyr who, towards the end of her legend, will out-argue the fifty most eminent pagan scholars in the world. She is famous for her brain. Her extraordinary prescience in the parliament scene may be an instance of her intelligence. So, on the one hand, it may seem that the hagiographer will make his heroine clairvoyant rather than conceive of a singleness that is not actually attachment-in-waiting; on the other hand, Katherine may appear to be a girl with only one future, not because female choice is unthinkable, but because an alternative future to marriage with Christ is instinctively unthinkable ("I fele wyth gret reson") to a woman whose choices are intelligent. Her fore-destination might be her own exertion of preference and not a reflex of her author's patriarchal ideology.

With both these readings entirely possible, perhaps the most that can be said is that a development away from an entirely relational way of thinking about the female is guaranteed by the fact that the life-story form stretches to include such a scene. A Katherine life-story must tell of a stage in her life where her *Sponsa Christi* future is necessarily a matter of her discretion. For whilst the *LMEPK* Katherine speaks like the *passio* Agnes, the crucial difference is that Agnes's narrative begins *after* she has become Christ's bride: "He *has placed* a wedding ring on my finger." (The same is a naturalized pretext in Agatha's narrative where it is implicitly relevant for the narrative to introduce unannounced the counter-attachment prospect of Quintianus.) Agnes speaks like a *Sponsa Christi* when the prospect of alternative destinies has been totally foreclosed by the narrative form. Her speech is thus not an expression of preference or subjective desire but is the reflex of the one-dimensional creation she is. For the pagan Katherine it is necessarily different. She is a heroine for whom marriage with Christ is an attractive prospect from an alternative position. She is close to an attachment, closer than she knows: Christ, we are told, is *near* her, but this is quantitatively and significantly different from Agnes whose attachment ("he has united his body to mine") is presupposed in her narrative representation. The heroine's subjective preference for a heavenly bridegroom is a possibility encoded in the longer form of Katherine in precisely the way that it is elided by *passio* narratives.

The hagiographer may be minimizing or maximizing this possibility. Whichever is the case, his notion of female choice or of female destiny still extends only to the question of which partner the female shall have, and not whether she will have a partner at all. This ultimate move is made, however, by John Capgrave's *Katharine*, a text written eighteen to twenty-five years later. Capgrave, a friar of the hermits of Augustine, was born in 1393.[22] In his teens Capgrave entered the Augustinian convent at Lynn, where he was fully ordained probably around 1417. After ordination Capgrave studied at his order's *studium generale* in London before moving to study theology at Cambridge, where he was incepted as a *magister* in 1427. There

---

[22] These details of the life of Capgrave are taken from M. C. Seymour, "John Capgrave," in *Authors of the Middle Ages,* vol. 3 (Aldershot, 1996), 201–56.

is no evidence of Capgrave's movements from this date until late 1439, by which time he had returned to Lynn, although several of his theological tracts can be assigned to this period. Capgrave was prior of the convent at Lynn from 1441 to 1453. He then became prior provincial until 1457. He died in 1463, the author of a substantial amount of biblical scholarship and commentary, and, in the vernacular, of the *Abbreuiacion of Chronicles*, the *Solace of Pilgrimes* (a pilgrimage guide to Rome), and four saints' lives: Norbert, Augustine, Gilbert and Katherine. These lives have tended to be dismissed as literary creations: M. C. Seymour described them as an "addition, not an adornment to . . . literature."[23] Whilst more sympathetic, Thomas J. Heffernan stressed the archaic nature of Capgrave's hagiography, the "last burst of bloom from a withered stock."[24]

In recent years, however, Capgrave's *Katharine* has been the focus of a good deal of critical attention.[25] Much of this scholarship has attempted to salvage it from the rather dismissive judgment that its only distinction within the hagiographic corpus is its length. Particularly telling for this discussion is Karen A. Winstead's suggestion that "Capgrave's Katherine differs most obviously from conventional virgin martyrs because her point of view is so thoroughly shaped by her personal experience."[26] Winstead draws our attention to the degree to which Capgrave's text enters into the day-to-day (rather than the clairvoyant) concerns of a woman who becomes a martyr. In the parliament scene, where Queen Katherine is urged to marry, Capgrave uses an internal monologue to present the inner anxieties of a young woman suddenly confronted by the prospect of an unwanted marriage:

> I supposed ful welle to leue now at myn eese:
> Now must I leeve my stody & my desyre,
> My modyr, my kyn, my puple if I wyll plese;
> I most leeve stody & wasch my boke in myre,
> Ryde owte on huntyng, vse all new a-tyre!
> Godd, þou knowyst my preuy confessyon,
> I haf made al a-nothyr professyon!
> If I myght kepe it, I shal yet, & I may,
> Contynue same, to godd I make a vowe.
> Schuld I now chaunge my lyffe and myn aray,
> And trace þe wodes a-bowte undyr þe bow?
> I loued it nevur, how schuld I loue it now? (2. 183–194)

---

[23] Seymour, "John Capgrave," 235.

[24] Thomas J. Heffernan, *Sacred Biography: Saints and their Biographers in the Middle Ages* (Oxford, 1988), 171.

[25] In addition to the Capgrave scholarship listed above and below, an important recent study is Karen A. Winstead, *Virgin Martyrs: Legends of Sainthood in Late Medieval England* (Ithaca, NY, 1997), 167–80.

[26] Karen A. Winstead, "Piety, Politics and Social Commitment in Capgrave's *Life of St. Katherine*," *Medievalia et Humanistica* 17 (1991): 59–80, here 66.

In doing so, he explores the desires and frustrations of a vocational single woman, one who longs to live "at myn eese" in a way that has "no precedent in Middle English hagiography."[27] As Winstead points out, such sentiments may represent an allusion to a very different heroine, Chaucer's Criseyde. Mulling over the prospect of a relationship with Troilus, Criseyde, like Katherine, also reflects on the benefits of feminine singleness: "I am myn owene womman, wel at ese."[28] The similarity emphasizes the degree to which Katherine is being presented as a self-possessed, pagan woman.

There is a further significant development. As we have seen, the *LMEPK* Katherine finally puts down the pressure on her to marry by agreeing to marry, but only if a man meeting her seemingly impossible criteria can be found. This stipulation is an effective way of trumping the pressure being put on her. In the *LMEPK*, however, it is clear that Katherine is not only using it as a final argumentative resort. This heroine intuitively feels that such a man exists. The fact that both she and her society are presently blind to his existence is because "þer is a trew wey that we be clene out of, overfore we be in derknesse, and tyl þe light of grace come, we mow not see þe cler wey." In the context of a saint's life it would be unthinkable for a martyr-to-be to adumbrate a Christian faith for duplicitous purposes. As part of an ideological hankering, Katherine's desire to marry only a Christ-type figure is an earnest motivation that testifies to her instinctive piety: "And qwan hym list to come, he xal voyde alle þe derk clowdes of ignoraunces and schewe hym clerly to me, that myn hert so fervently desyryth and lovyth." In the face of similar pressure, Capgrave's Katherine also concedes that she will marry, but she also will marry only a man whose impossibility is preclusive: "yet schall þis lordes lyff / Be eterne" (2. 1435–1436). The medieval reader will, of course, grasp the dramatic irony here, but as far as Katherine is concerned she is ruling out an attachment, not predicting her marital future. Capgrave's version, for instance, does not feature the *LMEPK* Katherine's prescient stipulation that her husband must have a virginal mother. Insofar as the impossible husband of Capgrave's Katherine does not specifically resemble Christ, her singleness is far less of a commitment undertaken in respect of the transcendent attachment she will form in her future. Capgrave's Katherine is not single because she is saving herself for Christ, as is clearly the case in the *LMEPK*. Capgrave's Katherine is single, at this point, because she wants to be, and her description of the impossible husband that she would

---

[27] Karen A. Winstead, "John Capgrave and The Chaucer Tradition," *The Chaucer Review* 30 (1996): 389–400, here 391.

[28] Geoffrey Chaucer, *Troilus and Criseyde*, in *The Riverside Chaucer*, gen. ed. Larry D. Benson (Boston, 1987), Bk 2. 750. There are many potential relationships between Chaucer's *Troilus* and Capgrave's *Katharine*. Notably, Capgrave divides his story into five books, à la *Troilus*, and uses the same stanza form as Chaucer, rhyme-royal. For further discussion, see Winstead, "John Capgrave and The Chaucer Tradition"; Mary-Ann Stouk, "Chaucer and Capgrave's *Life of St. Katharine*," *American Benedictine Review* 33 (1982): 276–91, here 290; and Derek Pearsall, "John Capgrave's *Life of St. Katharine* and Popular Romance Style," *Medievalia et Humanistica* 6 (1975): 121–37, esp. 123–24.

deign to marry is an expediency to that effect. Winstead even goes so far as to suggest that, as a device of pure evasion, Katherine's argument for an impossible husband is, when Christ appears, a joke on her.[29]

Why should a form that implicitly embraces female self-destination on the question of marriage, and that can even stretch to the prospect of feminine singleness, become particularly popular in mid-fifteenth-century England? The reason is a matter of audience and consumerism. The fifteenth-century developments in the Middle English tradition of Katherine are part of a larger movement "in which lay folk appropriated for themselves traditional religion."[30] The significant appropriation, for our discussion, is the laicization of the production of religious literature. According to Vincent Gillespie, "the fifteenth century witnessed an extensive and consistent process of assimilation by the laity of techniques and materials of spiritual advancement, which had historically been the preserve of the clerical and monastic orders."[31] Moreover, as a wealth of recent scholarship has shown, there was a considerable lay female contribution to this development. For instance, Susan Groag Bell has claimed that, excluded from the other forms of religious life, women readers found a substitute religious contribution in the role of a private reader.[32] In hagiography, a type of literature previously produced in connection with vocational religious life (as discussed below), such readers found a way to experience and appropriate significant features of that religious vocation. This finding is supported by Carol M. Meale's work on the books of fifteenth-century noblewomen.[33] Felicity Riddy calls this lay female piety a "late medieval sub-culture," in which "it seems clear that the literary culture of nuns in the late fourteenth and fifteenth centuries and that of devout gentlewomen not only overlapped but were more or less indistinguishable."[34]

A case in point is another mid-fifteenth century East Anglian clerical hagiographer, and one with connections to John Capgrave, Osbern Bokenham (1392–

---

[29] Winstead, "Piety, Politics and Social Commitment in Capgrave's *Life of St. Katherine*," 66.

[30] Eamon Duffy, *The Stripping of the Altars: Traditional Religion in England c. 1400–c. 1580* (New Haven, 1992), 7. The increasing role of the laity in the construction of "traditional religion" is discussed in 9–89.

[31] Vincent Gillespie, "Vernacular Books of Religion," in *Book Production and Publishing in Britain, 1375–1475*, ed. J. Griffiths and D. Pearsall (Cambridge, 1989), 317. See also Ann M. Hutchison, "Devotional Reading in the Monastery and in the Late Medieval Household," in *De Cella in Seculum: Religious and Secular Life and Devotion in Late Medieval England*, ed. Michael G. Sargent (Cambridge, 1989), 215–27.

[32] Susan Groag Bell, "Medieval Women Book Owners: Arbiters of Lay Piety and Ambassadors of Culture," *Signs* 7 (1982): 742–68.

[33] Carol M. Meale, " '. . . alle the bokes that I haue of latyn, englisch, and frensch': Laywomen and their Books in Late Medieval England," in *Women and Literature in Britain 1150–1500*, ed. eadem (Cambridge, 1993), 128–58.

[34] Felicity Riddy, " 'Women Talking about the Things of God': A Late Medieval Sub-Culture," in *Women and Literature in Britain*, 104–27, here 110.

1463).³⁵ Between 1443 and 1447, Osbern Bokenham produced thirteen legends of female saints (including a Katherine *passio*).³⁶ Six of these legends were explicitly written for noblewomen within Bokenham's East Anglian milieu. Even vignettes of female textual commission are provided. In the *Prolocutory* to his legend of Mary Magdalen, for instance, Bokenham tells us how this legend was asked of him on Twelfth Night in 1445 by Isabel Bourchier:

> "I haue," quod she, "of pure affeccyoun
> Ful longe tym had a synguler deuocyoun
> To þat holy wumman, wych, as I gesse,
> Is clepyd of apostyls þe apostyllesse;
> Blyssyd Mary mawdelyn y mene . . .
> Whos lyf in englysshe I desyre sothly
> To han maad . . . "³⁷

Isabel was a direct descendant of King Pedro of Spain and Edward III of England; her brother, Richard Neville, Duke of York, would maintain a claim on the throne of England in the Wars of the Roses. Bokenham is far from alone in having such auspicious female patrons. The Chaucerian acolyte and poet laureate, John Lydgate, another contemporaneous East Anglian, wrote a version of the virgin martyr Margaret for one Ann Mortimer, Lady March; his *Fyftene Ioyes of Oure Lady* was produced for Isabella Despenser, Countess of Warwick; *The Virtues of the Mass* was probably written for Alice Chaucer; and his *Invocation to St. Anne* was composed for Anne, Countess of Stafford.³⁸

More specifically, John Capgrave's hagiographic corpus contains clear evidence of a female interest. He wrote his lives of Augustine and Gilbert of Sempringham

---

³⁵ A recent study of Osbern Bokenham, which contains the most biographical detail, is Sheila Delany, *Impolitic Bodies: Poetry, Saints, and Society in Fifteenth-Century England: the Work of Osbern Bokenham* (New York, 1998). See also *A Legend of Holy Women: A Translation of Osbern Bokenham's Legends of Holy Women*, trans. Sheila Delany (Notre Dame, IN, 1992), ix–xxxv; and Winstead, *Virgin Martyrs*, 112–46. Bokenham was incepted as a *magister* at Cambridge only two years before Capgrave (Seymour, "John Capgrave," 213). He evidently knew of Capgrave and his *Katharine* as he refers to both, "My Fadrys book, maystyr Ioon Capgraue," in his own *passio* of Katherine: see Osbern Bokenham, *The Legendys of Hooly Wummen*, ed. Serjeantson, 6356.

³⁶ For edition see above, n. 4. The most likely production scenario for Bokenham is that he was a hagiographic pamphleteer, producing legends to order for a gentrified clique consisting of many women: see A. S. G. Edwards, "The Transmission and Audience of Osbern Bokenham's *Legendys of Hooly Wummen*," in *Late-Medieval Religious Texts and their Transmission*, ed. Alistair Minnis (Cambridge, 1994), 157–67.

³⁷ *Legendys of Hooly Wummen*, ed. Serjeantson, 5065–5073. For details about Bokenham's other female readers/commissioners, see Delany, *Impolitic Bodies*, 15–22.

³⁸ See Meale, " '. . . alle the bokes that I haue of latyn, englisch, and frensch,' " 137–41. For these texts of Lydgate see *The Minor Poems of John Lydgate*, vol. 1, ed. Henry Noble MacCracken, EETS e.s. 107 (London, 1911), 173–93 (*Margaret*), 87–115 (*The Virtues*), 130–33 (*Invocation*), 260–67 (*Fyfftene Ioyes*). See also Edwards, "Transmission," 162.

for a "noble creatur, a gentill woman."[39] No such explicit statement can be found in relation to his *Katharine* but, as Jacqueline Jenkins has shown, two of the four extant *Katharine* manuscripts suggest a connection with a female readership.[40] The *LMEPK* is tantalizing in this respect. For example, one copy of this text is to be found in Corpus Christi College, Cambridge, MS. 142, a volume containing selected legends from the *Gilte Legende*, and featuring the inscription "Thys ys betrys beuerley's book" on the verso of folio 126.[41] The *LMEPK* is also found in London, British Library, MS. Harley 4012. This book appears to have been designed for the devotional needs of a female reader and was at some time in the possession of one Anne Harling.[42]

Anne, of East Harling, Norfolk, was born in 1426 to the Norfolk knight Sir Robert Harling and Jane Gonville.[43] Anne died in 1499. Orphaned in 1435, Anne had her wardship sold to her father's uncle and, at sixteen, was married off to Sir William Chamberlain, some fifteen years her senior. She would be widowed three times by the time of her death. An acquaintance of Henry VII, she was a woman of considerable wealth and power: "She owned and supervised nineteen manors and five advowsons in Norfolk and a number of estates in Suffolk and Essex, which made her a political as well as economic force in both of those counties. She always retained her own Harling coat of arms . . . She was a literate and learned member of the country aristocracy, a member of the bookish East Anglian circle presided over by Alice Chaucer, Duchess of Suffolk (and granddaughter of Geoffrey Chaucer)."[44] Wealthy and accomplished, Anne was also deeply pious: McMurray Gibson's account details Anne's many charitable bequests to religious establishments, one of the most significant being her foundation of a chantry chapel of St. Anne, her patron, namesake saint, in East Harling church. St. Anne, the mother of the Virgin, miraculously conceived Mary in old age after having led a barren life. She was clearly the focus for Anne Harling's charged and emotional devotion for, in her testament, Anne referred to herself as "the woman to whom God had denied the

---

[39] See John Capgrave, *Lives of St. Augustine and St. Gilbert of Sempringham, and a Sermon*, ed. J. J. Munro, EETS 140 (London, 1910), 1, 15–16.

[40] See Jenkins, " 'Such peple,' " 129. The manuscripts in question are London, British Library, MSS. Arundel 168 and 396. The contents of Arundel 168, the *LMEPK*, Marian material, and lives of female martyrs, suggest that it is a collection concerned with female piety. Arundel 396 contains a statement of ownership linking it to the Austin nuns of Campsey in Suffolk. Jenkins, " 'Such peple,' " 125–57, argues that Capgrave's bookish heroine was a model for female reading practices.

[41] *Three Lives from the Gilte Legende*, ed. Hamer, 32.

[42] See Jenkins, " 'Such peple,' " 65–66.

[43] See Gail McMurray Gibson, *The Theatre of Devotion: East Anglian Drama and Society in the Late Middle Ages* (Chicago, 1989), 96–106. See also Jenkins, " 'Such peple,' " 60–90; Jenkins's argument, that the Katherine text in MS. Harley 4012 reflects the importance of Anne Harling, is generally analogous to my own. See Anne M. Dutton, "Piety, Politics and Persona: MS Harley 4012 and Anne Harling," in *Prestige, Authority and Power in Late Medieval Manuscripts and Texts*, ed. Felicity Riddy (Woodbridge, 2000), 133–46.

[44] McMurray Gibson, *Theatre of Devotion*, 96.

blessing of children."⁴⁵ To alleviate this disappointment she donated funds for the establishment of a free grammar school at Rushworth in order to facilitate the education of thirteen children. Thus, as her testament movingly details, she "will still leave children of her own who shall call her blessed."⁴⁶ A further indication of her piety, and one in keeping with Bell's and Riddy's observation about secular women encroaching upon the vocations of religious women, is that Anne was a lay sister at four local Suffolk and Norfolk monasteries as well as at the convent of Syon near London.

As a wealthy, learned, noble, and pious East Anglian woman, Anne is typical of those females who came to commission, consume, and, I would suggest, affect the form of hagiographical texts in the fifteenth century. The form of the Middle English Katherine legend develops to embrace a female protagonist whose commitment to Christ is not a given of her representation, but is a choice from an alternative position. It does so at a time when pious female noblewomen contribute to the production of devotional material. These are noblewomen for whom the religious life is not an option excluding all others, but is a *part* of their life. An illustrative comparison here is the collection of female martyr legends (Katherine, Margaret, Juliana) written for a female readership around 1200, a collection known as the "Katherine Group."⁴⁷ The female readers to whom these texts are directed are vocational female religious, recluses, anchoresses.⁴⁸ These legends are associated or circulate with literature (*Hali Meiðhad* [*Holy Maidenhood*], *Ancrene Wisse* [*The Guide for Anchoresses*]) that extols the virtues of or provides guidance for women who completely dedicate their lives and their sexuality to Christ.⁴⁹

This literature forcefully articulates the notion that a female religious vocation is utterly oppositional to its alternative, married life, that it is a marriage in itself, and one which totally consumes the prospects of the woman involved to the

---

[45] McMurray Gibson, *Theatre of Devotion*, 105.

[46] McMurray Gibson, *Theatre of Devotion*, 106. The allusion is to Mary's *Magnificat*.

[47] See *Seinte Marherete*, ed. Frances M. Mack, EETS 193 (London, 1934; repr. London, 1958); *þe Liflade ant te Passiun of Seinte Iuliene*, ed. S. R. T. O. d'Ardenne and E. J. Dobson, EETS 248 (London, 1961); and *Seinte Katerine*, ed. S. R. T. O. d'Ardenne, EETS s.s. 7 (Oxford, 1981).

[48] On the subject of the female religious audience of the "Katherine Group" and related texts, see E. J. Dobson, *The Origins of Ancrene Wisse* (Oxford, 1976); the introduction to *Medieval English Prose for Women*, ed. Bella Millett and Jocelyn Wogan-Browne (Oxford, 1990), xi–xxxviii; Elizabeth Robertson, *Early English Devotional Prose and the Female Audience* (Knoxville, 1990), 1–12; Anne Clark Bartlett, *Male Authors, Female Readers: Representation and Subjectivity in Middle English Devotional Literature* (Ithaca, NY, 1995), 1–33; and *Anchoritic Spirituality: Ancrene Wisse and Associated Works*, introd. Anne Savage and Nicholas Watson (New York, 1991), 7–32. Consideration of a wider audience is argued for in Bella Millett, "The Audience of the Saints' Lives of the Katherine Group," *Reading Medieval Studies* 16 (1990): 127–55.

[49] The "Katherine Group" appears in two manuscripts of the early thirteenth century, one of which, Oxford, Bodleian Library, MS. Bodley 34, also includes *Hali Meiðhad*. D'Ardenne, *Seinte Iuliene*, xlvii, holds that these texts, as well as those known as the "Wooing Group" and the *Ancrene Wisse*, were the products of a center (the dialect would indicate the South West Midlands) that was active in the early thirteenth century.

complete exclusion of others. Thus the anchoress, at the beginning of her vocation and upon entry to her cell, underwent a funereal ceremony of enclosure: the author of the *Ancrene Wisse* asks rhetorically "for hwet is ancre hus bute hire burinesse?" — for what, except for her grave, is an anchoress' house?[50] The anchoress' death-synonymous removal from the world emphasized her life-consuming dedication to Christ who, in the *Ancrene Wisse*, is imagined to be her wooing courtly knight.[51] Similarly, in *Hali Meiðhad* the would-be vocational virgin is encouraged in terms of the total and spousal life-commitment as performed by those female martyrs who died for it:

> þench o Seinte Katerine, o Seinte Margarete, Seinte Enneis, Seinte Iuliene, Seinte Lucie, ant Seinte Cecille, ant o þe oþre hali meidnes in heouene, hu ha nawt ane ne forsoken kinges sunes ant eorles, wið alle worldliche weolen ant eorðliche wunnen, ah þoleden stronge pinen ear ha walden neomen ham, ant derf deað on ende. þench hu wel ham is nu, ant hu ha blissið þeruore bituhe Godes earmes, cwenes of heouene.[52]

> [Think of St. Katherine, of St. Margaret, of St. Agnes, St. Juliana, St. Lucy, St. Cecilia, and of the other holy virgins in heaven, how they not only renounced the sons of kings and noblemen, with all worldly riches and earthly pleasures, but suffered cruel tortures rather than accept them, and a painful death at last. Think how happy they are now, and how they rejoice accordingly in the arms of God, as queens of heaven.]

The associated *passio* narrative of Katherine, the *Katerine*, is thus directed at women who live a religious life which, constructed as an all-consuming, committed, and exclusive marital relationship, is unimaginable as a partial vocation or as a course compatible with marriage or secular life. The *Sponsa Christi* trope is a prominent emphasis in the *Katerine* and its sister texts because it characterizes the absolutist nature of the female religious life in this respect. Thus the *Katerine* heroine answers her tormentor's offer to make her his second queen:

> He [Christ] haueð iweddet him to mi meiðhad wið þe ring of rihte bileaue, ant ich habbe to him treowliche itake me. Swa wit beoð iuestnet ant iteiet in an, ant swa þe cnotte is icnut bituhhen us tweien, þet ne mei hit liste, ne luðer strengðe nowðer, of na liuiende mon lowsin ne leoðien. He is mi lif

---

[50] *Ancrene Wisse*, ed. J. R. R. Tolkien, EETS 249 (London, 1962), 58, l. 7. For details of this ceremony see Ann K. Warren, *Anchorites and their Patrons in Medieval England* (Berkeley, 1985), 76–77; and Sharon K. Elkins, *Holy Women of Twelfth-Century England* (Chapel Hill, NC, 1988), 151–52.

[51] For the *Ancrene Wisse*'s depiction of Christ as a lover-knight, see *Ancrene Wisse*, ed. Tolkien, 198–200.

[52] *Hali Meiðhad*, ed. Bella Millett, EETS 284 (London, 1982), 23, ll. 2–7.

ant mi luue, he is þet gleadeð me — mi suðe blisse bu[u]e me, [mi] weole ant mi wunne, ne nawt ne wilni ich elles.[53]

[He has wedded himself to my maidenhood with the ring of true faith and I have truly devoted myself to him. Thus we are united and bound in one and the knot is so knit between us two that neither the guile or cruel force of any living man may loosen or slacken it. He is my life and my love, he is that which gladdens me, my true bliss above me, my wealth and my joy; nor do I desire anything else.]

Where female religiosity is itself a marriage, it underscores the degree to which it is incompatible with marriage in the conventional sense. The words of Katherine, "He is my life," reflect the commitment of the vocational female religious who will read them. That relational terms are here a way of thinking about women is obvious insofar as there is only one female future — marriage — choice being confined to the nature of the husband. But what is more important is the way this minimal variety is rigidified: the female can only have a relationship and she can have only one kind: marriage or piety.

A woman such as Anne Harling challenges such categories within hagiography customized for consumers like her. It is not so much that she resists the either/or nature of religiosity and marriage, of piety and secularity; it is that by doing so she resists being totally defined by one set of relational terms: she is not a bride of Christ but neither is she divorced from a *Sponsa Christi*'s religious devotion by her marital status and place in the world. In having access to one kind of life from another she maintains choice and fluidity in both and is thus implicitly resistant to the kind of one-dimensional model found in the literature of female religious and in the *passio* narrative. The Middle English Katherine legend develops the choosing, discerning heroine of the *LMEPK* because women like Anne Harling would be reading it. Such a woman evades the model of relational totalization previously inscribed by the female martyrological tradition, and thus produces changes in that tradition.

The concept of feminine singleness in Capgrave's *Katharine* is just such a change if we assume that this text reflects the kind of female readership that Anne Harling represents. Such a readership is likely given Capgrave's other hagiographic works, the manuscript evidence, and his place within the East Anglian milieu of Bokenham, Lydgate, and their well-to-do female patrons/commissioners/readers. Certainly, as her narrative progresses, Capgrave's heroine becomes a fully-fledged *Sponsa Christi* and conceives of her virginal piety in utterly relational terms. But she has chosen this vocation from a position of feminine singleness: she has chosen from a position in which she is not assumed to be the total of a relational destiny. This is because she will be read by women whose similar relational destiny (Anne Harling was married off at sixteen) will also not foreclose on the question of their choice in

---

[53] *Seinte Katerine*, ed. d'Ardenne, 552–59.

later life. The unique desire to be alone of Capgrave's Katherine may become a more conventional desire for marriage but, in this context, and for her independent late medieval female readers, it is *that* she chooses, not *what* she chooses that is significant.

Paul Price
University of Bristol

3

GENDER, MARRIAGE, AND KNIGHTHOOD:

Single Ladies in Malory

"But one thyng, sir knyght, methynkes ye lak, ye that ar a knyght wyveles, that ye woll nat love som mayden other jantylwoman ... But hit is noysed that ye love quene Gwenyvere, and that she hath ordeyned by enchauntemente that ye shall never love none other but hir, nother none other damesell ne lady shall rejoyce you; wherefore there be many in this londe, of hyghe astate and lowe, that make grete sorow."

"Fayre damesell," seyde sir Launcelot, "I may nat warne peple to speke of me what hit pleasyth hem. But for to be a weddyd man, I thynke hit nat, for than I muste couche with hir and leve armys and turnamentis, batellys, and adventures. And as for to sey to take my pleasaunce with paramours, that woll I refuse. ..." (270.18–33)[1]

It may seem odd to begin a consideration of single women in Malory's *Arthuriad* (also commonly referred to as the *Morte D'Arthur*)[2] by quoting Lancelot's rejection of the wedded state, and his desire to remain a single *man*. Indeed, Lancelot is best known for his relationship with Queen Guenevere, and that relationship derives almost all of its significance from the fact that the queen is most emphatically not a single woman, but married to Lancelot's lord and friend, King Arthur. But if Lancelot is correct in his fears, and marriage would derail his career as the "floure

---

[1] All citations are from Sir Thomas Malory, *The Works of Sir Thomas Malory*, ed. Eugène Vinaver, rev. P. J. C. Field, 3rd ed., 3 vols. (Oxford, 1990). Subsequent citations to the *Arthuriad* will be made parenthetically.

[2] I concur with scholars such as Stephen Knight in choosing to refer to Malory's text as the *Arthuriad*. See Stephen Knight, *Arthurian Literature and Society* (New York, 1983), 105.

of chyvalry," then Guenevere would at first seem an appropriate object of devotion for Lancelot: distant and unattainable, she will not distract him from his knightly endeavors, and since she is the highest-ranking lady of the land, it seems only fitting that the greatest knight should seek out adventures in order to win her favor. At the same time, the fact of her marriage to Arthur leaves Lancelot free to assist other women and thereby gain even greater renown for his prowess and courtesy. Put another way, Lancelot's response to the maiden's criticism is to argue that he will not be able to serve any and all ladies — as he does repeatedly throughout the *Arthuriad* — if he is married to just *one*, whose presence will curtail his ability to pursue adventures. Willing to risk his life to succor a damsel in distress, Lancelot cannot risk marriage because of the potential consequences to his knightly career.[3]

I have argued elsewhere[4] that in Malory's text, the devoted relationship between a knight and his lady[5] is one of the foundational elements of chivalric society. If the project of chivalry is what defines the collective identity of the Arthurian community, then the men who act as the agents of that community need a series of knightly tasks, the successful execution of which helps to reinforce both individual and communal identity in the terms of chivalry. The desire of a knight to establish and maintain his reputation as a heroic and valorous agent of the chivalric community — and thus further solidify the reputation of the community itself as one which produces noble knights — is most easily facilitated through courteous service to ladies, or what in other circumstances might be termed "courtly love" or *fin' amours*.[6] Whether it be maidens who come to court seeking a champion, or dam-

---

[3] See Janet Jesmok's discussion of Lancelot's refusal to take a wife in "'A Knyght Wyveles': The Young Lancelot in Malory's *Morte Darthur*," *Modern Language Quarterly* 42 (1981): 315–30, esp. 322.

[4] Dorsey Armstrong, "Gender and the Chivalric Community: The Pentecostal Oath in Malory's 'Tale of King Arthur'," *Bibliographical Bulletin of the International Arthurian Society* 51 (1999): 293–312. See also idem, "Malory's Morgause," in *On Arthurian Women: Essays in Memory of Maureen Fries*, ed. Bonnie Wheeler and Fiona Tolhurst (Dallas, 2001), 149–60.

[5] I use the term "lady" here — as opposed to "woman" — to signify the importance of class and noble status in the chivalric community. Malory's Arthurian society is significantly unconcerned with non-aristocratic women and men; with one or two notable exceptions, the common people are almost invisible in the world of the *Arthuriad*.

[6] I do not propose to engage at any great length in the debate surrounding whether or not so-called "courtly love" existed as a real phenomenon, either historically or in romance literature; rather, my point is that the *Arthuriad* repeatedly models knightly devotion to noble women as a source of communal-identity establishment and maintenance, and that such relationships are accurately described as "courtly." Maureen Fries has argued that "In spite of the claims of proponents of the so-called and recently identified 'demise' of even literary courtly love, as a system it served Malory and his knights very well, as long as it maintained the social approval and personal moderation which led to worship"; see eadem, "How Many Roads to Camelot? The Married Knight in Malory's *Morte Darthur*," in *Culture and the King: The Social Implications of the Arthurian Legend*, ed. Martin B. Shichtman and James P. Carley (Albany, NY, 1994), 203. C. Stephen Jaeger has suggested that medieval romance literature offers a distorted reflection of a "cult of refined love" in *The Origins of Courtliness: Civilizing Trends and the Formation of Courtly Ideals, 939–1210* (Phila-

sels in distress encountered while knights are out questing in the forests of adventure, again and again Malory's text demonstrates that opportunities for knightly career-building swirl around the locus of women's bodies, needs, and desires, clustering most thickly around single ladies.

For much of the text, the relationship between Lancelot and Guenevere stands as the pre-eminent example of the knight–lady association, functioning for all intents and purposes as a relationship between an unmarried man and woman; the ultimately destructive impact of their relationship offers a suggestive comment on the feasibility of this ideal as a viable foundational support. While an analysis of the Arthur–Lancelot–Guenevere triangle discloses how the ideals of love, marriage, and devotion operate within the chivalric community, upon further examination it also suggests a corollary: the *existence* of these knight–lady relationships is less important in understanding how communal identity in Malory's Arthurian society is established and maintained than the particular *quality* of these relationships. In other words, it is the state of either singleness or marriage — and perhaps even more crucial, *the movement within the knight–lady relationship from one to the other* — that is most important in understanding what impact the states of matrimony and bachelor/maiden-hood have on the chivalric community.

If Lancelot's assertion is correct, and marriage has the power to unmake a knight's reputation and abilities, in Malory's text its antecedent — the romantic devotion between unmarried knight and lady — is indeed the *very foundation* of a noble knightly identity. Lancelot's response to the damsel who chides him for being a "knyght wyveles" neatly sidesteps the rumors surrounding his relationship with the queen, but in his expressed fear that marriage would affect his knightly abilities and reputation, this greatest of all knights hints at an important truth about the structure of the chivalric community depicted in the *Arthuriad*. It is the activity of chivalry and knighthood — ruling, questing, fighting — that defines the Arthurian community, and thus the chivalric society in the *Arthuriad* depends upon its knightly agents not only for defense and rescue, but also for definition. As the "floure of al knyghtys," Lancelot is the prime exemplar of the chivalric ethos, and his actions, even more than Arthur's, help consolidate and maintain the identity and reputation of the community. While taking a wife may damage that reputation, Lancelot, like all other knights, is also dependent upon the presence of the feminine — a presence almost always manifested in the form of an unmarried lady — to help make the reputation that marriage would seem to undermine. Should Lancelot take a wife and give up arms and tournaments, the consequences will reach far beyond his own knightly reputation: the entire community will be adversely affected.

---

delphia, 1985), 267. On the development of a courtly love ethic by southern French troubadors, see Sarah Kay, "The Contradictions of Courtly Love and the Origins of Courtly Poetry: The Evidence of the *Lauzengiers*," *Journal of Medieval and Early Modern Studies* 26 (1996): 209–53. See also Roger Boase, *The Origin and Meaning of Courtly Love: A Critical Study of European Scholarship* (Manchester, 1977); and Moshe Lazar, *Amour courtois et "Fin'Amors" dans la littérature du XIIe siècle* (Paris, 1964).

To understand how and why the knight–lady relationship functions as it does, consider the moment in Malory's text that creates the ideals that, in turn, set up a model of gender in which the quality of singleness — particularly that of ladies — is so important: the swearing of the Pentecostal Oath by the knights of the Round Table.

> ... the kynge stablysshed all the knyghtes and gaff them rychesse and londys; and charged them never to do outerage nothir mourthir, and allwayes to fle treson, and to gyff mercy unto hym that askith mercy, uppon payne of forfiture of their worship and lordship of kynge Arthure for evirmore; and allwayes to do ladyes, damesels, and jantilwomen and wydowes socour: strengthe hem in hir ryghtes, and never to enforce them, upon payne of dethe. Also, that no man take no batayles in a wrongefull quarell for no love ne for no worldis goodis. So unto thys were all knyghtis sworne of the Table Rounde, both olde and yonge, and every yere so were they sworne at the hyghe feste of Pentecoste. (120.15–27)[7]

While the Pentecostal Oath is instituted to regulate the entire community, it is significantly only the members of the all-male Round Table sub-community who swear to uphold its strictures. In essence, the Oath effects a disciplinary production of gender in both its particular focus — a gaze that locates knights at the center, looking outward at the rest of the society — and in the particular strictures it legislates, such as the so-called "ladies clause": "and allwayes to do ladyes, damesels, and jantilwomen and wydowes socour: strengthe hem in hir ryghtes, and never to enforce them, upon payne of dethe." Embedded in the center of the Oath, this particular stricture suggests a similar embeddedness of gender in the formation and refinement of identity in Malory's chivalric society.

Not surprisingly, the model of gender that defines identities in the chivalric community of Malory's *Arthuriad* most frequently represents gender as derivative of biological sex. Feminist and gender theorists such as Judith Butler and Eve Sedgwick have challenged the concept of sex-derivative gender, with Butler arguing that "gender" is always only a performance, "an identity tenuously constituted in time, instituted in an exterior space through a *stylized repetition of acts*," and further, "that if gender attributes ... are not expressive but performative, then these attributes effectively constitute the identity they are said to express or reveal."[8] Butler's defi-

---

[7] Malory's primary source for this tale — the thirteenth-century French text commonly called the *Suite du Merlin* — is lacking any such injunction; thus, this moment has been regarded by scholars as key to understanding Malory's personal vision of the chivalric ideal. See Vinaver's commentary in the *Works*, 3: 1330.

[8] Judith Butler, *Gender Trouble: Feminism and the Subversion of Identity* (New York, 1990), 140, 141 (her emphasis). Eve Kosofsky Sedgwick theorizes that in relation to biological sex, gender "is the far more elaborated, more fully and rigidly dichotomized social production and reproduction of male and female identities and behaviors — of male and female persons — in a cultural system for which 'male'/'female' functions as a primary and perhaps model binarism affecting the structure

nition of gender — that the visible marks or observable behaviors by which one is categorized "masculine" or "feminine" are not the expression of a pre-existing gender identity, but rather the appearance or repeated performance of these marks or behaviors *is* gender itself — sheds light on the role of single ladies in the *Arthuriad*. While not specifically engaged with medieval gender categories, Butler's discussion of an idealized and "compulsory heterosexuality" that functions as a generative aspect of gender identity has relevance to the model of gender that Malory's text enacts; in the *Arthuriad* "heterosexual desire" (to use modern terminology) is repeatedly looked to or invoked as a means of safely maintaining and legitimizing the homosocial knightly sub-community of the Round Table as the masculine, stable center of power within the larger Arthurian community.[9]

In his theorization of power systems, Michel Foucault has argued that juridical power systems in fact create the subjects that they supposedly represent.[10] In both form and content, the Pentecostal Oath constructs male and female in terms of a binary which opposes active, aggressive masculinity to passive, helpless femininity.

---

and meaning of many, many other binarisms whose apparent connection to chromosomal sex will often be exiguous or nonexistent"; see eadem, *Epistemology of the Closet* (Berkeley, 1990), 27–28.

[9] The phrase "compulsory heterosexuality" was first coined by Adrienne Rich, "Compulsory Heterosexuality and Lesbian Existence," in *Women, Sex and Sexuality*, ed. Catherine R. Stimpson and Ethel Spector Person (Chicago, 1980), 62–91. Although it has been argued — particularly in Foucault's distinction between the "sodomite" and the "homosexual" — that categories of sexual identity such as "homosexual" and "heterosexual" did not exist in the Middle Ages, I choose to use such terminology simply as a matter of convenience. Allen Frantzen has articulated the reasoning behind use of these categories of identity when discussing the medieval period: "We use modern terminology to discuss the sexual acts and habits of the Middle Ages because medieval people did not have a vocabulary for doing so": "Between the Lines: Queer Theory, the History of Homosexuality, and the Anglo-Saxon Penitentials," *Journal of Medieval and Early Modern Studies* 26 (1996): 255–96, here 257. Karma Lochrie has also discussed medieval sexuality in terms of Foucault's contention that bodies and pleasures, not "sex-desire," should serve as the focus for inquiry into the history of sexuality: "Desiring Foucault," *Journal of Medieval and Early Modern Studies* 27 (1997): 3–16. See also Frantzen, *Before the Closet: Same-Sex Love From Beowulf to Angels in America* (Chicago, 1999); and Mark D. Jordan, *The Invention of Sodomy in Christian Theology* (Chicago, 1997). Joan Cadden, among others, has challenged the notion that there was in fact no understanding of the category of homosexual identity, pointing to medical and scientific texts which discuss men who enjoy anal stimulation "from birth": *Meanings of Sex Difference in the Middle Ages: Medicine, Science, and Culture* (Cambridge, 1993) and eadem, "Sciences/Silences: The Natures and Languages of 'Sodomy' in Peter of Abano's *Problemata* Commentary," in *Constructing Medieval Sexuality*, ed. Karma Lochrie et al. (Minneapolis and London, 1997), 40–57. I use the term "homosocial" here in keeping with Eve Kosofsky Sedgwick's definition and description of the term: " 'Homo-social' is a word . . . [which] describes social bonds between persons of the same sex; it is a neologism, obviously formed by analogy with 'homosexual,' and just as obviously meant to be distinguished from 'homosexual' ": *Between Men: English Literature and Male Homosocial Desire* (New York, 1985), 1.

[10] See Michel Foucault, *History of Sexuality*, trans. Robert Hurley, Vol. 1, *An Introduction* (New York, 1978), esp. the final chapter, "Right of Death and Power over Life."

Even as the Pentecostal Oath seems to offer explicit protection to women in the "ladies clause," it also simultaneously and deliberately constructs them as helpless, needy, and vulnerable to attack. The threat of sexual violence — and the need to protect women from it — provides knight after knight with the circumstances by which his prowess and knightly worship may be tested and proven. Kathryn Gravdal notes that "What has rarely been said is that rape (either attempted rape or the defeat of a rapist) constitutes one of the episodic units used in the construction of a romance. Sexual violence is built into the very premise of Arthurian romance. It is a genre that by its definition must *create* the threat of rape."[11] Affirmation of knightly identity is largely dependent upon how well a knight fulfills the "ladies clause," and thus, to establish his reputation as a knight of courtesy and prowess, a chivalric agent of Arthur's court quite literally needs a vulnerable, helpless woman, or more correctly — to push Gravdal's point to its ultimate articulation — a knight needs "woman" to signify as vulnerable and helpless.

The instantiation of the Oath creates a model for communal and individual identity similar to what Butler has elsewhere described as "a false stabilization of gender in the interests of the heterosexual construction and regulation of sexuality within the reproductive domain."[12] The "false stability" of gender identity in Malory's text is demonstrated in the continuous acts of service that unmarried knights seem compelled to perform for unmarried ladies; the goal of such courteous behavior is clearly the establishment of a romantic relationship, and the existence of that relationship helps to define both parties involved as conforming to the heteronormative gender ideal of the Arthurian community. The ultimate affirmation of this conformity is the state of matrimony; once married, both knight and lady are usually considered safely and permanently heterosexualized.

Although married ladies occasionally need the assistance of a Round Table knight, it is *single* ladies who provide the greatest opportunity for deeds of valor. In the patriarchal society of Malory's Arthurian community, noble wives are appropriately most often rescued and defended by their husbands, whereas single ladies in distress not only provide a questing knight with the chance to perform an act of rescue or service, but also afford that knight an opportunity to repeat such actions through the establishment of an attachment, or what we might term a "love relationship." As the knight seeks to win the ultimate favor, the lady's hand in marriage, he is spurred to perform greater and more impressive feats of valor, thereby further enhancing and consolidating his chivalric reputation and that of the community he represents. In converting the desirable single woman into his wife, however, the knight effectively undermines his career by removing any impetus to perform noble deeds of martial prowess. A wife must be protected and defended; a single woman must be won. In the *Arthuriad*, the elective activities of winning and

---

[11] Kathryn Gravdal, *Ravishing Maidens: Writing Rape in Medieval French Literature and Law* (Philadelphia, 1991), 43.

[12] Butler, *Gender Trouble*, 135.

wooing demand and inspire more glorious and impressive acts from knights than do the compulsory duties of protection and defense.

Thus, although at first it may seem that the main pursuits of the chivalric community — activities such as ruling, questing, and fighting — lie almost exclusively within the domain of the masculine knightly agents of the community, closer scrutiny reveals that, almost without exception, all of these knightly actions are dependent upon a feminine presence for initiation, mediation, and completion/validation.[13] When that presence is manifested in the form of a single — or "available" — lady, a particular knight's success and honor generally seem to be greater than when he undertakes chivalric tasks at the behest or request of married women or of other knights.

Claude Lévi-Strauss's work on kinship systems and social structures can help to clarify our understanding of how single women are valued in the *Arthuriad*, and why they occupy the position they do. Lévi-Strauss identifies the transfer or exchange of women as the means by which men within a society form and maintain relationships:

> The total relationship of exchange which constitutes marriage is not established between a man and a woman . . . but between two groups of men, and the woman figures only as one of the objects in the exchange, not as one of the partners . . . This remains true even when the girl's feelings are taken into consideration as, moreover, is usually the case. In acquiescing to the proposed union, she precipitates or allows the exchange to take place; she cannot alter its nature.[14]

Lévi-Strauss further identifies the incest taboo as an important element in the formation of kinship systems, arguing that such a constraint amplifies the possibilities for wide-ranging social relationships and linking of kinship groups:

> The prohibition on the sexual use of a daughter or a sister compels them to be given in marriage to another man, and at the same time it establishes a right to the daughter or sister of this other man . . . The woman whom one does not take, and whom one may not take, is, for that very reason, offered up.[15]

Gayle Rubin, discussing Lévi-Strauss's work in her now-classic essay "The Traffic in Women: Notes on the 'Political Economy' of Sex," notes that in such a system

---

[13] For more on the situation of women generally in the *Arthuriad*, see Geraldine Heng, "Enchanted Ground: The Feminine Subtext in Malory," in *Courtly Literature: Culture and Context*, ed. Keith Busby and Erik Kooper (Philadephia, 1990), 283–300, repr. in *Arthurian Women: A Casebook*, ed. Thelma S. Fenster (New York, 1996), 97–113.

[14] Claude Lévi-Strauss, *The Elementary Structures of Kinship*, ed. Rodney Needham, trans. James Harle Bell and Richard von Sturmer (Boston, 1969), 115.

[15] Lévi-Strauss, *Kinship*, 51.

there is a sharp distinction between "gift" and "giver." Only those who are the "givers" enjoy the benefits of social linkage with one other, while women — "gifts" — do not derive any similar benefit from their own circulation: "As long as the relations specify that men exchange women, it is men who are the beneficiaries of the product of such exchanges — social organization."[16] While there are a few notable exceptions in Malory's text,[17] it is single women who circulate and are exchanged among men, and who are valuable for the way in which desire for them can affect knightly behaviors and relationships.[18] We see an example of the worth of single women within the chivalric community in the episode of King Uther's marriage to Igrayne, wife of his dead rival, the Duke of Cornwall. Uther, enacting the role of the patriarch in relation to Igrayne's daughters, exchanges them for political alliances:

> And kynge Lott of Lowthean and of Orkenay thenne wedded Margawse . . . and kynge Nentres of the land of Garlot wedded Elayne: al this was done at the request of kynge Uther. And the thyrd syster, Morgan le Fey, was put to scole in a nonnery . . . And after she was wedded to Kynge Uryens of the lond of Gore . . . (10.5–12)

This is the first time that the theme of "wedding proliferation" occurs in Malory; the pattern will be insistently repeated by the text, each time pointing to the importance of such unions in affirming social bonds and the critical role that women — particularly single women — play in this exchange of power and alliance.

Once married and potential mothers, women in Malory largely lose their power to facilitate the construction of knightly identity. They become, in the terms of feminist theorist Luce Irigaray, "use value,"[19] and are therefore removed from the marketplace of patriarchy: ". . . mothers, reproductive instruments marked with the name of the father and enclosed in his house, must be private property, excluded from exchange."[20] In Malory, they are thus also largely barred from participation in the project of chivalry. No other episode in Malory so sharply demonstrates the

---

[16] Gayle Rubin, "The Traffic in Women: Notes on the 'Political Economy' of Sex," in *Toward an Anthropology of Women*, ed. Rayna Reiter (New York, 1975); repr. in *The Second Wave: A Reader in Feminist Theory*, ed. Linda Nicholson (New York, 1997), 27–62, here 37.

[17] Uther's desire for Igrayne, the wife of Gorlois of Cornwall, and Arthur's adulterous relationship with Morgause, King Lot's wife are two such examples. Lancelot's relationship with Guenevere, while at first seemingly transgressing the values of chivalry and patriarchy, is actually appropriate given the circumstances, as I discuss below.

[18] Felicity Heal has made a similar point about acts of exchange and alliance in the great households of the medieval period; see Felicity Heal, "Reciprocity and Exchange in the Late Medieval Household," in *Bodies and Disciplines: Intersections of Literature and History in Fifteenth-Century England*, ed. Barbara A. Hanawalt and David Wallace (Minneapolis, 1996), 179–98.

[19] See Luce Irigaray, *This Sex Which is Not One*, trans. Catherine Porter with Carolyn Burke (Ithaca, NY, 1985), 173.

[20] Irigaray, *This Sex*, 185.

power and importance of the single woman in constructing knightly identity — and the justification for Lancelot's expressed fear that marriage would "unknight" him — than the "Tale of Sir Gareth of Orkney." The Gareth episode depicts in its entirety the inception, development, and conclusion of a knightly career. More clearly here than anywhere else in Malory, we see the powerful influence exerted by an unmarried noblewoman on the actions of a knight, and the way in which the fulfillment of the knight's desire for the available lady — achieved through a repetitive and continuous performance of knightly prowess and skill — effectively brings both the performance and his knightly career to an end.

Gareth's story beings at the feast of Pentecost, a time when Arthur traditionally refrains from eating until "som mervayle" has occurred. On this particular occasion, that occurrence is the arrival of a young man, "the fayrest that ever they all sawe" (293.29), who enters the great hall and asks for three gifts:

> And they shall nat be unresenablé asked but that ye may worshypfully graunte hem me, and to you no grete hurte nother losse. And the fyrste do[n]e and gyffte I woll aske now, and the tothir two gyfftes I woll aske this day twelvemonthe, wheresomever ye holde your hyghe feste. (294.6–11)

The first gift that the unknown knight requests is to be supplied with room and board until the time of his asking for the other two gifts. Arthur encourages him to ask for more, but the young man refuses, and is thus sent to the kitchens, where he lives for a year in drudgery. He is constantly mocked by the ever-troublesome Sir Kay, who christens him with the sarcastic sobriquet "Beawmaynes," or "fair hands" — a most unlikely name for a kitchen knave.

The unknown young man is, of course, Sir Gareth, Arthur's nephew and brother to Sir Gawain, who does not recognize his own sibling. Gareth's deception of the court is a calculated move to create the circumstances that will allow him to establish a knightly reputation free from any hint of preference or partiality due to his kinship with the king. This plot device — often described as the motif of the "Fair Unknown"[21] — is common in medieval romance literature, a genre that is quite obviously concerned with matters of nobility and blood.[22] By obscuring his blood-

---

[21] Susan Crane has noted that "romance plots ... concur with estates literature in demanding that men deserve their estate through behaviour suitable to it. A familiar way of representing the double source of identity in lineal right and personal deserving is to obscure a young man's lineage so that he is thrown back on his own capacities to demonstrate his birthright": see eadem, *Gender and Romance in Chaucer's Canterbury Tales* (Princeton, 1994), 99. The figure of Gareth is not the only instance of this motif; in the "Tale of King Arthur," Torre, King Pellinor's son by a peasant woman, reinforces the noble of myth of heredity. Torre is obsessed with knightly activity from infancy, and is described as much better looking ("well-made") than the peasant woman's other sons, father by the cowherd Ayres.

[22] Although the *Arthuriad* borrows fom other literary genres, its primary and predominant generic mode is romance. Elizabeth Sklar, one of many scholars who have questioned the *Arthuriad*'s generic status, notes that "What we have in the *Morte Darthur* is the stuff of romance ... em-

line, a hero in disguise is better able to prove his inherent aristocracy; his rightful place within the chivalric society is affirmed through completion of challenges or tasks that only the most noble of men could possibly accomplish.[23] By deliberately choosing a position on the margin of the courtly community, Gareth elects to prove his worth by working his way up the chivalric social ladder from an "entry-level" position. His success is all the more notable in that his knightly career at Arthur's court begins from a position of prejudice rather than preference. And as is often the case within Malory's text, the establishment of his knightly reputation is effected through desire for — and thus service to — a single woman.

At the end of his year in the kitchens, a young maiden named Lyonet comes to Arthur's court to request assistance: "'Sir,' she seyde, 'I have a lday of grete worshyp to my sustir, and she is beseged with a tirraunte, that she may nat oute of hir castell. And bycause here ar called the noblyst knyghtes of the worlde, I com to you for succoure'" (296.20–23). At this moment, Gareth steps forward and asks to be granted his two remaining requests. His first request is to be given the task of assisting the damsel, the second to be knighted by Sir Lancelot, the greatest knight of the realm. Arthur grants both wishes, and, much to the astonishment of the court, Gareth (still known to all as Beawmaynes, the kitchen knave) suddenly appears before the court in a fine suit or armor, takes his leave, and sets off on an equally fine horse.

While Gareth may be happy with his assignment, Lyonet is none too pleased: "'Fy on the,' seyde the damesell, 'shall I have none but one that is your kychyn knave?' Than she wexed angry and anone she toke hir horse" (297.21–23). Gareth follows after her, as does the rest of the court to see what will transpire. Before he has gotten properly on his way, Kay challenges Gareth, and in the ensuing conflict Gareth handily defeats him, taking the other knight's shield and spear as trophies. Afterwards, he is more courteously challenged by Sir Lancelot, who "mervayled of his strengthe" (298.35–299.1), and suggests that they call a draw. Gareth eagerly asks Lancelot, "'Hope ye so that I may ony whyle stonde a proved knyght?' 'Do as ye have done to me,' seyde sir Launcelot, 'and I shall be your warraunte'" (299.15–18). Lancelot then confers the order of knighthood upon Gareth.

Thus Gareth begins his knightly career auspiciously. He proves his prowess to the assembled court in defeating Sir Kay, and he confirms that his victory is not occasioned by accident or chance, admirably acquitting himself in what might be termed "polite combat" with the greatest knight of the realm; so impressed is Lancelot that he not only affirms that Gareth is worthy of knighthood but also agrees to confer that honor upon him with his own hand. Although Gareth has proven himself a worthy knight in the eyes of Arthur's court, in the eyes of Lyonet he is

---

bedded in a matrix that mutates from history to religious vision to tragedy, forcing a continual readjustment of generic expectation. . . ." See eadem, "The Undoing of Romance in Malory's *Morte Darthur*," *Fifteenth Century Studies* 20 (1993): 309–27, here 311.

[23] See Jeanne Drewes, "The Sense of Hidden Identity in Malory's *Mort Darthur*," in *Sir Thomas Malory: Views and Re-views*, ed. D. Thomas Hanks, Jr. (New York, 1992), 7–23.

still a "bawdy kychyn knave." As his tale progresses, so does his knightly reputation. Gareth is called upon to prove his abilities to the knightly agents of other chivalric communities. Significantly, Lyonet withholds her approval of Gareth as a champion and knight longer than anyone else, vituperatively insisting that he is not worthy to be her escort or to engage in combat with other knights. When he is successful in any contest of knightly ability, she bemoans the fact that ever a mere "kychyn knave" defeated a knight. As Andrew Lynch has pointed out, "[Lyonet's] instincts are sound. It would be unacceptable for a kitchen knave to fight, let alone defeat, knights. 'The Tale of Sir Gareth' toys with the idea of true valour in a churl, in order to deny it."[24]

Throughout the tale, Lyonet mocks, berates, and scorns Gareth, refusing to acknowledge his clear display of innate nobility even though Gareth conducts himself as befitting a knight of the court of King Arthur: rescuing other noble knights in distress, defeating miscreant knights who seek to do harm to himself or to Lyonet, and perhaps most remarkably, enduring the constant jibes of his reluctant companion with grace and courtesy. For example:

> "What art thou but a luske, and a turner of brochis, and a ladyll-washer?"
> "Damesell," seyde sir Beawmaynes, "sey to me what ye woll, yet woll I nat go fro you whatsomever ye sey, for I have undirtake to kynge Arthure for to enchenve your adventure, and so shall I fynyssh hit to the ende, other ellys I shall dye therefore." (300.13–19)

And later:

> "Alas," she seyde, "that ever suche a kychyn payge sholde have the fortune to destroy such two knyghtes...."
> "Damesell ... ye may sey what ye woll, but whomsomever I have ado withall, I truste to God to serve hym or I and he departe, and therefore I recke nat what ye sey, so that I may wynne your lady." (302.12–22)

Despite her constant harassment — or indeed because of it — Gareth works hard to adhere to the highest standard of knightly behavior. Although he has won the admiration of his own court — and, as his victories mount, the respect of knights from other communities — Lyonet refuses to recognize his innate nobility. If anything, she redoubles her criticism of her companion as he defeats knight after knight, and, tellingly, it is her criticism that matters much more to Gareth than the approval or admiration he receives from any other quarter. As Gareth's words indicate, his ultimate goal is to "wynne" her, and thus, he cannot be satisfied with his achievements until she is won. As a single woman, Lyonet plays a far more important role in creating and shaping Gareth's knightly identity and reputation than do

---

[24] Andrew Lynch, *Malory's Book of Arms* (Cambridge, 1997), 64. See also his full discussion of blood and nobility as represented in the Gareth episode, 62–68.

those knights with whom he engages in direct conflict, for she is the catalyst that creates the opportunities for such conflicts.

That she is the most powerful force in the transformation of Beawmaynes the kitchen knave into Sir Gareth the Round Table knight is further demonstrated in the scene following Gareth's defeat of the Green Knight, who requests mercy:

> "All is in vayne," seyde Beawmanynes, "for thou shalt dye but yf this damesell that cam with me pray me to save thy lyff. . . ."
>
> "Lat be," seyde the dameselle, "thou bawdy kychyn knave! Slay hym nat, for and thou do thou shalt repente hit."
>
> "Damesell," seyde Beawmaynes, "your charge is to me a plesure, and at your commaundemente his lyff shall be saved, and ellis nat." (306.12–36)

Granted his life, the grateful Green Knight pledges homage to Gareth, and expresses puzzlement at Lyonet's verbal abuse of so obviously noble an escort.[25] Moments later, an almost identical scene is played out with the Red Knight: once again Gareth defeats his opponent, and once again he asks Lyonet to choose whether the other knight should live or die. After having his life spared, the Red Knight also marvels that "allwayes this damesell seyde many foule wordys unto Beawmaynes" (310.16–17).

Gareth himself finally gives a clear explanation for his patient endurance of Lyonet's abuse:

> "Damesell . . . ye are uncurteyse so to rebuke me as ye do, for mesemyth I have done you good servyse, and ever ye thretyn me I shall be betyn wyth knyghtes that we mete but ever for all youre boste they all lye in the duste or in the myre. And therefore y pray you, rebuke me no more, and whan ye se me betyn or yoldyn as recreaunte, than may you bydde me go from you shamfully, but erste, I let you wete, I woll nate departe from you; for than I were worse than a foole and I wolde departe from you all the whyle that I wynne worshyp." (310.34–36; 311.1–7)

It is her criticism and scorn that compel Gareth to challenge yet bigger and stronger knights. Every time he successfully counters her disdain with victory in a contest of knightly ability, his reputation is enhanced and solidified; soon Gareth is famous as the valorous knight accompanied by a verbally abusive maiden. Yet had Lyonet changed her opinion of him after his first victory and acknowledged his martial ability, he might not have met each knightly challenge with such eagerness. Gareth does not rest until he has the approval of his chosen lady; the withholding of that

---

[25] As Lynch notes, unless the Green Knight accepts the fact that "victory 'proves' nobility of blood . . . he must confess himself guilty of begging mercy from a churl. Beawmaynes *must* become Gareth, or ruin the economy of honour": *Malory's Book of Arms*, 65.

approval makes him a better knight. At long last, Lyonet offers praise for Gareth's behavior, and the terms of her approbation are significant, as is Gareth's response:

> "... mervayle have I," seyde the damesell, "what manner a man ye be, for hit may never be other but that ye be com of jantyll bloode, for so fowle and shamfully dud never woman revyle a knyght as I have done you, and ever curteysly ye have suffyrde me, and that com never but of jantyll bloode."
> "Dameself," seyde Bewmaynes, "a knyght may lytyll do that may nat suffir a jantyllwoman, for whatsomever ye seyde unto me I toke none hede to your wrodys, for the more ye seyde the more ye angred me, and my wretthe I wrekid uppon them that I had ado withall ... the mysseyyng that ye mysseyde me in my batayle furthered me much and caused me to thynke to shew and preve myselffe at the ende. ..." (312.29–36; 313.1–6)

It is only after she has expressed her approval of his knightly conduct that Gareth shares with Lyonet the secret of his lineage, and the fact of his knighting at the hands of Sir Lancelot. The news of his identity is pleasing to Lyonet, as it further confirms that his knightly actions arise from an appropriately noble source.

In the figure of Lyonet, then, we can clearly see the powerful force exerted by single ladies on the shaping of knightly identity; it is her words, Gareth acknowledges, that spur him on to perform deeds of valor. Once she has given her approval of his actions, however, Lyonet loses the influence she was previously able to wield over Gareth's career. That power is immediately and seamlessly transferred to Lyonet's imprisoned sister, Lyones. While in an immediate sense Gareth's adventure has been the result of Lyonet's request for assistance, the ultimate catalyst for his knightly career is the maiden who is truly in distress. Lyones is not only single, but also the object of desire of another knight whose advances she has long resisted, finally barricading herself in her castle. In the patriarchal structure of the chivalric society, her value thus automatically increases due to her apparent desirability, but ultimately, as a single noblewoman in the Arthurian community, she is truly valuable in terms of how she can benefit those knights who seek to possess her. Gareth has derived all the benefit he can from his relationship with Lyonet; once she is no longer useful in helping him consolidate and maintain his masculine knightly reputation, Gareth looks for another woman to fulfill that role, to help him further enhance his already admirable heteronormative chivalric identity.

As Gareth arrives on the battlefield to fulfill the obligation he undertook back in Arthur's court, he asks to have the woman for whom he is fighting pointed out to him. After seeing her from afar, he remarks "I aske no better quarrell than now for to do batayle, for truly she shall be my lady and for hir woll I fyght" (321.28–29). When Lyones's attacker, the Red Knight,[26] claims her for his own lady, Gareth rebukes him, and further claims that "I love hir and woll rescow hir, othir ellys to dye therefore" (322.8–9). Although he has never spoken with her, the fact of her

---

[26] This Red Knight is different from the one Gareth defeated earlier in his Tale.

availability as a potential wife and the extreme quality of her distress are enough to provoke Gareth to proclamations of love and devotion. If his patient endurance and service to Lyonet are born out of a sense of duty and obligation to a damsel in need, the more desperate need of Lyones leads him to declare himself her lover, and one singularly devoted to her. This particular challenge, more than any other he has encountered on the long road leading up to it, will afford Gareth the opportunity not only to enhance his own reputation, but also to win for himself the devotion of an available lady clearly deemed desirable by the standards of the community.

When Gareth and the Red Knight engage in battle over the lady Lyones, it is, appropriately, the most difficult contest of his knightly career thus far: the battle rages for an entire day. Every time Gareth tires, Malory tells us, he need only be reminded of the desperate situation of his newly proclaimed lady-love to find renewed strength and energy with which to continue the fight. Lyonet herself plays on this: "A sir Bewmaynes! Where is thy corrayge becom? Alas! My lady my sister beholdyth the, and she shrekys and wepys so that hit makyth myne herte hevy" (324.14). Not surprisingly, Gareth redoubles his efforts and finally defeats the Red Knight, who asks for mercy. Gareth hesitates to grant the request, as the Red Knight has "shamfully" been responsible for the deaths of many other "good knyghtes" and, in Gareth's estimation, deserves to die. When the Red Knight asks for a chance to explain himself, the excuse he offers is the only one that could possibly save his life: all of his "shamfull" actions were done at the request of his former lady. Upon learning this, Gareth grants him his life: "But insomuche all that he dud was at a ladyes requeste I blame hym the lesse . . ." (325.24–25). Gareth's act of mercy is the result of his recognition that, for a knight, the request of an unmarried lady — so powerful in helping to shape that knight's identity — is a command that cannot be disobeyed.

As Gareth's tale plays out, it becomes clearer and clearer that the construction of masculine chivalric identity in the *Arthuriad* is a repetitive process that is deeply dependent upon the presence of the subjugated feminine for enactment and completion. In its instantiation, the annual ritualized swearing of the Pentecostal Oath clearly identifies a masculine homosocial sub-community as the center of power within the larger Arthurian society, the existence of which is facilitated and legitimated by the presence of vulnerable and helpless female characters in constant need of knightly assistance.[27] As Gareth seeks to establish his right to belong to the Order of the Round Table by following the guidelines set forth in the Pentecostal Oath, his example demonstrates that the intersection of the two ideals of knightly prowess and romantic love is the site where masculine knightly identity is constructed. On any foray into the forest of adventure, a knight is sure to encounter other knights *with* whom he may affirm his masculine sameness through a display of martial capabilities; he will also encounter women *against* whom he may affirm his masculine difference through courteous behavior. These two types of encounter

---

[27] See Maurice Keen, *Chivalry* (New Haven, 1984), 116.

are crucial to the continual process of establishing and maintaining identity in the Arthurian community. As Gareth's narrative reveals, opportunities for this kind of identity construction primarily cluster around the position of single ladies in the text.

Although Gareth has proven his martial capabilities in combat against Kay, Lancelot, and the variety of other knights encountered in his quest, although he has proven his courtesy by graciously defending Lyonet and enduring her verbal abuse, and although he has even proven his right to love and defend the desirable Lyones by defeating the powerful Red Knight, he has not yet won the right to call her his lady. When he turns from his victory on the battlefield to regard Lyones at her window, instead of immediately granting him her love, she calls out:

> "Go thy way, sir Beawmaynes, for as yet thou shalt nat have holy my love unto the tyme that thou be called one of the numbir of the worthy knyghtes. And therefore go and laboure in worshyp this twelve-monthe, and than ye shall hyre newe tydyngis." (327.7–11)

As a consolation, she promises to be true to Gareth while he is gone and to love him until her death, but she withholds the possibility of marriage — the ultimate prize — until he has affirmed his status as a knight worthy to be her husband. She thus provokes him to achieve still greater heights of glory and nobility, to spread the news of his valorous reputation still further. Lyones uses this delay to try to discover his lineage, for although Gareth seems to be a man of noble birth, she cannot possibly consider marriage to him until she knows for certain: "for tyll that I know what is his ryght name and of what kyndrede he is commyn shall I never be myrry at my herte" (328.17–19). Once she learns his lineage, she suspends the twelve-month assignment, and "than they trouthe-plyght other to love and never to fayle whyle their lyff lastyth" (332.35–36). Their marriage is postponed, however, until Gareth — in a new disguise, so that none might know him — returns to Arthur's court, where he performs admirably in a tournament in which all the greatest knights of the Round Table compete. His career has thus come full circle, and he returns in triumph to the court where he began his knightly adventures as a kitchen knave.

Once unmasked and saluted, acknowledged, and lauded by his fellow knights, Gareth and Lyones are married at the feast of Michaelmas. In honor of the event, another tournament is held, but this time, significantly, Malory tells us that "the kynge wolde nat suffir sir Gareth to juste, because of his new bryde; for, as the Freynsh boke seyth, that dame Lyonesse desyred of the kynge that none that were wedded sholde juste at that feste" (362.22–26). There could not be a stronger piece of evidence to suggest that the office of knighthood and the state of matrimony cannot successfully co-exist in the chivalric community. With his marriage, Gareth has achieved the prize toward which all his efforts as a knight have been directed; his reward for exemplary behavior as a knight, however, also ironically ends his chivalric career. Once married, he all but disappears from Malory's text.

If we return to the example of Lancelot, then, it would seem that he is correct in fearing that marriage will hurt his career. Janet Jesmok has suggested that in the maiden's criticism of Lancelot's status as a "knyght wyveles," Malory is attempting to characterize the greatest knight as misled in the reasons he offers for his bachelor status, claiming that "the love affair ... of Gareth ... which end[s] in marriage, enhance[s] his chivalry and Arthur's society."[28] If Lancelot were to follow this model, according to Jesmok his marriage, too, would enhance the Arthurian community. However, while the events leading up to the marriage of Gareth follow the pattern of the questing knight and positively reinforce the idea of knightly devotion to the feminine and the role that female characters play in the constitution of knightly identity, Gareth largely disappears from the progression of the larger narrative after his marriage. When he — and other married knights, such as Sir Pelleas — do appear again, it is usually as helpless, imprisoned, or vulnerable; they occupy a state that looks remarkably like that in which women are expected to be found, providing an opportunity for other knights to demonstrate their abilities and reinforce their reputations through rescue and assistance. Indeed, Gareth's most unknightlike final appearance — weaponless, vulnerable, and accidentally in the path of Lancelot's sword — is also the occasion of his destruction. Larry Benson has argued that Gareth's marriage "symbolizes a lower order of knighthood than that of Lancelot,"[29] and Maureen Fries, concurring with Benson, notes that "Malory is unable to use marriage as a continuing impetus for knightly worship ... he ... seems unable to imagine postmarital martial reputations even remotely analogous to Lancelot's. ..."[30] What neither scholar quite articulates is that not only does the example of Gareth suggest that marriage is detrimental to a knight's career, but it also makes plain that single ladies — marriageable but not married — are a critical component in the formation and maintenance of masculine knightly identity. Marriage may destroy knightly reputations, but the courtship that precedes matrimony is somewhat paradoxically the strongest support of masculine chivalric identity.

In light of the example of Gareth, then, it might seem that Lancelot has hit upon the perfect solution: his object of devotion, the catalyst that spurs him on to deeds of noble valor, is the ultimate unattainable woman: Queen Guenevere. And while his devotion to her in some measure helps shape his identity as the "floure of al knyghtes," his need to hide that relationship simultaneously compels him to seek out other women — single women — to whom he may render service or assistance. In the third Tale of Malory's *Arthuriad*, "A Noble Tale of Sir Launcelot du Lake," Lancelot's identity as the protector of women in general exists in easy relationship to his other identity as the devoted champion of the queen. In fact, it is due to his desire to accrue honor in the name of Guenevere — and for himself in Guenevere's eyes — that he departs from the court to "preve" himself in "straunge adventures" which generally involve damsels in distress.[31] As the narrative pro-

---

[28] Jesmok, "'A Knyght Wyveles,'" 323.
[29] Larry D. Benson, *Malory's Morte Darthur* (Cambridge, 1976), 107.
[30] Fries, "How Many Roads to Camelot?" 199–200.
[31] As Heng has said of Lancelot, "the emotional logic of serving a particular lady translates

gresses, however, it becomes clear that Lancelot's double devotions — to ladies in general and to Guenevere in particular — cannot successfully co-exist.

In the early pages of Malory's text, the relationship between Arthur's queen and his greatest knight seems to be born out of mutual admiration and chivalric courtesy. In the opening of "A Noble Tale," Malory tells us that Lancelot surpassed all other knights, "*Wherefore* quene Gwenyvere had hym in grete favoure aboven all other knyghtis, and so he loved the quene agayne aboven all other ladyes..." (253.15–17; emphasis mine). Malory's statement here suggests that their devoted relationship has arisen logically, given that Lancelot is the greatest knight and Guenevere the highest-ranking lady of the land; it is status and prowess that are invoked here, not love or desire. Yet, although Lancelot is certainly hailed as the "floure of chyvalry" at this moment in the narrative, it is not until much later — when his relationship with the queen has transgressed the boundary between chaste devotion and adulterous desire — that he achieves his most remarkable feats of arms. In other words, not until Lancelot recasts his relationship with the married Guenevere into the same terms as that of the unmarried Gareth and Lyones does he hit his knightly stride, as it were.

Although Guenevere functions as a single lady for Lancelot, it is impossible to forget that she is in some sense the "most married" of all the women encountered in Malory's text; if a man's wife is off-limits to other men within the structure of patriarchy, then the wife of the patriarch must represent the height of unattainability. Interestingly, the queen's position as Lancelot's forbidden lover manages further to enhance his knightly reputation, in that he is compelled to serve a multitude of single ladies to hide his singular devotion to Guenevere. At the same time, his attachment to the queen precludes the possibility of matrimony with any of the other ladies he assists. For much of the text Lancelot manages successfully to balance between the two extremes of the knightly career: the honor and enhanced reputation that arise from unmarried devotion, and the oblivion of wedlock.

When Lancelot sets off to seek adventures in his Tale, it seems that around every bend in the road, behind every tree, within every castle or village encountered by the hero, there is a maiden who requires of him some service. Indeed, Malory alters his sources to emphasize the importance of single ladies in the making of a knightly career. Part way through "A Noble Tale," Lancelot encounters a maiden who asks for his assistance:

"Sir," seyde the damesell, "here by this way hauntys a knyght that dystressis all ladyes and jantylwomen, and at the leste he robbyth them, other lyeth by hem."

"What?" seyde sir Launcelot, "is he a theff and a knyght? And a ravyssher of women? He doth shame unto the Order of Knyghthode, and contrary unto his oth. Hit is pyté that he lyvyth!" (269.19–26)

---

polysemously for him into dedication to a feminine principle, affirmed in the enormous variety of requests successfully made of him by women": "Enchanted Ground," 103.

Lancelot's strident outrage affirms the ideal of knightly behavior toward women articulated in the "ladies clause" of the Pentecostal Oath. Interestingly, however, in the parallel passage in Malory's source, the French *Prose Lancelot*, the maiden says:

> Je vos maing ... combatre a .I. chevalier qui ci pres maint en ceste forest, qui sert d'un mauvés mestier dont toz li mondes le devroit blasmer, car il destourne touz cels qui par devant lui passant, pour qu'il am puist venir au dessus.[32]

> [I am taking you ... to do combat with a knight who lives nearby in this forest and performs an offensive office that everyone should condemn, for he turns aside all those who pass in front of him so that he can conquer them.][33]

Malory transforms the recreant knight's offensive behavior in the source into a specific attack on ladies; the masculine pronoun "cels" here suggests that in the *Prose Lancelot* the knight is guilty primarily — or only — of attacking other knights. Although the evil knight is effectively attacking the institution of knighthood itself as expressed in the "ladies clause" of the Pentecostal Oath, at the same time such attacks are essential in that they provide the opportunity for other knights to perform their masculine identities through defense of helpless ladies. Malory's transformation of the scene permits Lancelot, in redressing this wrong through combat, to affirm his masculinity through service to unmarried ladies.

Similarly, in another adventure Lancelot fights two giants who stand guard over a castle. They are taken care of quickly, after which success

> ... there com afore hym three score of ladyes and damesels, and all kneled unto hym and thanked God and hym of his delyveraunce. "For," they seyde, "the moste party of us have bene here this sevene yere theire presoners, and we have worched all maner of sylke workys for oure mete, and we ar all gret jentylwomen borne. And blyssed be the tyme, knyght, that ever thou were borne, for thou haste done the moste worshyp that ever ded knyght in this worlde." (272.1–8)

In the *Prose Lancelot*, it is quite a different group of people who are freed after the defeat of the giants:

> Lors fu la porte del chastel ouverte; si conmancerent a venir dames et damoiseles et chevaliers et dient a Lancelot que bien soit il venuz comme cil qui des or en avant sera lor sires et lor mestres.[34]

---

[32] Alexandre Micha, ed., *Lancelot: Roman en prose du XIIIe siècle* (Geneva, 1980), 5: 39.

[33] Norris J. Lacy, gen. ed., *Lancelot-Grail: The Old French Arthurian Vulgate and Post-Vulgate in Translation*, 5 vols. (New York, 1993–1996), 3: 215.

[34] Micha, ed., *Lancelot*, 5: 44.

[Then the castle gate was opened; ladies, maidens, and knights began pouring forth to welcome Lancelot as the one who henceforth would be their lord and master.][35]

The courtly community of Malory's source has become a homosocial sub-community of gentlewomen who not surprisingly wish to know the name of their rescuer. When Lancelot tells them who he is, their collective response is typical of all those who encounter this greatest knight. " 'A, sir,' seyde they all, 'well mayste thou be he, for ellys save yourself, as we demed, there myght never knyght have the bettir of thes two jyauntis; for many fayre knyghtes have assayed, and here have ended. And many tymes have we wyshed aftir you, and these two gyauntes dredde never knyghte but you" (272.14–19). That the giants have "dredded" Sir Lancelot speaks to his knightly prowess; that the maidens have "wyshed aftir" Lancelot specifically is indicative of Lancelot's reputation as the particular champion of women and of the crucial role that single ladies play in the formation and maintenance of masculine knightly identity.

The briefest perusal of the *Arthuriad* reveals many similar examples of the critical function of unmarried (but marriageable) ladies for knights. Even relationships with single noblewomen that initially seem to blemish Lancelot's career ultimately enhance the reputation of Arthur's greatest knight: although deceived into sleeping with the unmarried Elaine, the product of that union, the holy Galahad, reflects positively back on Lancelot; near the end of the text, the Fair Maid of Astolat dies of her unrequited love for Lancelot, but before she does he performs marvelous feats of arms as her champion in a tournament. Her very death strengthens his identity as the greatest — and most desirable — of knights. He is a knight to die for.

Clearly, however, Lancelot's simultaneous devotion to all single women and to Guenevere cannot exist indefinitely. Angry at his relationships with both Elaine and the Fair Maid, the queen demands more of Lancelot's attention, and thereby precipitates the undoing of the Arthurian community. Arthur's nephews become suspicious of the relationship between Lancelot and Guenevere, and contrive to trap them together in the queen's chamber. Although unarmed when he is taken with the queen, Lancelot manages to fight his way free, killing all except Mordred, and escapes back to his nephew, Sir Bors. Guenevere is left to face punishment for her crime of treasonous adultery. Lancelot, correctly assuming that Arthur will in "thys hete and malice jouge the quene unto brennyng" (1171.15), indicates that he is compelled to rescue Guenevere. Significantly, Bors agrees and tells Lancelot that he must save the queen:

And also I woll counceyle you, my lorde, that my lady quene Gwenyver, and she be in ony distres, insomuch as she ys in payne for youre sake, that ye knyghtly rescow her; for and ye ded ony other wyse all the worlde wolde speke you shame to the worldis ende. Insomuch as ye were takyn with her, whether ye ded ryght othir wronge, hit ys now youre parte to holde wyth

---

[35] Lacy, ed., *Lancelot-Grail*, 3: 217.

the quene, that she be nat slayne and put to a myschevous deth. For and she
so dye, the shame shall be evermore youres. (1171.26–33)

Lancelot must defend Guenevere, regardless of whether or not it is "ryght othir
wronge," because it is through his actions that she will be brought to the stake.[36]
Within the value system of the community, Lancelot has no choice but to rescue
the queen from burning. For him she has fulfilled the role usually occupied by a
single lady; he cannot abandon the lady whose devotion and favor have made him
the greatest of all "erthly knyghtes," even though to do so will ensure that he in-
curs the enmity of some of those men whom he once held in close alliance: "I
must do much harme or I rescow her, and peradventure I shall there destroy som
of my beste fryndis, and that shold moche repente me" (1172.27–29). Indeed, in
the process of saving Guenevere, not only does Lancelot kill some of his "beste
fryndis," but also kills the man that he loves most in the world, Arthur's nephew,
Sir Gareth. Almost entirely absent from the text since his marriage to Lyones, he
makes his final appearance neither as the patiently courteous escort of Lyonet, nor
the valiant rescuer of Lyones, nor the heroic champion of the tournament; rather
he stands weaponless, without armor, vulnerable in the path of Lancelot's sword.

As Lancelot accidentally strikes down Gareth — his greatest friend and most devoted ally, the man whom he himself created knight with his own hands — he simultaneously deals the fatal blow to the ideal of chivalry upon which Malory's
Arthurian community has constructed itself. This is the final act that seals the destruction of the Round Table, dividing it against itself and ensuring the inevitability
of "evermore warre" between the factions of Lancelot and Arthur.[37] As the prime
exemplar of the chivalric ethos, and the most important representative of the chivalric community, Lancelot — from the moment he dismisses the maiden's charge
that he is at fault for remaining a "knyght wyveles" — has recognized that his ability to represent that community successfully (and thereby enhance its reputation) not
only is dependent upon remaining unmarried, but also necessitates devoted service
to ladies. The more strident his devotion, the greater his chivalric achievements.
The example of Gareth, in demonstrating the power of the single woman to push
her sworn knight to ever-greater heights of glory, simultaneously makes clear that
the married woman fulfills the inverse function for her husband, diminishing his
reputation. Thus, in its particular construction of feminine gender identity, the
courtly society of the *Arthuriad* places the single woman at the center of the process

---

[36] See C. David Benson, "Gawain's Defence of Lancelot in Malory's 'Death of Arthur'," *Modern Language Review* 78 (1983): 268–72, here 270.

[37] In the *Mort Artu*, Arthur's main reason for waging war on Lancelot is his affair with the
queen; Malory has altered his sources to emphasize the king's love for his nephew Gawain and
Arthur's desire — indeed, compulsion — to help Gawain exact vengeance in the slaying of
Gareth. In *Characterization in Malory: A Comparison with His Sources* (Chicago, 1934), Robert H.
Wilson calls attention to Malory's revision of his source material to demonstrate a particularly close
and devoted relationship between Arthur and Gawain, and the importance of his kin relationship
with Gareth; see especially 106–9.

of both individual and communal chivalric identity-making. For such an organizational scheme to function successfully, the relationships of knights and ladies must constantly increase in devotion, moving toward a marriage that must constantly be deferred. To sustain such an ideal proves impossible, and the chivalric community of the *Arthuriad* is finally destroyed by the very forces it has attempted to employ as supports.

Dorsey Armstrong
Purdue University

PART II:

Repudiating Marriage

4

TO BE OR NOT TO BE MARRIED:

Single Women, Money-lending, and the Question of Choice in Late Tudor and Stuart England[1]

I have no humour to marry, I love to lie o' both sides o' th' bed myself ... marriage is but a chopping and changing, where a maiden loses one head and has a worse i' th' place.[2]

Despite evidence of the consistent elevation of the estate of marriage above celibacy in the Tudor and Stuart periods, recent demographic calculations indicate that from the late sixteenth century onwards a rising number of individuals never entered the marital estate.[3] Though the relative proportions of men and women who remained single could not initially be separated out, more recent work by Roger Schofield has indicated that the proportion of women who did not marry appears to have shifted from a figure of ten percent in the birth cohort of 1566 to reach its peak of twenty-two percent in that of 1641.[4] Evidence to suggest a likely

---

[1] The research on which this paper is based was undertaken at the diocesan archives of Lincoln and Chester as part of a doctoral thesis on the subject of early modern celibacy that was kindly funded by the Economic and Social Research Council of Great Britain.

[2] T. M. Middleton and T. Dekker, *The Roaring Girl* (1611), ed. A. Gomme (London, 1976), 2.2.35–44.

[3] The term "celibacy" can be used to describe a period of abstinence from sexual intercourse. In this chapter, however, the term is used in its most literal form to denote the state of not being (and not having been) married.

[4] E. A. Wrigley and R. S. Schofield, *The Population History of England, 1541–1871* (Cambridge, MA, 1981), 257–65; Roger Schofield, "English Marriage Patterns Revisited," *Journal of Family History* 10 (1985): 5; idem, "English Marriage Patterns Revisited: Once More," 6 (un-

rise in the incidence of female celibacy is not restricted to the work of modern historians. According to the author of at least one seventeenth-century ballad,

> A young man need never take thought how to wive,
> For widows and maidens for husbands do strive,
> Here's scant men enough for them all left alive,
> They flock to the Church, like Bees to the hive.[5]

Contemporary writers may have been unsure of the exact extent of the problem, but rising concern over the belief that such a situation existed solicited anxious attempts at explanation. The estate of monogamous marriage, which lay at the very heart of the Tudor and Stuart social system, provided the basis for internal stability, household order and external security. Its survival therefore appeared crucial to the continued success of the commonwealth.

The documentary evidence of this concern, manifested most visibly in the Restoration period, reflected the perception that marriage had undergone decline. Driven by a mercantilist philosophy predicated on the need to increase the numerical strength of the nation, emerging political economists sought to locate depressed levels of fertility within a context of nuptiality; since marriage, in contemporary discourse, was constructed as the prime locus of procreative behavior, a fall in the number of those entering this particular estate emerged as the most plausible explanation for the evident demographic stagnation. Contemporary discourse also shaped the parameters of the ensuing investigation. Dominant constructions of femininity in the Tudor and Stuart periods revolved around the concept of woman as wife and mother, and marriage for women therefore appeared in the literature as a stage in the life-cycle that was at once desirable, necessary, and inevitable.[6] Within the context of the common law, marriage for women was revealed as an expectation rather than a recommendation. As T. E., the anonymous author of *The Law's Resolutions*, was wont to insist, "All of them [women] are understood either married or to be married."[7]

The evident preference of all members of the female sex for the state of wedlock was perhaps most eloquently expressed by the anonymous author of the late seventeenth-century conduct book *The Batchelor's Directory* in 1694. It was his firm opinion that "tho' a Maid never asks to Marry, because she has modesty, yet there is nothing she desires with greater passion. . . . It must be confessed likewise that it is

---

published typescript dated 1998, cited by kind permission of the author). This change in behavior is now believed to be largely responsible for the slowing of population growth during the early seventeenth century, and the subsequent stagnation in population levels.

[5] Cited in Alan MacFarlane, *Marriage and Love in England: Modes of Reproduction, 1300–1840* (Oxford, 1986), 150.

[6] Kate Aughterson, ed., *Renaissance Woman: A Sourcebook: Constructions of Femininity in England* (London, 1995), esp. chaps. 1, 2, and 4; and in Joan Larsen Klein, ed., *Daughters, Wives, & Widows: Writings by Men about Women and Marriage in England, 1500–1640* (Urbana and Chicago, 1992), 32.

[7] T. E., *The Law's Resolutions of Women's Rights* (1632), 6.

her true state, and that there is no better party for her to take."[8] Yet the concept of marriage as the most definitive aspect of female existence has parallels in a much earlier period. For example, in the work of the most renowned English playwright of the Renaissance era, though the life of a man was most famously represented by a series of seven stages, that of a woman revolved more simply around a mere three: those of maid, wife, and widow.[9]

Lesser writers too concurred in presenting a comparable portrait of the female life-cycle. In Samuel Rowlands's ballad "'Tis Merrie When Gossips Meete" (1602), a wife and a widow take the opportunity of an impromptu meeting in an alehouse to enlighten a young maid regarding her best course of action. In the opinion of the wife,

> Maydes must be married, least they mar'd should bee
> I will be sworne, before I saw fifteene,
> I wish't that I my wedding day had seene.[10]

In "The Bride" (1617), a further example of the same genre, Rowlands allowed his eponymous heroine to take an even stronger line against recalcitrant maidens. Since marriage was clearly the ultimate aim of all young women, those who preferred the single life were characterized not only as "fooles," but also as flawed and abnormal:

> Unperfect female, living odde you are,
> Never true even, till you match and paire.[11]

Neither was the critical significance of marriage for women lost on contemporary moralists, and they appear to have taken considerable pains to remind their female audience of this fact. As the Protestant preacher Robert Wilkinson indicated in his formal address to the wedding guests of the newly married Lord and Lady Hay in January of 1608, "All the time of your life you have been gathering for this day."[12]

---

[8] *The Batchelor's Directory: Being a Treatise of the Excellence of Marriage* (1694), Advertisement. When John Verney's suit to Angel Harrington was refused, he assumed she wanted more money, since he could not imagine that a woman would choose to remain single. See Susan E. Whyman, *Sociability and Power in Late-Stuart England: The Cultural Worlds of the Verneys, 1660–1720* (Oxford, 1999), 120.

[9] William Shakespeare, *As You Like It*, 2.7.139–66; idem, *Measure for Measure*, 5.1.171–80; in *The Riverside Shakespeare*, ed. G. Blakemore Evans, 2nd ed. (Boston, 1997).

[10] Samuel Rowlands, "Tis Merrie when Gossips Meete" (1602), sig. C3.

[11] Idem, "The Bride" (1617), sig. C2, C3.

[12] Robert Wilkinson (dates unknown), *The Merchant Royall* (1608), 38.

I. A Single Woman Perforce

The boundaries of contemporary understanding therefore determined the nature of the problem. Since constructions of nuptial behavior created entry into marriage as a natural, logical, and desirable feature of the female life-cycle, it seemed most reasonable from a seventeenth-century viewpoint to address falling marriage rates by recourse to availability, in this case the problems women were experiencing in finding willing husbands. Pamphlets, of both a serious and a satirical nature, had highlighted the specific effects of the fighting on marriage opportunities during the period of the Interregnum.[13] By the 1660s and 1670s, however, in the wake of a century of conflict, half a century of indentured emigration and the persistent ravages of the plague, the irretrievable loss of large numbers of fertile young men formed a key element in contemporary explanations:

> The two last great plagues, the Civil Wars at home, and the several wars with Holland, Spain, and France, have destroyed several hundred thousands of men ... besides, vast numbers have transported themselves, or been transported into Ireland and other our foreign plantations ... and the loss more mischievous to the kingdom than merely the death or removal of so many persons, considering that they were men in the prime of their years in perfect strength; such, who had they not died, or been killed, or removed, might every year have begotten children, and thereby increased the world.[14]

Yet while falling female marriage rates may have been most easily discernible within the context of depressed marital opportunity, there were those who preferred instead to focus on the growth of certain anti-matrimonial tendencies among the male population. Thomas Hodges, a Protestant minister vehemently opposed to any suggestion of celibacy, especially among the clergy, even indicated that such attitudes had been encouraged by uncharitable female behavior: "The pride & peevishness of some Wives to their Husbands in our dayes, hath brought an ill report on Matrimony; and 'tis to be feared, hath frightened many from the remedy of Marriage, into the Disease of Adultery and Uncleanness."[15]

In the ecclesiastical sphere, it was clearly the moral implications of falling marriage rates that proved to be of particular concern, but in the atmosphere of sexual promiscuity that unfolded around the royal court, the licentious behavior thought to accompany the state of celibacy became more readily associated with the ranks

---

[13] *The Mid-wives just Petition, or the complaint of divers good Gentlewomen of that faculty* (1643); *The Virgins Complaint for the losse of their Sweet-Hearts*, 2nd ed. (1642).

[14] From "The Grand Concern of England explained, in several Proposals offered to the Consideration of Parliament ... by a lover of his Country and Well-wisher to the Prosperity both of the King and Kingdoms" (1673), in *Seventeenth-Century Economic Documents*, ed. Joan Thirsk and John P. Cooper (Oxford, 1972), 742.

[15] Thomas Hodges (d. 1688), *A Treatise of Marriage* (1673), 5.

of the elite.[16] A satirical pamphlet of 1675 went so far as to suggest that "A whore is become a necessary Appurtenance, and to keep her nobly part of the character of a gentleman,"[17] and by the end of the century a perceived preference for bachelorhood was increasingly related to the promiscuous behavior of men in the higher status groups: "Neglect and abuse of marriage lies most among the Men of Quality, and the Rich, who partly out of debauched principle; and partly out of a covetous humour forbear to marry."[18] However, the single male at all social levels proved a major source of anxiety. Some of the more extreme Protestant sects had already argued in favor of polygamy on theological grounds, and though it never received a substantial amount of support, a number of political economists recognized it to have been a possible solution to the problem of depopulation that threatened to menace society.[19] Far more acceptable to the majority, though, were the solutions offered by economists such as William Petty and Charles Davenant, who both ventured to suggest a higher tax rate for bachelors by way of compensation. The mercantilist critique crystallized in the passage of the Marriage Duty Act in 1695, which levied taxes on births, marriages, and deaths, and in addition imposed a poll tax on bachelors and childless widowers.[20]

There was little discussion of any comparable increase in the desire to remain single among women, although satirical attacks on the idea of the spinster in the later seventeenth century suggest that concern may have been an issue.[21] The homily on the state of matrimony in 1562 had hinted at the independence women must relinquish in order to marry, but no teaching was directed to the praise or encouragement of independence in women, even those that were unmarried.[22] Explanations for the failure of women to marry may then have been divergent — men were either unavailable or unwilling to enter the bonds of matrimony — but they had at their root one common feature: the understanding that celibacy was the antithesis of female desire.

Yet ideological pressure on women to marry was not absolute. A closer reading of the printed literature of the sixteenth and seventeenth centuries reveals that marriage was never inordinately advocated for all and sundry, even in the context of Tudor and Stuart England. Though there appears to have been a genuine accep-

---

[16] Lawrence Stone, *The Family, Sex and Marriage in England, 1500–1800*, abridged ed. (New York and London, 1979), 328.

[17] Anon., "The Maids Complaint Against the Batchelors" (1675), 6.

[18] *Marriage Promoted. In a Discourse of its Ancient and Modern Practice* (1690), 28.

[19] Ian Watt, *The Rise of the Novel: Studies in Defoe, Richardson, and Fielding* (Berkeley, 1957), 147. See also Christopher Hill, *The World Turned Upside Down. Radical Ideas During the English Revolution* (Harmondsworth, 1975), 314.

[20] D. V. Glass, "Two Papers on Gregory King," in *Population in History*, ed. D. V. Glass and D. E. C. Eversley (London, 1965), 170.

[21] Satirical offerings such as *The Maiden's Complaint Against Coffee* (1663) and *The Women's Complaint Against Tobacco* (1675) suggested that women were "reduced" to considering a preference for celibacy, in opposition to their "natural desire" for marriage, because men indulged in drinking coffee and smoking tobacco.

[22] Doris Mary Stenton, *The English Woman in History* (London, 1957), 117.

tance of the generalized necessity for marriage, commentators were aware that there were certain categories of people for whom only celibacy could be the recommended course of action. All those intending to marry were required to fulfil the necessary canonical precepts, observing first "the distinction of sex" — couples must contain one member of each sex — and second, the "just and lawful distance of blood." However, in addition to the third and usual requirement that the parties be legally free to marry, conduct literature also recommended that those intending to marry be physically capable of carrying out all their matrimonial duties. William Perkins therefore suggested that it was unlawful to marry "such a person, as is unfit for the use of mariage, either by naturall constitution of body or by accident. For example, in regard of sicknesse, or of frigiditie, or of the palsie uncurable, or lastly of the deprivation of the parts belonging to generation."[23] Furthermore, since marriage was recognized by contemporaries to have been both physically and emotionally demanding, those perceived to have been unable to cope with the hardship and rigors of matrimonial existence were likely to have been cautioned against it. Ellin Stout, sister of William, the Lancashire grocer and Quaker, apparently had several offers of marriage from men "of goode repuite and substance" (her father had left her £80), but, according to William, "being always subject to the advice of her mother, was advised, considering her infermetys and ill state of health, to remain single, knowing the care and exercises that always attended a married life, and the hazerd of hapiness in it."[24]

Aside from the constraints of physical inability, early modern society was not blind to the numerous personal factors that served to undermine the efforts of any individual to marry, both in the short term and in the long. Marriages were clearly prevented for any number of courtship problems, and relationships often fell at the first hurdle. For others, the discovery of a potential soulmate merely constituted a further, and frequently greater hurdle — that of convincing family and friends of the fitness of the match. Disapproval and opposition could result in the termination of the suit, or at the very least place the relationship in jeopardy. Yet there is little doubt that in general advice to marry remained the keynote of female experience. The ideological underpinning of the marital estate underwent little significant change over the early modern period, and support for marriage remained the dominant discursive theme.

Modern historians, heavily influenced by the doctrine of this Protestant marriage ideal, have also sought to address rising levels of female celibacy almost exclusively through recourse to the inability to marry. After much investigation, the factor that appears to have been most effective in impeding a woman's progress towards marriage in the late Tudor and early Stuart periods has proved to be financial. As much

---

[23] William Perkins, *Christian Oeconomy: Or A Short Survey of the Right Manner of Erecting and Ordering a Family, according to the Scriptures* (1609), 54.

[24] J. D. Marshall, ed., *The Autobiography of William Stout of Lancaster, 1665–1752* (Manchester, 1967), 87. Ellin's mother probably had genuine concerns, but she and her sons benefited as a result. Ellin kept house for her mother and each of her brothers, and she also helped William in the course of his business.

of the contemporary printed advice cautioned against a marriage that was economically unsound, this explanation, in addition to enjoying a considerable measure of current support, has a great deal of historical resonance. From the conduct manuals of Henry Bullinger, who in 1541 argued that it was "not mete for every man to mary" for "many poore maryages make many beggars," to the work of Thomas Hilder almost a century later, moralists continued to proselytize on the virtues of self-sufficiency: "a discreet Christian will not marry until he can comfortably conclude that his present or future meanes will be sufficient to keep him from poverty, pinching poverty, and destruction, and from lying as a burthen on others."[25] Moral precepts were reinforced by more familiar proverbs and aphorisms. "First thrive and then wive," and "there belongs more to marrying then foure bare legs in a bed" formed part of the greater cultural directive designed to offer prospective marital candidates a constant reminder of the need for economic security.[26]

The significance of such security in early modern marital opportunity should not be downplayed. As J. Hajnal was able to demonstrate in the 1960s, household structure in England consisted largely of nuclear-type family units, each unit containing only one married couple, or none at all.[27] This "simple" model, which prevailed over much of northwest Europe at the time, determined the extent to which economic security was a necessary factor in the decision to marry, for once married the relevant couple became responsible for the creation and management of an entirely new household unit. Marriage partners required goods and a measure of capital in addition to a large slice of psychological and sexual compatibility. In the circumstances of demographic expansion and spiraling inflation that dominated the later Elizabethan and early Jacobean periods, it would not therefore have been remarkable to find that a considerable number of women found their search for a willing husband increasingly problematic. Indeed, decisions by single men to defer marriage arrangements indefinitely could easily be interpreted as the most rational course of action. "Bachelors," as Lis and Soly have indicated, "were least threatened with hunger, but families generally existed in a state of chronic need. Marriage for most workers brought misery, and the unskilled in particular had to tighten their belts at marriage."[28]

Moreover, in allocating the control of all marital property to the husband, common law in turn demanded that the obligation of the husband be to maintain his

---

[25] Henry Bullinger (1504–1575), *The christen state of matrimony . . . newly set forth in Englyshe* (1546?), fol. xxix; T. Hilder (dates unknown), *Conjugal Counsell* (1653), 11.

[26] J. Clarke, *Paroemiologia anglo-Latina in usum scholarum concinnata. Or Proverbs English and Latine* (1638), 230, 65.

[27] J. Hajnal, "Two Kinds of Pre-industrial Household Formation System," in *Family Forms in Historic Europe*, ed. Richard Wall, Jean Robin, and Peter Laslett (Cambridge, 1983), 68–69. Laslett's study of one hundred English communities between 1574 and 1821 revealed that of the 5,843 households examined, only thirty-nine contained a married child living with spouse and married parents, of which twenty-nine couples were living with the husband's parents and ten those of the wife: Peter Laslett, "Mean Household Size in England since the Sixteenth Century," in *Household and Family in Past Time*, ed. idem and R. Wall (Cambridge, 1972), 149.

[28] Catharina Lis and Hugo Soly, *Poverty and Capitalism in Pre-Industrial Europe* (Brighton, 1982), 19.

wife, regardless of the amount of wealth she brought to the marriage.[29] While the wealthy bride became an economic asset, a bride without capital was at best a drain on resources and at worst a financial millstone. By the seventeenth century, the English marriage portion — the amount of capital (or productive goods) a bride brought to a marriage — consequently appears important to the idea and conclusion of marriage agreements at every social level. Economic prudence was especially valued as a female virtue. The lack of a portion then not only provided an indicator of material failings, but in addition implied the existence of moral ones. Richard Gough, Shropshire yeoman and orthodox Anglican, in discussing the marriage of a man to his servant maid, was openly caustic about the character of the latter — "a wanton gadding dame, who had neither goods nor good name."[30] Consequently, since the lump sum brought by the woman often proved a key element in marriage negotiations, it may have been the case that during this period the inability of the bride to provide a suitable portion constituted the most likely reason for the failure of a couple to reach a marriage agreement.[31] John Sheppard of Somerset apparently preferred to flee the country rather than marry Mary Robins, "because she was not able to bring with her any portion or sufficient value to help pay for the purchase of their living."[32]

Most young women of middling status and above probably received the bulk of their portion from their close family, but those lower down the social scale relied on a combination of sources: inheritance from parents; gifts and legacies from employers, friends, and relatives; charitable bequests; and money saved from wages. Penurious young women with little or nothing in the way of inherited assets would have expected to accumulate their entire portion through time spent in gainful work, and it is their situation that appears most critical. Though girls generally began to work outside their natal households in their mid-teens, and continued in paid employment, where possible, until such time as they married, the need to add to a small portion or indeed raise one at all was increasingly at odds with existing remunerative opportunities. In an overstocked labor market in which they were already at a disadvantage, their chances of obtaining waged work in service, in a trade, and even in the more general field of laboring appear to have become increasingly circumscribed.[33]

---

[29] Margaret R. Sommerville, *Sex and Subjection: Attitudes to Women in Early-Modern Society* (London, 1995), 101, 103.

[30] Richard Gough (1634–1723), *The History of Myddle* (Harmondsworth, 1981), 113.

[31] Laslett has argued that a woman needed certain "possessions or accomplishments" in order to marry, one of which was a dowry. See Peter Laslett, *The World We Have Lost Further Explored* (London, 1983), 99–100.

[32] G. R. Quaife, *Wanton Wenches and Wayward Wives: Peasants and Illicit Sex in Early Seventeenth Century England* (London, 1979), 97.

[33] Ann Kussmaul, *Servants in Husbandry in Early Modern England* (Cambridge, 1981), 4; J. A. Sharpe, *Early Modern England: A Social History, 1550–1760* (London, 1987), 210; I. K. Ben-Amos, "Women Apprentices in the Trades and Crafts of Early Modern Bristol," *Continuity and Change* 6 (1991): 236–37; Donald Woodward, *Men at Work: Labourers and Building Craftsmen in the Towns of Northern England, 1450–1750* (Cambridge, 1995), 115. While male wage rates for building

There is clear evidence of a common understanding that marriage failure to a large extent was rooted in economic failure, especially in relation to the provision of a portion. Testators in the late fifteenth century, for example, had been aware of the problems poor girls encountered in accumulating sufficient resources to marry. William Covert willed that every poor maiden lacking the funds to marry within five miles of his home was to have 6s. 8d. towards her marriage; others like Robert Benjamen and John Buckland bequeathed goods in the form of pots, pans, vessels, or bedding to assist poorer girls in the setting up of a house.[34] In the Tudor and Stuart periods, similar examples of charitable bequests reflected both the importance of a portion and the relative value of its size in improving marital opportunity. Jane Pearson of Wrinehall in Cheshire left £20 to the three daughters of Robert Gormell, "to be set forth for the use and benifitt of the abovesaid three daughters for their better preferment in marriage."[35] Employers, too, were often active in improving the marriage prospects of their employees. Samuel Pepys gave his servants Jane Birch and her prospective husband Tom Edwards £40 by way of a portion on the occasion of their marriage, and Joyce Jeffreys was particularly generous in the marriage gifts she extended to her hired staff: one maid was given a present of £100, and another received the sum of £20. She even gave 10s. to the maid of one of her tenants.[36]

By the seventeenth century, however, such awareness had also taken on institutional dimensions. In recognizing its responsibilities towards impoverished youngsters in the area of its jurisdiction, the Laud Charity, a trust based on land given to Reading by the Archbishop of Canterbury of the same name, had tailored the nature of its giving towards improving the chances of destitute children. Unashamedly gendered in its application, the details of the charity's payments at once reveal the symbiotic nature of the relationship between women and marriage in early modern thought: poor boys were to receive assistance in finding an apprenticeship; poor servant girls, on the other hand, were to be given £20 in the form of a marriage portion.[37] By the late seventeenth century, in the climate of moral panic over the perceived decline in marriage rates, continued faith in the efficacy of a young girl's portion to facilitate her entry into marriage even encouraged at least one social commentator to recommend nothing less than state provision. The anonymous author of the pamphlet entitled *Marriage Promoted* (1690) suggested that those who

---

laborers at Durham may have doubled between the 1520s and 1570s from 3d or 4d to 6d per day, female workers' wages over the same period remained static at around 2d per day: Woodward, *Men at Work*, 112. The fact that women received around three-fifths of the male rate had biblical authority: see Leviticus 27:3–4.

[34] Mavis E. Mate, *Daughters, Wives and Widows after the Black Death* (Woodbridge, 1998), 28.

[35] Chester Record Office (hereafter C.R.O.), WS 1671.

[36] Robert Latham and William Mathews, eds., *The Diary of Samuel Pepys*, vol. 10 (London, 1983), 195; R. G. Griffiths, "Joyce Jeffreys of Ham Castle," *Transactions of the Worcestershire Archaeological Society* 10 (1933): 22.

[37] M. Fellgett, "Revealed Women — Widows and Spinsters in Seventeenth-Century Reading" (M.Phil. diss., University of Reading, 1990), 104.

chose to remain single be appropriately taxed and the resulting money made available "for Portions to young Maids who are under Forty Years of Age" in order to facilitate their marriage.[38]

The extent to which lack of access to a portion determined the marital opportunities of young women in the Tudor and Stuart periods remains a matter of ongoing debate. Richard M. Smith has suggested that the marginalization of women in the late fifteenth and early sixteenth centuries, rather than delaying marriage, instead encouraged a situation in which they more readily sought out marriage, possibly at an earlier age, and almost certainly in higher proportions than had previously been the case.[39] David R. Wier, too, has questioned the validity of a model that requires people to postpone a marriage in order to increase the size of their nest egg, when the amount that could be saved was so small as to render the prospect of marriage in the foreseeable future extremely unlikely.[40]

Nevertheless, economic pressures remain a vital part of the overall picture. Unlike a number of other countries in central Europe, England had no direct system of marriage prevention in the early modern period.[41] Concern with untimely marriages had caused both the Henrician and the late Elizabethan parliament to flirt with the idea of tighter regulation of marriage, but in the event national legislation proved unnecessary.[42] After the terrible harvest crises of the 1590s the Overseers of the Poor in a number of counties took it upon themselves to prevent economically unsound marriages, particularly those of migrants, and wage earners born outside the parishes they proposed to enter were also refused settlement if they had dependent families or intended to marry. Clergymen colluded in such actions by refusing to marry immigrants whom parishioners sought to exclude. Such restrictions, in the view of Ralph Houlbrooke, played a not inconsiderable role in diminishing the number of marriages.[43]

Houlbrooke is not alone in voicing these concerns. Historians allied to the ideology of social control have viewed the implementation of the Elizabethan Poor Law as a key factor in the shift towards a later age of marriage and a higher inci-

---

[38] *Marriage Promoted*, 56.

[39] Richard M. Smith, "Geographical Diversity in the Resort to Marriage in Late Medieval Europe: Work, Reputation, and Unmarried Females in the Household Formation Systems of Northern and Southern Europe," in *Woman is a Worthy Wight*, ed. P. J. P. Goldberg (Stroud, 1992), 45.

[40] David R. Wier, "Rather Never than Late: Celibacy and Age at Marriage in English Cohort Fertility, 1541–1871," *Journal of Family History* 9 (1984): 340–54, here 341.

[41] In Central European parishes clergymen were "forbidden by law to marry indigent persons without a marriage permit issued by the local judiciary." See Michael Mitterauer and Reinhard Sieder, *The European Family: Patriarchy to Partnership from the Middle Ages to the Present* (Oxford, 1982), 123.

[42] A policy paper sent to Cromwell suggested preventing the marriages of young men until they were "of potent age," and in the parliamentary session of 1597–1598 an abortive bill aimed at preventing "sundry great abuses by licences for marriages without banes" was proposed. See S. Hindle, "The Problem of Pauper Marriage in Seventeenth-Century England," *Transactions of the Royal Historical Society* ser. 6, 8 (1998): 71–89, here 79 n. 33.

[43] Ralph A. Houlbrooke, *The English Family, 1450–1700* (London, 1984), 68.

dence of lifetime celibacy, both of which are visible in the demographic data of the seventeenth century.[44] Though the impetus to the implementation of control can usually be located within the severe depression of the 1590s, examples of parish officers refusing to allow couples to marry continue to manifest themselves in the records of a number of English communities in the first half of the seventeenth century. Even as late as the Restoration period, cases in which local officials denied partners the opportunity to marry, according to Steve Hindle, can be interpreted as a process of exclusion in which community representatives ostracized those they considered guilty "of imprudent and potentially burdensome marital behaviour."[45] The fact that much of the operation of such control was likely to have been unofficial conceals the very extent of its effect. However, it was a recognized weapon in the battle to reduce the poor rate: Sir Dudley North believed local officers regularly attempted to defend their parish from charges, taking "great care to prevent the mareage of those that they have, hindering all they can possibly the matching of young ones together."[46] Some objections were formulated around parish relief: Edward Marten and Jane Goodwin of Frampton in Lincolnshire, for example, were refused permission to marry until they could offer proof that they would not be a drain on parochial resources.[47] Others were focused more strongly around the provision of accommodation: in 1596 all vestrymen of the town of Swallowfield in Wiltshire were ordered to have "an especyall care to speake to the mynyster to stay the maryage of such as wolde mary before they have a convenient house to lyve in according to their callynge"; in 1628 the minister of Nether Compton in Dorset complained that Anne Russed "hath no house nor home of her own and very like to bring charge on the parish, and therefore will hardly be suffered to marry in our parish."[48] Control of marital opportunity then constituted one official, if illegal, strategy by which parishes sought to discourage economically unsuitable marriages.[49]

Other strategies prove more difficult to document. In spite of the absence of legislation directed specifically towards the prevention of unsuitable marriages, a number of statutes operated indirectly to reduce their incidence. In 1556, the age for the earliest termination of London apprenticeships had been fixed at twenty-four in a deliberate attempt to check "over hastie maryages and over sone settyng upp of householdes of and by the youthe," and in 1563 this was prescribed by statute for all cities and corporate towns. In 1589 an act was passed which prevented

---

[44] Richard Smith, "Charity, Self-interest and Welfare: Reflections from Demographic and Family History," in *Charity, Self-Interest and Welfare in the English Past*, ed. Martin Daunton (London, 1996), 24.

[45] Hindle, "Pauper Marriage," 83.

[46] Hindle, "Pauper Marriage," 85.

[47] Hindle, "Pauper Marriage," 77.

[48] Hindle, "Pauper Marriage," 80–81; Martin Ingram, *Church Courts, Sex, and Marriage in England, 1570–1640* (Cambridge, 1987), 131.

[49] William Gouge indicated that denying marriage on the grounds of poverty contravened Christian law: "For Mariage is honourable in all, or among all, namely in, or among all sorts of people: wherein it is accounted a Doctrine of devils to forbid to marry": Gouge, *Of Domesticall Dutie. Eight Treatises* (1622), 183.

the building of cottages without the benefit of four acres of land, and strictly regulated the subletting of rooms in order to discourage such activity.[50] Furthermore, there is some evidence to suggest that charity payments were geared towards excluding the claims of those who had recently married. Robert Dallington of Geddington, whose will in 1636 endowed a charity with £300 "for the distribution of twenty-four three-penny loaves everie Sunday to twenty-four of the poor of the parish," ensured that the criterion of residence necessary for eligibility automatically excluded servants, apprentices, and young married couples.[51] These provisions may have been echoed in other rural charities.

The prosecution of those who erected cottages with less than the required amount of land, and the eviction of lodgers likely to prove financially burdensome to the poor rate, in addition to the withholding of charity payments from young married couples, clearly had the capacity to affect marriage decisions, although the overall effectiveness of this plethora of preventative practices is hard to gauge. Couples intent on matrimony could usually manage to circumvent parish decisions, if sufficiently determined, for while local officials may have refused settlement, rogue priests were often happy to marry anyone for an appropriate fee. In Somerset in the 1620s the parishes of Milverton and Pitney and the peculiar jurisdiction of Illminster appeared as early English equivalents of Gretna Green, and other couples prevented from marrying in Somerset made their way to the neighboring counties of Devon, Gloucester, and Dorset in search of more sympathetic wedding locations.[52] The poor inmate did become a particular problem for towns, but regulations were concerned less with the prevention of marriages and more with the problem of pregnant single women who were likely to become a burden on the parish. However, declining opportunities for permanent settlement clearly had the ability to delay marriage decisions, if not render them impossible. Research on migration patterns in the Tudor and early Stuart periods has led Anthony Salerno to suggest that lack of settlement opportunities in Wiltshire resulted in the existence of a higher age at first marriage in this area between 1581 and 1660 than in other areas of the country.[53]

Though both contemporary and modern researchers have labored under similar assumptions about women's affinity for marriage, in contrast to the modern fascination with problems of accumulation and the role of community as matrimonial guardian, much of the contemporary discourse, as indicated earlier, was concerned to highlight the availability — or lack of availability — of eligible single men. Though little weight has been attributed to the notion of deteriorating sex ratios in more recent historiography, it does not seem unreasonable to argue that a woman's

---

[50] Houlbrooke, *English Family*, 68.

[51] S. Hindle, "Fuel, Dole and Bread: Order and Expediency in a Forest Economy, c. 1600–1800," unpublished paper for Sussex 'Cultural and Community Studies' seminar (Brighton, 6 November 1997), 16–17; by kind permission of the author.

[52] Quaife, *Wanton Wenches*, 96.

[53] Anthony Salerno, "The Social Background of Seventeenth-Century Emigration to America," *Journal of British Studies* 19 (1979): 31–52, here 49.

chances of marriage were to a considerable extent reliant upon the pool of available partners. A holistic investigation of falling marriage rates should then at the very least consider the potential effects of sex imbalances on marriage chances, whether such imbalances were temporary — as a result of migratory patterns — or of a more permanent nature, induced by disease, emigration, or war.[54]

There is considerable evidence to indicate the existence of a highly mobile unmarried population in the early modern period. Severe underemployment, tremendous variation in annual mortality, and the small size of communities all interacted to induce single people who lacked stable positions to travel in search of work.[55] In urban areas, it was the system of apprenticeship that dominated the migration process: seventy-five percent of all apprentices listed in the Bristol registers in the early seventeenth century originated from outside the city; studies of London indentures over the same period reveal that eighty-five percent of all apprentices there were migrants.[56] Moreover, a considerable number may have traveled over long distances to take up their positions: of one hundred four inhabitants of Whitechurch and Stepney between 1580 and 1639, as few as fourteen had been born in one of the London suburbs or other parts of Middlesex.[57] The internal dynamics of migration in the countryside may have been very different, but young rural servants in particular were highly mobile. Although they frequently did not venture further than fifteen kilometres at a time, they generally moved on between annual contracts, and often circulated widely around their home region.[58]

Local and regional opportunities clearly affected migratory practices, and the effects of structural change on employment opportunities could feasibly have constituted an exacerbatory factor in the reduction of marriage chances. Thus from early in the seventeenth century, the sex ratio at burial in the Devonshire community of Colyton, for example, became distinctly skewed. Whereas the pattern of burials in the 1550s had witnessed four male examples for every three female, by the 1650s the opposite was the case, a situation that appears to have had a negative effect on women's marriage opportunities.[59] Pamela Sharpe, while recognizing the difficulty of measuring sex ratios with any accuracy, has ventured to suggest that the bias in burials during the mid-seventeenth century may have been the result of differential patterns of migration. For though women in the Colyton region tended to move from one village or small town to another in search of employment, men were

---

[54] Distortions in sex ratios resulting from patterns of regional specialization have been cited by David R. Wier as a possible explanation for the increase of celibacy in the seventeenth century: Wier, "Rather Never Than Late," 349.

[55] David Levine, *Family Formation in an Age of Nascent Capitalism* (New York, 1977), 35.

[56] Ilena Krausman Ben-Amos, *Adolescence and Youth in Early Modern England* (New Haven, 1994), 86.

[57] David Cressy, "Occupations, Migration and Literacy in East London, 1580–1640," *Local Population Studies* 5 (1970): 57.

[58] Ben-Amos, *Adolescence*, 69.

[59] Pamela Sharpe, "Literally Spinsters: A New Interpretation of Local Economy and Demography in Colyton in the Seventeenth and Eighteenth Centuries," *Economic History Review*, 2nd ser., 44 (1991): 47–48.

more likely to join streams of migrants heading for the larger towns or cities, or bind themselves apprentice on a ship heading for America.[60] The sporadic and *ad hoc* nature of much of the subsistence migration before the Interregnum was likely to have militated significantly against the incidence of marriage in other areas too. Before 1650 a significant number of migrants were poor itinerant workers who moved from place to place in a system of relatively undefined and undifferentiated migration. Localized movement tended to merge into longer distance traveling and was based primarily on crude subsistence or push factors.[61] Anecdotal evidence indicates that servants led highly mobile and relatively isolated lives, and if, as Eversley has suggested, between seventy-five and eighty percent of marriages were either between residents of the same parish or between residents of parishes within a five-mile radius, then subsistence migration was likely to have been an important factor in reducing nuptial opportunity.[62]

However, while the full extent of temporary migratory patterns on marriage chances remains elusive, the permanent loss of a large number of marriageable young men in the second quarter of the seventeenth century appears as a definitive episode in English population history. Despite the reluctance of modern demographic historians to attribute any significant weight to the sudden disappearance of a considerable number of marriageable young men, contemporary writers were quick to recognize the extent of the problem, and keen to elaborate on its causes:

> That we have fewer people than formerly is imputable not only by the hand of God on the late visitation, but more especially to the long continued diverting of the young and prolific people to the plantations, and to the repeopling of Ireland besides those whom the late civil wars devoured in England.[63]

---

[60] Sharpe, "Literally Spinsters," 50–51.

[61] Peter Clark, "Migration in England During the Late Seventeenth and Early Eighteenth Centuries," in *Migration and Society in Early Modern England*, ed. idem and David Souden (London, 1987), 215.

[62] Of the twenty-six servants appearing in the local census listing for Cogenhoe, Northamptonshire, in 1628, only Elizabeth Stocking had been among the twenty-eight listed in the earlier 1618 census; "even she had been out of the village in 1621 and had changed households between 1624 and 1628." See Peter Laslett, *Family Life and Illicit Love in Earlier Generations: Essays in Historical Sociology* (Cambridge, 1977), 72. The work of V. Brodsky Elliott has indicated that some London servants were well-traveled and had few friends. She has also suggested that mobility was a powerful force, capable of delaying marriage independently of status. See Elliott, "Mobility and Marriage in Pre-industrial England" (Ph.D. diss., University of Cambridge, 1978), 231, 291. Also D. E. C. Eversley, "Population History and Local History," in *An Introduction to English Historical Demography from the Sixteenth to the Nineteenth Century*, ed. E. A. Wrigley (London, 1966), 21–22.

[63] From "An Essay concerning the Decay of Rents and their Remedies, written by Sir William Coventry about the year 1670," in *Seventeenth-Century Economic Documents*, ed. Thirsk and Cooper, 80.

Premature death as a result of infectious disease formed part and parcel of early modern existence, but the erratic and in many cases cataclysmic "visitations" of the plague could not fail to strike terror into the heart of every individual during the Tudor and early Stuart periods. With little or no appreciation of its epidemiology and a misguided policy on its containment, attempts to prevent the plague were most frequently ineffective; consequently, death rates were high and sorrow widespread: "In every house griefe striking up an Allarum: servants crying out for maisters: wives for husbands, parents for children, children for their mothers."[64] Yet though the threat of death from the plague was an innate feature of both male and female experience, there were those who believed that certain visitations were more detrimental to one sex than another. In 1604 Francis Hering, M.D., a member of the Royal College of Physicians, wrote of the general understanding that "six or ten" men died for every woman during the plague outbreak of 1603, and in the last recorded year of the plague popular opinion amongst the male population of the capital was reportedly convinced that the presence of such a bias had resulted in a gross female surplus. "Most men do believe," noted John Graunt, London haberdasher and early demographer, "that there be three Women for one Man."[65]

In modern times the existence of a bias in levels of morbidity and mortality as a result of the plague has received a measure of support. In its twentieth-century manifestation the disease has demonstrated a definite propensity for healthy young adult males, with individual men apparently being twice as likely as women to become infected with the plague and five times as likely to die from it.[66] The extent to which such patterns have a historical precedent, however, remains contentious. In 1971, a study by Mary F. Hollingsworth and T. H. Hollingsworth, based on evidence gathered from the parish of St. Botolph's without Bishopsgate in London, indicated that mortality as a result of the plague had been significantly greater among men in the early seventeenth century than it had been among women. The figures were extremely suggestive. Within the parish as a whole the sex ratio of male burials to those of females was 200:100 in 1603 and 190:100 in 1625, compared with a pre-plague figure of 72:100, a fact the couple attributed to the greater cleanliness of women and their avoidance of the areas most likely to be rat-infested.[67]

The problem confronting demographic historians, however, has been that the pattern the Hollingsworths uncovered in St. Botolph's did not repeat itself in similar studies of early modern plague-related deaths either at Colyton in Devon or Eyam

---

[64] Thomas Dekker, *The Wonderfull Yeare, 1603* (1604–1607?), sig. C4.

[65] Francis Hering, *A Modest Defence of the Caveat given to the Wearers of impoisoned Amulets* (1604), cited in F. P. Wilson, *The Plague in Shakespeare's London* (Oxford, 1927, repr. 1999), 3–4 n. 3; J. D. Graunt, *Natural and Political Observations Made upon the Bills of Mortality*, 3rd ed. (1665), 124. Graunt, on the other hand, believed there to be "fourteen Men for thirteen Women" in London at that time.

[66] Stephen R. Ell, "Iron in Two Seventeenth-Century Plague Epidemics," *Journal of Interdisciplinary History* 15 (1985): 445.

[67] Mary F. Hollingsworth and T. H. Hollingsworth, "Plague Mortality Rates by Age and Sex in the Parish of St. Botolph's without Bishopsgate, London, 1603," *Population Studies* 25 (1971): 145.

in Derbyshire.[68] Later research by Roger Finlay has done little to resolve this particular historical conundrum. Although in numerical terms more males than females died from the plague in the six London parishes Finlay analyzed, death rates were not relatively higher for men except in 1603. In addition, there were wide variations between individual parishes, and the relative significance of male and female mortality fluctuated both chronologically and according to wealth. Why males appear to have been unusually susceptible in 1603 remains puzzling. Consequently Finlay had little option but to conclude that "The study of differential plague mortality between males and females is therefore exceptionally difficult and little sense can be made of it."[69]

Unlike the problematic nature of sex-specific mortality rates, patterns of emigration and premature death as a result of war offer not only more self-evident variables in the search for the factors underlying differential sex ratios, but ones that are more easily quantified. Unmarried young males constituted the greater proportion of all indentured servants who left Bristol for the West Indies during the 1650s, and a study of the occupational structure of indentured servants leaving Bristol for all the main American colonies between 1654 and 1662 has shown that of the 5,133 individuals who emigrated during this period less than a quarter (1,264) were female.[70] A similar picture is revealed by the research of Anthony Salerno in the county of Wiltshire. Of one hundred and ten Wiltshire emigrants leaving Southampton between 1635 and 1638 bound for Massachusetts, by far the majority were male and single, and between the ages of sixteen and thirty.[71] In his opinion, the nature of this out-migration contributed to the significant demographic decline in the Wiltshire region between the 1630s and the 1650s, a situation that was especially acute in the areas around Warminster and Trowbridge.[72]

Many of the young men who chose to serve their country in the armed forces rather than seek their fortune abroad were also unwittingly removed from the pool of available marriage partners. England was involved in a number of conflicts during the Tudor and Stuart periods as successive monarchies regularly crossed swords with Spain and France and later Holland. Yet the loss of life as a result of combat before the mid-seventeenth century was insufficient to make deep inroads into marriage opportunities; it was the civil wars at home that were to prove most detrimental to the marriage prospects of young single women in the Tudor and Stuart periods. Contemporary statistics of those lost in battle were little more than rudimentary:

---

[68] Roger Schofield, "An Anatomy of an Epidemic: Colyton, November 1645 to November 1646," in *The Plague Reconsidered*, Local Population Studies Supplement (Matlock, Derbyshire: S. S. R. C. Cambridge Group for the History of Population and Social Structure, 1977), 95–126; Leslie Bradley, "The Most Famous of All English Plagues: A Detailed Analysis of the Plague at Eyam, 1665–6," in *The Plague Reconsidered*, 63–94.

[69] Roger Finlay, *Population and Metropolis: The Demography of London 1580–1650* (Cambridge, 1981), 130–31.

[70] David Souden, " 'Rogues, Whores and Vagabonds'? Indentured Servant Emigrants to North America, and the Case of Mid-Seventeenth-Century Bristol," *Social History* 3 (1978): 37, Table 6.

[71] Salerno, "Social Background," 32–33.

[72] Salerno, "Social Background," 43–44.

Thomas Hobbes reckoned that some 100,000 English men had perished during the conflagrations; William Petty put the figure much higher at 300,000.[73] Modern estimates, too, remain nebulous, but have been grounded in a more secure statistical reality. Figures collated from some 635 recorded incidents of confrontation, from the bloodiest battle of Marston Moor to a skirmish in Doncaster where one man was killed, reveal an estimate of around 85,000 casualties.[74] To the numbers of those killed in combat must be added those who lost their lives either accidentally or as a result of illness. Daily accidents were commonplace — "We bury more toes and fingers than we do men" — and weapons were inherently dangerous, even in the hands of skilled operators.[75] Moreover, before the advent of modern medical practices and an awareness of public health, more soldiers may have died from war-related disease than combat itself. Allowing for slightly more indirect than direct deaths and a number of accidents may therefore raise the final toll to a figure of 185,000. Loss of life among Englishmen would then have been more significant, in proportionate terms, than it was to prove in the most destructive of all subsequent European conflicts, the First World War.[76]

II. A Single Woman by Choice

In their eagerness to isolate the most likely explanation for the inability of single women to marry in the Tudor and Stuart eras, the majority of modern historians, heavily informed by contemporary marriage theory, have failed to recognize the possibility that an increasing number of women may have made a deliberate decision in favor of celibacy. Yet the concept of female choice appears not only as a theoretical, but also as a tangible reality: the raised profile of female celibacy, together with the heightened concern over the decline of marriage as an institution, falls in the immediate aftermath of the steady deterioration in marriage rates visible from the late sixteenth century. The factors that appear to have been most influential in effecting an increase in the desire to remain single therefore form the following section of the discussion.

According to Jean-Louis Flandrin, the seventeenth century witnessed the development of a greater level of freedom of choice in marriage partner, a theory that has received further elaboration in the work of Lawrence Stone.[77] Stone's suggestion of a general shift away from an emphasis on the primacy of the community

---

[73] Cited in Charles Carlton, "The Impact of the Fighting," in *The Impact of the English Civil War*, ed. John Morrill (London, 1991), 17.

[74] Carlton, "Impact of the Fighting," 18.

[75] Carlton, "Impact of the Fighting," 19.

[76] The estimated size of the population size during the Interregnum was approximately 5,200,000: Wrigley and Schofield, *Population History*, 532, Appendix A3.3. As much as 3.6 percent of the population may then have perished as a result of the Civil Wars, compared with 2.6 percent in the First World War and 0.6 percent in the Second: Carlton, "Impact of the Fighting," 20.

[77] Jean-Louis Flandrin, *Families in Former Times*, trans. Richard Southern (Cambridge, 1979), 135.

towards a new interest in the self has ramifications in many areas aside from marriage. His theory of the rise of "affective individualism" in the seventeenth century is especially significant in this context, however, because it postulates a new recognition of the need for personal autonomy and the individual pursuit of happiness.[78] While such a recognition may, in many cases, have served to defeat the best-laid plans of families and friends, the existence of a greater measure of choice in the matter of betrothal partners could also have facilitated the development of increased levels of self-determination in matters of celibacy versus marriage. Indeed, this would help account for much of the later seventeenth-century preoccupation with the concept of celibacy. In attempting to defend the institution of marriage in the 1670s from "the unjust attacques of this Age," the anonymous author of *An Account of Marriage* revealed the extent of contemporary anxiety: "Many indeed (but unjustly) cry out of marriage, as a condition of care and perplexities, and celebrate single living, for its freedom and repose."[79]

Yet documented exemplars of such self-determination are relatively rare. An early case in point is that of Blanche Perry of Hereford. Employed at the royal court as a maidservant to the young Elizabeth, she died in 1589 at the age of eighty-two, claiming to have chosen a single life in preference to marriage in order to devote herself to the service of her monarch:

> So that my tyme I thus did passe awaye
> A maed in court, and never no man's wife,
> Sworne of Queene Ellsbeth's hedd chamber allways,
> With Maeden Queene a mayde did end my lyfe.[80]

Much more common in the writings of known celibates, however, are the narratives which frame individual states of celibacy within the dominant cultural context of marriage failure: William Stout recorded in his autobiography his continued inability to find a suitable partner; Hester Pinney found she was unable to marry George Booth, the love of her life, after a rise in his family's social status rendered such a marriage socially and financially impossible; Joyce Jeffreys appears to have preferred to leave the responsibility for her failure to marry in the hands of a greater power, residing in 1640 as an elderly spinster in Hereford "to God's pleasure."[81]

In spite of the overall significance of marriage in the contemporary discourse, the problematic nature of married life, especially from the male viewpoint, was regularly parodied in ballads and pamphlets. *A Discourse of the Married and Single Life, herein by Discovering the Misery of the one is plainly declared the felicity of the other* (1621) and *The batchelors delight* (1622) constituted two examples of a genre that

---

[78] Stone, *Family, Sex and Marriage*, esp. Part 4.
[79] B. G., *An Account of Marriage* (1672), 35.
[80] Cited in Stenton, *English Woman in History*, 135.
[81] Marshall, *Autobiography*, 141–42; Pamela Sharpe, "Dealing with Love: The Ambiguous Independence of the Single Woman in Early Modern England," *Gender and History* 11 (1999): 209–32, here 217; British Museum Egerton MS. 3054, fol. 37.

sought to juxtapose the idyllic happiness of a single life with the manifold miseries attending the matrimonial estate. However, there were also more serious offerings from male authors who chose to champion the celibate cause. In his essay entitled "Of Marriage And Single Life," Francis Bacon, for example, elected to outline the distractive nature of married life, and pointed instead to the benefits society could expect to gain from those who decided to remain single: "Certainly the best workes, and of greatest Merit for the Publike, have proceeded from the Unmarried or Childlesse Men."[82] The notion that the activities of families were a seductive and dangerous diversion from service to the public cause — an idea of central importance in classical republican thought — constituted an influential element in political discussion prior to the onset of the civil wars.[83] However, in the immediate aftermath of the conflict the concept of celibacy received even greater articulation as the imagery of the independent citizen, active in the service of the state, helped legitimate male arguments in favor of celibacy. Arguments spilled over into the religious sphere, too, effecting a limited revival of the debate over priestly celibacy. Once again the notion of the individual was influential; freed from limitations of sexual activity and family responsibility, priests would prove better servants to their Lord on earth, eliciting for themselves in the process "a higher reward and crown in the world to come."[84]

By the later seventeenth century a number of female writers had also taken up the challenge to the Protestant ideal, and in doing so significantly raised the profile of female celibacy. There had been an understanding for some time that it was acceptable for women to remain unmarried in the service of God — books written for single women before the Civil Wars were intended for those in religious orders — but prior to 1640 there was no serious discussion or acceptance of permanent celibacy for women outside the ecclesiastical sphere.[85] In the post-war period, however, the focus shifted to the civic dimension as women such as Margaret Cavendish, Duchess of Newcastle, and later Aphra Behn experimented in the medium of print with the concept of female friendship and the single existence.[86] It was Jane Barker's damning exposé of social attitudes towards spinsters, however, and her insistence that single women could be of civic benefit that marked out her poem "A Virgin Life" as one of special significance: in adopting the Baconian rhetoric of altruistic rationality, she offered a view of the single woman as chaste, pious, caring, and kind, and as obedient as any man in the service of her country and community.[87]

---

[82] Francis Bacon, *The Essays or Counsells, Civill and Morall. Newly enlarged* (1625), no. 8, "Of Marriage and Single Life," 36.

[83] A. Hughes, "Women, Men and Politics in the English Civil War," University of Keele Inaugural Lecture, 8 October 1997 (Keele University), 12.

[84] A. Woodhead, *A Discourse Concerning the Celibacy of the Clergy* (Oxford, 1687), 4.

[85] Suzanne W. Hull, *Chaste, Silent & Obedient: English Books for Women 1475–1640* (San Marino, CA, 1982), 96.

[86] See, for example, Margaret Cavendish, *The Convent of Pleasure* (1668); Aphra Behn, *Ten Pleasures of Marriage* (1682).

[87] Jane Barker, "A Virgin Life" (1688), in Germaine Greer et al., *Kissing the Rod: An Anthology of Seventeenth-Century Women's Verse* (London, 1988), 360.

Though the full articulation of female choice appears most prominently in the literature of the later seventeenth century, there is little reason to suspect that its apparent availability was anything other than the culmination of a trend whose origins can be traced back to much earlier generations of single women. In this more nuanced interpretation of demographic change, the negative shifts in fertility visible in the first half of the seventeenth century may not have been caused so much by the failure of women to marry as by the decision of women to remain single.[88] Yet in order to remain single, women clearly required a minimal level of financial stability: the desire for celibacy may have been a function of the growth of an individualist ideology, but without the ability to maintain economic independence, the realization of it on a day-to-day basis would have proved impracticable. To that end research undertaken on the medieval period has already revealed the existence of a link between female marriage levels and economic autonomy. Richard Smith, for instance, has argued that in the conditions of demographic malaise of the late fourteenth and early fifteenth centuries labor shortages gave rise to a substantial expansion of unmarried women working outside their natal household, often in towns, and especially in service. The consequence of this was a sharp rise in the proportions of those who never married.[89] P. J. P. Goldberg, too, has hypothesized that the greater the economic autonomy of medieval women, the greater the control they exercised over their own lives, the later their marriages would tend to be, and the lower the associated marriage rate.[90]

This clearly has continuing relevance in the context of the Tudor and Stuart eras. Alice Wandesford, later to become Mrs. Alice Thornton, need never have entered the marital estate. She had no romantic inclinations towards William, her future husband. Furthermore, she recognized that she had the capacity to maintain an independent existence: "As to the fortune left by my father, it was faire, and more then competent, soe that I needed not fear (by God's blessing) to have bin troublesome to my friends." But under the weight of continued pressure from friends and relatives Alice finally conceded and accepted William's suit, convinced that the marriage "might tend to the good of the whole family."[91] Economic security, as the case of Alice indicates, was insufficient in itself to determine celibacy. Marriage decisions were also contingent upon a host of psychological, social, and religious factors, in addition, of course, to the availability of suitable partners.

Yet relatively few women would have enjoyed the benefit of Alice's considerable financial advantage. Consequently, traditional accounts of marriage behavior have tended to problematize the position of the greater proportion of women below the level of the gentry, who may have sustained considerable difficulty in attempting to

---

[88] For a full explanation of demographic change in the early modern period, see Wrigley and Schofield, *Population History*.

[89] Smith, "Geographical Diversity," 44.

[90] P. J. P. Goldberg, " 'For Better, For Worse': Marriage and Economic Opportunity for Women in Town and Country," in *Woman*, ed. Goldberg, 108–9.

[91] Alice Thornton, "The Autobiography of Mrs Alice Thornton of East Newton, Co. York," *Surtees Society* 62 (1875): 75, 62.

subsist in the long term without access to the resources of a partner. A major stumbling block to the revision of such attitudes so far has been the failure of historical accounts to integrate a theory of increased economic autonomy into the scenario of female employment: the image of women's work in the Tudor and Stuart periods is largely one of marginalization, underemployment, and low remuneration.[92] However, there was one activity that did have the capacity to offer security and allow economic independence to single women who enjoyed access to at least a measure of liquid capital. To date that activity — lending money for profit — has been largely neglected by historians.

The practice of lending money was not an early modern phenomenon, for a mass of ecclesiastical and secular legislation on the subject of usury testifies amply to the prevalence of lending and borrowing throughout the Middle Ages.[93] But the legalization of the taking of interest by the statute of 1571, and the decision to set official interest rates at ten percent, injected new life into the credit business, regulated its workings, and further encouraged its development.[94] Nevertheless, there are significant problems in attempting to measure the nature and extent of money-lending in the early modern period, for credit mechanisms were widely diffused across the social and economic strata of early modern communities as part of a larger pattern of social behavior.[95] The lack of sufficient specie ensured that credit, in terms of both deferred payment and money-lending, was a necessary and widespread market tool, a factor that often renders problematic scholars' attempts to separate profitable or formal money-lending *per se* from the mass of more informal credit arrangements.[96] Interest-bearing lending was increasingly secured by contractual agreements, but the mere absence of contract should not lead to the assumption that interest was not charged.[97] In addition, it is the money-lending activities of single women in the early modern period that are most heavily obscured in the historical record. The relative absence of women from all surviving documentation, for the most part the result of their inferior legal status, has ensured that the parameters of lending activity have largely been established around a small number of wealthy single women of middling or genteel status, most notably Hester Pinney and Joyce Jeffreys.[98]

---

[92] Judith M. Bennett, "'History that Stands Still': Women's Work in the European Past," *Feminist Studies* 14 (1988): 278.

[93] Thomas Wilson, *A Discourse upon Usury* (1572), intro. by R. H. Tawney (London, 1925), 19.

[94] Craig Muldrew, *The Economy of Obligation: The Culture of Credit and Social Relations in Early Modern England* (Basingstoke, 1998), 114.

[95] Muldrew, *Economy of Obligation*, esp. chap. 5.

[96] Formal lending in this context is defined as all lending secured by formal credit instruments. This includes inventory references to bonds, bills, and mortgages; informal lending refers to all other unspecified lending.

[97] Muldrew, *Economy of Obligation*, 315.

[98] Joyce Jeffreys of Ham Castle in Worcestershire indulged both in farming and in horse breeding and dealing, but the main source of her income was derived from the "toleration" or "consideratio" for money on mortgage or loan; in 1638 she had £3,250 invested in bonds at an

However, new research on lending can now reveal the involvement of single women in the lending network to have been much more extensive than has previously been suspected. Though earlier work on probate inventories from the east Midlands and Norfolk in the period between 1650 and 1720 suggested that around forty percent of all testators were engaged in various combinations of formal and informal lending, analysis of documents from the Lincolnshire and Cheshire regions between 1601 and 1700 shows a clear indication of the much higher levels of participation amongst single women: on average, fifty-six percent of the Lincolnshire documents contained some reference to lending, and in the case of Cheshire this figure reached the much higher level of sixty-three percent.[99]

Moreover, while it has already been recognized that it was not unusual for wealthy spinsters to invest their capital in credits, the evidence offered here suggests that all wealth groups represented in the probate sample were involved to a greater or lesser degree in money-lending, their lending ability apparently determined more often by their desire to do so than by the level of assets at their disposal. Though there were a number of affluent spinsters in the sample — Anne Wright of Nantwich, for example, a wealthy gentlewoman whose total personal assets exceeded a thousand pounds, had lent out £246 in bonds — there were many other lenders in Cheshire and Lincolnshire who enjoyed access to more modest cash sums: Alice Buckley, a servant from Wrenbury in Cheshire, had no personal assets other than the £4 she had lent out in bills; Margit Bettes from Gretham in Lincolnshire had £6 owing to her "upon specialitie"; Margaret Ferribie, a resident in the small market town of Barton upon Humber (also in Lincolnshire), had lent out a total of £10 to various locals in bonds and bills. She supplemented her income from lending by spinning cloth.[100]

Details of the range of amounts lent out by the single women surveyed in the study are outlined more clearly in Table 1.

---

annual rate of eight percent. Hester Pinney, too, displayed a considerable measure of entrepreneurial spirit. In addition to the joint running of the family lace business, she was successfully engaged in extensive financial dealings before she reached the age of thirty, acting as a banker to country relations and making numerous personal loans: Griffiths, "Joyce Jeffreys," 12; Sharpe, "Dealing with Love," 218.

[99] B. A. Holderness, "Credit in English Rural Society before the Nineteenth Century, with Special Reference to the Period 1650–1720," *Agricultural History Review* 24 (1976): 102.

[100] C.R.O. WS 1634; C.R.O. WS 1649; Lincoln Archive Office (henceforth L.A.O.) INV 119/381 (1616); L.A.O. LCC AD 1628/101. A loan on "specialty" was arranged by special contract, under seal, similar to a bond.

Table 1: Proportional spread of debts in percentages in the probate documents of Cheshire and Lincolnshire single females, 1601–1700

Amount	Cheshire women (%)	Lincolnshire women (%)
Less than £5	9	20
£5 to £9	12	19
£10 to £49	49	47
£50 to £99	17	7
£100 or more	13	7
Total	100	100

As Table 1 indicates, the bulk of all female lenders in Lincolnshire and Cheshire were owed on average between £10 and £50, although the spread of the Cheshire debts was skewed more heavily towards the upper end of the range than was the case in Lincolnshire. Nevertheless, from the poorest woman in the sample with less than £5 to offer to the richest spinster with cash resources in excess of £2000, the single women surveyed in this study appear to have been prepared to make their assets available to the community in the form of credit.

What is perhaps most interesting in the present context, however, is the fact that a rising proportion of the single women who were lending appear to have been doing so on a formal basis for the purpose of profit.[101] The proportion of women's inventories that included one or more references to specific instruments of debt — in the form of bonds, bills, mortgages or loans "with speciality" — rose markedly over the course of the seventeenth century, at the same time as the proportion of those solely recording informal lending underwent decline. In order to represent this shift more clearly, an analysis and comparison of the extent of formal and informal lending in seventeenth-century Cheshire and Lincolnshire is outlined in Tables 2 and 3 below.

---

[101] Informal lending in the context of this research does not, as indicated earlier, preclude the possibility of profitable lending, but the appearance of formal credit instruments is taken to be a clear indication of profitable intent.

Table 2: Proportion of Cheshire single women involved in lending, 1601–1700[102]

Decade	Number (Total = 449)	% lending[103]	% formal lenders	% informal lenders	Formal as % of all lenders
1601–10	18	72	33	39	46
1611–20	35	69	31	38	46
1621–30	41	76	37	39	48
1631–40	36	64	44	19	70
1661–70	87	68	53	15	78
1671–80	80	66	43	24	64
1681–90	85	52	37	15	70
1691–1700	67	57	48	9	84

Table 3: Proportion of Lincolnshire single women involved in lending, 1601–1700

Decade	Number (Total = 267)	% lending	% formal lenders	% informal lenders	Formal as % of all lenders
1601–10	18	50	17	33	33
1611–20	38	63	31	32	50
1621–30	41	41	17	24	41
1631–40	43	56	30	26	54
1661–70	44	75	55	20	73
1671–80	36	58	42	17	71
1681–90	24	46	42	4	91
1691–1700	23	57	30	26	54

[102] Since the number of documents surviving from the Interregnum is very small, and the possibility of bias therefore greatly increased, the decades of the 1640s and 1650s have not been included in the statistical sample.

[103] The combined figures for informal and formal lending may not always equal that for total lending as a result of rounding.

Though the two regions display differing tendencies towards overall lending activity — in Cheshire the absolute proportion of all lenders falls from seventy-two percent to fifty-seven percent over the course of the seventeenth century, while in Lincolnshire the comparable figure rises from fifty percent to fifty-seven percent — in both regions there is evidence of a shift away from informal towards more formal lending arrangements. Though the proportion of formal lenders in Lincolnshire falls back during the final decade of the century, the move towards formalized lending in both counties is clear.[104] The balance between formal and informal lending, heavily weighted in favor of the latter at the beginning of the century, had by the end undergone a complete reversal.

This situation no doubt reflects in part the increasing emphasis on the contractual nature of interpersonal economic relationships, but may also have been the means by which single women attempted to secure their economic independence. In terms of annual income, a relatively modest cash sum enjoyed considerable economic potential. Access to a figure of around £20 — an amount a sizeable proportion of husbandmen's daughters may feasibly have received as their marriage portion and one that was not uncommon among charitable trusts — could, under the prevailing interest rate of ten percent, have provided an annual income of £2 in the early seventeenth century.[105] Clearly such revenue would have been entirely dependent upon the prompt payment of the interest due on the loan. Yet though interest was always charged on bonds because of the high demand for secure credit, sadly there is no way of recovering with any accuracy the full extent of either the interest that was paid, or more significantly, that which was in default.[106] A small number of inventories referred to the amount of interest owed by debtors, and occasionally there were indications of interest payments that were overdue, but in practical terms the success of lending as an income-generating activity must at present remain speculative.[107]

Nevertheless, in theory, lending could have offered single women with free capital a route to economic independence. The bulk of the women in both the Lincolnshire and Cheshire regions were in control of liquid assets valued at between £10 and £50. Under standard conditions of repayment the annual income they

---

[104] The most likely explanation for this is the harvest failures of the 1690s. The proportion of formal lenders also fell back in Lincolnshire in the 1620s during an earlier period of agricultural depression.

[105] Though the amount a young girl received as her portion reflected her individual economic and social status, local studies can offer some idea of the amounts involved. Alan MacFarlane has suggested that husbandmen's daughters in one Westmoreland parish received between £10 and £50, but mostly less than £20, and laborers' daughters between £1 and £5: MacFarlane, *Marriage and Love in England*, 264. In eighty Selby wills, most unmarried daughters' bequests were for £20 for yeomen and more substantial craftsmen's daughters, or £10 for the daughters of husbandmen, laborers, and poorer craftsmen and yeomen. Orphans of the Red Maids School might be given £10 or £20 on marriage: Amy Louise Erickson, *Women and Property in Early Modern England* (London, 1993), 88. (See above for the £20 donation from the Laud charity.)

[106] Muldrew, *Economy of Obligation*, 113.

[107] The amount of debt litigation involving single women awaits further investigation.

could have expected to obtain through money-lending in the early decades of the seventeenth century would have fallen somewhere in the range of between £1 and £5. Even after the legal interest rate had fallen to eight percent in 1624, a factor that would have reduced this figure to between 16s. and £4, this still represented a generous return relative to the other remunerative opportunities.[108] The likely salary for women in service, whether as servants in husbandry or household maids, ranged between £1 and £2 per annum with room and board.[109] Any young woman not contracted to a household would of course have had to take the cost of her board and lodging into consideration, but since the economy was geared towards female dependency (a woman was expected to live under her father's or master's roof until she married, and then under that of her husband), women's earnings in other employment sectors failed to reflect the full cost of their upkeep. Outside of service a woman could expect to earn little more than 1s. a week, or a little over £2 per annum if work was regular and forthcoming.[110] Lending had an additional advantage in that it did not place undue restrictions on women's time or energy. While lending for many unmarried women may have constituted their single most important source of income, it would rarely have been their only source. Inventory records of single women in Lincolnshire and Cheshire indicate their customary participation in a number of complementary enterprises, which varied widely from farming, renting out animals, and producing dairy goods to include spinning, weaving, sewing, washing, ironing, and innumerable examples of other menial, irregular, and poorly paid tasks. For a considerable proportion of single women independence, in addition to having been possible, may also have proved comparatively comfortable. If, as Donald Woodward has suggested, a man could have enjoyed a relatively nutritious diet for 2d. per day, a cash sum of £30 invested wisely in the early seventeenth century would have been capable of providing a woman with a more than tolerable living standard.[111] It proves not insignificant then that almost half the single women in the Chester region between 1600 and 1625 had at least £30 at their disposal.

The extent to which single women perceived this benefit purely in personal terms, however, must remain subject to interpretation: marriage was neither constructed nor envisaged merely in terms of individual benefit. In the same way as the marriages of some aristocratic daughters may have been "sacrificed" in order to improve the prospects of their sisters, so the portions of young women lower down the social ladder may have constituted an essential element in family survival strate-

---

[108] The legal interest rate fell to eight percent in 1624 and six percent in 1651: Sidney Homer, *A History of Interest Rates* (New Brunswick, 1963), 126.

[109] Erickson, *Women and Property*, 85. Henry Best's female servants, for example, were paid anything from 10s. to £1 4s. per annum in the 1620s and 1630s, depending on duties, age, and experience. See *The Farming and Memorandum Books of Henry Best of Elmswell, 1642*, ed. Donald Woodward (Oxford, 1984), 178–91.

[110] Erickson, *Women and Property*, 15.

[111] Woodward, *Men at Work*, 216.

gies, particularly under conditions of economic exigency.[112] As Pam Sharpe has suggested, for middling families like the lace-making Pinneys, "economic vicissitudes and greed could force them to delay or exert significant pressure against daughters' marriages in this era."[113] Because scope for individual action was inevitably restricted by family circumstance, shifting patterns of celibacy must be located in the familial and the communal as well as the individual context. Lending in the seventeenth century was constructed in terms of a mixture of Christian theology, the ethics of neighborliness, and classical notions of obligation: "Every man is to his neyhbour a debtor, not onely of that which himselfe borroweth, but of whatsoever his neyghbour needeth."[114]

Moreover, Holderness's detailed study of inventories in the century after 1650, which indicated peaks of lending activity in periods of crisis when prices for local cash commodities were high, has led him to assume that the distribution of credit obeyed "a clearly defined and explicable logic within a well-developed and sophisticated credit system."[115] Viewed in these terms, the lending activities of single women in particular appear as a flexible and necessary feature of the local credit system, and their liquid assets as a valuable local resource. Since inventories of such women that do indicate the direction of the loan suggest that most were lending within their own community, those with capital and few commitments can perhaps most accurately be characterized as the metaphorical "back pocket" of seventeenth-century society. In addition, two particular aspects of inheritance practice rendered this characterization increasingly probable. Firstly, testamentary evidence suggests that, in the event of the premature death of their fathers, most daughters gained access to their portion either on marriage or on reaching the age of majority (occasionally eighteen but more usually twenty-one), whichever occurred first. The lateness of the average age at first marriage — around twenty-six in the seventeenth century — and the fact that at least half of all young women may already have lost their fathers by this point in time may then have enabled a considerable number of women to gain access to their portion prior to the occasion of their marriage.[116]

---

[112] Olwen Hufton, *The Prospect Before Her* (New York, 1996), 111–12. Sir Ralph Verney withheld his sisters' portions because of the unfavorable financial situation of the family. See Whyman, *Sociability and Power*, 127.

[113] Sharpe, "Dealing with Love," 226.

[114] Muldrew, *Economy of Obligation*, 319; J. Blaxton, *The English Usurer; or Usury Condemned by the Most Learned Divines of the Church of England*, 2nd impression (1634), 11.

[115] Holderness, "Credit in English Rural Society," 105.

[116] Wrigley and Schofield, *Population History*, 255, Table 7.26; cited in Erickson, *Women and Property*, 93. It is also possible that increasingly young women may have been granted access to their portion before their marriage. Christine Peters has identified a trend in the sixteenth and seventeenth centuries towards giving portions to daughters at specified ages rather than on the occasion of their marriage. See eadem, "Gender, Sacrament and Ritual: The Making and Meaning of Marriage in Late Medieval and Early Modern England," *Past and Present* 169 (2000): 89–91. In addition, transmission of property was often a gradual process, with ante-mortem gifts and settlements being frequent rather than unusual. See Diana O'Hara, *Courtship and Constraint: Rethinking the Making of Marriage in Tudor England* (Manchester, 2000), 167.

Secondly, cash as a commodity for female legatees may have assumed greater relative importance in probate settlements during the course of the seventeenth century. Not only has it been shown that testators in regions as varied as Yorkshire, Sussex, and Lincolnshire regularly favored daughters over sons with gifts of cash, but also that money legacies to girls (and also boys) over the course of the Tudor and Stuart periods were becoming steadily more common than any other type of bequest: by the mid-seventeenth century gifts to godchildren, grandchildren, and other kin were predominantly in the form of ready cash.[117]

The discovery of a relationship between lending and celibacy allows for the possibility of a new approach to the understanding of falling marriage rates in the early seventeenth century. While the expansion in money-lending clearly reflects female opportunities in the labor market, and highlights the different accumulation strategies of men and women, it also requires that the concept of economic autonomy be incorporated into the theory of marriage behavior in the seventeenth century. Since the occasion of marriage, in common law, transferred all property of the bride to her husband, money-lending and marriage for women at least, appear to have been largely incompatible.[118] In addition, investment opportunities for women with a measure of liquid capital were steadily increasing. The secularization of the lending process, in which the taking of interest was irrevocably divorced from theological control, finally culminated in the introduction of the Jacobean usury statute of 1624.[119] Increasingly defined solely in terms of its economic necessity, lending therefore constituted a progressively more acceptable and necessary part of early modern life.[120] Moreover, the fall in the legal rate of interest from ten to eight percent which accompanied the Jacobean legislation and the deepening economic recession of the 1620s would have manifested themselves most visibly in terms of increased levels of demand for credit facilities. In this context of heightened demand, at the very least the idea of financial independence sits comfortably alongside existing theories of developing autonomy and freedom of choice.

Some women may have visualized lending merely as a means of achieving greater control over their choice of life-partner or the timing of their wedding; others

---

[117] Erickson, *Women and Property*, 81, 85.

[118] Erickson has highlighted the fact that under equity law married women could make legal provision to retain the right to their own property, including outstanding debts. See Amy Louise Erickson, "Common Law Versus Common Practice: The Use of Marriage Settlements in Early Modern England," *Economic History Review*, 2nd ser., 43 (1990): 21–39. However, she notes that arrangements for "separate estate" were more common in settlements negotiated on the occasion of a second marriage, when the bride was "older, perhaps wealthier, and wiser at least in the ways of legal coverture" than had previously been the case: eadem, *Women and Property*, 123. In Claire Cross's admittedly small sample of married women's wills, again the majority — four out of the six who made wills — had been married before: C. Cross, "Northern Women in the Early Modern Period: The Female Testators of Hull and Leeds 1520–1650," *Yorkshire Archaeological Journal* 59 (1987): 86.

[119] 21 Jac.1.c.17. See N. L. Jones, *God and the Moneylenders: Usury and Law in Early Modern England* (Oxford, 1989), 197–98.

[120] Prejudicial attitudes towards Jewish moneylenders linger through the nineteenth century in English literature. I am grateful to Dorothea Kehler for drawing this to my attention.

may have conceived of their lending (or alternately it may have been socially constructed) as much in terms of social benefit as individual gain: as late as mid-century, Alice Wandesford visualized her putative role as money-lender, a function in her own estimation of her not inconsiderable fortune, in charitable rather than profitable terms.[121] For others still, the decision to lend may have represented a conscious desire to avoid marriage, for lending activity was not bounded solely by duty and obligation. Marriage might well raise the total amount of resources available to a woman at the outset, but in the longer run, and especially in times of economic recession, increasing numbers of children posited a potentially dangerous strain on resources, which themselves were being contemporaneously undermined by the inability of the mother to work. Under such circumstances even a laborer's daughter with access to a small amount of capital may have questioned the long-term benefit of marriage as a stratagem. For as Alice Clark succinctly indicated, "The full misery of the labourer's lot was only felt by the women."[122]

In any event, while the decision to lend may not have militated against the idea of marriage *per se*, regardless of the manner in which women visualized their lending activity, the very nature of that activity and their high levels of involvement may have functioned to compromise both their present and future marital choices. The financial rewards of lending were inclined to be greatest while women remained single, and marriage was unlikely to be a realistic consideration until the debt had been recouped. Indeed, problems of this nature may have refocused the priorities of a number of single women in the wake of the 1620s. The pronounced shift towards formal lending visible in the lending patterns of both the Lincolnshire and Cheshire women in the 1630s suggests a more businesslike attitude to debt management, although the extent to which this was determined by marital considerations remains unclear. In addition, the use of formal instruments of debt did not in itself guarantee repayment; Judith Sweete of Grimoldby in Lincolnshire was owed a total of £9 2s in 1617, the two bonds in question being two and three years overdue.[123] Even so, formal lending among single women and proportions of women never married underwent a synchronous rise in the seventeenth century, until both reached a peak during the 1660s. Since interest rates had fallen again in the previous decade to six percent, and inflationary pressures were leveling out, the impetus to lend during this period can perhaps be more feasibly interpreted in terms of supply rather than demand: the proportion of female inventories referring to the existence of formal lending reached record proportions in the 1660s, precisely at the time when Roger Schofield's birth cohort of 1641 — the cohort most likely never to marry — were at the peak of their marriageability.[124] Given the cumulative effects of emigration, disease, war, and structural shifts in employment

---

[121] Thornton, "Autobiography," 75.

[122] Alice Clark, *Working Life of Women in the Seventeenth Century* (London, 1919), 86.

[123] L.A.O. INV 119/570, 1617.

[124] Because of the dearth of probate material that has survived from the Interregnum, it is not possible to know whether lending was even higher in the 1650s when interest rates had fallen to six percent.

opportunities, decisions to remain celibate may have been superfluous. The more likely scenario at this particular juncture could well have been one of enforced rather than elected female celibacy, financed and supported by lending activity.

Although the proportions of single women involved in formal lending did fall back in Lincolnshire and Cheshire after the 1660s (as the marriage rate began to recover), single women appeared considerably more conspicuous within the ranks of formal lenders towards the end of the century than had been the case at the beginning. Economic difficulties may once again have been a key factor. A wet autumn in 1692 ushered in six years of bad harvest, and demographic data suggest that the numbers of marriages in this decade on a national basis fell back to their lowest point for nearly fifty years.[125]

By the final years of the century, however, the decision of women with capital to remain celibate can perhaps be more readily interpreted in relation to their desire to remain independent. Literature had provided evidence of a new confidence in the single life and in the ability to sustain it, and as opportunities for investment expanded dramatically — in the Bank of England, in government annuities, and in merchant trading companies — single women with relatively large amounts of capital proceeded to take full advantage of their resources.[126] As a result the later seventeenth century witnessed a massive increase in personal wealth among the inventories of female lenders, with a corresponding rise occurring in the mean amount lent.[127]

§

As the profile of female celibacy reached unprecedented heights in the later seventeenth century, a broader scope for investment allowed wealthy women extensive opportunities to consider the relative benefits of marriage and the single life, a situation that may have contributed in no small part to the rising proportion of aristocratic women who chose to remain unmarried during this period.[128] The question that remains, however, is the extent to which the decisions of single plebeian women in the earlier seventeenth century were similarly formulated. Was their celibacy largely a function of their inability to marry, as current marriage theory would suggest, or did they enjoy a more positive element of choice?

There is little doubt that economic difficulties bore down heavily on the marital opportunities of poorer single women in the Tudor and early Stuart periods. The inability to amass a sizeable enough portion may have been more likely to delay

---

[125] R. B. Rose, "Eighteenth Century Price Riots and Public Policy in England," *International Review of Social History* 6 (1961): 281; Wrigley and Schofield, *Population History*, 498, Table A2.3.

[126] P. G. M. Dickson, *The Financial Revolution in England: A Study in the Development of Public Credit, 1688–1756* (London, 1967), 256.

[127] In Lincolnshire, the mean female debt amongst those formally lending increased from £10 in the 1600s to £111 in the 1690s, with the greatest gains being made in the Restoration period. Comparable figures in Cheshire were £42 rising to £156.

[128] T. H. Hollingsworth, "The Demography of the British Peerage," *Population Studies* 18 (1964 Supplement): 20.

marriage decisions than render them impossible in the short term, but in the long term a prolonged recession had the capability to make a permanent impact on the rate of marriage. It also remains feasible that informal institutional controls were successful in deterring an unknown number of women from effecting a marriage — the local financing of poor relief gave those responsible for its administration a direct pecuniary interest in maintaining a manageable demographic and economic balance — and problems of institutional control could have been exacerbated by a variety of external constraints. Though demographic historians have downplayed the effectiveness of structural change in significantly affecting marriage chances, clearly any shift in the sex ratio, either temporary or permanent, had the potential to affect marriage behavior adversely. Migratory patterns and shifting employment opportunities, often favoring one sex at the expense of another, have been documented at both regional and local levels; emigration was largely concentrated around indentured single men; and though the extent of premature death among young men as a result of the plague remains unclear, the mid-century conflict was to prove disastrous for a generation of single women reaching maturity in its wake. Females born in the year 1641 were more likely than any others in the seventeenth century to retain their celibate status.

Yet the desire to remain single may also have contributed significantly towards the rise in the levels of celibacy. Though the strength of the early modern marital discourse has militated against the notion that a considerable number of women during the Tudor and Stuart periods would have chosen the single life in lieu of marriage, the rising profile of celibacy and the ability of women with capital to be self-supporting requires historians to incorporate the concept of choice into discussions of marriage behavior. For while a full elaboration of the proto-feminist challenge to the Protestant marital ideal had to await the literature of the Restoration, the seeds of this challenge were germinating much earlier in the century.

Paradoxically, it was prior access to monies set aside for the purpose of betrothal that enabled young women to formulate the basis of their independence.[129] The growth in the demand for credit facilities after the legalization of interest-bearing loans in the late sixteenth century ensured that the one factor traditionally constructed as the prime indicator of marriageability — a cash portion — suddenly became the most significant element in the realization of celibacy. For women without the benefit of liquid capital, the ideology of failure has continuing resonance. Many lacked even the basic resources necessary to initiate the probate process, and for these women the boundaries of choice would inevitably have been severely circumscribed. It also remains unclear as to what extent single women who did have access to capital enjoyed full autonomy in the provision of credit, for the decision to remain celibate may have been affected as much by familial and social concerns

---

[129] Amy Froide's work on Southampton has suggested that some single women were able to trade in their own right because they received bequests of money and goods from their relatives. Moreover, she has indicated that a number of women with choices preferred to remain unmarried. Cited in Sara Mendelson and Patricia Crawford, *Women in Early Modern England 1550–1720* (Oxford, 1998), 169–70.

as individual ones. Attempts to isolate the impetus to lend in the early seventeenth century are complicated by the existence of an ethical understanding of credit based around the concept of individuals as socially responsible: "Liberty ceaseth," in the words of Thomas Hobbes, "where obligation begins."[130]

Yet in the final instance, it seems likely that a rising number of single women in the first half of the seventeenth century envisaged formal lending as a route to increased autonomy. As contractual lending steadily increased its share of the total lending network, marriage rates spiraled downward in a contemporaneous decline that was not arrested until later in the Stuart era. A number of women may not have initiated loan agreements with the intention of remaining permanently unmarried, but the prospect of a regular income from lending may have militated significantly in favor of celibacy, especially in situations of acute economic hardship. Moreover, there was an added element of circularity insofar as lending money for profit provided women not only with the means to remain single, but also with the reason to do so. Decisions to remain celibate were of course individually formulated and dependent upon a host of variables too complex and too personal to allow proper investigation. Nevertheless, the fact that they existed at all is significant. The dominant construction of marriage for women as necessary, desirable, and inevitable is therefore revealed as little more than a cultural myth designed primarily to bolster the status quo.

Judith M. Spicksley
University of Hull

---

[130] Cited in Muldrew, *Economy of Obligation*, 331.

5

A STRANGE HATRED OF MARRIAGE:

John Lyly, Elizabeth I, and the Ends of Comedy

It might strike some as odd to find an essay on Elizabethan comedy in a book devoted to single women. After all, Northrop Frye long ago demonstrated the affinities between comic structure and the institution of marriage.[1] From a feminist perspective, comic conventions enforce what Judith Butler, appropriating and revising Adrienne Rich's term, calls "compulsory heterosexuality" — the paradigm for desire necessary to patriarchal order and propagation.[2] Comic heroines typically pass from the control of fathers to the control of husbands, enacting dramatically the "normal steps in an unfolding life pattern" that would take an early modern woman from daughter to wife.[3] Most Elizabethan comedies appear to follow dominant Tudor ideology in not presenting "singleness" — the establishment of an identity independent of men — as a viable option for young women. Even the initially autonomous Rosalind of *As You Like It*, for example, functions as the object of an exchange that affirms and consolidates relations among men.[4] By marrying Rosalind, Orlando forges a political and economic alliance with Duke Senior; their reciprocity, however, can be instituted only through Rosalind's submission to matrimo-

---

[1] See for example Northrop Frye, *The Anatomy of Criticism* (Princeton, 1957), 163–86.
[2] See Judith Butler, *Gender Trouble: Feminism and the Subversion of Identity* (New York, 1990), 18, and 151, n.6.
[3] Olwen Hufton, *The Prospect Before Her: A History of Women in Western Europe* (New York, 1996), 255.
[4] The status of Rosalind as an object of exchange is especially evident in 5.4.116–17, where she "gives" herself both to her father ("To you I give myself, for I am yours") and to her husband ("To you I give myself, for I am yours"). On *As You Like It* and male–male relationships, see also Louis Adrian Montrose, "The Place of a Brother in *As You Like It*: Social Process and Comic Form," *Shakespeare Quarterly* 32 (1981): 28–54. All references to *As You Like It* are to *The Riverside Shakespeare*, ed. G. Blakemore Evans, 2nd ed. (Boston, 1997).

nial hierarchy. Hymen, the god of comic marriage, preserves patriarchal order by matching women to their lords. Deviance from his rule is not tolerated: poor Phoebe loves Rosalind but must learn to "accord" to Silvius instead, for she cannot, given the patriarchal orientation of her culture, "have a woman to [her] lord" (5.4.133–34), or, for that matter, remain single.

Yet the resistance of characters like Phoebe to social and comic convention raises some important questions: Must women always marry *men*? Must women always *marry*? *As You Like It* answers these questions in the affirmative; however, not all romantic comedies follow suit. In her initial deviance from accepted norms, Phoebe recalls John Lyly's court plays, especially *Gallathea*. This play, in which the two heroines marry after a divinely authored sex-transformation makes marriage possible, is as close as Lyly comes to celebrating matrimony. He rarely presents more traditional marriage as a desirable goal for young women.

Lyly's unusually skeptical attitude towards marriage contradicts official Tudor ideology, which emphasized marriage as the only trajectory to be taken by young women.[5] Actual demographics failed to accord with the official position as well: historians estimate that between five and twenty-seven percent of the English population remained unmarried during the early modern period.[6] Single women did exist in early modern England. Strikingly, however, such women received little representation in the literature of the time. According to Sara Mendelson and Patricia Crawford, this lack of representation reflects the fact that "contemporary wisdom declared that woman was made for man, [that] any adult woman without a husband was an anomaly" and that "by ignoring the single woman and refusing to acknowledge her existence, contemporaries contributed to her invisibility."[7] Certainly, the drama of the period participates in this erasure of single women. Its female characters tend not to deviate from the prescribed roles of maid, wife, and widow. Even potentially monstrous or rebellious women like Lady Macbeth or Cleopatra fit the profile, for Lady Macbeth is a wife and Cleopatra a widow who might like to be a wife. In the histories and tragedies, the very few exceptions to the approved life pattern for women, like Joan in *1 Henry VI* or the witches in *Macbeth*, are demonized and dismissed. Lyly is the only early modern dramatist whose plays routinely feature single women.

The generic characteristics of comedy facilitate Lyly's interest in unmarried women. Ironically, despite its association with marriage, romantic comedy gives more, and more complex, representation than other dramatic genres to the idea of the single woman. Even the most ideologically conservative exemplars must entertain the possibility that their attractive young heroines might not marry, since this

---

[5] According to Linda T. Fitz, the early modern period witnessed the institutionalization of the "restrictive marriage-oriented attitude towards women that feminists have been struggling against ever since": " 'What Says the Married Woman?': Marriage Theory and Feminism in the English Renaissance," *Mosaic* 13 (1980): 11.

[6] Sara Mendelson and Patricia Crawford, *Women in Early Modern England, 1550–1720* (Oxford, 1998), 166–67.

[7] Mendelson and Crawford, *Women in Early Modern England*, 165.

possibility forms the basis of the dramatic conflict. Elizabethan comedy takes a social process — the passage of young women from maid to wife — described by the official Tudor discourses as inevitable and emphasizes instead all the impeding problems, obstacles, and desires, all the possible deviations from the accepted pattern. Frye conflates the end of comedy with the ends of most comedies. But comedy might just as easily be about *not* marrying. As a genre, comedy has the potential to subvert "compulsory heterosexuality" by emphasizing the artificiality of this construct, by calling attention to its subjection of women, by exploring alternative paradigms for desire, or by refusing to close with the "obligatory" marriage.

This potential is realized in Lyly's court plays: *Campaspe* (1584), *Sappho and Phao* (1584), *Gallathea* (1585), and *Endymion* (1588). Except for Campaspe, the central female characters in these plays either do not marry or do not marry men. Although Lyly is widely credited with developing Elizabethan romantic comedy, his resistance to "conventional" comic closure has been accounted a failure. Mary Beth Rose, for example, invokes Frye's establishment of "the necessary structural relationship between fulfilled sexual love and the form of romantic comedy" as perfected by Shakespeare and concludes that Lyly "fails to unite love with marriage."[8] Unfamiliar with Frye, Lyly was presumably also unaware of the "necessary structural relationship" between romantic comedy and heterosexual marriage. In any case, his plays upset both conventional endings and conventional marriages, suggesting that neither is finally "necessary." Lyly catalogues different types of unmanned women, from chaste goddesses and queens (Cynthia in *Endymion*, Sappho in *Sappho and Phao*) to unmarried virgins (Haebe, Phillida, and Gallathea in *Gallathea* and Campaspe in *Campaspe*) to old hags (Sibylla in *Sappho and Phao*, Dipsas and Bagoa in *Endymion*). In the world of his plays, the woman without a husband is not anomalous but normal.

Lyly's attitude towards his single female characters is conflicted, ranging from admiration to sympathy to contempt.[9] But the plays share a basic perception of heterosexual marriage as a compulsory institution, designed to enhance patriarchal power at the expense of women. This perception owes something to Lyly's in-

---

[8] Mary Beth Rose, "Moral Conceptions of Sexual Love in Elizabethan Comedy," *Renaissance Drama* 15 (1984): 1–29, here 15. Rose's emphasis on Lyly's "negative and skeptical portrayal of love" (14) is shared by David Bevington, "Jack hath not Jill: Failed Courtship in Lyly and Shakespeare," *Shakespeare Survey* 42 (1990): 1–13. I owe a debt to both these critics for pointing me in the direction of this essay.

[9] As several critics note, Lyly's attitude towards women generally is conflicted. The plays go out of their way to flatter Lyly's royal mistress; however, they are not without their misogynist moments. On␣Lyly's occasional misogyny, see Philippa Berry, *Of Chastity and Power: Elizabethan Literature and the Unmarried Queen* (London, 1989), 111–33; and David Bevington, "Introduction to *Sappho and Phao*," in *"Campaspe" and "Sappho and Phao,"* ed. G. K. Hunter and idem (Manchester, 1991), 175. Many of Lyly's male characters have negative opinions of women, but these opinions are frequently undermined by their own poor conduct, as is the case with Endymion, who insists on women's deceptiveness even as he is deceiving Tellus.

volvement in court culture.[10] All these plays were performed for Elizabeth I, the most famous single woman in England, and they reflect the ongoing debate regarding the desirability of the queen's marriage. The queen responded to this debate by developing strategies for not marrying while avoiding the social stigma visited on single women. Typically, scholars who write about Elizabeth assume that she, as a powerful unmarried woman, was exceptional but not exemplary. The focus has been on how Elizabeth's exceptionality affected her male subjects, not on how the queen might have offered a model for her female subjects. The latter are usually left out of the discussion altogether. Louis Montrose, for instance, justifies this exclusive concern with male anxiety by noting that the "political nation" was "wholly a nation of men," who frequently found it "frustrating or degrading to serve a prince who was, after all, merely a woman."[11] But no doubt some women found Elizabeth's example inspiring rather than "frustrating" or "degrading." Lyly's comedies encourage such a view by generalizing on the queen's status. Far from presenting the queen as the exception who confirms patriarchal rule, Lyly offers a way of extending the implications of the queen's behavior to a consideration of other single women.

Among the plays presented at court in the earlier part of Elizabeth's reign, romantic comedies were especially common. The Spanish ambassador Guzman de Silva noted their popularity in 1564, explaining to King Philip II that these plays "generally deal with marriage."[12] De Silva reports in two separate letters Elizabeth's irate reactions to comedies: in March 1565, when a court comedy decided a debate between Diana and Juno about the desirability of marriage in favor of

---

[10] Bevington calls attention to the possibility that Lyly's ambivalence regarding marriage is attributable to court culture: "Introduction to *Sappho and Phao*," 175. The nature of the relationship between Lyly's plays and the Elizabethan court has been the subject of a good deal of critical debate. Scholars have treated the plays as commentaries on political issues ranging from the actual courtships of Elizabeth I, to her treatment of her courtiers, to her use of the monarch's two bodies; see, for example, Bevington, who emphasizes Lyly's flattering enshrinement of the queen as divine goddess: *Tudor Drama and Politics* (Cambridge, MA, 1968), 171–86, and who reads *Campaspe* and *Sappho and Phao* as celebrations of royal power: "John Lyly and Queen Elizabeth: Royal Flattery in *Campaspe* and *Sappho and Phao*," *Renaissance Papers* [1966] (1967): 57–68. Theodora A. Jankowski, *Women in Power in the Early Modern Drama* (Urbana, 1992), argues against readings that emphasize Lyly's flattery of the queen. According to Jankowski, *Sappho and Phao* initially offers "an idealized and flattering portrait of a woman ruler," but eventually shows Sappho as "incapable . . of controlling her womanish/irrational emotions" (126–27). Berry views Lyly's plays as attempts to define the relationship between queen and courtier through the creation of "a secluded and interior mode of courtliness" (*Of Chastity and Power*, 111).

[11] Louis A. Montrose, "*A Midsummer Night's Dream* and the Shaping Fantasies of Elizabethan Culture: Gender, Power, Form," in *Rewriting the Renaissance: The Discourses of Sexual Difference in Early Modern Europe*, ed. Margaret W. Ferguson, Maureen Quilligan, and Nancy J. Vickers (Chicago, 1986), 81. This seminal essay is one of the best examples of the exclusive focus on the "collective" (male) "anxiety" generated by Elizabeth I, or "this perplexing creature" as Montrose calls her (71, 80).

[12] *Calendar of Letters and State Papers Relating to English Affairs, Preserved Principally in the Archives of Simancas (1558–1567)*, ed. Martin A. S. Hume, 4 vols. (London, 1892–1899), 1: 367.

Juno, the queen turned to de Silva and told him "this is all against me."[13] Two years later, the ambassador writes that "the hatred this Queen has of marriage is most strange. They represented a comedy before her last night until nearly one in the morning, which ended in a marriage, and the Queen, as she told me herself, expressed her dislike of the woman's part."[14] As David Bevington suggests, the queen disliked these comedies because she suspected that they constituted attempts to advise her on the matter of marriage.[15] De Silva's second report also implies that the queen made a more far-reaching judgment. Elizabeth did not like plays that ended in marriage because she objected to the "woman's part." Did she object to the "woman's part" in the play or in marriage? And to what extent might the queen's objections to plays that end in marriage, or to marriage itself, be the objections of a woman to early modern marriage generally rather than those of a queen regnant to a particular marriage?

The official documents of the Tudor government promoted the virtues of marriage. According to "An Homily on the State of Matrimony" marriage was designed by God to help human beings avoid "the snares of the devil and the unlawful lusts of the flesh."[16] In its emphasis on the salubrious effects of matrimony and the "filthiness" risked by those who choose to abstain, the homily registers the marked elevation of the institution in post-Reformation English culture.[17] The language of infection employed by the homily had its literal correlative in medical practices: doctors might, for example, prescribe marriage as a cure for the menstrual disorders of young virgins.[18] An instrument of control over troublesome female bodies, marriage also worked to control women's behavior. The homily enjoins newlyweds to adhere to divinely instituted patriarchal norms and defines marriage in terms of the proper subjection of wife to husband, reminding the husband that "the woman is a frail vessel and thou art therefore made the ruler and head over her."[19] By likening the husband to a king and the wife to his obedient subject, the homily implies that a well-ordered marriage reflects and contributes to a well-ordered state: both result from a strict observance of divinely instituted hierarchies.

For those who found the "woman's part" in marriage distasteful, singleness did not necessarily provide a viable alternative. All women fit the category of "maid" at one time or another; however, this category was a transitory one, occupied by

---

[13] *Calendar of Letters and State Papers*, 1: 404–5.

[14] *Calendar of Letters and State Papers*, 1: 633.

[15] Bevington, *Tudor Drama and Politics*, 8–9.

[16] "An Homily of the State of Matrimony" from *The Second Tome of Homilies* (London, 1563), repr. in *Daughters, Wives, and Widows: Writing by Men about Women and Marriage in England, 1500–1640*, ed. Joan Larsen Klein (Urbana, 1992), 24.

[17] "An Homily of the State of Matrimony," 14. On the value attributed to marriage in post-reformation Tudor culture, see Fitz, "'What Says the Married Woman?'," passim; Lawrence Stone, *The Family, Sex and Marriage in England, 1500–1800* (New York, 1979), 136–42; Keith Wrightson, *English Society, 1580–1680* (London, 1982), 66–118; and Mendelson and Crawford, *Women in Early Modern England*, 66–69, 124–48.

[18] Mendelson and Crawford, *Women in Early Modern England*, 25.

[19] "An Homily of the State of Matrimony," 22.

women in the period that separated sexual maturation from sanctioned sexual consummation. Maidenhood did not provide the control implied by the idea of singleness, for maids remained under the authority of male relatives until the wedding ceremony transferred that authority to their husbands. A failure to negotiate the transition from maid to wife involved severe social repercussions. The pamphleteer Joseph Swetnam attacked "vnmarried wantons," for example, for having made them "selues neither maidens, widowes, nor wiues."[20] Through no fault of her own, Shakespeare's Mariana in *Measure for Measure* is such an "vnmarried wanton," caught in transition. "Neither maid, widow, nor wife," she is vulnerable to Lucio's construction of her as a "punk."[21] Mariana in her melancholy moated grange is an apt figure for the marginal status occupied by single women in the early modern community. The "single" woman — the woman not clearly related to a male authority figure — was abnormal and risked being placed in the negative categories available to describe women. As Mendelson and Crawford put it, "Women could be good, proceeding from virginity to marriage and maternity, and die after a virtuously spent widowhood. Or they could be wicked: scolds, whores, or witches."[22] They could also, of course, be queens.

The Tudor queens regnant complicated early modern society's rigid system of categorization: Mary, who was widely perceived as wicked, was married, while Elizabeth, who became very popular, remained single. The challenge Mary and, to a greater extent, Elizabeth posed to received wisdom on the matters of marriage and of categorizing women created something like what Victor Turner calls a "social drama": a breach in the fabric of normative social structure.[23] Although this breach was contained by the exceptionality of the women involved, it nevertheless generated serious conflicts, pitting the queens against their male subjects, and these subjects against one another. Comedy, with its focus on the passage of young women from maidenhood to adulthood (usually figured as wifehood), was eminently suited to reflecting on these conflicts. As de Silva's letters indicate, to at least one participant in the social drama — Elizabeth herself — court comedies qualified as attempts to redress the marriage crisis by forcing a specific resolution. The anxieties generated by the queen's singular status thus form an important context for understanding Elizabethan comedies generally and Lyly's comedies specifically.

Mary and Elizabeth drew unprecedented attention to the passage of a young woman from maidenhood to adulthood, itself one of the major focuses of comedy. In their different ways, both queens challenged cultural expectations regarding the desirability of "the plot of ... 'maid, wife, and widow'."[24] Although Mary wed,

---

[20] Joseph Swetnam, *The Araignment of Lewde, idle, froward, and vnconstant women: Or the vanitie of them, choose you whether* (1615), STC 23533, 27.

[21] *Measure for Measure*, in *The Riverside Shakespeare*, 5.1.177–80.

[22] Mendelson and Crawford, *Women in Early Modern England*, 17. On this, see also Linda Woodbridge, *Women and the English Renaissance: Literature and the Nature of Womankind, 1540–1620* (Urbana, 1984), 84.

[23] Victor Turner, *From Ritual to Theatre: The Human Seriousness of Play* (New York, 1982), 10–11.

[24] The expression is that of Mendelson and Crawford, *Women in Early Modern England*, 76.

and thus conformed to the idea that a woman should be manned, her marriage was a personal and political disaster. Elizabeth, meanwhile, deviated from conventional life patterns for women and ultimately proved the deviation desirable. Thus, while Tudor society attributed ever greater value to marriage, England was successfully governed by a queen who, despite her participation in various courtships, remained single. Conventional comedies, such as the ones that Elizabeth attended in de Silva's company, tended to emphasize the queen's nonconformity to cultural systems of categorizing. They were "all against" Elizabeth because the unmarried queen eluded the social conventions celebrated in such comedies.

The contradictions posed by the queens regnant to early modern paradigms provoked contentious commentary. For English subjects at this time "the problem of the authority of a *married* queen regnant was particularly urgent. What was her authority to be with respect to her husband, her social and political superior?"[25] The writers who participated in the so-called queenship debate frequently reduced the question of female monarchy to the vexed issue of marriage. The debate's most notorious pamphlet, John Knox's *The First Blast of the Trumpet Against the Monstrous Regiment of Women* (1558), argues that "woman in her greatest perfection, was made to serve and obey man, not to rule and command him."[26] Citing Genesis, Knox claims that God decrees the subordination of women to their husbands, and uses this marital subjection as grounds for arguing against a female monarch: "no woman can euer presume to reigne aboue man, but the same she must nedes do in despite of God."[27] Knox's thinking on the issue of marriage is congruent with official discourse on the matter; indeed, his metaphors and biblical citations echo the ones used by the homily on marriage. His argument against queens extends the subjection of the wife to her husband into a more general feminine subjection to *all* masculine authority. The "woman's part" in marriage, in other words, provides the blue print for her "part" in patriarchal society generally.[28] Such arguments might well explain Elizabeth's lack of enthusiasm for conventional comic endings.

Even the writers eager to defend Elizabeth's right to reign shared many of Knox's assumptions about feminine subjection. In *An Harborowe for Faithfull and Trewe Subjectes,* John Aylmer counters that although a woman must indeed be subject to her husband, she is not therefore subject to all men. Furthermore, a queen might obey a husband as his wife and nevertheless command him as his monarch. However, a queen should privilege the duty "she oweth to the commōweale" over what she owes to her husband; otherwise "is she a louing wife to him and an euel head to the countrey."[29] Ultimately, Aylmer's pamphlet construes marriage as in-

---

[25] Constance Jordan, "Woman's Rule In Sixteenth-Century British Political Thought," *Renaissance Quarterly* 40 (1987): 421–51, here 426.

[26] John Knox, *The First Blast of the Trumpet Against the Monstrous Regiment of Women* (1558; repr. Amsterdam, 1972), 13ʳ.

[27] Knox, *Monstrous Regiment,* 15ʳ.

[28] Although certainly they would disagree about the desirability of the end served, Knox and Butler thus agree about the sort of cultural work performed by "compulsory heterosexuality."

[29] John Aylmer, *An Harborowe For Faithfull And Trewe Subiectes* (1559; repr. Amsterdam, 1972), G3ʳ. On this famous passage in Aylmer, see Patricia-Ann Lee, "A Bodye Politique to Governe:

compatible with successful female sovereignty: a "louing" head takes the risk becoming an "euel" wife. His valiant attempt to separate the queen's role in marriage from her role in society ends in contradiction.

As these pamphlets show, the social categories by which Elizabeth might understand her options and take action were hopelessly at odds with one another. Simply by being a female monarch, she had activated her culture's "'classificatory' *oppositions*" and initiated a social drama.[30] Good women married and became obedient wives: feminine virtue consisted of conforming to this role.[31] Good monarchs did not, however, hand over sovereignty to anyone, particularly not foreign princes, even if these princes were their husbands. How could the wife's part and the monarch's part be reconciled? As the epilogue to *Gallathea* implies, Elizabeth was put in the position of "working things impossible in [her] Sexe."[32] For not reconciling marriage and monarchy might be worse: her subjects wished to secure the succession and pressed her to choose a husband. Whether she liked it or not, marriage initially appeared to be Elizabeth's destiny, just as it was the social destiny of most young women in early modern culture.

Even while she was being badgered to marry, Elizabeth was continually reminded of the loss of sovereignty that marriage entailed. No wonder, then, that the queen evinced a "most strange" hatred of matrimony. Although during the early years of her reign "everyone assumed that Elizabeth would marry, including the queen herself,"[33] Elizabeth showed little taste for the role that she was destined to play. In her 1566 response to the parliamentary request that she marry, for example, the queen evoked the homily on marriage by sternly reminding Parliament that *she* was the "head" and they the "feet." Having established her authority, she nevertheless promised to marry "assone as I can convenyentlye."[34] But she also asserted that of her "own dysposycion [she] was not enclyned thereunto"[35] and that she

---

Aylmer, Knox and the Debate on Queenship," *The Historian* 52 (1990): 242–61. Lee notes that "in considering the relation between male authority and female subordination in marriage, Aylmer argued that the woman became subordinate to her husband because she was a wife, not because she was a woman. In other words, the difference derived from function rather than nature" (251).

[30] Turner, *From Ritual to Theatre*, 11.

[31] Mendelson and Crawford, *Women in Early Modern England*, 17 and 33.

[32] John Lyly, *Gallathea*, in *The Complete Works*, ed. R. Warwick Bond, 3 vols. (Oxford, 1902), 2: 472. All further references to *Gallathea* are to this edition.

[33] John N. King, "Queen Elizabeth I: Representations of the Virgin Queen," *Renaissance Quarterly* 43 (1990): 30–74, here 39. King offers an important corrective to the prevalent view that "Elizabeth I set in motion her cultic celebration by means of esoteric literary and artistic symbolism when she made a youthful vow to remain a virgin" (31–32) held by scholars like Montrose and Roy Strong, *The Cult of Elizabeth: Elizabethan Portraiture and Pageantry* (London, 1977). King argues that this view derives in part from the mythologizing of the queen's first historians, and instead proposes that in the early years of the reign the queen was perceived as a marriageable virgin, not as a virgin goddess. King has influenced the shape of my argument in that I take the queen's single status to be the result of a gradual and contested process of deferment.

[34] Elizabeth I, "Queen's Speech to Delegation from Both Houses, 5 November [1566]," in *Proceedings in the Parliaments of Elizabeth I*, ed. T. E. Hartley (Leicester, 1981), 1: 147.

[35] Elizabeth I, "Queen's Speech," 1: 147.

would "never be by vyolence constreyned to doo anye thynge."[36] Elizabeth's speech, with its multiple references to death, violence, and exile, makes amply clear her ambivalence about her apparently inevitable fate. Despite her assertions of independence, she felt that she was being "constreyned" into playing a "woman's part" for which she had no inclination.

Where the parliamentarians handled their anxiety about the queen's deferment by repeatedly petitioning her, courtiers often relied on entertainments to make their point. In advancing one suit to the detriment of another, however, these men generated images of marriage that must have confirmed the queen's worst fears about the institution. Robert Dudley, for example, sought to promote his own eligibility by serving as patron to a series of performances.[37] A 1561 entertainment given by Dudley used allusions to the Andromeda myth to signal the superiority of a native over a foreign match. In this myth, Neptune attempts to rape the virgin Andromeda, offered to him as a sacrifice; however, Perseus intervenes in time and saves the virgin from her grim fate. As Marie Axton notes, the rape represents the "national threat to religion and quiet government" posed by the possibility of a foreign marriage. Elizabeth could neutralize this threat by marrying Dudley, an English Perseus.[38] Another series of entertainments planned by Dudley at Kenilworth in 1575 also included the rescue of a virgin (this time, the Lady of the Lake) from rape by a valiant knight. Again, the purpose seems to have been to encourage Elizabeth to marry.[39] Dudley's rhetorical skills left something to be desired, for the analogies among marriage, rape, and virgin sacrifice seem unlikely to encourage marriage of any sort. Had he tried, Dudley could hardly have come up with a more vivid representation of the threat that marriage posed to feminine sovereignty.

Thus, whereas in the culture marriage was thought to present the only positive choice for young women, at court assessments of the institution were more conflicted. Elizabeth herself regarded marriage with suspicion and encouraged others to follow suit. Although she initially presented herself as eligible, with the failure of the Alençon courtship in the early 1580s it became clear that, despite the maneuv-

---

[36] Elizabeth I, "Queen's Speech," 1: 148.

[37] Among these was the comedy which Elizabeth, according to de Silva, judged to be "all against" her, and also Thomas Sackville and Thomas Norton's *Gorboduc* (1561–1562), performed at the same time as the Andromeda masque. *Gorboduc*, too, attempted to convince Elizabeth of the wisdom of marrying an English subject; on this, see Henry James and Greg Walker, "The Politics of *Gorboduc*," *English Historical Review* 110 (1995): 109–21; and Norman Jones and Paul Whitfield White, "*Gorboduc* and Royal Marriage Politics: An Elizabethan Playgoer's Report of the Premiere Performance," *English Literary Renaissance* 26 (1996): 3–16. Dudley was a favorite of Elizabeth's at this time; for her relationship to him, see Wallace MacCaffrey, *Elizabeth I* (London, 1993), 71–75; Christopher Haigh, *Elizabeth I* (London, 1988), 12–15, 53, 89; and Carole Levin, *"The Heart and Stomach of a King": Elizabeth I and the Politics of Sex and Power* (Philadelphia, 1994), 45–49.

[38] Marie Axton, *The Queen's Two Bodies: Drama and the Elizabethan Succession* (London, 1977), 44; for a detailed description of Dudley's entertainment, see 40–45.

[39] The entertainment was designed by George Gascoigne on the occasion of the queen's visit to Dudley at Kenilworth. Gascoigne published the scripts as *The Princely Pleasures at Kenelworth Castle* (1575); for a more thorough description and discussion of these events, see King, "Queen Elizabeth I," 45.

erings of her parliaments, her counselors, and her courtiers, the queen would never play the "woman's part."[40] Her first historian, William Camden, argues that Elizabeth remained single in part because "Her Glory . . . whilst she continued unmarried she retained intire to herself and uneclipsed, she feared would by Marriage be transferred to her Husband."[41] Camden's analysis shows that the queen's continuance in the single state drew her contemporaries' attention to what would be "transferred" in a marriage, to the way that marriage would make the queen — and by extension perhaps other women — less than "intire." As she aged, Elizabeth's "strange" hatred of marriage extended to her entourage: she was famously antagonistic to the marriages of her ladies-in-waiting. She imprisoned several of them for marrying against her wishes, and a number of couples, including Dudley and his wife, were forced to hide their nuptials for fear of the queen's wrath.[42]

Elizabeth deferred marriage for so long that she transformed a transitory state into a permanent one. This strategy (if strategy it was) allowed her to refuse a role for which she was "not enclyned" while avoiding some of the repercussions of being single.[43] According to Turner, the "winners of social dramas positively require cultural performances to continue to legitimate their success."[44] By the 1580s, when Lyly wrote his plays, the conflict about the queen's marriage was for all intents and purposes over.[45] Now remained the task of assigning meaning to this conflict, of making sense of the queen's unorthodox status. Lyly rose to the occasion by contributing to the emerging cult of Elizabeth as a virgin goddess.[46]

---

[40] King sees this period as the turning point where the marriageable virgin became "perpetually virgin goddess" in Elizabethan iconography: "Queen Elizabeth I," 43. This period of transition coincides with the performance at court of Lyly's comedies.

[41] William Camden, *The History of the Most Renowned and Victorious Princess Elizabeth, Late Queen of England*, ed. Wallace T. MacCaffrey (Chicago, 1970), 137.

[42] See Haigh, "Elizabeth I," 93–96.

[43] As the impressive amount of unsavory gossip about the queen suggests, she was not able to avoid such repercussions altogether. For this gossip, see Levin, "*The Heart and Stomach of a King*," esp. 65–91. As Levin notes, in the stories circulating about the queen's alleged illegitimate children, for example, Elizabeth was dismissed "as a whore" (70), almost certainly reflecting the fact that she "refused to marry" despite her many suitors (66).

[44] Turner, *From Ritual to Theatre*, 74.

[45] Some scholars persist in viewing the plays as partaking in marriage politics (see, e.g., Ellen M. Caldwell, "John Lyly's *Gallathea*: A New Rhetoric of Love for the Virgin Queen," in *Women in the Renaissance*, ed. Kirby Farrell, Elizabeth H. Hageman, and Arthur F. Kinney [Amherst, MA, 1988, 69–87]; and Jankowski, *Women in Power*); however, the queen was by this time in her fifties. Already in 1579, John Stubbs had undiplomatically called attention to the fact that her age made marriage inappropriate: see *The Discoverie of a Gaping Gulf Whereinto England is Like to be Swallowed . . .*, in *John Stubbs's "Gaping Gulf" with Letters and Other Relevant Documents*, ed. Lloyd E. Berry (Charlottesville, VA, 1968), 51, 72.

[46] The plays most frequently cited in connection with the elevation of Elizabeth into a virgin goddess are *Endymion* and *Sappho and Phao*. For an excellent overview of Lyly's flattery of Elizabeth in these plays, see David Bevington's "Introduction to *Endymion*," in idem, ed., *John Lyly: Endymion* (Manchester, 1996), 1–72, esp. 27–37, and idem, "Introduction to *Sappho and Phao*," 164–72, as well as the works cited above. Some scholars have also attempted to connect *Gallathea* with the elevation of Elizabeth as a virgin goddess; see, for example, Caldwell, "New Rhetoric of

But Elizabeth's behavior also seems to have inspired Lyly to a broader critique of the institution of marriage. Lyly posits the possibility that the queen's singleness, rather than just being exceptional, should be exemplary.

The queen's distrust of the "woman's part" created conditions conducive to an interrogation of matrimony from the point of view of women. Lyly's plays generalize on the queen's resistance to marriage, using the themes and topos of the social drama to "desacralize" one of early modern society's most cherished institutions.[47] All the plays focus on young women caught in the transition between maidenhood and adulthood; all these women appear destined for traditional sexual unions for which they are not "enclyned"; all the prospective sexual unions are described in imagery (of rape, exile, death, and virgin sacrifice) associated with the conflict over the queen's marriage; and all the plays finally refuse to endorse dominant Tudor ideology on the salubriousness of heterosexual marriage. Instead, Lyly touts the virtues of singleness on the one hand and of reciprocal (as opposed to hierarchical) relationships on the other. Significantly, the latter frequently involve a homosocial pairing, rather than the heterosexual pairings favored by patriarchal culture and by conventional comedy.

In his presentation of heterosexual love, Lyly focuses on the issues of subjection and sovereignty raised in the debates regarding the queen's marriage. As I argued earlier, pamphleteers like Knox and Aylmer dwelt on structures of authority and obedience to the exclusion of other aspects of matrimony. Lyly adapts common Petrarchan motifs to examine such power structures in heterosexual relationships.[48] Petrarchism figures love as a violent experience, emphasizing the lover's feelings of pain and his or her exaggerated subjection to the beloved. Its conventional tropes include metaphors of war, torture, and imprisonment: in *Campaspe*, Alexander contrasts his "triumphs" in war with his "torments" in love.[49] As this example indicates, Petrarchism highlights disparities of power; it is thus uniquely unsuited to the conventional comic pursuit of sexual union. Shakespeare wittily makes the point by having the connubially minded Rosalind cure Orlando of his Petrarchism before she marries him. Contrasting Lyly to Shakespeare, Bevington argues that the endings of Shakespeare's comedies reflect a "wider acknowledgement of moral prestige in love and marriage, and greater acceptance of a kind of equality in the marital relationship."[50] But, as feminist historians have demonstrated, the increased "moral prestige" attributed to marriage produced only the illusion of "greater equality."

Love," 69–87, or Jacqueline Vanhoutte, "Sacrifice, Violence, and the Virgin Queen in Lyly's *Gallathea*," *Cahiers Elisabéthains* 49 (1996): 1–14.

[47] The desacralization of a society's "most cherished values and beliefs" is one of the functions of theatre described by Turner, *From Ritual to Theatre*, 11.

[48] On Lyly's use of Petrarchism, see also Bevington, "Jack hath not Jill," and Rose, "Moral Conceptions of Sexual Love."

[49] Lyly, *Campaspe*, in *"Campaspe"; "Sappho and Phao,"* ed. Hunter and Bevington, 2.2.22–23. All references to *Campaspe* and to *Sappho and Phao* are to this edition and will be indicated parenthetically.

[50] Bevington, "Introduction to *Sappho and Phao*," 175.

Mendelson and Crawford show that in court, "a wife's subjection was interpreted as a measure of her affection for her spouse."[51] Love and power were inextricably intertwined in early modern heterosexual relationships. Like most conventional comedies, *As You Like It* romanticizes the connections between love and power; Lyly, however, criticizes them. In his plays, heterosexual love assumes the shape of violence. Sappho's lady-in-waiting Mileta, for example, dreams of being in love as being "all in a gore of blood" (4.3.29–33). Such graphic images are amplified by Lyly's characterization of Venus. The goddess of love routinely thinks about sexual affection as a form of subjection: in *Sappho and Phao*, she articulates her intention to "yoke [Sappho's] neck that yet never bowed" (1.1.37–38). Venus's plans for Sappho illustrate the fusion of "love and obedience" that Mendelson and Crawford identify as characteristic of the woman's role in marriage.[52]

Although Lyly's men and women are equally likely to feel the "yoke" of love, it weighs more heavily on female characters, who risk political as well as amorous subjection. Alexander experiences "torments" as a result of his unrequited passion for the "unfit" Campaspe (2.2.23, 24); yet despite its inappropriateness his love does not endanger his position.[53] When the princess Sappho falls in love with the ferryman Phao, on the other hand, she faces political and social degradation. As Camden noted in reference to Elizabeth, a female ruler who "married a Subject" would "disparage herself by the Inequality of the Match."[54] For Alexander, love is a temporary distraction from rule; for Sappho, love potentially spells an end to rule. Her experience of love is correspondingly more traumatic.[55] The low class of her beloved further complicates the situation. A relationship with Phao might disrupt gendered hierarchies since Sappho's status disqualifies her as a wife. If she is to marry at all, she should marry a "great lord" (3.3.112), one whose husbandly authority will be appropriate as well as inevitable. Ultimately, Sappho remains single, thus solving the contradictions posed by marriage and monarchy in the same way that Elizabeth did. Her final allegorical conquest of Venus signifies her achievement, for as the goddess notes, "When Venus ceaseth to love, let Jove cease

---

[51] Mendelson and Crawford, *Women in Early Modern England*, 133.
[52] Mendelson and Crawford, *Women in Early Modern England*, 133.
[53] For Phao and Endymion, a consummation would actually lead to a marked social elevation.
[54] Camden, *History*, ed. MacCaffrey, 136.
[55] See also Bevington, "John Lyly and Queen Elizabeth," 64, and Jankowski, *Women in Power*, 126–31. Both note the extremity of Sappho's affliction in comparison to Alexander's. Jankowski concurs with Bevington that this extremity is hardly flattering to Elizabeth, if indeed we are to take Sappho as a direct representation of the queen. However, as Bevington points out, a strictly allegorical reading may not be appropriate. Rather than functioning as direct reflections of the queen, Lyly's ruler figures seem to work as foils: they are at once like and unlike Elizabeth. Sappho's exaggerated lovesickness underlines Lyly's thematic interest in subjection as a consequence of heterosexual desire for women in patriarchal society; however, Lyly's depiction of the amorous princess need not be a comment on Elizabeth's own affective tendencies. Also, according to Jankowski, the intensity of Sappho's passion reflects Lyly's anxiety regarding female rule (see above n.10). But this intensity is commensurate with what is at stake for Sappho. Moreover, Sappho *does* control her emotions, as the allegorical battle with Venus indicates.

to rule" (4.3.44–45). By rejecting the fusion of love and obedience, by opting for singleness, Sappho has neutralized patriarchal law. Her neck will suffer no "yoke"; like Lyly's queen, she will remain unmastered.

Similarly, Cynthia in *Endymion* is an unmarried ruler besieged by a lower-class lover, whose advances she ultimately rejects. For Sappho and Cynthia, as for Elizabeth, singleness is the only alternative compatible with successful sovereignty. But Lyly is careful to show that the problems of female subjection raised by traditional heterosexual unions are not limited to ruling women. The main difference between the ruler-figures and the other female characters is that the rulers have the resources to reject marriage, whereas the other female characters frequently find themselves in intolerable positions, "constreyned" to marry despite their inclinations.

This distinction is best illustrated by *Endymion*, which also recounts the amorous tribulations of Cynthia's courtiers. *Endymion* is the only one of Lyly's comedies that ends in multiple heterosexual pairings. All these pairings involve secondary characters, a result of the tyrannical imposition of patriarchal norms that Cynthia herself eludes. In a marked departure from Elizabeth, who preferred to keep the women around her unmarried, Cynthia uses marriage as a punitive institution, forcing her unruly ladies-in-waiting to take husbands of her choosing. She exchanges the rebellious Tellus's prison for marriage to Corsites, the prison guard. Presumably, as a husband, Corsites will control Tellus's "thoughts" and her "body" more effectively than prison has.[56] The homily on marriage likens the relationship between husband to wife to that between king and subject, thus idealizing husbandly authority. Through his analogy to a guard and his prisoner, Lyly instead casts a critical light on the distribution of power in early modern marriage. Nor is Tellus alone in suffering the tyrannical punishment of matrimony. Cynthia also peremptorily constrains Semele, entirely innocent of wrongdoing, first to be silent, then to become a wife. When Eumenides interprets Semele's enforced silence as consent, the appalled girl defends herself eloquently: "A hard choice, madam, either to be married if I say nothing or to lose my tongue if I speak a word" (5.4.220–21). Semele's "hard choice" highlights the problem of mistaking feminine silence or passivity for consent. Like most young women in early modern culture, both Semele and Tellus eventually comply with Cynthia's orders and make the transition to wifehood. But their weddings are hardly of the celebratory comic variety. Marriage in *Endymion* is compulsory, a form of containment that strips women of sovereignty and silences feminine opposition. The strained artificiality of *Endymion*'s ending signals the constraining nature of the institution.[57] Cynthia may be able to decide that "nothing pleaseth her but the fairness of virginity" (4.1.74), but her female subjects, who also desire "sovereignty" (3.3.19), do not yet have the same luxury.

---

[56] See the dialogue at 3.3.6–12 in *Endymion*, ed. Bevington. All citations of *Endymion* are from this text.

[57] The point is emphasized by the fate of Dipsas, the conjurer who assists Tellus in her punishment of the unfaithful Endymion. In her pursuit of the "devilish art" of enchanting (5.4.27), Dipsas deserted her husband; Cynthia, however, forces the old woman to give up her art and return to her husband.

Even when he represents deviant women like Dipsas or Sibylla in *Sappho and Phao* in unflattering ways, Lyly is attentive to the political phenomena that explain their deviancy from the normal path of maid, wife, and widow. Sibylla, for example, had the "hard choice" of accepting Apollo's unwelcome advances or suffering unpleasant consequences. She chose the latter, and lost youth, beauty, and social status, going from "young maid" to "grave matron" without first passing through the stage of wife (2.1.50–90). Relegated to a cave, like Shakespeare's Mariana to her grange, Sibylla demonstrates the fate of women who fail to comply with patriarchal power. To be sure, she now preaches the false doctrine of compulsion to Phao, assuring him that women "would be overcome. Force they call it, but such a welcome force they account it that continually they study to be enforced" (2.4.105–08). But the play is careful to take note of Sibylla's bitterness and to undermine her claims. Certainly, Sappho shows no interest in being forced.

The type of sexual oppression advocated (and suffered) by Sibylla occurs repeatedly in Lyly's plays, for all that his women never "welcome" such "force." His comedies are suffused with allusions to rape, mutilation, and sacrifice. These references frequently recall Elizabeth's speeches, in which she presented marriage as an inevitable sacrifice, or entertainments like the two rape masques patronized by Dudley.[58] Lyly uses courtly rape and sacrifice motifs outside of their political context in order to problematize heterosexual power structures. More particularly, in *Gallathea* and *Campaspe*, he presents the "woman's part" in marriage as a form of sexual oppression disguised as destiny. Where destiny cannot be averted, however, Gallathea, Phillida, and Campaspe follow Elizabeth in avoiding the role that they are expected to play. Despite Lyly's own occasional ambivalence, his two plays about non-ruling women imply a far-reaching critique of the options available to young women in early modern patriarchal society. *Gallathea* even suggests that feminine "destiny" in patriarchal society is a matter of social custom, and that social customs may be altered.

Lyly emphasizes the precarious position of average women within patriarchal culture by staging relationships that exaggerate the power differential between the sexes. *Campaspe* concerns the fate of a young girl taken prisoner by Alexander and forced to become his "paramour" (3.5.32). It opens with the arrival on stage of Campaspe, Timoclea, and others, all "captives whose necks are yoked by force" (1.1.45–46). Where Sappho is able to resist Venus's "yoke," these captives have no resources. Lyly's language calls attention to their vulnerability vis-à-vis Alexander, whose goal is "To bring all under his subjection" (1.1.53). When Timoclea assures one of the Macedonian officers that feminine "virtue" cannot be so subdued, her own history defeats her claim. As Lyly's courtly audience knew, a soldier had raped Timoclea during her capture, and feminine "virtue" and chastity were synonymous

---

[58] Rape was a favored political metaphor at court, a convenient shorthand for threats to the queen: see Axton, *The Queen's Two Bodies*, 45. Various works closely related to the court make use of rape to signal political crises. *Gorboduc*, for example, depicts England as a woman and figures a foreign invasion as a rape of the motherland.

in the period.[59] Campaspe poignantly evokes the threat of rape when she hopes that Alexander will "save our honours" (1.1.64–65). But instead Campaspe may have to face the "destiny" of young women at the hands of their conquerors (1.1.44). Upon meeting her, Alexander promptly makes sexual advances: he "doth love and therefore must obtain" (2.2.112–13). In *Campaspe*, "love" is a form of masculine conquest, a violation of female captives "by force."

Although Lyly does not explicitly show that Alexander "obtain[s]" Campaspe's virginity, the play does insist on rape as a distinct possibility. Alexander seems to derive pleasure from forcing obedience: he comments on the alluring mix of Campaspe's "sweet consent" and "chaste disdain" (3.4.140). *Campaspe* frames the central relationship between Alexander and Campaspe through allusions to rape myths: the pictures in Apelles's shop, for example, all represent women "ravished" (3.3.22) by a Jupiter intent on "obtain[ing] his desire" (3.3.20). Such references establish the normative heterosexual relationship within the play as one in which a woman is subjected to a man through violence or deception. Campaspe herself connects the myths to her own situation when she remarks that "In kings there can be no love but to queens; for as near must they meet in majesty as they do in affection. It is requisite to stand aloof from king's love, Jove, and lightning" (4.5.33–36). Explicit is the idea that a power differential between partners renders mutual "love" impossible; implicit is the idea that such sexual relationships must be based on the "enforced" (2.2.116) subjection of the weaker partner. The relationship between Campaspe and Alexander literalizes and thus exaggerates the relationship between husband and wife as delineated in the homily on marriage: he is her king, she his subject. *Campaspe* associates the loss of sovereignty that ensues from this fusion of "love and obedience" with rape, thus tainting a hierarchy usually typed as desirable.

Where Dudley's court entertainments failed to recognize that presenting a specific marriage as a rape had implications for marriage generally, Lyly capitalizes on these implications. In *Campaspe*, he employs mythological allusions to undermine the validity of "love" in hierarchical relationships. *Gallathea* makes even more radical use of these motifs. It, too, features a virgin about to be sacrificed to Neptune. However, rather than being saved by a male hero, Lyly's virgin simply fails to meet her destiny, and falls in love instead with another girl. Foregoing "compulsory heterosexuality," the play renders explicit the superiority of equitable (and homosocial) relationships left implicit in Lyly's other plays.

Like Dudley's masques, *Gallathea* is structured around a homology between marriage and virgin sacrifice.[60] In order to preserve peace with Neptune, a small Eng-

---

[59] For the court's familiarity with Timoclea's story, see G. K. Hunter, "Introduction to *Campaspe*," in *"Campaspe" and "Sappho and Phao,"* 8–9.

[60] On the correlations between marriage and sacrifice in this play, see also Caldwell, "New Rhetoric of Love," who notes that the play presents "a thinly veiled allegory of a woman's reluctance to face the sexual demands of marriage" (70); Vanhoutte, "Sacrifice, Violence, and the Virgin Queen," who argues that *Gallathea* presents Elizabeth's refusal to marry as a form of public sacrifice; and Theodora Jankowski, " 'Where There Can Be No Cause of Affection': Redefining Virgins, Their Desires, and Their Pleasures in John Lyly's *Gallathea*," in *Feminist Readings of Early Modern Culture: Emerging Subjects*, ed. Valerie Traub, M. Lindsay Kaplan, and Dympna Callaghan

lish community sacrifices its "fairest and chastest virgine" every five years (1.1.43). Gallathea and Phillida both qualify for this undesirable "desteny" (1.1.62), but their over-attached fathers forego the "custom of this Countrey" (1.3.2) in order to hide the girls, disguised as boys, in the pastoral woods. As in Dudley's entertainment, Neptune might signal the threat posed by a suitor; certainly, his monster, Agar, seems to embody masculine sexual aggression. The sacrifice in *Gallathea* parallels marriage practices in a number of other ways. Early modern marriages consolidated relations between men through the exchange of women; in the same way, the "horror" that young girls "endure" (1.1.51) at the hands of Agar guarantees peaceful relations between their fathers and Neptune.[61] Both systems work as long as men are willing to use their daughters as objects of exchange and as long as women consent to these exchanges. As Butler puts it, "The relation of reciprocity established between men . . . is the condition of a relation of radical nonreciprocity between men and women and a relation, as it were, of nonrelation between women."[62] By violating this condition, *Gallathea* calls into question the inevitability of patriarchal forms of social organization. Despite what Hymen tells Phoebe, *Gallathea* shows that women do not have to "accord" to patriarchy.

The unfortunate Haebe, selected to take Gallathea and Phillida's place, establishes that marriage/sacrifice serves the interest of men. While preparing for the apparently inevitable loss of her "chastitie," Haebe suggests that "the custom, the bloodie custom" of virgin sacrifice reflects a patriarchal organization of culture: "men will haue it so, whose forces commaund our weake natures" (5.2.12–14). Her emphasis on masculine volition and force undermines the Augur's claims that marriage/sacrifice is fated (5.2.1). Meanwhile, her long invocation to Agar, that "vnsatiable Monster of Maidens blood" (5.2.49), connects heterosexual sex and violence, reconfiguring the passage from maid to wife as a process of ingestion and digestion: the "misfortune of a mayden" (5.2.5–6) involves allowing the "deuourer of beauties bowels" to "Teare these tender ioynts wyth [his] greedie iawes, these yellow lockes with [his] black feete, this faire face with [his] foule teethe" (5.2.49–52). These (admittedly ludicrous) images gesture towards the erasure of feminine sovereignty in marriage, as the girl's body is covered, controlled, and consumed by the monster. Like many a virgin before her, Haebe appears destined to be destroyed in the exchange between men and gods.

But Haebe fails to negotiate the passage from maidenhood, and joins the ranks of Lyly's single women instead. The offended Neptune, intent on "obtain[ing] loue" (2.2.18) only from "the fairest," refuses the poor substitution and abolishes the "bloodie custom." The reciprocity between men is thus interrupted, opening

---

(Cambridge, 1996), 253–74. Jankowski's emphasis on "society" and hence the social rather than the political implications of *Gallathea* corresponds with my argument in a number of ways, although she is engaged primarily in the play's presentation of the "position" of "non-marrying virgins . . . relative to desire or pleasure" (255).

[61] See Jankowski, "Redefining Virgins," 257.
[62] Butler, *Gender Trouble*, 41.

a space for "an alternative sexual economy."[63] Once this "condition" of patriarchy is suspended, other conditions that had appeared to be a matter of destiny are revealed as arbitrary and chosen. These include, famously, gender: one of the girls disguised as a boy actually becomes a boy so as to be able to marry the other girl.[64] The second construct revealed as mere "custom" is that of "compulsory heterosexuality." Under the old dispensation, Gallathea and Phillida were both destined to be sacrificed to Neptune's lust. Gallathea initially resists her father's strategy for avoiding this grim fate, observing that "Destenie may be deferred, not preuented" (1.1.69). As it turns out, however, the girls do prevent their destiny by deferring it, thus successfully adapting Elizabeth's strategies for avoiding the threat posed by the Neptunes of this world. While deferring their destinies in the pastoral woods, Gallathea and Phillida meet and fall in love. The suspension of compulsory heterosexuality allows for the exploration of more palatable alternatives: in Lyly's comic world, a young woman can have another young "woman to [her] lord."

Or perhaps the point is that a young woman needs no lords at all: in *Gallathea*, love and obedience are no longer fused. Lyly underlines the likeness of his two heroines. The two are so similar, in fact, that they are interchangeable: Phillida describes herself as loving "one that I feare mee, is as thy selfe is" (4.4.38). The confusion of pronouns that attends such declarations of love points to the utter absence of differentials, including power differentials, between Gallathea and Phillida. Unlike the "love" between Sappho and Phao, between Cynthia and Endymion, between Alexander and Campaspe, or between Tellus and Corsites, the love between Gallathea and Phillida is based on a thoroughgoing reciprocity.[65] Despite Venus's promise to change one of the girls into a man, the play's resolution leaves us with an image of two "Maidens" who "loue one another" (5.3.116). The perfect mutuality of this union stands in stark contrast to the marriages at the end of *Endymion*, to marriage as it is described in the Tudor homily, even to the marriages of *As You Like It*. Indeed, the final coupling of *Gallathea* is a sort of fantastic anti-marriage. It subverts the hierarchical structure that is the *sine qua non* of early modern marriage, and it replaces the "nonrelation" between women in patriarchal culture with a perfect reciprocity. Here is a new "state" altogether, one in which women, to use the words of the servant boy Raffe, take "No more Maisters" (5.1.1). Elizabeth could find nothing wrong, surely, with these women's parts.

Gallathea's resolution, radical though it appears, is in keeping with Lyly's other endings, in which characters consistently reject inequitable relationships. The rulers, Sappho and Cynthia, both remain single because reciprocal relationships are impossible for them, although Sappho, to be sure, is tempted by Phao. So much is made

---

[63] Butler, *Gender Trouble*, 41. Jankowski makes a similar point: "one particular form of patriarchal oppression is stopped forever. Virgins' bodies are no longer to be used to forge alliances between men and gods" ("Redefining Virgins," 258).

[64] On *Gallathea*'s construction of gender as arbitrary and on its celebration of androgyny, see the definitive essay by Phyllis Rackin, "Androgyny, Mimesis, and the Marriage of the Boy Heroine on the English Renaissance Stage," *PMLA* 102 (1987): 29–41.

[65] On this reciprocity, see also Caldwell, "New Rhetoric of Love," 70, who notes that Lyly avoids the extremes of Petrarchan language in *Gallathea*.

of Phao's low rank that it must account in part for Sappho's attraction: she might love such a "mean" man (4.1.18) without giving up sovereignty, and might redefine the "woman's part" without foregoing heterosexual marriage. A woman of high estate who loves a man of lower status can adjust the imbalance of power inherent in early modern heterosexual relationships (as Shakespeare's Desdemona or Webster's Duchess of Malfi both attempt to do). This sort of recalibration marks the relationship between Campaspe, elevated by Alexander's love for her, and Apelles, the lowly court painter. Ultimately, they are matched in "majesty" as in "affection." Alexander gives up the attempt to "enforce marriage" where he "cannot compel love" (5.4.126–27), and prefers the homosocial bond that he shares with Hephestion to the dissatisfaction of an unequal relationship. *Campaspe* thus moves towards the possibility of more satisfying and reciprocal relational structures in the fairly traditional pairing of its heroine with Apelles and in the non-traditional pairing of its hero with his friend. The joys of homosocial congress are gestured at also by Eumenides's friendship with Endymion, by Diana's nymphs in *Gallathea*, and, obliquely, by Sappho's own status as a historical figure associated with love between women.[66] Lyly's comic endings repeatedly refuse to present traditional heterosexual marriage as a desirable end in life; instead, they encourage — and in the case of *Gallathea*, enact — the search for alternatives.

Far from constituting a failure, Lyly's rejection of "normal" marriage is one of his most important contributions to comic tradition. For although later comedies increasingly conform to patriarchal orthodoxy by ending in hierarchical marriages, many plays also continue to examine the value of alternatives by creating characters like Shakespeare's Phoebe or his Olivia who resist dwindling into a wife and who recall Lyly's heroines and his queen.[67] Initially, Olivia seems intent on moving from the category of maid to the category of widow without ever becoming a wife. In mourning for her brother, she defers marriage for at least seven years, imitating Elizabeth by discouraging her suitor.[68] As in Lyly's plays, Olivia's attachment to her own sovereignty is expressed first as the desire to remain single and second as the urge to form a nontraditional bond (with the disguised Viola). Even if eventually characters like Olivia are brought to give up their interest in androgynous, non-dominant partners and to conform to the heterosexual paradigms of early modern culture, they nevertheless call attention to options that patriarchal ideology

---

[66] It is highly likely that both Lyly and his audience would have been aware of this association; see Berry, *Of Chastity and Power*, 123, and Bevington, "Introduction to *Sappho and Phao*," 153.

[67] Leah S. Marcus calls attention to the resemblance of Shakespeare's cross-dressing heroines to Elizabeth: "Shakespeare's Comic Heroines, Elizabeth I, and the Political Uses of Androgyny," in *Women in the Middle Ages and the Renaissance*, ed. Mary Beth Rose (Syracuse, 1986), 135–54. However, unlike Gallathea and Phillida, Shakespeare's cross-dressers usually don disguise in order to enhance their chances of traditional marriages. In their initial investigation of alternatives to such "normal" marriages, Phoebe and Olivia reflect more closely the sort of threat posed by Elizabeth to her culture's way of imagining the woman's part. Levin also finds similarities between Olivia and Elizabeth, "*The Heart and Stomach of a King*," 136–37.

[68] William Shakespeare, *Twelfth Night*, in *The Riverside Shakespeare*, 1.1.25.

would disguise. And they keep alive the possibilities generated by Elizabeth's extraordinary example while preparing the way for heroines like Moll in *The Roaring Girl*, who unequivocally states that she will not be married until women are "manned but never pandered. ..."[69]

Jacqueline Vanhoutte
University of North Texas

---

[69] Thomas Middleton and Thomas Dekker, *The Roaring Girl*, ed. Paul A. Mulholland (Manchester, 1987), 5.2.220.

PART III:

Imaginary Widowhood

6

Chaucer's Sely Widows

It is perhaps not surprising that the English concept of widowhood was, at least until the late Middle Ages, both gender specific and closely connected to the status of the female body. The term "widewe" or "widwe" derived from the Indo-European root *widh* — "to be empty, separated" — suggesting that the surviving spouse continued life as only half of her former and thriving married identity.[1] Yet the idea that the survivor lived something of a marginal or half life applied only to women; not until the fourteenth century did the derivative male form of the English word, "widower," appear. Whereas women who survived the death of their spouses were considered to be "unheaded" and were easily disenfranchised of their marital protections and rights, widowers retained all the physical and material aspects of their married selves.[2] The volatile gendered category that widows tend to occupy in the Middle Ages is reflected in this ultimate form of marginalization.

---

[1] *Oxford English Dictionary*, s.v. "widow." Anna Roberts points out that a similar concept is embedded in the French *veuve*, which derives from the Latin *vidua*, "deprived of": "Helpful Widows, Virgins in Distress: Women's Friendship in French Romance of the Thirteenth and Fourteenth Centuries," in *Constructions of Widowhood and Virginity in the Middle Ages*, ed. Cindy L. Carlson and Angela Jane Weisl (New York, 1999), 25–47, here 25.

[2] The sentiment that the widow is "unheaded" seems to derive from St. Paul, 1 Corinthians 11:3: "The head of every man is Christ, and the head of the woman is the man." Gratian's *Decretum* states that ". . . the man is the head of the woman and the woman is the body of the man" (2. 33.5 [PL 187.1653 B]), while Aquinas writes in his *Summa Theologiae*, 1a 92, art. 1, that "With man male and female are not only joined together for purposes of procreation, as with the other animals, but to establish a home life, in which man and woman work together at some things, and in which the man is the head of the woman." The idea had great resonance in the antifeminist tradition: Jacques de Vitry writes in Sermon 66 that though "the married couple is equal as regards the carnal debt, in other things the husband is his wife's head, to rule her, correct her (if she strays), and restrain her (so she does not fall headlong)." All three texts may be found in Alcuin Blamires, trans., *Woman Defamed and Woman Defended* (Oxford, 1992), 83–87, 91–93, 144–47.

If husband and wife are united in marriage, the widow's very identity is disembodied and dislocated as a condition of her husband's death.

Thus a contradictory set of assumptions regarding the social and sexual behavior expected of widows appears in the official discourse and literary popular imagination of the time. Both evince a cultural anxiety concerning these "unheaded" women that reflects an open suspicion about widows' sexual experience and sometimes a certain envy or distrust of their economic autonomy. As women who had essentially "paid their dues" through marriage, widows, unlike most single women, could at least in theory live independent of direct male authority and control their own households and financial affairs. Widows were protected in medieval England by laws that granted one third or as much as one half of the husband's estate for their maintenance, although the remainder of the estate passed to their husband's other heirs.[3] They could continue their husband's businesses, retain certain guild privileges, manage their property, negotiate business affairs, and, in short, enjoy a degree of autonomy not granted married women or maidens.[4] Yet despite these privileges widows commonly found themselves forcibly displaced by aggressive heirs and compelled to litigate their dower claims before the royal courts.[5] Widows who were to be successful in their claims had to be knowledgeable about property law and adept in asserting their legal rights.[6] Considering the formidable obstacles that might beset the presumably bereft widow, it might be more advantageous for the widow to remarry. But remarriage offered problems, too: concerns regarding the patrimonial claims of former children and the demands of the widow's prior family upon her emerged as a potentially debilitating social handicap.[7]

As women who had once been married, moreover, widows retained the traditionally feminine characteristics associated with sexuality and, potentially, childbearing. Thus while on the one hand canon law granted widows the privilege of remarrying and thereby reentering traditional systems of kinship and patriarchy, on the other it repudiated the continuing sexuality and fertility remarriage implied, instead encouraging widows to adopt lives of humble poverty, or to attain what

---

[3] For a useful compilation of European legal documents concerning women and their rights, see Emilie Amt, ed., *Women's Lives in Medieval Europe: A Sourcebook* (New York, 1993). See also the discussion by Barbara A. Hanawalt in "Remarriage as an Option for Urban and Rural Widows in Late Medieval England," in *Wife and Widow in Medieval England*, ed. Sue Sheridan Walker (Ann Arbor, 1993), 141–64.

[4] Hanawalt, "Remarriage," 141.

[5] On the widow's dower and experience in the royal courts, see Barbara A. Hanawalt, "The Widow's Mite: Provisions for Medieval London Widows," in *Upon My Husband's Death: Widows in the Literature and Histories of Medieval Europe*, ed. Louise Mirrer (Ann Arbor, 1992), 21–45; Sue Sheridan Walker, "Litigation as Personal Quest: Suing for Dower in the Royal Courts, circa 1272–1350," in *Wife and Widow in Medieval England*, 81–108.

[6] Walker, "Litigation," 82. Hanawalt estimates that the widow's chances of winning her plea were barely more than fifty percent. See "The Widow's Mite," 35.

[7] Barbara Todd, "The Remarrying Widow: A Stereotype Reconsidered," in *Women in English Society, 1500–1800*, ed. Mary Prior (London, 1985), 55, 71, 74.

Chaucer's Parson calls "the seconde manere of chastitee."[8] But unlike the virgin's body, which could be measured and evaluated for its purity, the widow's body could not reveal impropriety or promiscuity because it had already experienced the marriage bed. Hence the problem encountered by the good widow of the Friar's Tale, who is described as living a life of humble poverty that would seem by all the public markers to adhere to public mores: she is victimized by a summoner who accuses her of adultery despite her unblemished reputation. The summoner's taunt, that he once "payde at hoom" for the widow's "correccioun" (l. 1617), implies he is willing to claim that it was he with whom she committed the act — an accusation against which she is powerless. Her horrified reaction reminds us of that dual role assigned to widows: though she rigorously defends herself, swearing that she was never anything but "trewe" in body (l. 1621), she has been consigned to uncleanness via a swift renegotiation of the widow's stereotype.

Such depictions of widows conflate disparate concerns over regulating their "headless" bodies. Bereaved widows are alternatively portrayed through official and popular discourse as sexually overcharged or curiously divested of their reproductive capability. Pierre Bourdieu, Mary Douglas, and other social anthropologists have suggested that entire social systems and their values are both read through the body and enacted by it. The body, indeed, stands in as a microcosm for the tensions of societies. According to Bourdieu, "em-bodied" social principles are curiously detached from conscious processes;[9] gender stereotypes, for example, can be surmounted only with deliberate effort because they normally are not recognized as anything other than essential and therefore cannot be made explicit through language. The social and mental categories that distinguish various bodies in accordance with their perceived social value maintain a sense of tradition and fitness and distribute power unequally between the sexes: "Sexual potency," as Bourdieu observes, is "inseparable from social potency."[10] By extending Bourdieu's hypothesis, we can see that the widow's figurative headlessness renders her not autonomous but masterless, bereft of the rightful head that should rule her unruly body.

The transformation of normative symbols across cultures can either subvert or reinforce values already in place; what is important is that the renegotiation is constantly active. Bourdieu is useful in such formulations because he allows us to see the more marginal positions, such as those occupied by widows, not just as transgressive, but as malleable and easily adapted according to their social use value. Marginal categories, including those in-between categories of women and especially their potentially contaminating bodies, are in Mary Douglas's view seen as liminal and potentially dangerous, because they test and expose the limits of our social con-

---

[8] *The Parson's Tale*, l. 943. All quotes from Chaucer are from *The Riverside Chaucer*, gen. ed. Larry D. Benson (Boston, 1987). On medieval canon law and widows, see James A. Brundage, "Widows and Remarriage," in *Wife and Widow in Medieval England*, 17–31.

[9] Pierre Bourdieu, *Outline of a Theory of Practice*, trans. Richard Nice (Cambridge, 1977), 94.

[10] Bourdieu, *Outline*, 93.

cepts of biology and behavior.[11] Yet though Douglas is right to flag the margins as sociological stress points, she nonetheless fails to account for how the marginalized may be symbolically invested with seemingly contradictory values that, far from testing the limits of the dominant ideological system, instead actually preserve its social needs.[12] One might argue, using Douglas's account, that widows transgress medieval concepts of marriage as a unity between the body of the husband and wife — he is the head, she the body — in continuing on beyond the death of the husband. In such a view, this capacity should expose the limits of an ideology that defines a widow as only half the marital body. Widows as such might be thought to represent a form of transgression or pollution: they transgress the limits of patriarchal control by outliving the deceased head of the household, thereby demonstrating the limits of patriarchy in constraining and controlling the female body. Yet countless historical and literary examples demonstrate how easily that "unheadedness" seamlessly becomes integrated back into the ideological system — as, indeed, my assessment of the treatment of widows in Chaucer, below, attests. A more flexible position, drawing on Bourdieu, might thus instead show how official discourse attempts to appropriate the role of the deceased husband by imposing new limits on the widowed body — such as by insisting that the widow should devote herself to God and chaste living — only to have this discursive act itself transform into yet other manifestations. For even as official discourses demarcate the widow's unheaded soul as a model for spiritual piety, her body becomes useful surplus for other kinds of appropriation. That unheaded physical body is, for example, a convenient site for enacting and practicing the sexual power of otherwise unmaturated or unmarried males. Transfiguration becomes transgression again, as the widow's humble exterior is successfully relocated within other contexts that preserve the unequal balance of power.

This paper will examine the concept of widowhood in Chaucer. While Chaucer's works do not necessarily foreground widows as a particular social category or issue, widows nonetheless are scattered throughout his texts, and Chaucer's treatment of them reveals a certain awareness of their excluded social status and how it affects their assertions as individuals. Though Chaucer's most famous widow is the sexually aggressive Wife of Bath, widows more often than not appear as "sely" women who have been superfluously invested with the sexual anxieties of the men surrounding them. The Middle English term Chaucer associates particularly with the character of Dido, paradoxically bringing together the multifarious conditions of happiness, innocence, haplessness, and ignorance, seems especially indicative of the widow's condition. Indeed, Chaucer uses the category of widowhood to add psychological complexity to the situations of some surprising women: both Dido and Cleopatra in the *Legend of Good Women* are widows; Criseyde as a young widow provides the ideal partner in a clandestine and passionate love affair. Particularly

---

[11] Mary Douglas, *Purity and Danger: An Analysis of Concepts of Pollution and Taboo* (New York, 1966; repr. London, 1981), 122.

[12] See also Judith Butler's critique of Douglas in *Gender Trouble: Feminism and the Subversion of Identity* (New York, 1990), 131–34.

notable is the prevailing powerlessness of his widows' voices. Widows are acknowledged only when they speak as part of the marital bond — when they function as ventriloquists, in other words, for their dead husbands. Such is the case when the Theban widows plead to Theseus to avenge their husband's deaths in the Knight's Tale. When widows speak for themselves, however, their voices — with the sole exceptions of Criseyde and the Wife of Bath — tend to be feeble and protesting or easily disengaged.[13] The widow of the Nun's Priest's Tale, portrayed according to the institutional ideal of humility in adversity, is patient and quiet, supporting herself and her two daughters as best she can on their simple farm. She speaks not at all; her animals are the ones who talk, and who, in their talking, take on larger-than-life characteristics. Indeed, her voice is heard only as shrieks of dismay when Chaunticleer is stolen by the fox, and then she is described not as producing coherent discourse but rather as creating an undecipherable cacophony that blends with the braying of the beasts: "Out! Harrow and weylaway! Ha, ha! The fox!" (ll. 3380–81; 3383–96). Her garbled shouts have no effect on the outcome of the narrative. If a widow's voice possesses any threatening vitality, it is neutralized as part of the normal resolution of events.

In Chaucer's imagining, the widow's status as "unheaded" woman opens curious avenues for exploring the relationship between identity and language, the controlling medium of any social organization. In general, the widow's matrimonial headlessness caused by the death of her husband translates into her own metaphoric headlessness, whereby her voice, thoughts, and inner being are treated as essentially nonindependent of the critical discourses that define and regulate her, and her own essential being and autonomy drop away. The widow's headless body, deprived of will, subjectivity, or even an audible voice that might assert itself against wrongdoing, is further frequently portrayed as a seizable asset that can be used and discarded with impunity. Young widows are particularly vulnerable to male abuse, as Chaucer makes very clear. Yet even older widows who have retired into lives of humility and poverty, as the widow of the Friar's Tale attests, are targets for male fantasy.

Sely Widows

It is interesting to note that despite cultural assumptions about their sexual independence and their threatening *joie de vivre*, Chaucer's younger widows seem to prefer the wedded state to the unwedded. Those widows who remain of marriageable age tend to express or at least imply a desire to be wedded again. Dido insists on labeling herself a wife, despite the fact that no formal ceremony has taken place. Cleopatra remarries. Even the Wife of Bath expresses her desire to remarry. Frequently the wedded state is denied these women by their love interests, despite opportunity and, sometimes, the promise to wed. Widows both young and old, regardless of

---

[13] Chauncey Wood includes the Prioress and the Second Nun among this category, stating that they can be considered widows of Christ. See "Three Chaucerian Widows: Tales of Innocence and Experience," in *A Wyf Ther Was: Essays in Honour of Paule Mertens-Fonck*, ed. Juliette Dor (Liège, 1992), 282–90.

how carefully they guard their reputations, are largely portrayed in Chaucer's sympathetic characterization as embodying opportunities for men who have agendas of their own. Even when the widows don't physically become involved, their widowed status offers a safe site on which Chaucer posits the sexual fantasies of the unmaturated male, who can take advantage of the widow's social "disembodiment" by making lewd or otherwise unsupportable accusations. In Chaucer not widows but the concept of widowhood is sexually charged — a stereotyping that reflects more on the men who encounter these women than on the women themselves.

Both Dido and Cleopatra are portrayed historically as widows, a fact that is stated explicitly in the *Legend of Good Women* as an excuse for the characters' openly sensual yet still innocent natures. Dido is described alternately as "sely" (l. 1157), "amorous" (l. 1189), and "lusty" and "freshe" (l. 1191), a selection of terms that combines the sense of her sexual experience with naivete about the hidden natures of men. When she describes her longing for Aeneas with the simple sentence, "I wolde fayn to hym ywedded be; / This is th'effect" (ll. 1179–1180), she expresses Chaucer's sense that "good women" are naturally domestic and thus drawn to the state of marriage, by implication echoing the sentiment that widowhood is an unnaturally "emptied" or "separated" state. Even the powerful Cleopatra, who is traditionally unmarried during her torrid love affair with Antonius, "wax" as his "wif" in Chaucer's version of the story (l. 615). Her beauty, like Dido's, is described in axiomatic courtliness — "she was fayr as is the rose in May" (l. 614) — yet her sexual experience is also conveyed through the deceptive observation that once married, she "hadde hym as hire leste" (l. 615). As Florence Percival observes, this line very possibly reveals Chaucer's continued interest in the problem of sovereignty in marriage.[14] But more to the point of this essay, Cleopatra achieves her working identity through the marriage, attaining control over Antonius and her environment in the process. Cleopatra's power in the physical world is portrayed in Chaucer as an extension of her marital embodiment in Antonius: she goes with him as his wife on his campaign against Octavian, flees when he flees, dies when he dies.

Dido, unlike Cleopatra, is offered no physical embodiment through the sanctioned identity of marriage. As vocalized by a widow and unremarried lover, all Dido's utterances either remain unheard or evoke no material response, as if her "unheaded" voice and her lack of male protectors guarantee the ultimate impossibility of her own fulfillment in Chaucer's classic world. When Aeneas finds himself alone with her he elaborates a conventional lover's tale of pain, swearing fidelity to the hapless Dido; she in return "tok hym for husbonde and becom his wyf / For everemo, whil that hem laste lyf" (ll. 1238–1239). In her eyes the sexual union is equivalent to the promise of marital union, which itself signifies the passing of her identity from her old and deceased husband to her new. But these vows, exchanged unwitnessed in a cave amidst a storm, have no bearing in the Carthage to which they return.[15] Dido's near-hysteria at discovering Aeneas's intention to leave her

---

[14] Florence Percival, *Chaucer's Legendary Good Women* (Cambridge, 1998), 227.
[15] Cf. Sheila Delany, *The Naked Text: Chaucer's Legend of Good Women* (Berkeley, 1994), 198. Delany is sympathetic to Dido's belief in the validity of the clandestine marriage.

is especially trenchant, for from her perspective her very identity and right to speak is stripped from her when Aeneas revokes his promise. As Marilyn Desmond points out, Chaucer's Carthage, unlike Virgil's, shows no signs of decay because of Dido's affair.[16] The violence incurred through her actions affects her alone and is displayed only through the boundaries of her own physical body, impregnated by the recreant Eneas. Dido vows to slay herself — making him free to marry again — if only he will marry her before he leaves (ll. 1319–1322). That dignity denied her also, she turns to a letter as the last option for embodiment — a letter which will itself, ironically, likely remain unread: "But syn my name is lost thorugh yow," she writes, "I may wel lese on yow a word or letter" (ll. 1361–1362). Dido's lost words and letters are emblematic of the identity lost through the death or betrayal of the men in her life. The hopeless tone of her final words indicates her own conviction that suicide as a *wife* is considerably more significant than suicide as an abandoned lover: the wife has an identity through her husband, but the lover, widowed already and having moreover given up the emotional attachment to her deceased husband, dies bodiless and identityless. Dido's suicide lacks the righteous virtue of Cleopatra's or even Phyllis's, and invokes pity rather than indignation in its pathetic aspect.

By contrast, Cleopatra's self-immolation is portrayed in Chaucer as the ultimate in voyeuristic excess. After first digging a pit next to Antony's shrine, Chaucer's Cleopatra fills the grave with serpents, then flings herself, naked, into it. The added gratuitousness of the pit full of asps and the conspicuously naked body in part repudiate the image of chaste wife. The twice-widowed Cleopatra is twice as sensuous, twice as extravagant in her suicide as the more pathetic Dido. But she is also twice as bereft. Her final speech invokes the cultural stereotype that links the widow's body to her dead husband's: "... I yow swor to ben al frely youre," she says, and "Ye nere out of myn hertes remembraunce" (ll. 683 and 686). Because she sees her utterances as wife as having lasting resonance, she proclaims her final sacrifice to Antonius as the fulfillment of her marital covenant:

> And in myself this covenaunt made I tho,
> That ryght swich as ye felten, wel or wo,
> As fer forth as it in my power lay,
> Unreprovable unto my wyfhod ay,
> The same wolde I fele, lyf or deth —
> And thilke covenant whil me lasteth breth
> I wol fulfille.... (ll. 688–694)

In spectacularizing her own death, Cleopatra essentially delivers her body back to society, imagined as a widow true to the memory of her husband yet at the same time fully invested with medieval society's obsessive preoccupation: the sexual aspect of the widowed body. The imagistic effects of the *Legend of Good Women*, displayed not just here but also in the legend of Dido, where Eneas looks on the

---

[16] Marilyn Desmond, *Reading Dido: Gender, Textuality, and the Medieval* Aeneid (Minneapolis, 1994), 159.

aftermath of the Trojan war as it is displayed in tablets in Dido's temple, ultimately replace speech as a more trenchant remnant of the feminine. Words and deeds are for the patriarchy, images and tableaux for unheaded women.[17]

Appropriation and Re-embodiment

Yet language has great power for Chaucer's widows, even if that power is frequently the tool by which the widowed identity is fractured and marginalized. In Chaucer's fictive world, discourse can uncover the means by which the widow's victimization is enacted, and when used by particularly savvy practitioners, it can rebound upon the victimizer. Such is the case when the widow of the Friar's Tale curses the hell-bent summoner after he accuses her of adultery. "Thou lixt," she avers, repudiating his claims, "Unto the devel blak and rough of hewe / Yeve I thy body and my panne also!" (ll. 1618; 1622–1623). Oddly, though the tale's interrogation of language centers up to that moment on the word "entente," expressing the idea that intentions have greater value than the superficial words uttered (and which may not actually be meant), the widow's "entente" at this moment overpowers the summoner's. It would seem that she has the power to consign *his* soul to the devil:

> And whan the devel herde hire cursen so
> Upon hir knees, he seyde in this manere,
> "Now, Mabely, myn owene mooder deere,
> Is this youre wyl in ernest that ye seye? (ll. 1624–1627)

When the widow concurs, saying she wishes that the summoner die if he fails to repent, the devil whisks the summoner off. Her discourse has power because it reveals the truth about others' intentions.

The same is true of the two most expressive widows in Chaucer's canon: Criseyde and the Wife of Bath. Both are portrayed as speakers — and in Criseyde's case, even a writer — and both attempt to narrate or inscribe justifications of their behavior and motivations, perhaps in tacit acknowledgment of their inscrutability as widows. The extent to which the two characters are able not only to speak for themselves but also to have their speech affirmed by their contemporaries is of course debatable. Even contemporary scholars (let alone medieval ones) doubt the success of the Wife of Bath's attempt to forge a viable feminine speaking voice. And both the male characters of *Troilus and Criseyde* and the majority of her medieval mythographers treat Criseyde's excuses scornfully, despite Chaucer's stated sympathy for her.[18] Yet Criseyde and the Wife differ from Chaucer's other widows in

---

[17] Note also Philomela, who, once bereft of her tongue, can only weave pictures into tapestry to describe the outrageous wrong done to her.

[18] The scholarly debate over whether the Wife successfully establishes her voice against the anti-widow rhetoric of the institution has been extensive. See particularly the two opposing positions occupied by Carolyn Dinshaw, who argues that the Wife "appropriates the methods of the

their open acknowledgment of a marginal, dislocated status and their attempts at compensation. Both widows speak and act *as widows* rather than as typical single women insofar as both characterizations are informed by a sense of social displacement in the wake of their widowhood. The Wife of Bath's famous lament against the patriarchy is notably inspired by injunctions against remarrying — a social judgment that applies exclusively to widows. Criseyde's initial introduction in her own tale is also that of a woman for whom traditional avenues of behavior are closed. Widowed and abandoned by a traitor father, she is described as no longer knowing "how to read," or how to behave or judge her circumstances. Her sudden change of circumstance renders her marginal and vulnerable, unable to act according to her past wont. For both women, then, their self-presentation and inscrutable behavior may be seen as attempts to embody the widowed voice through manipulation of the social discourses that otherwise exclude them.

Chaucer's interest in both characters' strategies for survival in part lies in his pervasive empathy for marginalized women. Certainly it could be argued that the Wife of Bath's attempt to debunk official assumptions about women and marriage and to formulate through authorized language the experiences and concerns that constitute her feminine voice and subjectivity merely replicate or even further the antifeminist tradition she seeks to repudiate.[19] The Wife misunderstands many of the texts that concern her, such as the parable of the Samaritan Woman, which she believes to be an indictment of multiple marriages rather than of unsanctioned intercourse. Yet even when she gets it wrong, she engages the discourse: she thinks, questions, and measures stereotypes of behavior against her own experiences. By becoming what we might call "a good reader" of the texts of the patristic tradition — reading through the discourse and paying attention to the language that instills behaviors

---

masculine, clerkly *glossatores* themselves, thus exposing techniques that they would rather keep invisible" (*Chaucer's Sexual Poetics* [Madison, 1989], 120), and Elaine Tuttle Hansen, who believes that the Wife dramatizes "an important instance of women's silence and suppression in history and language" (*Chaucer and the Fictions of Gender* [Berkeley, 1992], 27–28). See also Barbara Gottfried, "Conflict and Relationship, Sovereignty and Survival: Parables of Power in the *Wife of Bath's Prologue*," *Chaucer Review* 19 (1985): 202–24; Donald C. Green, "The Semantics of Power: *Maistrie* and *Soveraynetee* in the *Canterbury Tales*," *Modern Philology* 84 (1986): 18–23; Peggy A. Knapp, "Alisoun of Bathe and the Reappropriation of Tradition," *Chaucer Review* 24 (1989): 45–52; Walter C. Long, "The Wife as Moral Revolutionary," *Chaucer Review* 20 (1986): 273–84; Barrie Ruth Straus, "The Subversive Discourse of the Wife of Bath: Phallocentric Discourse and the Imprisonment of Criticism," *English Literary History* 55 (1988): 527–54. Criseyde's authenticity as a speaker has been interrogated from a somewhat different angle: see David Aers, "Criseyde: Woman in Medieval Society," *Chaucer Review* 13 (1979): 177–200; J. D. Burnley, "Criseyde's Heart and the Weakness of Women: An Essay in Lexical Interpretation," *Studia Neophilologica* 54 (1982): 25–38; E. Talbot Donaldson, *Speaking of Chaucer* (London, 1970), 65–83; Maureen Fries, " 'Slydynge of Corage': Chaucer's Criseyde as Feminist and Victim," in *The Authority of Experience: Essays in Feminist Criticism*, ed. Arlyn Diamond and Lee R. Edwards (Amherst, MA, 1977), 45–59; Jill Mann, *Geoffrey Chaucer* (New York, 1991), 21–31.

[19] For an in-depth discussion of the Wife of Bath's discursive strategies, see Jeanie Grant Moore's essay in this volume, "(Re)creations of a Single Woman: Discursive Realms of the Wife of Bath."

and even processes of thought — the Wife uncovers the strategy of a symbolic system that creates ideology through its very discourses. Her prologue, contextualizing the story of her own marital experiences against the glosses of the clerics, demonstrates the importance of understanding the discourses that shape social and personal identity. The Wife has a personal motive for taking on the authorities in her prologue, insofar as husband number five, Janekyn, read to her constantly from his Book of Wicked Wives in order to indoctrinate her as to the failings of her sex. "[I]t is an impossible / That any clerk wol speke good of wyves," she remarks (ll. 688–689), confirming Carolyn Dinshaw's conclusion that "self-interestedness ... is always potential in the act of glossing."[20] Her derogatory words, however self-interested, have the effect of diminishing the more "authoritative" discourse of the scholars' rhetorical display. Her use of repetition and context certainly reveals the exegetes' objectivity as less than objective, her revelation being a magnificent accomplishment in itself. What the Wife accomplishes, essentially, is the deconstruction of discourse to reveal the structures of ideology and self-interest that always lie behind it.

The Wife's engagement with the authorities reveals that an insightful individual may appropriate and reformulate problematic discourses so as to accommodate a greater diversity of life practices. The Wife, though she may very well be illiterate, refers to the words of the authorities as "texts" (l. 346), adopts a posture of seasoned disbelief, and refers to her own experience of widowhood as a means of refutation. Her combative engagement with the discourse unmasks the gendered equations that are instilled through language. Her prologue may seem absurd and finally dismissable by her fellow pilgrims, but even heretical discourse, as Bourdieu notes, ultimately derives its own legitimacy by gaining the attention of the "authorized" group.[21] By uttering what has been unsaid, by making publicly known those experiences that would otherwise have remained unformulated, the unorthodox may also eventually achieve legitimation.

Although the newly widowed Criseyde's discursive and behavioral tactics, almost deliberately minimizing her own effectiveness as a judge and decision maker, seem superficially more passive than the Wife of Bath's, they too initially replicate an ideological and discursive tradition that exploits all single women and widows in particular. Criseyde differs from her counterpart, Dido, in that the former reflects upon the dilemma of the widowed state. But because she is (at least initially) not a good judge of people or consequences, and because she models a reactive rather than active decision process, she exercises only a minimal effect upon her environment. Not until she becomes an adept manipulator of the very discourse that objectifies and delimits widows — that is, not until she becomes the Wife of Bath — can she effect the kinds of changes in her situation that will ensure her survival.

Criseyde's initial appearance in widow's garb signals the extent to which she attempts to mold her body to prescribed notions of widowhood. Her black dress, her isolated position as she watches public ceremonies, her avoidance of public appear-

---

[20] Dinshaw, *Chaucer's Sexual Poetics*, 122.
[21] Bourdieu, *Outline*, 171.

ance, and her mention of the obligatory period of mourning conform to the standards of medieval conduct books concerned with regulating the behavior of the widow's marginalized body.[22] Yet Criseyde's attempts to adhere to the outward signs of humility conflict with her still sensuous physical body, which attracts the gaze of the unmaturated Troilus. Indeed, Criseyde's widowed status seems at least part of the attraction she holds for the stricken Troilus. The description of her "makeles" beauty follows fast upon her most noticeable feature, the "widewes habit blak" that she wears (I.170–172). The one seems almost dependent on the other:

> Nas nevere yet seyn thyng to ben preysed derre,
> Nor under cloude blak so bright a sterre
> As was Criseyde, as folk seyde everichone
> That hir behelden in hir blake wede. (I.174–177)

As Criseyde stands "ful lowe and stille allone" (I.178), Troilus passes. Curiously, Troilus himself is scanning the crowds, looking at each of the ladies to see "[w]her so she were of town or of withoute" (I.270). He judges each woman, in other words, according to her social appropriateness to the city — how and where she fits into Troy itself. These details indicate that it may be Criseyde's isolation as a widow, combined with Troilus's unspoken interest in locating socially detached ladies, that makes her particularly attractive to him. We know her widowhood makes her vulnerable, because her defenselessness is stated explicitly in the text: when Pandarus accosts her with the tale of Troilus's love, she "wel neigh starf for feere" that Pandarus might abandon her if she does not agree to meet Troilus, for "she was the ferfulleste wight / That myghte be" (II.450–451). Yet paradoxically her attempts to conform to a standard of humble bereavement and to speak and act according to the narrow societal expectation for widows make her not only more attractive, but also more available.

Even in these first appearances Criseyde attempts to use the discourses available to widows in order to prolong Pandarus's protection of her. She is not entirely without the resources to survive, although as a tyro in handling her new position she is easily manipulated by Troilus and Pandarus. She understands the necessity of performing roles, enjoining herself to go along with Pandarus's outrageous plea ("It nedeth me ful sleighly for to pleie," II.462), and she also understands the importance of reading her surroundings, even if she is unsure of how to go about grounding those readings. Indeed, language manipulation seems to be the key to her survival. Yet her "headlessness" becomes apparent when repeated attempts to read or to speak — two kinds of language acts that might otherwise inform and project the feminine viewpoint — are deliberately interrupted by the men in her life who would rather see her embodied in another role. Repeated references to moments of interrupted reading and writing surround Criseyde, signaling both her attempt to engage language acts and her inability to complete them. Pandarus

---

[22] See Margaret Hallissy's description of these rules in *Clean Maids, True Wives, Steadfast Widows: Chaucer's Women and Medieval Codes of Conduct* (Westport, CT, 1993), 140–41.

prevents Criseyde from finishing a history of Thebes in Book II, hinting that a more appropriate kind of reading might be a book about love (II.94–97); critics have noted that had she been allowed to continue, Criseyde might have gained insight into Troy's fate by noting its analogous relationship to Thebes'.[23] She would certainly have empathized with the widows and war wives of Statius's epic, who are allowed untypically large space for expressing their anger and grief at their abandonment.[24] Yet this moment of potential self-discovery is obstructed, as is the possibility of connecting on a psychological level with the experiences of other widowed women.

These moments of interrupted reading are complemented by incidents signaling that Criseyde's role is being actively "written" for her by her antagonists. Pandarus (and to some extent Troilus) attempts to force a romanticized role upon Criseyde that not only neglects but aggravates the complicated set of fears with which she grapples. Criseyde's famous dream, in which an eagle rips out her heart and replaces it with Troilus' (II.925–931), does not merely indicate that she has fallen in love with Troilus. The violence portrayed in the tearing out of her own physical heart and the implanting of another that is not her own powerfully suggests that Criseyde has implicitly accepted the re-embodiment Troilus and Pandarus imagine for her. In a scene immediately following, Pandarus thrusts Troilus's letter forcefully down Criseyde's "bosom" (II.1155) because she will not accept it willingly, imposing an inscription of love upon her that metaphorically mirrors the reinscription of self that has already begun. Moreover, it is not enough that simply following their desires for her is, for the time being, in her best interest. She must truly make those desires her own. She must love Troilus, become for him the courtly heroine, and acknowledge, with her dream, that the fantasy element inherent in her widowed status has for all intents and purposes erased her previous selfhood.

In Criseyde, then, we witness a curious phenomenon in which the widow not only provides a fantasy site upon which the unmaturated male may project his own longings and ideals, but actually enacts that fantasy, as if she herself begins to believe in the image thrust upon her. This fantasy remains only as long as Criseyde remains single and widowed. Although the affair lasts over three years, the possibility of remarriage never emerges, despite the threat of the lovers' imminent separation. Troilus briefly contemplates the option of asking his father for Criseyde, but rejects the idea out of hand with the double justification that his father, having already agreed to Criseyde's trade for Antenor, would not alter a decision once made, and that, furthermore, to request Criseyde would be a kind of "accusement" against her (IV.556). Both excuses seem weak, given their lack of explanation or justification in the text, especially since Chaucer deliberately omits the more legitimate justification Boccaccio provided in his original version: that Criseida was of too low

---

[23] See especially Winthrop Wetherbee, *Chaucer and the Poets: An Essay on Troilus and Criseyde* (Ithaca, NY, 1984); David Anderson, "Theban History in Chaucer's *Troilus*," *Studies in the Age of Chaucer* 4 (1982): 109–33; Catherine Sanok, "Criseyde, Cassandre, and the *Thebaid*," *Studies in the Age of Chaucer* 20 (1998): 41–71.

[24] Sanok, "Criseyde, Cassandre, and the *Thebaid*," 43.

a degree for Troiolo's father to consent to their match. Boccaccio plausibly explains the impossibility of their forging a public relationship. But Chaucer offers no such condition; to the contrary, Criseyde has been described as being of equal worth to Troilus: she is "of good name and wisdom and manere ... and ek of gentilesse" (I.880–881). Instead Troilus offers to steal away with her — a much less honorable suggestion, and one which provokes Criseyde's sorrowful sighs. In the absence of convincing explanations, Troilus's unwillingness to publicly protect his mistress is suspect. The fantasy element of the relationship is contingent upon Criseyde's singleness; only as long as she allows Troilus to play the role of courtly lover does she fulfil his projection of himself as a masculine presence in Troy.

It is only when her own safety is jeopardized by her role in this game that Criseyde begins to reject it and to create a new identity for herself outside Troy. Book V is permeated by a new kind of action, as Criseyde begins to appropriate the discourses of the feminine for her new purpose. The first instance of this emerges when Criseyde invents a ruse to deceive her father: she will "enchaunten [him] with . . . sawes" (IV.1395) in order to hide her intention to escape. The wording is significant insofar as it underscores Criseyde's growing awareness of the power of a language that superficially corresponds to expectation but in reality provides a mask for a concealed agenda. Chaucer's inserted comment on the intended deceit — "treweliche ... I fynde / That al this thyng was seyd of good entente" (IV.1415–1416) — seems to indicate his own conviction that lies may be justified when love is at stake. But more important, it draws attention to the change that most characterizes the once-more-to-be-abandoned Criseyde. By the end of the book she recognizes the importance of fashioning her identity for males who are ready and willing to impose stereotypes of widowhood upon her. The cruel letter Criseyde writes to Troilus from the Greek camp, after she has already involved herself with Diomede, is the model of deception and innuendo, fully exploiting the expectations she knows Troilus has for her and at the same time making it plain that she can see through his own game. Deliberately rendering the inclination of her own heart ambiguous, she tells Troilus that his letters of complaint, conspicuously splattered with tears, "Conceyved hath myn hertes pietee" (V.1598). Have Troilus's letters "comprehended" the pity of Criseyde's heart, or have they merely "conceived" them? The evasive wording makes both interpretations possible. She further points out that Troilus thinks only of his own "plesaunce" (V.1608) when he imagines his relationship with her, and that he "ne do but holden ... [her] in honde" (V.1615), a comment that again resonates with a back-handed reprimand. Instead of decisively breaking off the relationship, however, Criseyde uses the very language Troilus has already used regarding his own lack of action toward her, claiming that she must not return at once lest people talk. This almost deliberately false-seeming concern might be construed as a desire on Criseyde's part to maintain amity with her old lover: that is, Criseyde certainly seems aware of the necessity of keeping her reputation at home as untainted as possible. But it may also be read as the redeploying of the very discourses that had been used on her to inscribe her as the type of courtly lady Troilus desired. The departing Criseyde understands not only how she has been embodied through language, but also how she can use it to re-embody herself.

Criseyde's later medieval mythographers failed to read her character as sympathetically as Chaucer. Despite the narrator's many attempts to mitigate or contextualize the widow's actions, Criseyde's abandonment of Troilus for another more expedient protector merely fulfilled already entrenched expectations about faithless widows. For later medieval writers, the only conceivable motivation for a woman's "slydynge corage" [V.825] is her intransigent lust and inherently fickle nature. In the least vituperous accounts, Criseyde's faithlessness is compared with the falseness of Lady Fortune.[25] In others, following Henryson, Criseyde is punished with prostitution and leprosy for her betrayal — the latter disfiguration deemed a commensurate recompense for the misuse of a body intended for fidelity.[26] The elaborate subjectivity elaborated by Chaucer, in which the individual's will is buried behind layers of institutionalized discourse and bias that restrict its powers of self-enactment, reverts either to pure reductivism or gendered willfullness among the later Chaucerians. Further, the widow's double role of penitent and harlot elide in the form of a sophisticated beguiling seducer, who, following Criseyde and the Wife's examples, uses artifice and play-acting to manipulate social judgment and create a space for further acts of wantonness. Society's implication in the creation of "sely" widows remains ignored.

Laurel Amtower
San Diego State University

---

[25] See, for example, John Lydgate's *Troy Book*, ed. Henry Bergen, EETS e.s. 97, 103, 106, 126 (London, 1906–1935; repr. New York, 1975), and his "Amor Vincit Omnia Mentiris Quod Pecunia," in which he refers to Criseyde as "A false serpent of chaunge and variaunce" (l. 20), in *The Minor Poems of John Lydgate, Part 2*, ed. Henry Noble MacCracken, EETS o.s. 192 (London, 1934), 744–49; Stephen Hawes' *The Pastime of Pleasure*, ed. William Edward Mead, EETS o.s. 173 (London, 1928), 1332 ("full of doublenesse"); and John Skelton's *Phyllyp Sparowe* in *The Complete English Poems*, ed. John Scattergood (Harmondsworth, 1983), 88–89 (lines 677–723).

[26] Robert Henryson, *The Testament of Cresseid and Other Poems*, ed. Hugh MacDiarmid (Harmondsworth, 1973), 31.

7

(RE)CREATIONS OF A SINGLE WOMAN:

Discursive Realms of the Wife of Bath

Alone among the pilgrims, the Wife of Bath bears a title suggesting her marital status. She might have been designated the "Weaver of Bath," a name reflecting her occupation, like that of the other travelers. However, while the narrator of the *Prologue* praises her skill at the craft of weaving, her profession appears inconsequential. She is primarily seen as a weaver of tales, whose craft is manipulation and whose art lies in matters of love. Although the appellation "Wife" implies that her social function is based on marriage rather than on her work, the word "Wife" in medieval times could refer more broadly to all women, married or not.[1] The more inclusive title allows for the multitude of representations of her and by her, as wife and widow — a married woman and a single woman.

Astute readers should not allow Alisoun's title, "Wife," to contain her linguistically, since as a teller of tales on the pilgrimage she is not a wife, but a single woman: a widow. As a widow she creates a new category of single woman that draws on the experience of marriage but is activated only after she is free of marriage. As a widow she has more freedom to travel and to speak; the pilgrimage itself provides the venue for discursive manipulation. Her ability to gloss scripture, her androgynous characteristics, her independence as a single traveler: all help to form a picture of her as single woman with agency and power, a single woman who often eludes the social constructs that would limit her.

Admittedly, the images of Alisoun in marriages to five different husbands reinforce the idea of her as "Wife" in its narrow sense, and the imagined possibilities she creates in the *Tale* ultimately lead to marriage. Yet the narrative voice that creates the fictions of texts, the fictions of identity, and the fictions of marriage is a single voice of a single woman: a widow who tells the tales of wives. Only after

---

[1] Originally "Wife" was synonymous with "woman in general"; see the *Oxford English Dictionary*, s.v. "wife," 1.

her marriages have ended can she relate the experience of wifehood; only after she is widowed, in other words, can she construct her married identity at all. Although Alisoun's colorful discursive creations of marriage may act to obfuscate her singlehood, she simultaneously foregrounds her singleness in practice as an independent woman, alone on her journey. Moreover, her singleness allows her an authoritative space as narrator. The power that she seeks in both her *Prologue* and *Tale* — the power of female sovereignty in marriage — pales beside the power of discourse that she manipulates through the constructive narratives of a single woman. The spaces that she creates for agency within and without marriage are created discursively, and because she understands the dynamics of roles, she is powerful in a variety of discursive contexts. She can hold her own in the story, in whatever roles she creates for herself, and she can hold her own as a single woman — a story-telling pilgrim alone on her journey.

Many critics have noted Alisoun's discursive proficiency by focusing on the creations of her narrative — portraits, as it were, of herself in her marriages. However, focusing on the speaker is as important as examining the content of her speeches. It is as a *femme sole* that Alisoun takes us on a semantic journey through her *Prologue* and *Tale*, creating spaces for agency, appropriating male narratives, tracing roles of power, and exploring various imagined possibilities for social practice.[2] In the first words of her *Prologue*, Alisoun establishes the centrality of text, discourse, and construction. Striking a flagrant pose, she, a single woman, usurps the position of the single cleric as she recognizes and challenges the textual constructions of the Church Fathers, replacing them with her own. Later, the textual constructions of her husband Janekyn become the focus of the crucial confrontation with him. Near the end of the *Prologue*, just before she is about to create her own *Tale*,[3] she indicates her consciousness of the power of discourse:

> Who peyntede the leon, tel me who?
> By God, if wommen hadde writen stories,
> As clerkes han withinne hire oratories,

---

[2] Lee Patterson uses the term *femme sole* in its legal sense: "In Chaucer's world a woman in business would have been identified as a *femme sole*, a single woman, whether she was married or not": " 'Experience woot well it is noght so': Marriage and the Pursuit of Happiness in the *Wife of Bath's Prologue* and *Tale*," in *Geoffrey Chaucer: The Wife of Bath*, ed. Peter G. Beidler, Case Studies in Contemporary Criticism (New York, 1996), 133–54, here 135.

[3] Bartlett J. Whiting states, "There can be little doubt that Chaucer originally intended what is now the *Shipman's Tale* for the Wife of Bath": "*The Wife of Bath's Tale*" in *Sources and Analogues of Chaucer's Canterbury Tales*, ed. W[illiam] F[rank] Bryan and Germaine Dempster (New York, 1941), 223.

The connection between the *Prologue* and the *Tale* is most often seen in the similarities between Alisoun and the Hag. See Muriel Bowden, *A Reader's Guide to Geoffrey Chaucer* (London, 1965), 40; Derek Traversi, *The Canterbury Tales: A Reading* (London, 1983), 117–19; and Anne Wilson, *Magical Thought in Creative Writing: The Distinctive Roles of Fantasy and Imagination in Fiction* (Exeter, 1983), 91.

> They wolde han writen of men moore wikkednesse
> Than al the mark of Adam may redresse.[4]

It might seem that Alisoun is doomed before she begins to paint her own Lion, since she cannot escape social constraints: equipped only with the tools society has given her, she paints with textual pigments already discolored by misogyny on a canvas of limited space; as a result, her *Tale* may seem only to replicate her own world and reinforce some of its binarisms. And yet, overall, her narratives in both the *Prologue* and the *Tale* buoyantly register challenges and successes: through a dazzling series of fictions, Alisoun re-creates socially constructed dichotomies only to invert or deconstruct them. The initial dichotomy of married/not married is collapsed by her ability to occupy both polarities simultaneously; moreover, the spaces created within the constraints of marriage are discursive formations, and they are the creations of a single woman.

Crucial to understanding Alisoun and the effect of her discourse is the recognition that she re-presents and enacts several binarisms simultaneously. In addition to seeing her play both roles in the single/married dichotomy, we can see her also as both controller and controlled. This binarism relates directly to another: male/female. The influence of Venus and Mars at Alisoun's birth suggests androgyny, and in her texts she adopts both male and female roles. Her own narrative voice is androgynous: underlying it is the male poet's voice, and indeed the very words she speaks about herself are often taken from misogynistic texts. At the same time, she uses the controlling male roles of narrator and/or preacher to speak with a woman's voice as she re-creates herself. Even while she embodies the misogynistic views of women, she asserts her right to be that which she has discursively formed from the perspective of a single woman: a woman who challenges those views within or without marriage. Alisoun appears androgynous not only in her role as narrator, but also in the roles she adopts, as she assumes the male prerogative of glossing texts and preaching, or as she becomes the dominant partner in each of her marriages. Finally, she creates resemblances between herself, a single female traveler, and the male wanderer in her *Tale*, the Knight, as she simultaneously enacts male and female roles and continues to invert and collapse them.

At the beginning of her *Prologue*, the image of Alisoun as a "prechour" emphasizes her widowed status, even as she argues for marriage. She is a solitary figure playing the single role of a clergyman, attempting to create a space that allows her agency. She appropriates the discursive power of the ecclesiastical authorities as she steps into their role. Her interpretative manipulation is necessary since the texts themselves create a distorted view of women and reduce them to stereotypes.[5]

---

[4] Geoffrey Chaucer, *The Wife of Bath's Prologue and Tale* in *The Riverside Chaucer*, gen. ed. Larry D. Benson, 3rd ed. (Boston, 1987), ll. 692–696. All quotations are taken from this edition. Subsequent citations are given parenthetically.

[5] For an insightful discussion of this issue see R. W. Hanning, "Roasting a Friar, Mis-Taking a Wife, and Other Acts of Textual Harassment in Chaucer's *Canterbury Tales*," *Studies in the Age of Chaucer* 7 (1985): 3–21. Also see E. Talbot Donaldson, who recognizes the "willful inaccuracy"

When Alisoun assumes a male role, she creates an enlarged space for female roles, and the androgynous moment challenges the male/female dichotomy. It is not so much that she pits her "experience" against the "authority" of the Church Fathers as that she manages to occupy both the female position of experience and the male position of "auctoritee." When she turns the tables on "auctoritee" by using the tactics she has learned from the authorities, the power structure is not only inverted but even collapsed for a moment as she manages to occupy, simultaneously, polar positions: male/female; experience/"auctoritee."

Alisoun is highly defensive; she has apparently been accused of breaking ecclesiastical law by having been married five times. Since scripture records that Christ had gone to only one wedding, for some theologians it follows that she should have married only once. This interpretation of the gospel (John 2:1) comes directly from St. Jerome's *Epistola Adversus Jovinianum*;[6] the first glosser we see distorting texts, then, is not Alisoun, but her unnamed accuser, following Jerome, who provides the original misinterpretation. The second basis of her alleged misbehavior comes from another of Jerome's distortions: the story of Christ's encounter with the Samaritan woman who has had five husbands. Again interpreting beyond the text, Jerome admits he is baffled by Christ's statement, "Ye [the Samaritan woman] have noon hosebonde; for thou hast hadde fyue hosebondis, and he that thou hast, is not thin hosebonde."[7] Apparently Jerome has failed to understand that Christ is objecting not to the woman's five previous marriages, but to the fact that she is not married to the man with whom she is now living. Defending herself, Alisoun calls upon a conflicting passage from Jerome himself, one that supports remarriage and cites biblical examples of its validity. Jerome's authoritative text that would instruct her is exposed as distorted when she makes its contradictions visible. This single woman makes a solid point in arguing for her right to remarry.

Alisoun makes use of Church authority — distorted or not — to support her case once again as she calls upon St. Paul, who sanctions marriage directly in the scriptures. She can thereby validate her own behavior: "so nys it no repreve / To

---

of St. Jerome: *The Swan at the Well: Shakespeare Reading Chaucer* (New Haven, 1985), 136. On the other hand, there are a surprising number of modern critics who still condemn Alisoun and her strategies of glossing. For instance, Dieter Mehl describes her as a "shrew of the first order, obsessed by her lust for absolute power, as the ... quarrelsome, domineering ... female who ... suppresses, demoralizes and ruins her husbands" and refers to her glossing as a "pseudo-learned refutation of ... Christian ideals" that ultimately makes her position "appear as comical and absurd": *Geoffrey Chaucer: An Introduction to his Narrative Poetry* (Cambridge, 1986), 147. For a similar view see Robert O. Payne, *Geoffrey Chaucer*, 2nd ed., Twayne's English Authors Series (Boston, 1986), 119–20.

[6] Benson, *The Riverside Chaucer*, 865 n. 9–24.

[7] John 4:18, in *The Holy Bible Containing the Old and New Testaments, With the Apocryphal Books, in the Earliest English Versions Made From the Latin Vulgate by John Wycliffe and His Followers* (1850), ed. Josiah Forshall and Frederic Madden, 4 vols. (Oxford, 1982), 4: 244. I use this translation of the *Vulgate*, as it is contemporary with Chaucer.

wedde me, if that my make dye, / Withouten excepcion of bigamye" (84–86). Alisoun's repeated references to 1 Corinthians 7 occur in a passage which the Wycliffe translation of the Vulgate Bible designates as compulsory public reading:

> But for fornycacioun eche man haue his owne wijf, and ech womman haue hir owne hosebonde. The husband 3elde dette to the wijf, and also the wijf to the hosebonde. The womman hath not power of hir bodi, but the hosebonde; and the hosebonde hath not power of his bodi, but the womman.[8]

Of course, Jerome repeats some of this material as well, but the inconsistencies between texts and within the texts themselves enable Alisoun to recognize shrewdly that a misrepresentation of a higher authority is being imposed upon her. Having learned from "auctoritee" that texts may be manipulated, she can do more than point out contradictions: she can manipulate texts for herself. The first time she does so, she distorts through omission: "I have the power durynge al my lyf / Upon [my husband's] propre body, and noght he" (158–159). Absent from Alisoun's version is any mention of the preceding line of scripture endowing husbands with the same power over wives. Immediately, she elicits a reaction from the Pardoner, who starts up and exclaims, "'Now, dame,' quod he, 'by God and by Seint John! / Ye been a noble prechour in this cas'" (164–165). Significantly, he associates her with a churchman as soon as she is guilty of distortion, catching her in the act of discursive creation.

Throughout the *Prologue* Alisoun can be seen struggling to escape the authoritative texts which control her. Barbara Gottfried maintains that she cannot:

> Even as she attempts a deconstruction of patriarchal literature in an experiential revision of it, the Wife necessarily falls short of the goal of overcoming authority because she can only define herself in relation to that authority.[9]

---

[8] 1 Corinthians 7:2–4, in *The Holy Bible . . . by John Wycliffe*, 348.

[9] Barbara Gottfried, "Conflict and Relationship, Sovereignty and Survival: Parables of Power in the *Wife of Bath's Prologue*," *Chaucer Review* 19 (1985): 202–24, here 203. Among critics who agree with Gottfried on this issue is Lee Patterson: "Try as she (and Chaucer) might, she remains confined within the prison house of masculine language; she brilliantly rearranges and deforms her authorities to enable them to disclose new areas of experience, but she remains dependent on them for her voice": *Chaucer and the Subject of History* (Madison, 1991), 313. Carolyn Dinshaw disagrees, proposing that Alisoun "*mimics* the operations of patriarchal discourse" and that she is "[f]ar from being trapped within the 'prison house' of antifeminist discourse." Applying the words of Luce Irigaray to the case of Alisoun, Dinshaw states that Alisoun "'convert[s] a form of subordination into an affirmation'": *Chaucer's Sexual Poetics* (Madison, 1989), 115. Laurie Finke suggests that by placing misogynistic words in the mouth of Alisoun, Chaucer "re-contextualizes them" so that they "enter into a dialogue with the material and historical conditions of existence" for a middle-class woman of the time: "'All is for to selle': Breeding Capital in the Wife of Bath's Prologue and Tale," in *Geoffrey Chaucer: The Wife of Bath*, 173. Cf. Barrie Ruth Straus's excellent discussion, "The Subversive Discourse of the Wife of Bath: Phallocentric Discourse and the Imprisonment of Criticism," in *Chaucer*, ed. Valerie Allen and Ares Axiotis, New Casebooks (New York, 1996), 126–44. On "auctoritee" see Suzanne Reynolds, "Inventing Authority: Glossing,

When we see her embodying the stereotypes of anti-feminist literature, it does seem as though she cannot extricate herself from the misogynist texts which have formed her. As Judith Ferster points out, the unflattering picture of womanhood in the *Roman de la Rose* exactly parallels Alisoun's depiction of herself:

> She is, as others have noted, the embodiment of clerical antifeminism. Everything they accuse women of being, she claims to be. She admits her delight in sex ... her love of wealth and power, her ability to deceive men. But she claims to be not merely the antifeminists' nightmare ... but their creation. ...[10]

As a discursive creation of the patriarchy she fights, Alisoun might seem doomed to fulfill negative stereotypes. Yet in her narration Alisoun seems to me to escape that fate as she uses her discursive deftness to accrue power and to invert and collapse binary positions that would entrap her. She knows that her only defense is a strong offense and that her game threatens her life. Her various manipulations must succeed, she realizes, "Or elles often tyme hadde I been spilt" (388). "Spilt" is often interpreted as "ruined," but it could also mean "killed," and R. M. Lumiansky's edition translates it that way.[11] Benson interprets "spilt" to mean "ruined." The *OED* lists "killed" as an alternate meaning for the word. The latter usage is appropriate, since Alisoun has been a battered wife. Her demand for sovereignty arises from necessity: her literal and figurative survival depend on a reversal of power.

Although Alisoun is in control at the end of the *Prologue*, her tenuous victory is abated by the battle. Experience triumphs over authority, as evidenced by Janekyn's burned book, and that experience — or learning through sensory data — prevails, but Alisoun's senses pay a great price. "Auctoritee" — in the form of the book — literally damages her sense of hearing when Janekyn hits her with it; that injury is an outward sign of the inner damage authority has done to her. It is no surprise then that her ongoing struggle in the *Prologue* leads to the fantasy of uncontested female sovereignty in her *Tale*. Although the vivid creations of Alisoun are images of a married woman or one who wants to be married, her single state foregrounds the boundaries around her marital episodes. She narrates as a single woman, speaking from the gaps between marriages about marriage itself. In the *Prologue* a single Alisoun presents a narrative of her married selves; in her *Tale*, the storytelling single woman will align herself with single figures on a different sort of pilgrimage.

In *The Wife of Bath's Tale*, Alisoun constructs the kind of world to which she has alluded in the very first lines of her *Prologue*: a place where "authority" does not exist. Authority looms large in the realm of the *Prologue* and hinders the construction of a unified female subject in that sphere; her attempt to attach herself to the centricity of authoritative texts forges moments of challenge and success, but in

---

Literacy and the Classical Text," in *Prestige, Authority and Power in Late Medieval Manuscripts and Texts*, ed. Felicity Riddy (Woodbridge, 2000), 7–16.

[10] Judith Ferster, *Chaucer on Interpretation* (Cambridge, 1985), 124.

[11] R. M. Lumiansky, ed., *Chaucer's Canterbury Tales* (New York, 1971).

another way it emphasizes her marginality, since the binarisms re-assert themselves. In the fantasy of her *Tale*, however, she can try to create a world of experience alone.[12] Although Alisoun's foray into painting her own lion is not entirely successful, the discursive realm of fantasy having its limitations too, neither is it ultimately self-defeating.

Critics have often commented that Alisoun turns to inversion as a favorite strategy both in the *Prologue* and the *Tale*.[13] I want to advance an argument for the particular way that she accomplishes that inversion as narrator of the *Tale* by establishing a link between herself, a single wandering woman, and the subject of the *Tale*, the Knight, a single wandering man. Such a connection does not obviate the more evident parallels between the aging Alisoun and the old Hag, but by attaching herself to more than one role — the single woman as narrator, Hag, and Knight — she can enact both dichotomies of male/female oppositions. Alisoun's description of her astrological make-up in the *Prologue* foreshadows this androgyny, for she is not just a female Venus; she has been influenced by the male Mars as well:

> For certes, I am al Venerien
> In feelynge, and myn herte is Marcien.
> Venus me yaf my lust, my likerousnesse,
> And Mars yaf me my sturdy hardynesse;
> Myn ascendent was Taur, and Mars therinne. (609–613)[14]

The merging of male and female as an important part of Alisoun's character in the *Prologue* prepares us to find the double connection in the *Tale*, for Alisoun reflects

---

[12] Stewart Justman sees inversion in a different way: the bourgeois values that Alisoun voices are what turn the medieval world order upside down. He also views her *Tale* as an escape to romance so that she may elude "auctoritee," but he sees her construction of identity in economic rather than gender terms: "Trade as Pudendum: Chaucer's *Wife of Bath*," *Chaucer Review* 28 (1994): 344–45. Derek Traversi perceives Alisoun's fantasy not as taking the tale out of reach of authority but rather "out of the realm of common experience": *The Canterbury Tales*, 113.

See, for a valuable discussion of the way that the genre of fantasy can be used to re-shape the social order, Louise O. Fradenburg, " 'Fulfild of fairye': The Social Meaning of Fantasy in the *Wife of Bath's Prologue* and *Tale*," in *Geoffrey Chaucer: The Wife of Bath*, 205–20.

[13] Walter C. Long's discussion of inversion is especially astute. He sees Alisoun's rhetorical aim throughout as "the redressing of an imbalance" and recognizes that her "radical female 'maistree' is rhetorically necessary to counterbalance a masculine 'maistree' that *defines itself* as over against a feminine 'lack'." Any hierarchy, in which a superior defines itself by its inferior, may be undone, Long says, by reversal of those positions: "The Wife as Moral Revolutionary," *Chaucer Review* 20 (1986): 273–84, here 276.

[14] Walter Clyde Curry maintains that Mars has distorted Alisoun's physical appearance: Venus alone would have made her lovely, but the interference of Mars has caused her complexion to be ruddy, her personality boisterous, and her body stocky: *Chaucer and the Mediaeval Sciences* (New York, 1926), 108–9. In addition to these traditional male characteristics, the presence of Mars as God of War would have created another male component, since, as Caroline Walker Bynum points out, "images of warfare . . . were to medieval people clearly male images. . . .": *Jesus as Mother: Studies in the Spirituality of the High Middle Ages* (Berkeley, 1982), 139.

certain aspects of both Knight and Hag. The male aspects of her image augment the view of her as single: no longer is she creating stories about her married selves. In the *Tale* we see instead a representation of the single Alisoun, an independent traveler who has much in common with the Knight of her story. At the outset the Knight enjoys a privileged position as male subject, but as the fiction develops, he will enter the experience of women. The Hag, a single woman beginning as "other," will in some ways adopt the dominant position of men. Similarities between the *Prologue* and the *Tale* also link Alisoun to both figures, and an exploration of these likenesses discloses new discursive challenges to the status quo, as well as the limitations of female experience even in fairyland.

The *Wife of Bath's Tale* and Gower's *Tale of Florent*, which share elements of their common sources,[15] differ significantly in their main characters, the Knights. The "lusty bachelor" of Alisoun's *Tale* stands apart from his counterparts in all the source tales and analogues because he commits a rape. This most brutal form of male oppression curiously serves to connect him in several ways to Alisoun and to the *Prologue*. First, the rape is a sexual offense. Alisoun begins her *Prologue* with a defense of herself, since she has been accused of committing "sexual crimes" against the authority of the Church. The lust of both Alisoun and the Knight has placed them in opposition to law, a circumstance which establishes the second connection: the Knight, as criminal, becomes a disenfranchised figure with only a peripheral status in his society. The social position of the Knight is further marginalized when the central ruling authority, through Alisoun's reversal of the power structure, becomes female-dominated: Guinevere, not Arthur, will judge him. Now accountable to women for his behavior, the Knight, who has ruined a woman, begins to experience the state of women, who, since Eve, have been blamed for the ruin of man. Just as Alisoun, unconsenting inheritor of generations of guilt, must wrestle with the male authorities of her society, the guilty Knight must face the female authorities of his.

In addition to the "guilty" woman and the guilty Knight and their subsequent marginal social positions, a third connection between the *Tale* and the *Prologue* is established by the rape, which symbolically represents the conflict between authority and experience. The authority of the law says he "sholde han lost his heed" (892) for raping a maiden, but that punishment is not carried out. This reflects a similar discrepancy between theory and practice in Chaucer's world, where rape, technically a felony, was treated merely as a misdemeanor. Neither the Arthurian

---

[15] G. H. Maynadier exhaustively surveys the appearance of the "loathly lady" in the literature of western Europe in *The Wife of Bath's Tale: Its Sources and Analogues* (London, 1901; repr. New York, 1972). Whiting reprints three analogues: the contemporary *Tale of Florent*, by Gower, and two tales from the following century, the *Marriage of Sir Gawaine* and the *Weddynge of Sir Gawen and Dame Ragnell* (*Sources and Analogues*, 224–64). Anne Wilson discusses two Irish versions to which Chaucer may have had access, namely "Lughaid Laeighe" and the *Temair Breg*, in *Magical Thought in Creative Writing*, 82–83. See the excellent comparative study by Olga C. M. Fischer, "Gower's *Tale of Florent* and Chaucer's *Wife of Bath's Tale*: A Stylistic Comparison," *English Studies* 66 (1985): 205–25.

punishment for rape (castration and blinding) nor the fourteenth-century punishment (hanging) was effected in practice; the law forbade the crime, but society overlooked it.[16] A passage from *The Art of Courtly Love* by Andreas Capellanus even seems to encourage it:

> If you [male aristocrat] should, by some chance, fall in love with [a peasant woman] . . . do not hesitate to take what you seek and to embrace [her] by force. . . . [U]se a little compulsion as a convenient cure for their shyness.[17]

In this contradiction between authority and experience, the Knight is saved by experience; his escape from authority through experience mirrors the escape Alisoun desires. When Arthur relinquishes his right to judge to Guinevere, the reversal of agency from male to female is a direct part of Alisoun's wish-fulfillment in the *Tale*, since patriarchal rule has been suspended for her counterpart, the Knight. The inversion reflects back to the *Prologue*.[18] And yet, if we see Alisoun in both male and female roles, the scene of judgment is more complex than a simple reversal of the gendered power binarism might indicate: her gender identifies her with the authorities now in power, the judge, but she retains the connections established earlier with the Knight, the judged. Alisoun occupies multiple positions, and the moment is fantasy in perfection: females rule and their rule is wise, but their wisdom comes from having had the female *experience* of the Knight.

Authority also gives way to experience in the Knight's punishment, for it is not through texts that he must learn the answer to Alisoun/Guinevere's question, "What thyng is it that wommen moost desiren?" (905). The task is appropriate for a male who has utterly disregarded a female's choice by violating her, since he will now have to atone for the injury by concerning himself with her wishes. In such a way the key question establishes a direct link with Alisoun, since what will save the life of the male sexual offender will, figuratively, save her life as well. The pre-Freudian quest to know what women want is implicit in Alisoun's discursive search for self as a single woman. So, in a sense, the journey to gain insight upon which the Knight embarks is analogous to Alisoun's pilgrimage, and the Knight's need to discover what women want is her own.

When the Knight first begins to "wendeth forth his weye" (918), he receives as many incorrect answers to his question as Alisoun has been given in her life. Then suddenly the narrator digresses with a tale of Midas, ostensibly told to point out yet

---

[16] Robert J. Blanch, " 'Al Was This Land Fulfild of Fayerye': The Thematic Employment of Force, Willfulness, and Legal Conventions in Chaucer's *Wife of Bath's Tale*," *Studia Neophilologica* 57 (1985): 41–51, here 42–43. See also the discussion of "common law" and "statute law" concerning rape in H. Marshall Leicester, Jr., " 'My bed was ful of verray blood' ': Subject, Dream, and Rape in the *Wife of Bath's Prologue* and *Tale*" in *Geoffrey Chaucer: The Wife of Bath*, 244–48.

[17] Andreas Capellanus, *The Art of Courtly Love*, trans. John Jay Parry (New York, 1990), 150, quoted in Blanch, " 'Al Was This Land Fulfild of Fayerye'," 42.

[18] Anne Wilson notes these reversals in the *Tale* and the way that they transfer "power from men to women — an activity within her marriages which she has already recounted in her Prologue": *Magical Thought in Creative Writing*, 88–89.

another weakness of women. The story is no unrelated tangent, but provides interconnections between Alisoun and another male subject, Midas, and between Alisoun and the Hag. Each pairing replicates in a different way the tension between Alisoun's society and her struggle for power. The parallels between Alisoun and Midas reflect a common opposition to authority. In a musical contest between Apollo and Pan, Midas votes against Apollo, who then angrily changes Midas's ears to those of an ass. Since Apollo is associated with codes of law, and Pan "in general ... is amorous,"[19] Midas's choice represents a preference for love over law, and he is punished for making it. Alisoun has made a similar choice — in her case love over the law of the Church Fathers — and she too has been punished. The law of Apollo deforms Midas's ears; the law of the authoritative text literally damages Alisoun's ears.[20]

The secret in the Midas tale relates to female power and creates a link among three women: Midas's wife, the Hag, and Alisoun, since all have a secret they reveal. The picture of Midas's wife telling her husband's secret to the water is not unlike that of Dame Alisoun in the *Prologue*, who embarrasses her husbands by revealing the secrets they have told her ("To hire [her gossib] biwreyed I my conseil al," 533). The manipulative power implicit in "telling" or having a secret to tell is a small, rather ineffectual force in the relationships of husbands and wives, but one seized upon by Alisoun, who recognizes the discursive opportunity. The power in the Hag's secret has a similar, but greater import; magnified in fairyland it gives a woman complete dominance over a man, since his very life depends on learning it. As the *Tale* has it, the answer to the question, "What do women most desire?" is of course "sovereignty." This reversal of the hierarchy within the power structure, from male to female superiority, identifies Alisoun once again with both Knight and Hag, since in the *Prologue* she has played both parts: ruler and ruled.

The wedding-night encounter at the end of the *Tale* contains another series of interconnections among Alisoun, Hag, and Knight, which underscore limitations, fantasy, and sovereignty. The old woman, transformed to a young beauty, transparently reveals the aging Alisoun's wish for her lost youth; she has verbalized such a desire in the *Prologue*. The Knight can also be seen repeating an earlier experience of Alisoun's as he turns away with revulsion from the withered Hag. Alisoun, married to three old husbands in her youth, must have experienced some horror of her own in the bedroom. Although she remembers with amusement "how pitously a-nyght I made hem swynke!" (202), her sexual encounters with three old male hags — impotent besides — must not have been a romping good time for a young woman. Thus the desire for youth in the *Tale* can also be seen from the point of view of Alisoun as Knight, since both desire a younger sexual partner. The wishes of both are fulfilled: the young beauty who replaces the hag at the end of the *Tale*

---

[19] *The Oxford Classical Dictionary*, 2nd ed., ed. N. G. L. Hammond and H. H. Scullard (Oxford, 1970), 81 and 773. Cf. A. H. Griffith, s.v. "Midas," in *OCD*, 3rd ed., ed. S. Hornblower and A. Spawforth (Oxford, 1996), 978.

[20] For different connections between the Wife and Midas, see D. W. Robertson, Jr., "The Wife of Bath and Midas," *Studies in the Age of Chaucer* 6 (1984): 1–20.

reflects the youthful Janekyn who replaces the old husbands in the *Prologue*; no doubt he seems a fantasy to Alisoun after her previous mates.

The bedroom scene recalls the striking image of Alisoun as a single woman preaching in the *Prologue*, even as it continues to evoke Alisoun's earlier relationship with her fifth husband: instead of a female enduring a lesson from authoritative texts, we see a female who preaches to her husband. The single narrator of the *Prologue* and *Tale* again creates a space within marriage for women to speak. We can observe this kind of reversal elsewhere when Alisoun preaches to her old husbands and when she preaches to the pilgrims. Her sermonizing draws comment from her fellow travelers: first from the Pardoner who calls her a "noble prechour" (165), and then from the Friar who objects to her preaching: "And lete auctoritees, on Goddes name, / To prechyng and to scoles of clergye" (1276–1277). The reversal which occurs in the *Tale* identifies her closely with the Knight and repeats the attack on the authoritative texts which Janekyn has read her. At one point Janekyn torments her with anti-feminist material from the works of Valerius, presumably the *Epistola ad Rufinum*.[21] The Hag uses Valerius's tale of Tullius Hostilius (1165) to form part of her lecture for the Knight on *gentillesse*. Within her message concerning the leveling of hierarchy is an oblique reference to the Knight's conduct: "For vileyns synful dedes make a cherl," she says (1158). We see the Knight clearly entering Alisoun's experience as he listens to what might be called *The Book of Wicked Knights*.

The incongruity of Alisoun-behind-the-Hag as narrator of a sermon on equality and poverty is amusing. She seems at odds with the philosophy since the accumulation of property is one of her concerns, as is her need to assume her rightful status as the first to present the offering on Sundays. But, viewed in the light of the *Prologue*, perhaps Alisoun as the unlikely author of a lecture on *gentillesse* suggests hypocrisy in the writers of those authoritative texts and especially in Janekyn, who has read them to her. He, who has been a willing participant in a dalliance with Alisoun while she was still married to husband number four, is hardly justified in lecturing her on infidelity.

Within the *Tale*, the sermon the Hag preaches strikes an earnest note; her appeal to a higher authority resembles Alisoun's earlier need to escape from the authorities governing her. When the Hag states that "Thy gentillesse cometh fro God allone" (1162), she implies some awareness that the hierarchy which limits her and shapes her is itself a social construct; this parallels the understanding Alisoun has in the *Prologue* that the authoritative texts imposed upon her are the self-serving, man-made distortions of scripture.[22]

---

[21] Benson, *The Riverside Chaucer*, 114 n. 671–80.

[22] Stephen Knight sees a positive result from the Hag's sermon: "But when the old wife addresses her husband on what he has done wrong, the poem moves to a different plane, seeing women as a force for liberation from a whole world of masculine and aristocratic oppression, suggesting a new world of social and ethical values": *Geoffrey Chaucer* (Oxford, 1986), 102.

Only in fairyland could one break through such constructs, transcending gender and class distinctions to achieve happiness. Of course, the fantasy cannot completely overcome social codes. The Knight's choice at the end of the *Tale* reveals just how limiting the patriarchal system is to both men and women. Anti-feminist versions of female behavior appear when the Knight must decide whom he will have: a wife who is "Foul and old" but "Trew and humble" or one who is "young and fair" but who therefore attracts the attention of other men. The system which prescribes roles for women and shapes their behavior limits not only their possibilities but the choices of men as well; the Knight faces an either/or option, and it is the fictional discourse of a single female who re-shapes the notion of an ideal woman: one who collapses traditional polar stereotypes.

The Knight's voluntary subjection, which places him again in a feminine role, brings him joy — in fantasy land. His unrealistic decision to cede mastery unconditionally can perhaps be explained by the fairy-tale setting, but on a practical level it disregards his learning through the experience of occupying a female space: as a man or as a counterpart of Alisoun, he should know by now that it is better to control than be controlled. The lack of realism in his choice makes possible Alisoun's wish fulfillment since the fantasy establishes female dominance, but recognition of the resulting conclusion as preposterously unrealistic raises an intriguing question about the similar mutual bliss in the *Prologue*: was Janekyn's release of sovereignty another of Alisoun's fantasies? Earlier in the *Prologue* she has asked the other pilgrims not to be annoyed with her "If that I speke after my fantasye . . ." (190). "Fantasye" could mean "imagination" in the fourteenth century, and perhaps again Alisoun points toward the possibilities of discourse and construction.[23] If her sovereignty is fictional in the *Prologue* as well as the *Tale*, her claims based on "experience" may be diminished, but her discursive powers are thereby enlarged, and, whether Janekyn releases control or not, the possibilities for role-playing Alisoun creates are no less accessible to medieval women. If her re-creation of her marriage is fictional, then her stance as a single narrator is even more crucial. As a wife who lectures, Alisoun is beaten on the ear with her husband's book. However, as a single woman who narrates, she gets to have the last word by inventing a husband who believes in granting wives sovereignty.

Fairyland, however, does not allow Alisoun or her counterpart the Knight to elude binarisms, since they both must choose between the opposites of ruler and ruled. Even though she acts and reacts from a variety of polar positions, and, in simultaneously occupying them, collapses them, she does not consciously postulate

---

[23] In *The Riverside Chaucer* Benson interprets the line to mean "according to my fancy, desire," but the *MED* also lists "imagination" as a meaning of "fantasye" current in the fourteenth century.
Robert B. Burlin suggests that Alisoun's *Prologue* is as much "fictionalized autobiography" as the *Tale* is "autobiographical fiction": *Chaucerian Fiction* (Princeton, 1977), 222. Concurring, Lisa J. Kiser contends that Chaucer presents a narrator who deftly manipulates the distinction between fact and fiction: *Truth and Textuality in Chaucer's Poetry* (Hanover, NH, 1991), 136–37. Carolyn Dinshaw points out the similarity between the fantasy endings of both *Tale* and *Prologue*: *Chaucer's Sexual Poetics*, 129.

beyond inversion — to control rather than be controlled.[24] Alisoun discursively creates a situation of mutuality at the end of the *Tale,* but she neither sustains the concept nor presents it as a variant social practice. She re-asserts her contention that harmony is derived from female sovereignty, but, in fact, the relinquishing of mastery on both sides is the element which has effected happiness at the end of the *Tale*.[25] In this case, authority triumphs over experience: she experiences mutuality yet adheres to the binary notions inscribed within her society and authorized by it. Alisoun's identification with both the Knight and the Hag in the *Tale* allows her to move back and forth from opposite positions — and to invert them — but that flexibility offers possibilities beyond her preference for dominance; the binary opposition of ruler/ruled has been undone by a mutual relinquishing of sovereignty. Although Alisoun uses discursive power deftly, she does not seem to realize the full implications of that power and the emergent social possibilities it might suggest.

Neither the *Prologue* nor the *Tale* affords Alisoun total escape from the patriarchal ideology that has constructed her. The female position of the Knight in the *Tale* exposes but does not remove the limitations of Alisoun in the *Prologue*. The male experience of Alisoun does not make possible the creation of a self; she is able only to marginalize the Knight and make him an "other" too. And yet there are successes as she re-positions herself, inverts power structures, seizes control, challenges authority, and seldom capitulates. It is at least partly because of her "otherness" that she can create a space to speak out: as a secular single woman she is an

---

[24] Martha Fleming suggests that in the *Prologue* and the *Tale* Alisoun exacts only a token mastery: in both cases, once she attains it she promptly relinquishes it. "Maisterye" in Middle English, Fleming notes, implies "skill" and "the authority deriving from that skill" rather than the idea of simple dominance; what the Wife really wants is control of her own property: "Repetition and Design in the *Wife of Bath's Tale*," in *Chaucer in the Eighties*, ed. Julian N. Wasserman and Robert J. Blanch (Syracuse, 1986), 151–61, here 157. Once this is in hand, Fleming sees "no further mention of crude dominance but rather equilibrium, harmony, and restoration of order" ("Repetition and Design," 156, quoting Mary Carruthers, "The Wife of Bath and the Painting of Lions," *Publications of the Modern Language Association* 94 [1979]: 209–22, here 218 n. 12). A look at the text dims this idealistic conclusion, however. Alisoun certainly ends the *Tale* with something other than equilibrium in mind: a plea to Jesus to shorten the lives of husbands "That noght will be governed by their wives" (1262); she finishes the *Prologue* with the "bridel" in "hond," with not only control over her property but also "governance of hous and lond, / And of his tonge and of his hond also. . . ." (814–15). Her property and its control may be a crucial issue underlying her desire for mastery, but clearly she wants more than property rights, perhaps because she has learned that mastery is a non-negotiable absolute in her society. Bernard S. Levy maintains that what she really wants is not sovereignty, but love in marriage, which, he believes, to her means "good sex": "The Meanings of the *Clerk's Tale*," in *Chaucer and the Craft of Fiction*, ed. Leigh A. Arrathoon (Rochester, 1986), 385–409, here 386.

[25] Henry Ansgar Kelly cites several instances in Chaucer that depict harmony achieved in marriage through the release of mastery by both parties: *Troilus and Criseyde* 3.169–175 and the *Franklin's Tale* 728–798, as well as the *Wife of Bath's Prologue* and *Tale*. Kelly believes that Alisoun may be unaware of her own cause of bliss: "The Wife of Bath, whether she knows it or not, provides an example of mutuality, in her account of her marriage to her fifth husband, and also in the marriage of the knight to the Loathly Lady": *Love and Marriage in the Age of Chaucer* (Ithaca, NY, 1975), 33 n. 3.

"other" in medieval society. Outside the boundaries of marriage, she can comment on it and reshape it.

Even though this single woman moves toward marriage at the end of her *Prologue* and *Tale* and embraces that hierarchical institution, she has managed to invert the rules and demonstrate new possibilities for a woman as wife. Moreover, it is the narrative of a single woman's transgressive discourse that confronts the male establishment. The Wife of Bath's voice is also single in the sense of its being solitary, since it is the sole memorable female voice from *The Canterbury Tales*. And, in the profound challenge it presents, it is a singular voice. Alisoun is also a singular representation of a woman expanding the category of "single woman" to signify not only an unmarried woman, but also a female position that eludes the binarisms that contained medieval women.

Jeanie Grant Moore
University of Wisconsin Oshkosh

8

GOOD GRIEF:

Widow Portraiture and Masculine Anxiety in Early Modern England

A seemingly ordinary picture of a woman hangs in the Dulwich Picture Gallery in London (fig. 1). Depicted in a three-quarter pose and set obliquely against a plain, dark background, the sitter, simply veiled and dressed in black, stares calmly and directly toward the viewer. This picture can be situated within a distinct yet previously unnamed category of female portraiture, what I call widow portraiture: depictions of the woman during and after her husband's funeral when she is recognized as his widow. This genre can be generally characterized as follows: the woman is dressed in dark colors, her expression is sober, and she sometimes holds or wears a small attribute, such as a medal or ring, that connotes her status as someone's widow. (In the Dulwich picture, the sitter wears a strand of pearls, a reference to her virtue and chastity.)[1] Overall, widow portraiture tends to be noticeably static, though necessarily so, for this paradigm and its frequent repetition became a standard means of marking the social status of widowhood. Further,

---

[1] Despite the wealth of information about the socio-economic situation of widowhood in early modern England, there is a noticeable absence of such information within art-historical scholarship. Thus we do not find any references to the *representation* of widowhood in the following most recent canonical surveys of portraiture: Lorne Campbell, *Renaissance Portraits: European Portrait Painting in the 14th, 15th, and 16th Centuries* (New Haven, 1990); Andrew Moore with Charlotte Crawley, *Family and Friends: A Regional Survey of British Portraiture* (London, 1992); and Marcia Pointon, *Hanging the Head: Portraiture and Social Formation in Eighteenth-Century England* (New Haven, 1993). Two studies deserve special mention. Paul Binski, *Medieval Death: Ritual and Representation* (Ithaca, 1996) and, especially, Nigel Llewellyn, *The Art of Death: Visual Culture in the English Death Ritual, c. 1500–c. 1800* (London, 1991) examine visual representations produced in conjunction with the death ritual in early modern Europe; neither of these, however, offers a critical examination of the role of gender within ritual and representation. In all of the works cited here, widow portraiture, as a distinct category of female portraiture, remains undefined.

Figure 1.
"Jane Cartwright," oil on canvas by John Greenhill.
Dulwich Picture Gallery, London.
By permission of the Trustees of Dulwich Picture Gallery.

if such a visual marker also perpetuates the ephemeral nature of mourning ceremonial, in so doing it continues the widow's ritual act of grieving and thereby (ideally) maintains masculine memory. Thus, as we would expect, the majority of these portraits were commissioned by male patrons: fathers, sons, and grandsons. Some portraits of wives as widows were even commissioned prematurely, disclosing a project of pre-posthumous mourning, by which the husband positions his wife as the one who will be his widow and will have mourned for him. In other cases, wives were portrayed as widows, even though, were they to predecease their husbands, that role would never be filled.

Such is the case with the Dulwich picture, *Mrs Jane Cartwright*. The "widow" in question is Jane Hodgson, the third wife of the actor and bookseller, William Cartwright (1606/7–1686), who commissioned John Greenhill (c. 1640/45–1676) to paint his "Last wifes pictur, with a blacke vaile on her head."[2] She predeceased her husband, yet it is her status as his widow that is commemorated in this portrait.[3] Why did Cartwright impose widowhood upon his wife in this way? Nigel Llewellyn has suggested that this portrait "is a reference not so much to her emotional state but to his."[4] Indeed, Cartwright's selfish commission of his wife in a state of mourning, because it is not simply premature but is, in fact, erroneous, can be interpreted as a reflection of his *own* state of mourning. Yet beyond this, I clearly see a newly separable category of representation — women, at a particular cultural moment, caught in a situation of complex and complicating transformation — which is perhaps contingent upon what might be called early modern masculine anxiety. Does Cartwright commission the portrait of his never to be widowed wife because he fears that, without a widow, he will not be properly mourned and, thus, will be forgotten? Perhaps his anxieties can be justified, for he had already lost two potential widows. His first wife, Elisabeth Cooke, whom he married on 1 May 1633, died only a couple of years into their marriage.[5] Of note, Cartwright, no stranger to the stage, cast his wives in various supporting roles. He asked Greenhill to paint his "first wifes pictur Like a Sheppardess" (fig. 2);[6] this portrait of *Elisabeth Cartwright*, which also hangs in the Dulwich Picture Gallery, depicts his wife in the

---

[2] As cited by Llewellyn, *Art of Death*, 96. See also Eleanore Boswell, "Young Mr. Cartwright," *Modern Language Review* 24 (1929): 125–42; and Peter Murray, *Dulwich Picture Gallery: A Catalogue* (London, 1980), 62–63. On Greenhill, a student of the successful portrait painter, Sir Peter Lely, see C. H. Collins-Baker, *Lely and the Stuart Portrait Painters*, 2 vols. (London, 1912), 2: 8; E. K. Waterhouse, *Painting in Britain, 1530–1790* (London, 1953), 74–75; and Margaret Whinney and Oliver Millar, *English Art, 1625–1714* (Oxford, 1957), 179.

[3] We do not know the date of the portrait. The only secure date assigned to the sitter is her wedding date, 19 November 1654, which is recorded in the St. James, Clerkenwell, parish registry. That entry, as cited by Boswell, "Young Mr. Cartwright," 128, reads as follows: "Nov. 19. [1654] William Cartwright, of St. Giles in the Fields, and Jane Hodgson, of our parish." Therefore the painting must have been executed between Cartwright's marriage in 1654 and the death of Greenhill in 1676.

[4] Llewellyn, *Art of Death*, 96.

[5] Boswell, "Young Mr. Cartwright," 127.

[6] As cited by Murray, *Dulwich Picture Gallery*, 63.

guise of St. Agnes, virgin martyr. He married his second wife, Andria Robbins, on 28 April 1636; she died, without having had her portrait painted, on 12 May 1652.[7] Two years later, he married his third and last wife, Jane Hogdson. She would be cast as his widow — a role that would prove necessary insofar as Cartwright would die a "single man (Haveing neither wife nor childe . . .)"; worse (?), he would die without a grave marker.[8] Will his pictorial strategy, at least, be successful? That is to say, will his "widow" ensure his memory?

This essay attempts to explain why and how widows both mourned and were portrayed in early modern Europe, focusing on the traditions and revisions of the mourning ritual in England at that time. In my analyses of the rites of death, I work also with the idea, convincingly put forth by David Cressy, that "Early modern society was governed by principles of order and consensus, but countervailing tendencies of discord and dissension also gnawed at its heart."[9] Along these lines, I understand the widow as someone whose place was ambiguous yet necessary in the account of masculine memory of which she was always so signal a part; further, I bring to this account notions of the subversive and the destabilizing of the masculine, suggesting that the ambiguities of ritual performance and representation could result in a very precarious memory for both mourner and mourned in early modern England.

Why did Cartwright impose widowhood upon his wife? Historically, strategies of deferral or transcendence have been consciously devised as a response to what Henry Staten calls thanato-erotic anxiety: the fear within the dialectic of mourning not of loss of object but of loss of self.[10] The fear, then, of one's own death and the concomitant fear of being forgotten could and did result in auto-mourning: a premature and self-inflicted process of grieving. This initial act is eventually — and vengefully — transferred onto the bodies of women, for it is the woman's sexuality that undermines the man's authority. Her erotic allure is also a deathly allure an idea Staten refers to as "thanatoerotophobic misogyny."[11] This fear of being forgotten and the subsequent strategies of remembrance, which may become deeply misogynistic, can be understood further when considered in conjunction with the reading of early modern English society offered by Mark Breitenberg. He suggests that not

---

[7] Boswell, "Young Mr. Cartwright," 127.

[8] As cited by Boswell, "Young Mr. Cartwright," 128.

[9] David Cressy, *Travesties and Transgressions in Tudor and Stuart England: Tales of Discord and Dissension* (Oxford, 2000), 4.

[10] Henry Staten, *Eros in Mourning: Homer to Lacan* (Baltimore, 1995), xi–xii: "[The dialectic of mourning] begins with the process of attachment to, or cathexis of, an object, without which mourning would never arise . . . As soon as desire is something felt by a mortal being for a mortal being, eros (as desire-in-general) will always be to some degree agitated by the anticipation of loss . . . the loss of the beloved is a loss of self."

[11] Staten, *Eros in Mourning*, 108. Staten cites an early example (p. 38): "Akhilleus weeps, and makes women weep, for himself and for his loss. To wreak vengeance in the *Iliad* means finally: to be the cause of mourning, to transform the passive affect of grief into the active, compensatory pleasure of inflicting grief upon others and most conclusively upon women."

Figure 2.
"A Young Woman, called Mrs Cartwright," oil on canvas by John Greenhill.
Dulwich Picture Gallery, London.
By permission of the Trustees of Dulwich Picture Gallery.

only is masculinity inherently anxious, but that this anxiety is paradoxically both a cause and an effect of the patriarchal system:

> ... anxiety is so endemic to patriarchy that the issue becomes not so much its identification but rather an analysis of the discourses that respond to the compensatory or transferential strategies operating behind its representations and projections. Thus anxiety is both a negative effect that leads us to patriarchy's own internal discord, but it is also an instrument (once properly contained, appropriated or returned) of its perpetuation.[12]

Thus masculine anxiety is both inevitable and necessary, and, when channeled positively, this anxiety can become a strategic tool.[13]

By such an account, the role of women within the death ritual can be interpreted as a "compensatory or transferential" strategy of continuation, of guaranteeing masculine memory. Because the death ritual was enacted as a means of restructuring society, the categorization and repetition of gender roles within that ritual were essential for both the restoration and continuation of the constructed order. That is to say, at the especially vulnerable and disruptive time of death, social order could be restored through the repetitive, gender-specific practice of mourning,[14] and indeed, historically within the western tradition of grieving, women have been designated — and remain — the primary mourners or "memory specialists."[15] But if, according to Sharon Strocchia, "the fundamental human obligation to bury the dead was inextricably bound up with the social imperative to bury them well,"[16] then memory required the proper type and amount of mourning. In other words, a good death was determined by good grief.[17]

---

[12] Mark Breitenberg, *Anxious Masculinity in Early Modern England*, Cambridge Studies in Renaissance Literature and Culture 10 (Cambridge, 1996), 2.

[13] According to Stephen Greenblatt, *Renaissance Self-Fashioning: From More to Shakespeare* (Chicago, 1980), 9: "Self-fashioning is achieved in relation to something perceived as alien, strange, or hostile. This threatening Other — heretic, savage, witch, adultress, traitor, Antichrist — must be discovered or invented in order to be destroyed." Thus, the widow is, at once, constructed as a container of masculine memory *and* de-constructed as one of society's Others.

[14] Judith Butler established the basis for my discussion of the performance of identity. See especially *Gender Trouble: Feminism and the Subversion of Identity* (New York, 1990), 140: "... the action of gender requires a performance that is *repeated*. This repetition is at once a reenactment and reexperiencing of a set of meanings already socially established; and it is the mundane and ritualized form of their legitimation ... this 'action' is a public action ... gender is an identity tenuously constituted in time, instituted in an exterior space through a *stylized repetition of acts*."

[15] Patrick Geary, *Phantoms of Remembrance: Memory and Oblivion at the End of the First Millennium* (Princeton, 1994), 177.

[16] Sharon Strocchia, *Death and Ritual in Renaissance Florence* (Baltimore, 1992), 5–6.

[17] On the English death ritual, see especially David Cressy, *Birth, Marriage, and Death: Ritual, Religion, and the Life-Cycle in Tudor and Stuart England* (Oxford, 1997); Clare Gittings, *Death, Burial and the Individual in Early Modern England* (London, 1984); and Ralph Houlbrooke, *Death, Religion, and the Family in England, 1480–1750* (Oxford, 1998).

A successful performance revolved around the strategic staging of gesture and behavior, as well as of access, movement, and visibility within an urban space temporarily transformed into a ritual space. In an attempt to get things right, or to perform well, the structures and rules of ceremonial underwent constant permutation. This delicate operation, if well orchestrated, could, in turn, result in remembrance. But there was much at stake for the actors, actresses, and directors, who took their show on the road. The streets of early modern England held an attentive audience, who, soon enough, would be competing for recognition within the same urban landscape. Control of such an ephemeral performance within an equally ephemeral and penetrable ritual space would become essential. The role of the widow, in particular, would have to be re-written.

In the early modern period, the move to control or the attempt to territorialize public space by suppressing women's dramatic displays of grief[18] resulted in what has been called "the defeminization of the public sphere." Writing from a psychoanalytic perspective, Juliana Schiesari asks of this politicized re-staging:

> ... were these women's ritualized expressions of grief really disorder? How could they be disorder when mourning was part precisely of a symbolic order? I think what we need to see is that in the transition from a feminized symbolic (or one at least in which women had a more central role) to a masculinist symbolic, the 'disorder of women' becomes part of an ideological apparatus that would empower men to hegemonize the public sphere, hence to phallicize the symbolic.[19]

---

[18] In the sixteenth century, Juan Luis Vives called for an end to disorderly grieving by women in *A Very Fruitful and Pleasant Book Called the Instruction of a Christian Woman*, written in 1523 for Catherine of Aragon. One of the most influential women's conduct books of the sixteenth century, it was translated into English by Richard Hyrde, friend of Thomas More, in 1528–1529. Excerpts from Chapters 1, "Of the Mourning of Widows," and 3, "Of the Minding of Her Husband," of Book 3, as quoted by Joan Larsen Klein, ed., *Daughters, Wives, & Widows: Writings by Men about Women and Marriage in England, 1500–1640* (Urbana, 1992), 119–20, follow (italics mine):

[Upon her husband's death] may come honest weeping, sorrow, and mourning with good occasion, and wailing not to blame. It is the greatest token that can be of an hard heart and an unchaste mind, a woman not to weep for the death of her husband. Howbeit there be two kinds of women which in mourning for their husbands in contrary ways do both amiss: that is, both they that mourn too much and those that mourn too little. I have seen some women no more moved with the death of their husbands than it had been but one of light acquaintance that had died, which was an evident sign of but cold love unto their husbands. ... Let her keep the remembrance of her husband with reverence and *not with weeping*, and let her take for a solemn and a great oath to swear by her husband's soul and let her live and do so as she shall think to please her husband, being now no man but a spirit purified and a divine thing.

[19] Juliana Schiesari, *The Gendering of Melancholia: Feminism, Psychoanalysis, and the Symbolics of Loss in Renaissance Literature* (Ithaca, NY, 1992), 164.

Indeed, the desired result of this revision of female lamentation was a masculinization of the death ritual and of the spaces of that ritual. The goal of restoring order legitimated women's access into the privileged masculine sphere, and their repetitive performance, as newly regulated, continued to contribute to and maintain patriarchal structures.

And yet, this attempt to control women's mourning eventually backfires, insofar as the presence of the female mourner "reveals the very anxiety it is meant to suppress: it at once resists and represents the catastrophe of death."[20] If wives, mothers, and sisters, designated as the primary mourners, stabilize the public, masculine realm, they also contaminate it. That is to say, their very performance within the masculinist symbolic, no matter how contained and restricted, disturbs and challenges the stability of this new ideology, even if it simultaneously contributes to and maintains it:

> The supplement has not only the power of *procuring* an absent presence through its image; procuring it for us through the proxy of the sign, it holds it at a distance and masters it. For this presence is at the same time desired and feared. . . . Thus, the supplement is dangerous in that it threatens us with death. . . .[21]

If we read the widow as supplement, then we can characterize her as subversive in that her presence — or 'disorder' — is considered threatening. Moreover, insofar as the very performance of ritual points toward an unraveling of social order, or insofar as the possibilities of permutation within ritual suggest a potential failure of patriarchal fixity, it can be argued that this particular strategy, to rewrite the role of the widow during ceremonial, is not only dangerous but is, perhaps, even unsuccessful.

Despite women's role and reputation as memory specialists (now read as questionable), tension remained. That is to say, even beyond the space of ritual, the widow was guaranteed a place, albeit a limited one, within the public realm, where she was often able to reformulate her imposed containment, finding herself at the threshold of unlimited opportunity; this pregnant moment arose precisely upon her husband's death and continued until her own. In fact, the abundance of widows in early modern England did little to quell anxiety. One recent calculation estimates that 14.9 percent of adult women in England were widows, and that 12.9 percent of all households were headed by widows.[22] ". . . [F]ull of variation, contradiction,

---

[20] Sarah Webster Goodwin and Elisabeth Bronfen, *Death and Representation* (Baltimore, 1993), 14.

[21] Jacques Derrida's analysis of Rousseau's "supplement," as cited by Staten, *Eros in Mourning*, xii.

[22] See Amy M. Froide, "Marital Status as a Category of Difference: Singlewomen and Widows in Early Modern England," in *Singlewomen in the European Past, 1250–1800*, ed. Judith M. Bennett and Amy M. Froide (Philadelphia, 1999), 236–69. Froide bases her readings on the survey conducted in Peter Laslett, "Mean Household Size in England Since the Sixteenth Century," in *Household and Family in Past Time*, ed. idem and Richard Wall (Cambridge, 1972), 147.

[and] ambivalence" as those cohorts were,[23] even more disturbing than the number of these single women were their potential transgressions: will they play the role of chaste widow, or will they take lovers or remarry and, if so, forget their duty to mourn?

These were legitimate concerns in the early modern period. We might think of the opinions of Alexander Niccholes, as expressed in *A Discourse of Marriage and Wiving*, first published in London in 1615 and then again in 1620:

> At the decease of their first husbands, they learn commonly the tricks to turn over the second or third, and they are in league with death and coadjutors with him, for they can harden their own hearts like iron to break others that are but earth. And I like them the worse that they will marry, dislike them utterly they marry so soon. For she that so soon forgets the flower and Bridegroom of her youth, her first love and prime of affection (which like a color laid on in Oil, or dyed in grain, should cleave fast and wear long), will hardly think of a second in the neglect and decay of her age. ... *Who can love those living that he knows will so soon forget him being dead.* ... *Yet decease, and such a lethe of forgetfulness [oblivion] shall so soon overtake thee as if thou hadst never been.*[24]

Similarly, we might think of the surprising yet powerful comment upon widowhood by Lodovico Dolce, who wrote that women "rejoice at the death of their husbands as if they had been freed from the heavy yoke of servitude";[25] or of a witness at the court of Catherine de' Medici, who made the following observation:

> They want friends and lovers, but no husband, out of love for the freedom that is so sweet. To be out from under the domination of a husband seems to them paradise, and no wonder, they have the use of their own money ... everything passes through their hands ... they can pursue their pleasures and enjoy companions who will do as they wish. They remain widows in order to keep their *grandeur*, possessions, titles and good treatment.[26]

Writings such as these reflect what Christiane Klapisch-Zuber, writing on the situation in Italy, is prepared to call a marked degree of "anxiety among men."[27]

---

[23] Henrietta Leyser, *Medieval Women: A Social History of Women in England, 450–1500* (New York 1995), 168.

[24] As cited by Lloyd Davis, ed., *Sexuality and Gender in the English Renaissance* (New York, 1998), 222–23; italics mine.

[25] As cited by Giulia Calvi, "Reconstructing the Family: Widowhood and Remarriage in Tuscany in the Early Modern Period," in *Marriage in Italy, 1300–1650*, ed. Trevor Dean and K. J. P. Lowe (Cambridge, 1998), 275–96, here 276.

[26] As cited by Nancy Lyman Roelker, "Widowhood and Rational Domesticity: Modes of Independence for Women in Early Modern Europe," *Journal of Family History* 7 (1982): 376–78, here 377.

[27] Christiane Klapisch-Zuber, *Women, Family, and Ritual in Renaissance Italy*, trans. Lydia Cochrane (Chicago, 1985), 122.

And, if, as William J. Bouwsma pointedly put it, "all anxiety is anxiety about death,"[28] or as Clare Gittings specified, "the early modern period was characterized by an increasing anxiety over death" due to "growing individualism,"[29] then the collapse of both literal and figurative boundaries at this crucial time could and did cause considerable confusion within an otherwise strictly regulated social world. Indeed, if the consistently uncertain position of the widow during and after ritual magnified masculine anxiety, the widow, once more, would have to be put in her proper place.

The English Gentlewoman, written by Richard Brathwaite, can be read as just one example of a literary attempt to counter the anxiety-inducing deficiencies of ritual. Like other conduct books of the period, this one, published in 1631, provides counsel on how to live as a woman, be it as wife, mother, or widow. This text is set apart from many, however, insofar as it is addressed particularly to female readers. It is noteworthy that the frontispiece of the first edition contains a representation of Brathwaite's ideal English gentlewoman (fig. 3). She is, literally, boxed-in; we might even say *framed*. Surrounding her image, which is placed centrally and contains her motto, "Glory my goal, grace my guide," are eight scenes, each set within a different social, mainly domestic, setting. These scenes illustrate qualities of character and proper comportment: apparel, behavior, complement, decency, estimation, fancy, gentility, and honor.[30] One of those didactic images, in particular, "Fancy," attempts to make clear that choice and opportunity, especially concerning another man, whether he be a second husband or a new lover, are undesirable and are best avoided. The accompanying text reads as follows:

> Fancy is featured with a lovely and lively presence; fixing her eye intentively on a *Tablet*, presenting the portrature of her *Lover*. Drawing aside a Curtaine, she discovers an *amorous Picture*, and compares it with her *Tablet*, which enshrines her *best feature*. In the middle of the *Picture* is engraven a *wounded heart*, implying love's intimacy; above it, a *burning lampe*, importing love's purity; below it, a pair of *Turtles* mating, inferring love's constancy. All which expressive Emblemes of her minde, she seconds with this Moto: *My Choice admits no Change*.[31]

Both prescriptive and proscriptive, word and image work together here to discourage desire and transgression; in so doing, this literary and visual dissuasion points to the inherent anxiety of the author, and thus further calls attention to the

---

[28] William J. Bouwsma, "Anxiety and the Formation of Early Modern Culture," in idem, *A Usable Past: Essays in European Cultural History* (Berkeley, 1990), 162.

[29] Gittings, *Death, Burial and the Individual*, 102.

[30] See Suzanne W. Hull, *Chaste, Silent & Obedient: English Books for Women 1475–1640* (San Marino, CA, 1982), 32–35.

[31] For the explanatory tablet, see Kate Aughterson, ed., *Renaissance Woman: A Sourcebook: Constructions of Feminity [sic] in England* (London, 1995), fig. 5.

Figure 3.
"The English Gentlewoman."
Bodleian Library, Oxford.
By permission of the Bodleian Library.

complexity and urgency with which such apotropaic strategies, those intended to ward off evil, operated at this time.

Most interesting in this didactic image of "Fancy" is the use of portraiture, as directed both within the scene and toward the reading audience. The portrait of the lover is meant to function here as a marker and protector of masculine memory; and, indeed, this English gentlewoman, heeding the advice of Brathwaite, will contain any curiosity, suppress all temptation, and remain loyal to her lover. But if we take a closer look at the entire image, her obedience also can be read as disturbing and challenging to Brathwaite's ideal, a reading that speaks to the potential failure of male portraiture. Even though she "present[s] the portrature of her *Lover*," "Drawing aside a Curtaine," she displays both a voyeuristic gaze and a large, we might say 'erect,' "*amorous Picture*," which, once decoded, abets her decision to remain loyal to her lover. But "fixing her eye intentively" on his miniature portrait — already flat, 'limp' — her gaze, like the castrating stare of Medusa, is, ultimately, fatal, and *this* English gentlewoman can be read as subversive, *this* didactic image as counter-productive.

How, then, can the widow be so sanctioned that she ensures without erasing masculine memory? Building upon Staten's argument that the initial act of auto-mourning is eventually transferred onto the bodies of women, I propose that masculine memory in early modern England could be best maintained by transferring the task of commemoration from male portraiture to female portraiture. An unusual painting, the *Triptych Portrait of Lady Anne Clifford*, painted circa 1647 (probably by Jan van Belcamp), illustrates the ways in which this strategic transfer could both re-shape identity and construct a particular memory (fig. 4).[32] The left panel of the triptych depicts Lady Anne Clifford in 1605, the year of her father's death; this image of her commemorates an early period of mourning. Portrayed at the age of fifteen, she is situated appropriately among her schoolbooks, which, it is noteworthy, include Castiglione's *Book of the Courtier* and Ovid's *Metamorphoses:* two

---

[32] See Katherine O. Acheson, ed., *The Diary of Anne Clifford, 1616–1619* (New York, 1995), 32–35; eadem, "The Modernity of the Early Modern: The Example of Lady Anne Clifford," in *Discontinuities: New Essays on Renaissance Literature and Criticism*, ed. Viviana Comensoli and Paul Stevens (Toronto, 1998), 27–51; D. J. H. Clifford, ed., *The Diaries of Lady Anne Clifford* (Stroud, 1990), 97; Anthony Fletcher, *Gender, Sex & Subordination in England, 1500–1800* (New Haven, 1995); Alice T. Friedman, "Wife in the English Country House: Gender and the Meaning of Style in Early Modern England," in *Women and Art in Early Modern Europe: Patrons, Collectors, and Connoisseurs*, ed. Cynthia Lawrence (University Park, PA, 1997), esp. 121–25; Elspeth Graham et al., eds., *Her Own Life: Autobiographical Writings by Seventeenth-Century Englishwomen* (London, 1989), 35–38; Martin Holmes, *Proud Northern Lady: Lady Anne Clifford 1590–1676* (Chichester, 1975); Mary Ellen Lamb, "The Agency of the Split Subject: Lady Anne Clifford and the Uses of Reading," *English Literary Renaissance* 22 (1992): 347–68; Barbara K. Lewalski, "Re-Writing Patriarchy and Patronage: Margaret Clifford, Anne Clifford, and Aemilia Lanyer," *Yearbook of English Studies* 21 (1991): 87–106; Helen Wilcox, "Private Writing and Public Function: Autobiographical Texts by Renaissance Englishwomen," in *Gloriana's Face: Women, Public and Private, in the English Renaissance*, ed. S. P. Cerasano and Marion Wynne-Davies (New York, 1992), 47–62; and George C. Williamson, *Lady Anne Clifford, Countess of Dorset, Pembroke & Montgomery, 1590–1676: Her Life, Letters and Work* (Kendal, 1923).

Figure 4.
"The Great Picture" depicting Lady Anne Clifford, Countess of Dorset, Pembroke and Montgomery (1590–1676), 1646 (oil on canvas) by Jan van Belcamp (1610–53) (attr.).
Abbot Hall Art Gallery, Kendal, Cumbria.
By permission of the Bridgeman Art Library.

suggestive texts insofar as one is concerned with conduct, the other with bodily transformation. Addressed primarily to male readers, both texts suggest a future of performance and permutation. In addition, two portraits which depict her governess, Ann Taylor, and her tutor, Samuel Daniel, hang on the back wall. The central panel represents her immediate family in June 1589, one month after her conception: her parents, Margaret Russell, daughter of the Earl of Bedford, and George Clifford, third Earl of Cumberland, and her two brothers, Robert and Francis, both of whom died in infancy. Behind the family are four portraits, each depicting one of Anne's maternal aunts: Lady Warwick, Lady Bath, Lady Wharton, and the Countess of Derby. Presumably at least three of these women, dressed in plain black costume and wearing the characteristic 'widow's peak' head covering, are depicted as widows. In the right panel, Anne is portrayed at the age of fifty-six. As in the opposite wing of the triptych, she is positioned among a collection of portraits and books, and she is portrayed in a period of mourning; here, however, she no longer mourns her father but at least one of her husbands. Excerpts from her diary record the exact dates of each of her periods of widowhood:

> I lived Widdow to this Noble Richard Sackville, Earle of Dorsett about six yeares two monthes and fower or five daies over. ... On the 3rd Daie of June, after I have continewed a Widdow 6 yeares 2 monthes and 5 or 6 daies over, was I marryed in Chenies Church in Buckinghamshire to my 2nd Husband Philip Herbert, Earl of Pembroke and Montgomery, Ld Chamberlain of the King's Howsehold and Knight of the Garter; he being then one of the greatest subjects in the Kingdom. ... This second husband of myne dyed the three and twentieth of Januarie one thowsand sixe hundered and fiftie (as the Yeare begins on Newyeares daie) and was buryed the ninth of Februarie following in the great church at Salisburie. I was lying then at my castle at Aplebie in Westmorland.[33]

Her meticulous records, as cited here, demonstrate the seriousness with which she twice performed her social obligation to mark the memory of the dead. The portraits in the right wing depict her husbands, Richard Sackville, the third Earl of Dorset, and Philip Herbert, fourth Earl of Pembroke and Earl of Montgomery. The latter was not yet deceased, though he might well have been. Estranged, he was living in London at the time of the commission. Both portraits, framed and mounted, sit above what appears to be a memorial inscription. Moreover, depicted in black dress with a plain black veil on her head, Anne seems already to be in a state of mourning for him. Once a widow, always a widow? Even her books, which include More's *Map of Mortality* and Strode's *Anatomy of Mortality*, suggest that the duty to mourn remained a constant concern throughout her life.

Following Marcia Pointon's keen observation that "the ordering of imagery in particular spaces and settings produces meanings specific to those times and places" and that "[i]t is thus not only what is possessed that is significant but where and

---

[33] As cited by D. J. H. Clifford, ed., *Diaries*, 87, 89–91, 106.

how it is made visible,"[34] I propose that issues of mourning and memory consume the entire triptych, and that the insistence upon commemorating each of Anne's periods of mourning served a particular memorial purpose. If, as previously suggested, the work of mourning is better achieved by female mourners, and if the pictorial task of commemoration is redirected toward female portraiture, then widow portraiture in particular can be interpreted as a "compensatory or transferential" strategy of continuation, a more efficient means of guaranteeing memory. But whose memory, exactly, is recorded? In the particular case of the *Triptych Portrait*, I would suggest that the portraits of Anne Clifford mark the memories of her father, brothers, and husbands, as well as her own.[35]

On the one hand, widow portraiture can be read as a successful strategy because it kept women in the home. That is to say, the strict orchestration and almost 'archaic' style of the triptych as a whole, in addition to the form and display of the individual portraits contained within it, can be interpreted as a determined attempt to sanction, at least pictorially, the widow. For example, the framed portraits of Anne's (presumably) widowed aunts seem to forestall the potential transgressions of these single women. Similarly, Anne, who is literally contained within the side wings of the triptych, appears to occupy her proper place while performing her proper role as mourner. But if, by contrast, "the side panels of the painting show Clifford framing and containing her family,"[36] rather than *being* framed or contained, might we read these two 'marginalized' portraits as challenging to family memory? In other words, the ambivalence with which the portraits of Anne function suggest that there is yet another chapter to be written — or rewritten. Positioned at the edges of this memorial triptych, her pendant portraits resemble a pair of inverted bookends. Which story from the annals of her family history does Anne seek to reveal or conceal?

Significantly, Anne commissioned the *Triptych Portrait* herself; thus, it is she who selectively and strategically writes and rewrites this family history. In so doing, she also repositions herself within that history, seeking, perhaps, what she calls "a new role to play on the stage of this world."[37] Notably, her "self-immortalizing strategies"[38] revolve around the performances and permutations of gender. Situating herself within a powerful female genealogy, evident in the central panel, she is remembered as "an individual woman holding out against the combined patriarchal

---

[34] Pointon, *Hanging the Head*, 13. On the display of pictures, see also John Fowler and John Cornforth, *English Decoration in the Eighteenth Century* (London, 1974); Andrew Moore, "Hanging the Family Portraits," in Moore and Crawley, *Family and Friends*, 31–38; Francis Russell, "The Hanging and Display of Pictures, 1700–1850," in Gervase Jackson-Stops et al., *The Fashioning and Functioning of the British Country House* (Washington, DC, 1989), 133–53; Peter Thornton, *Seventeenth-Century Interior Decoration in England, France, and Holland* (New Haven, 1978); and idem, *Authentic Décor: The Domestic Interior, 1620–1920* (London, 1984).

[35] It could be argued that she is also mourning the loss of her five sons, all of whom died in infancy.

[36] Graham, *Her Own Life*, 37.

[37] As cited by Acheson, *Diary*, 34.

[38] Acheson, *Diary*, 35.

forces of father, uncles, husbands, lawyers, churchmen, and even the king."[39] And yet if she thereby seems to reconstitute gender difference, she also subverts that gender dichotomy, simultaneously positioning herself as both male and female. A passage from her autobiography reads as follows:

> I was very happy in my first constitution both in mind and body, both for internal and external endowments, for never was there child more equally resembling both father and mother than myself. The color of mine eyes were black like my father, and the form and aspect of them was quick and lively like my mother's; the hair of my head was brown and very thick, and so long that it reached to the calf of my legs when I stood upright, with a peak of hair on my forehead, and a dimple in my chin, like my father, full cheeks and round face like my mother, and an exquisite shape of body resembling my father.[40]

The portraits of Anne within the triptych reflect this gender blending. In the left panel, her portrait echoes that of her mother: head, hairstyle, and dress are similar in each. In the right panel, Anne's authoritative stance is similar to that of her father; her black veil, in particular, resembling his hairstyle.[41] This gender performance revealed in both text and image continued throughout her life and indeed was commemorated in her funeral sermon: "[t]he Subject here, *Woman*, we must allow to be so far figurative as ... by a Synechdoche, under one to comprehend both Sexes."[42]

Appropriately, recent writers have portrayed Anne as a "split" subject or "divided subject,"[43] who self-consciously and successfully repositioned herself within history by unsettling traditional codes of class and gender. Her oscillation between the roles of obedient daughter and wife and self-ruling and self-reliant aristocratic heir has been read as a sign of her modernity.[44] According to these terms, I would suggest that the paradoxical nature of her particular manner of self-fashioning can

---

[39] Graham, *Her Own Life*, 37.

[40] As cited by Acheson, *Diary*, 32–33.

[41] Black dress for women marked them as mourners; indeed, black is, traditionally, the color of death, of grief, and of loss. And yet, it has been adopted by men to represent not what they lack or have lost but what they have; it signifies, according to John Harvey, *Men in Black* (Chicago, 1995), 51, "the privileges claimed by grief." Indeed, black dress, for men, was a social uniform. According to Baldesar Castiglione, *The Book of the Courtier*, trans. George Bull (New York, 1976), 135, "the most agreeable colour is black, and if not black, then at least something fairly dark." At this time, among princes and courtiers, the color signified grace, seriousness, respect and distinction, not necessarily mourning. It can be argued, however, that Anne re-appropriates black dress, claiming for herself the authoritative and empowering gestures previously reserved for her father.

[42] Acheson, *Diary*, 33.

[43] Lamb, "Lady Anne Clifford," 349, 350.

[44] According to Acheson, "Modernity of the Early Modern," 42–43, "Anne Clifford is distinctively modern because she constructed herself, within a historiographic discourse, as separate from the present in which she lived."

Figure 5.
"William Cartwright," oil on canvas by John Greenhill.
Dulwich Picture Gallery, London.
By permission of the Trustees of Dulwich Picture Gallery.

be understood as a symptom of her widowhood or, at least, of her ability to mourn. That is to say, the reshaping of her own identity and, subsequently, the revision of her own memory are, in the case of the *Triptych Portrait*, contingent upon her social obligation to mourn the dead — a duty which, as already described, enabled her to transgress social boundaries (both geographical and, now, bodily) in order to record family memory. For example, if we look again at the right wing of the triptych, she plays both the traditional female role of memory specialist and the previously unscripted, but now permissible, male role of head of family; she is simultaneously portrayed as widow of her first husband and estranged wife of her second, and, having appropriated the body language of her father, as patriarch. If Anne is "capable of both *producing* and *being produced* by history,"[45] how do her performances and permutations affect masculine memory?

Reading the multivalence of the *Triptych Portrait* as representative of the ambiguities and complexities of the mourning ritual, we might even read the flexibility of the tripartite structure as a metaphor for the malleability of ritual at this time and, especially, for the tenuousness of memorial strategy insofar as the threefold relationship between the role of the widow, the representation of the widow, and the desired result of that representation seem to be precariously hinged. Indeed, if widow portraiture discloses a continuous project of pre-posthumous auto-mourning, enabling the male subject to mourn in advance his own death and thus perhaps even to ensure his own memory, the manipulations of this new category of representation also complicate the identities and memories of both mourner and mourned. That is to say, if the imposition of widowhood points toward an endless layering of deception and masquerade, and if, moreover, the widow's very performance can be read as suggestive of the fissures and fluidity of identity in early modern society, we might conclude that the widow assumes a very precarious place within the discourse on masculine memory.

Finally, what, then, can be said of the relationship between William Cartwright, himself a performer, and his "widow"? In other words, does the portrait of *Mrs Jane Cartwright* ensure his memory? Having unveiled this peculiar widow's portrait, perhaps not. Perhaps, then, for this reason, the always already anxious Cartwright commissioned Greenhill to paint another portrait — this one of himself "in a black dress with a great doge" (fig. 5).[46] If his wives could not mourn him, and if his "widow" might not, Cartwright would have to turn to man's best friend. A boy and his dog — good grief.

Allison Levy
Wheaton College

---

[45] Acheson, "Modernity of the Early Modern," 32.
[46] As cited by Boswell, "Young Mr. Cartwright," 139. We do not know the date of the portrait, but, like the portrait of *Mrs Jane Cartwright*, it had to have been painted before the death of Greenhill in 1676.

PART IV:

Sexuality and Revirgination

9

WORKING GIRLS:

Status, Sexual Difference, and Disguise in Ariosto, Spenser, and Shakespeare

In *The Lawes Resolution of Womens Rights*, T. E., the book's anonymous author, notes, "All of them [women] are understood either married or to bee married and their desires or subject to their husband, I know no remedy though some women can shift it well enough."[1] Despite this certainty regarding women's eventual marital status, statistical evidence suggests that the percentage of women who were temporarily and/or permanently single is larger than modern historians, and early modern social observers, would expect. According to Maryanne Kowaleski's review of the demographic picture, as many as thirty to forty percent of adult women were single at any given time in sixteenth-century northwestern Europe (including life-cycle and lifelong single women), and perhaps ten percent of women never married.[2] Given this predominance, why was the single woman seen as exceptional or anomalous? Perhaps the most obvious answer lies in the increased importance of marriage after the Protestant Reformation closed the convents. Marriage not only constituted the most basic social unit but also provided a ubiquitous metaphor for political relationships. Unlike the exceptional Queen Elizabeth, for many women virtue was defined primarily in relation to a married state that was, as T. E. assumed, always in the future or in the past, if not the present. And in many contemporary representations of women's social position, marriage remained the primary definitive event. Even Esther Sowernam's efforts to define an identity

---

[1] T. E., *The Lawes Resolution of Womens Rights: or, The Lawes Provision for Woeman* (London, 1632; repr. New York, 1978), 6.
[2] Maryanne Kowaleski, "Singlewomen in Medieval and Early Modern Europe: The Demographic Perspective," in *Singlewomen in the European Past, 1250–1800*, ed. Judith M. Bennett and Amy M. Froide (Philadelphia, 1999), 38–81, esp. 39, 45–46.

outside of marriage was primarily negative, since she called herself "neither Maide, Wife, nor Widdowe, yet really all."[3]

Since representations of early modern women vanished them into a marital state that occluded any distinct identity, many contemporary feminist scholars have responded by pursuing a project of historical recovery, attempting to unearth the single woman's remains. In tandem with this effort has come two assumptions: first, that single women, despite their singularity, were rarely alone; second, that if marriage obscures feminine identity in the early modern period, relations with other women will bring that identity into relief. This dual focus is evident in two recent ground-breaking anthologies entitled *Maids and Mistresses, Cousins and Queens: Women's Alliances in Early Modern England* and *Singlewomen in the European Past: 1250–1800*. Though the explicit thematic of each anthology is different, they both are deeply invested in the collective identities that buttressed the often marginal lives of early modern single women. But this interdependence between a single status "hidden from history" and the collective female identity that should abet its representation raises some troubling questions about the overall project of historical recovery, especially as it has been practiced by feminist historians and literary scholars. For example, Ann Rosalind Jones's "Maidservants of London: Sisterhoods of Kinship and Labor" in the volume *Maids and Mistresses* argues that a 1567 pamphlet, "A Letter sent by the Maydens of London," is a tour-de-force of collective bargaining, which promotes solidarity between maidservants and between maidservants and their mistresses.[4] Setting aside the problems of the pamphlet's authorship[5] and the relative unavailability of writing and publication to many women, Jones sees it as an authentic expression of the collective maidservants. She assumes that representation is transparent insofar as it constitutes a form for a pre-existent content; i.e., the beliefs and practices of the pamphlet's collective subject, the maidservants, are not significantly affected by the various discourses available or unavailable to them. Agency pre-exists representation, as, for example, in Ruth Mazo Karras's essay, "Sex and the Singlewoman," in the *Singlewomen* volume. In response to historical analyses of medieval women's sexuality that have emphasized danger over pleasure, Karras argues that ". . . we should not forget that despite the efforts of medieval society to deny to women other than the most degraded the possibility of sexual activity outside of marriage, women were still making choices for themselves, and those choices could include sexual activity."[6] But both Karras's and Jones's efforts

---

[3] Esther Sowernam, "Ester hath hang'd Haman," *Female Replies to Swetnam the Woman-Hater* (London, 1617; repr. Bristol, 1995).

[4] Ann Rosalind Jones, "Maidservants of London: Sisterhoods of Kinship and Labor," in *Maids and Mistresses, Cousins and Queens: Women's Alliances in Early Modern* England, ed. Susan Frye and Karen Robertson (New York, 1999), 21–32.

[5] In contradistinction to the pamphlet's editor, R.J. Fehrenbach: "A Letter sent by the Maydens of London (1567)," in *Women in the Renaissance: Selections from English Literary Renaissance*, ed. Kirby Farrell, Elizabeth H. Hageman, and Arthur F. Kinney (Amherst, MA, 1988), 28–47, here 37.

[6] Ruth Mazo Karras, "Sex and the Singlewoman," in *Singlewomen in the European Past, 1250–1800*, 127–45, here 140.

to restore the question of agency to the debate presume a liberal subject, for whom status and sexuality are instrumentalized. Their essays connect agency to visibility, such that the metaphorical axis of (aesthetic) representation is projected onto the metonymical axis of (political) representation. Political representation (the product of hegemony) is thus conflated with aesthetic representation (the product of mimesis), invisibility with oppression.[7]

Given the tendency of much male-dominated historical and historico-literary writing to ignore sexual difference, it is difficult not to take the historical recovery of women's lives as the solution. But this project, especially as enacted within the *Maids and Mistresses* and *Singlewomen* volumes, carries with it several unexamined and problematic assumptions. First, the feminist project usually presumes that the women represented in historical discourse identified themselves primarily as women and identified with other women.[8] Second, its political valence often produces a certain surplus: the historian's fantasized identification with the women whose visibility she delivers. Restoring women hitherto lost from history to historical representation becomes a politically virtuous and self-validating activity. As a consequence, identifications with women become primary, while other social differences (e.g., status or class) become secondary. But as Elizabeth Brown reminds us, if such identifications operate within relationships that are already structured according to a hierarchy of birth and breeding, they can produce not a collective which transcends status distinctions, but the erasure of the weaker partner's interests and desires.[9] Brown's essay raises the possibility that historical retrieval, with its presumed identifications between women, may result in the premature foreclosure of the problem of individual women's differences from other women, and hence the loss of those specific identities and desires which the project attempts to represent.

I am not suggesting that the project of historical recovery is misplaced; such work has been invaluable, and my own work remains greatly dependent on it. But I do want to propose that perhaps early modern feminist studies should not assume a unitary female subject (an agent) to be rendered visible in her relations with like

---

[7] See Gayatri Chakravorty Spivak, "Can the Subaltern Speak?" in *Marxism and the Interpretation of Culture*, ed. Cary Nelson and Larry Grossberg (Chicago, 1988), 271–313; Ernesto Laclau, *Emancipation(s)* (London, 1996), 97–101.

[8] For example, several of the essays in *Maids and Mistresses* rely on a notion of female homosociality (which presumes the similarity of the masculine and feminine psyches) to support their subjects' self-identification. See Simon Morgan-Russell, "'No Good Thing Ever Comes Out of It': Male Expectations and Female Alliance in Dekker and Webster's *Westward Ho*," in *Maids and Mistresses, Cousins and Queens*, 70–84, here 80.

[9] In Brown's reading of *Antony and Cleopatra*, Charmian's and Iras's devotion to their mistress, Cleopatra, results in the sacrifice of their own interests, and eventually, their own lives to Cleopatra's dynastic and erotic ambitions. See Elizabeth A. Brown, "'Companion Me with My Mistress': Cleopatra, Elizabeth I, and Their Waiting Women," in *Maids and Mistresses, Cousins and Queens*, 131–45, here 144.

female subjects.[10] Rather, we should be inspired by Wendy Brown's argument that contemporary feminists need "a historiography that emphasizes instead contingent developments, formations that may be at odds with or convergent with each other, and trajectories of power that vary in weight for different kinds of subjects."[11] Given the difficulties of representing single women (as single women, not as married women *manqué*), Brown's call for an archaeological mode of analysis that presumes the coherence neither of the category of women, nor of the early modern discourses that presumed to represent women, seems a useful strategy.

I have therefore attempted to dis-articulate the various early modern discursive productions that offered the false coherence of a feminine ideal defined as "chaste, silent, and obedient."[12] In order to focus on the discontinuities within and between representations of women, I have chosen to read three versions of the story of Ariodante and Ginevra, all produced during the 1590s in England: (1) Book 4 from John Harington's translation of Ariosto's *Orlando Furioso* (1591); (2) Spenser's retelling of that story in Book 2 of *The Faerie Queene* (1590); and (3) Shakespeare's adaptation of it in *Much Ado About Nothing* (ca. 1598–1599). In each of these texts, the self-identification of women as women (underwritten by homosocial relations with other women) is disrupted by the status difference between maid and mistress. Moreover, the ideal of marriage constructs the differential relation between them as one of envy. Because status difference is mapped onto marital difference, the maid disappears — an occlusion dramatized by her disguise as her mistress. As a consequence, the representation of the maid disrupts a notion of character that emphasizes agency, motivation, and choice. The disguise motif offers us, paradoxically, a character who "chooses" to vanish herself into another character. Disguise thus frustrates historical recovery.

Contemporary feminist literary criticism has often been concerned with restoring women to agency and mapping women's subjectivity; to be an agent is often seen as contingent upon being seen as a subject. For many feminist critics, despite a spate of post-structuralist critiques of the subject, to be a subject is to move past the traditional objectification predominant in representations of women and to enter into a realm of freedom. For early moderns, on the other hand, the subject did not connote freedom; to be a subject was to embrace (or be defined by) a subjection both social and political in character.[13] According to the 1547 *Certain Sermons or Homilies*, "Some are in high degre, some in lowe, some kynges and princes, some inferiours and subjectes, priestes and laimen, masters and servauntes, fathers and

---

[10] According to Jacques Rancière, making visible paradoxically results in making silent: Jacques Rancière, *The Names of History: On the Poetics of Knowledge*, trans. Hassan Melehy (Minneapolis, 1994), 46.

[11] See Wendy Brown, "The Impossibility of Women's Studies," *differences* 9 (1997): 79–101.

[12] Suzanne W. Hull has added this phrase to our lexicon by so entitling her survey of early modern conduct books: *Chaste, Silent & Obedient: English Books for Women, 1475–1640* (San Marino, CA, 1982).

[13] See Etienne Balibar, "Citizen Subject," in *Who Comes After the Subject?*, ed. Eduardo Cadava, Peter Connor, and Jean-Luc Nancy (New York, 1991), 33–57.

chyldren, husbandes and wifes, riche and porre, and evry one have nede of other. ..."[14] Subjection was total, since every member of the polity was subjected to someone else.

Though early modern elites were obsessively concerned with the intelligibility of a social field characterized by subjection and organized according to hierarchy and degree, sexual difference remained a point of potential unintelligibility, precisely because classification in terms of sexual difference could (and often did) conflict with the self-image of a society ordered according to status. Efforts such as the "Homily" to map hierarchical differences of status and economics onto a sexual difference located within marriage disguised marital and status/class differences between women themselves.[15] As a consequence, though men were differentiated according to status and occupation in contemporary descriptions of the social, women were cited *en bloc*. Keith Wrightson cites a mid-sixteenth-century pamphlet which lists "twelve several estats of men," including "beggars, servants, yeomen, priests, scholars, learned men, physicians, lawyers, merchants, gentlemen, magistrates, and women."[16] In the "Homily," women were excluded from the polity, except insofar as they could be registered (and subjected) as wives.[17] Political economy in early modern England naturalized women's marital status, despite differences of degree and hierarchy. This naturalization led to the representation of a homogeneous "woman," defined primarily in terms of virtue (or the lack thereof), which forestalled the recognition of social differences between women, including differences of marital and social status. But the homogenization of women was never complete, since status differentiation remained the primary schema for the

---

[14] "An Exhortacion concernyng Good Ordre and Obedience to Rulers and Magistrates," in *Certain Sermons or Homilies (1547)* . . . , ed. Ronald B. Bond (Toronto, 1987), 161–73, here 161.

[15] See Susan Dwyer Amussen, *An Ordered Society: Gender and Class in Early Modern England* (Oxford, 1988), 3–4; Cristina Malcomson, "'What You Will': Social Mobility and Gender in *Twelfth Night*," in *The Matter of Difference: Materialist Feminist Criticism of Shakespeare*, ed. Valerie Wayne (Ithaca, NY, 1991), 29–57, here 31; Jean E. Howard, *The Stage and Social Struggle in Early Modern England* (New York, 1994), 89.

[16] David Cressy, "Describing the Social Order of Elizabethan and Stuart England," *Literature and History* 3 (1976): 29–44, here 34–35; Keith Wrightson, "Estates, Degrees, and Sorts: Changing Perceptions of Society in Tudor and Stuart England," in *Language, History, and Class*, ed. Penelope J. Corfield (Oxford, 1991), 30–52, here 32. Recent research has uncovered evidence that many women were politically active, serving as justices of the peace, sextons, and even constables, and, surprisingly, voting. For an overview, see Sara Mendelson and Patricia Crawford, *Women in Early Modern England, 1550–1720* (Oxford, 1998), 49–58.

[17] In a description of the "degrees of people" to be found in Elizabethan England, William Harrison assumes four classes of men (gentlemen, citizens, yeomen, and artificers/laborers). Women are largely irrelevant to this discussion, probably since a woman's social status was defined by that of her father or husband. The only mention of women occurs when Harrison discusses how courtesy (though not common law) dictates that a woman who marries more than once retains the "most honorable" title: William Harrison, *The Description of England*, ed. Georges Edelen (Ithaca, NY, 1968; repr. New York, 1994), 103.

distribution of social, political, and economic goods.[18] Legal and political discourses continued to register their independent status, largely because, as Sherry Ortner has suggested, in hierarchical societies organized according to status, status ultimately trumps sexual difference.[19]

The single woman disappeared since she avoided (temporarily or permanently) what was regarded as the standard modality of women's subjection: marriage. But the example of Elizabeth reminds us that status remained one of the primary indicators of the fate of single women.[20] The imperatives of status, lineage, and inheritance demarcated a position for the independent woman. But as we move down the social scale, the situation of the unmarried working woman becomes very different. As many scholars have demonstrated, unmarried women were often perceived as a threat by the authorities, who went to considerable efforts to reincor-

---

[18] Though gentry and aristocratic women were more likely to be married (at least in the sixteenth century), by the eighteenth century, roughly twenty-six percent of aristocratic women became lifelong single women: Kowaleski, "Singlewomen," 61.

[19] Sherry B. Ortner, *Making Gender: The Politics and Erotics of Culture* (Boston, 1996), 107. Cf. Sir Thomas Smith: "And in this consideration also we do reject women, as those whom nature hath made to keepe home and to nourish their familie and children, and not to medle with matters abroade, nor to beare office in a citie or common wealth no more than children and infantes: except it in such cases as the authoritie is annexed to the bloud and progenie, as the crowne, a dutchie, or an erledome for there the blood is respected, not the age nor the sexe . . . For the right and honour of the blood, and the quietnes and suertie of the realme, is more to be considered, than either the base age as yet impotent to rule, or the sexe not accustomed (otherwise) to intermeddle with publicke affaires. . . ." See Sir Thomas Smith, *De Republica Anglorum*, ed. Mary Dewar (Cambridge, 1982), 64–65.

[20] As many feminist scholars have increasingly demonstrated, Queen Elizabeth's power and virgin state offered little to the masses of early modern women, including few opportunities for imitation or identification. See Susan Frye, *Elizabeth I: The Competition for Representation* (New York, 1993), 77. Elizabeth Brown has argued that, in contrast to Elizabeth's waiting women (who, despite being explicitly debarred from politics, played an important role, especially as intermediaries, in the court's various intrigues), the waiting women's devotion to Cleopatra removes them (including their mistress) from the kinship networks which were so important to the dissemination and exercise of political power in the early modern period. As a consequence, Cleopatra appears "isolated" and "exceptional," in other words, a fantasy of "female power stripped of its connections to the social world" (" 'Companion Me with My Mistress'," 144). In fact, Queen Elizabeth was often represented as exceptional, as chosen by God for an office for which, by nature, she was unfit. See, for example, John Aylmer, *An Harborowe for Faithfull and Trewe Subiectes* (Strasborowe [London], 1559), G¹; John Calvin's letter to Sir William Cecil in *The Zurich Letters*, ed. Hastings Robinson, 2 vols. (Cambridge, 1845), 2: 34–35; Edmund Spenser, *The Faerie Queene*, 5.5.25. And in a final act of historical irony, Queen Elizabeth's very visibility has often hindered research into the loves of those women, single or not, whose historical traces are so much more ephemeral. See Susan Dwyer Amussen, "Elizabeth I and Alice Balstone: Gender, Class, and the Exceptional Woman in Early Modern England," in *Attending to Women in Early Modern England*, ed. Betty S. Travitsky and Adele F. Seeff (Newark, DE, 1994), 219–40, esp. 219–20, 230–34.

porate such women into more traditional social arrangements.[21] The single women condemned by parish authorities were precisely those whose economic position rendered them the equivalent of "masterless men." This paternalism often had the consequence of rendering women's work invisible. Despite the many critiques of Alice Clark's ground-breaking *Working Life of Women in the Seventeenth Century*, Clark's work anticipates a theme evident in more recent research programs: the subordination of women's working lives, both practical and ideological, to the imperatives of family life.[22] Women's work was characterized by what Mary Prior called the "Jack Sprat Principle of the Division of Labor." In the early modern period, men's work tended to be specific and well-defined, often by occupational classifications which had important legal, political, and social functions as well.[23] Even when a man could practice his occupation only intermittently, his social and political identity was still largely determined by it.[24] Though women undoubtedly played a very important role in the early modern economy, frequently their "occupations" as brewer or baker grew out of work done for the family, and remained subordinate to the family.[25] Despite the evidence supporting the occasional woman's membership in a guild (usually because she had been widowed by a guild member), for most women work was not definitive of social or economic identity. Even service, a career which only single women pursued, did not constitute an occupational identity, since most early moderns tended to view service as merely a stage on the way to marriage.[26]

Service in particular demonstrates the interrelation between women's work and women's marriage and the failure of the presumed relationship between the two, as well as the problems that this relationship generates for late modern feminist historical projects. As the title of *Maids and Mistresses* demonstrates, two oppositions (single woman and married woman, servant and employer), two different modalities of identity, were mapped onto each other. This ambiguity points towards a crucial

---

[21] Amy M. Froide, "Marital Status as a Category of Difference: Singlewomen and Widows in Early Modern England," in *Singlewomen in the European Past, 1250–1800*, 236–69.

[22] Clark argues that prior to the onset of capitalism, the majority of industry was located within the domestic space, a situation which she sees as beneficial not only for family life, but also for women's position within the family. See Alice Clark, *Working Life of Women in the Seventeenth Century* (London, 1919, repr. 1982), 4–5, 290–95; Chris Middleton, "Women's Labour and the Transition to Pre-Industrial Capitalism," in *Women and Work in Pre-Industrial England*, ed. Lindsey Charles and Lorna Duffin (London, 1985), 181–206, here 183.

[23] Mary Prior, "Women and the Urban Economy: Oxford 1500–1800," in *Women in English Society, 1500–1800*, ed. eadem (London and New York, 1985), 93–117, here 95–96.

[24] Michael Roberts, " 'Words they are women, and deeds they are men': Images of Work and Gender in Early Modern England," in *Women and Work in Pre-Industrial England*, 122–80, here 136–44.

[25] Judith M. Bennett, "The Village Ale-Wife: Women and Brewing in Fourteenth-Century England," in *Women and Work in Preindustrial Europe*, ed. Barbara A. Hanawalt (Bloomington, 1986), 20–36, here 27.

[26] See Merry E. Wiesner, *Women and Gender in Early Modern Europe* (Cambridge, 1993), 93–94.

analytic problem: though marital and status differences cannot be equated, nevertheless they were frequently articulated together. As a consequence, the "maid" must be located at the intersection of a series of often conflicting discourses, which render her both unintelligible within and disruptive of hegemonic representations of women. Women were usually represented as strangely "class-less" (i.e., not represented as exercising privileges or prerogatives), even though their virtue implicitly signified an elevated social status. This effort to produce a representation of women that suppressed the discursive complexity of women's positions within the early modern polity rendered the maidservant — paradoxically, both a privileged and marginalized figure — a disturbance.[27] The maid is a witness to the culture's contradictory expectations of women: the reliance on degree and hierarchy, the expectation that women should embody a virtuous ideal of chastity, the importance of working women's contributions to politics and the economy.

It is in this context that the story of the maidservant masquerading as her mistress should be located. The story's retellings are frequently subordinated to the primary narrative material, which tells the story of a man's unfounded suspicion of his lover/fiancée, as usually instigated by an ostensible friend and rival for the woman's affections. Charles Prouty and Geoffrey Bullough, in their studies of Shakespeare's source material for *Much Ado About Nothing*, have identified two traditions in the retelling of this story, one deriving from Bandello's novella, the other derived from Ariosto's *Orlando Furioso*.[28] Whereas the former tradition usually provides no external cause for the lover's jealousy of his fiancée, the Ariostan tradition does furnish such an object, in the person of a maid masquerading as her mistress. It was the latter version that was most popular in Elizabethan England, occasioning at least four "translations," including three in the 1590s.[29] What follows focuses on what these three produced; though I have not attempted to place the following consideration of Ariosto/Harington, Spenser, and Shakespeare within a thick contextual description of that tumultuous decade, I remain impressed by how dislocations within the socio-economic fabric of late Elizabethan England placed considerable pressure on the mistress-servant relation. As I will argue, the maidser-

---

[27] Mark Thornton Burnett has recently examined the theatrical interest in figures of the working man, through whom problems of power and autonomy were often articulated, and has concluded that, for the most part, working women are remarkably silenced within early modern literature. Though his argument is convincing, I have argued that such silence is symptomatic, and that many early modern texts register the working woman's absence. See Mark Thornton Burnett, *Masters and Servants in English Renaissance Drama and Culture: Authority and Obedience* (New York, 1997).

[28] Charles T. Prouty, *The Sources of Much Ado About Nothing: A Critical Study, Together with the Text of Peter Beverley's Ariodanto and Ieneura* (New Haven, 1950); Geoffrey Bullough, ed., *Narrative and Dramatic Sources of Shakespeare* (London, 1958), 2: 61–139.

[29] See Miranda Johnson-Haddad, "Englishing Ariosto: *Orlando furioso* at the Court of Elizabeth I," *Comparative Literature Studies* 31 (1994): 323–50. In addition to Harington's translation of Ariosto, Spenser's version, and Shakespeare's play, Peter Beverley translated the story of Ariodante and Ginevra as "The Historie of Ariodanto and Ieneura" in 1566. Prouty includes the long poem in an appendix to *Sources*.

vant's masquerade as her mistress reveals with particular acuity the problematic representation of a working girl's desire and its general unintelligibility, given the attempted narrative consolidation of women's identity in marriage. Those narratives that examined the perils of courtship frequently attempted to stage how the antagonism of sexual difference gives way to the complementarity of marriage. Within this social imaginary, marriage becomes the mechanism by which other social disturbances are eased. It synecdochally represents the various relations (prince and subject, master and servant, parent and child) uniting the body politic. As a consequence, the specific identities and desires of working women are obscured by a narrative logic that privileges aristocratic marriage as the means to resolve antagonisms converted into contradictions and suture discontinuities within politico-economic discourses.

In Book 4, Ariosto's *Orlando Furioso* recounts the story of how Ariodante, a knight at the Scottish court, became convinced of the Scottish princess Ginevra's infidelity with the Duke of Albany, Polynesso: after seducing Ginevra's maid, Dalinda, Polynesso convinces her to masquerade as her mistress in a tableau set up for Ariodante's eyes. Maddened with jealousy, Ariodante apparently commits suicide, leaving Ginevra at the mercy of his brother, Lurcanio, who has accused her of dishonor. Because Scottish law equates a woman's virtue with her reputation, Ginevra's chastity must be proven by a champion; otherwise, she must be executed. Renaldo, one of Ariosto's heroes, decides to fight on Ginevra's behalf, but discovers that a disguised knight (later revealed to be Ariodante) has already stepped in. Renaldo interrupts the battle, reveals Polynesso's treachery, and then kills him in battle. Ariodante marries Ginevra and assumes Polynesso's title as Duke of Albany, while Dalinda leaves for a convent.

Though John Harington's marginal glosses to his translation twice identify the story as the "tale of Ginevra," she remains something of a mystery. Most of the tale is actually recounted by Dalinda, whom Renaldo rescues shortly after he has decided to travel to the Scottish court to defend Ginevra. From 4.56 until 4.74, she tells him the story of Polynesso's desire for Ginevra and the trickery he used to besmirch her honor. But the tale also describes at great length Dalinda's almost masochistic love for Polynesso. Given the intensive focus on Dalinda's affections, the story's omission of any similar treatment of Ginevra is remarkable. Only one stanza is devoted to the latter's inner life:

> O Lord what wofull words by her were spoken
> Laid all alone upon her restlesse bed?
> Oft did she strike her guiltlesse breast in token
> Of that great griefe that inwardly was bred. . . .[30]

The opening (rhetorical?) question raises the possibility that even here, when the narrator would apparently claim a privileged perspective into Ginevra's interiority,

---

[30] Ludovico Ariosto, *Orlando Furioso*, trans. John Harington, ed. R. McNulty (Oxford, 1972), 5.60; hereafter cited in the text by canto and stanza numbers.

it remains mysterious. One of the accompanying woodcuts confirms Ginevra's marginalization: whereas Dalinda is represented twice in the foreground, Ginevra only appears once, in the background. Her identity is subordinated to Dalinda's especially insofar as the "story of Ginevra" must be told by her maidservant. But the privilege to narrate has its price. Dalinda provides no model for an autonomous feminine agent; in her masquerade as Ginevra, her own desire is simultaneously uncovered and disguised by an identification with her mistress. As we will see, though Dalinda's first-person narrative apparently consolidates her identity, her subjectivity is actually articulated via and disintegrated within a series of unstable and oscillating identifications. These reveal the pressures of status differentiation on sexual difference.

The "Tale of Ginevra" maps efforts to "social climb" onto the tribulations of courtship. Certainly, Polynesso and Ariodante's rivalry for Ginevra's love is a not-so-subtle cloak for status differences as well. As Dalinda informs Renaldo,

> Not all of love but partly of ambition
> He [Polynesso] beares in hand his minde is onely bent;
> Because of her great state and hie condition
> To have her for his wife is his entent. (5.13)

Ginevra therefore represents not only an object of love, but also an avenue of social advancement, as Ariodante himself notes:

> For know, I am (though not in rents or land)
> Yet in my Princes grace no whit inferior
> And in his daughters greatly your superior. (5.30)

Ariodante's characterization of his relationship to Ginevra and her father as a "sound ... estate" (5.35) recapitulates a fundamental antagonism within early modern Europe: the tension between a more established feudal nobility (Polynesso, the Duke of Albany), and an educated, upstart "stranger," who has won the king's love through his fame and accomplishments. Ginevra therefore symbolizes, to both Polynesso and Ariodante, the princely affections that were necessary for success at court. Beyond this lesson in an incipient absolutism or state centralization, though, the Prince's grace and daughter's favor erases status differences, at least between gentlemen; in relation to the king, Ariodante and Polynesso are equals.[31] Harington's gloss plays up this interpretation of Ginevra's love, noting that "it is no disparagement for the greatest Emperesse in the world to marrie one that is a gentleman by birth ..." (68).

---

[31] This recalls Sir Philip Sidney's argument to Queen Elizabeth after his quarrel with the Earl of Oxford; when the Queen tried to remind Sidney of the difference in birth and estate, Sidney replied (according to Fulke Greville), "the difference of degrees between free men could not challenge any other homage than precedency." See Fulke Greville, "A Dedication to Sir Philip Sidney," in *The Prose Works of Fulke Greville, Lord Brooke*, ed. John Gouws (Oxford, 1986), 3–135, here 41.

Onto Ginevra and her favors is displaced the problem of status differences between men; ambition takes the form of rivalry for her affections. Ginevra's honor thus becomes a marker of socio-political fairness and desert, which perhaps explains Renaldo's own somewhat ambivalent attitude towards the "problem" of her honesty. Whereas initially Renaldo denounces the Scottish law because women should have the right to enjoy their lovers as much as men (4.50–54), after Dalinda's story,

> his corage was confirmed well
> That wanted erst a true and certaine ground,
> For though before for her he ment to fight,
> Yet rather now for to defend the right. (5.75)[32]

Despite Renaldo's initial defense of a woman's right to enjoy sex as she sees fit (in fact, a *demand* that she enjoy, since he criticizes "disdain"), here he reinforces the narrative's investment in Ginevra's honesty. Ginevra must be honest, so that Ariodante's claim to her love, and hence his own merit, may be confirmed. Concomitantly, sexual transgression must be displaced onto Dalinda, a servant who cannot serve as a reward. Though both Ariodante and Dalinda's positions are similar, and though erotic desire offers them both the best opportunity for social advancement, in the end their differences are emphasized and ascribed to gender. In other words, the narrative suggests that a meritocratic system of rewards for men must be underwritten by status differences between women that are disguised as a function of sexual behaviors, licit and illicit. This asymmetry is evident even in the tale's introduction: for men, nobility matters, since only a noble knight can undertake the defense of an accused woman; for women, sex outweighs status, since all women, base or noble, are subject to the harsh Scottish law. Both Ginevra and Dalinda are collapsed into a representation of "woman" which attempts to deny the importance of social status to women.

Dalinda's tale continues to disguise the problem of women's social ambitions as a problem of love. For Dalinda, love is the cause of her downfall:

> Till love (alas that love such care should bring)
> Envide my state and sought to do me shame. (5.7)

Dalinda's personification of love projects her emotions onto the external world, resulting in a fragmented subjectivity. Despite her insistence that erotic desire was responsible for her downfall, ambition nevertheless lurks within the metaphor: love envies her "state," a word that recalls "estate" as well as "status." And given Dalinda's later masquerade as her mistress, it is not too farfetched to see her identified with the love that she disavows, and her envy for her mistress displaced onto that love. As Valeria Finucci has argued, Ginevra constitutes Dalinda's "ego-ideal"; disguise offers her a way to overcome fantasmatically the status difference between the

---

[32] A viewpoint which merited from Harington a marginal comment ascribing it to Catholicism, and a moralistic condemnation following Book 4.

two. When she describes her habit of meeting Polynesso in Ginevra's chamber, she emphasizes that this was the room where "the things of greatest value lay" (5.9). When Polynesso asks her to masquerade as Ginevra, he asks her to wear Ginevra's richest clothing:

> Her gorgets and her jewels rich no lesse
> You may put on t'accomplish my desire. . . . (5.25)

Dalinda herself later provides a second description of her appearance as Ginevra, which reveals her desire to be exceptional:

> Not thus content, the vaile aloft I set
> Which only Princes weare. (5.47)

The result?

> Me thought before I was not much unlike her,
> But certaine now I seemed very like her . . . (5.49)

Assuming Ginevra's clothes allows Dalinda to forge an imaginary identification with her.

But as Finucci has also argued, the masquerade presumes a masculine spectator, and therefore the apparent subversion is in the service of masculine desire. When Dalinda masquerades to satisfy Polynesso's desire, she reveals that desire as desire of the Other, that her desire to be Ginevra derives from Polynesso's desire for Ginevra. Status and erotic desire are closely intertwined here; when Dalinda tells Renaldo, "God knowth how glad I was to worke his will" (5.16), she places her identity as Ginevra's maidservant in the service of Polynesso's own desires, resulting in the masochism which Finucci describes. According to Finucci, class identity and the performances to which it gives rise offer Dalinda an opportunity, perhaps, to escape from the rigid gendered norms that the "tale of Ginevra" ends up rigorously enforcing. Finucci has argued that Dalinda's class identity is conscious and hence manipulable; she therefore rationalizes Dalinda's character in order to give her a voice. But status is less manipulable than Finucci's analysis would allow us to believe.[33] Under the pressure of status differentiation, Dalinda's identity actually

---

[33] See Valeria Finucci, "The Female Masquerade: Ariosto and the Game of Desire," in *Desire in the Renaissance*, ed. eadem and Regina Schwartz (Princeton, 1994), 61–88. Finucci's essay raises an important historiographic problem: that of "class" versus "status." Though it might be true that class is a more voluntarily chosen identity (insofar as it has no necessarily biological component) for many in Western democracies, class or status functioned quite differently in early modern Europe, especially since status, unlike the more modern class, was an identity underwritten by birth and blood. As several essays on the topic reveal, neither class (an economic concept) nor status (a pre-modern ontology of blood) is sufficient to capture the complexities of early modern hierarchies. In large part, this may be because, as Fernand Braudel suggests in his magisterial *Civilization and Capitalism, 15th–18th Century*, early modern societies were marked by as many as five

fragments, caught between her sense of herself as fundamentally deprived and her fantasmatic identification with Ginevra.

This fragmentation of Dalinda's subjectivity is embodied in the form of her narrative. As she tells Renaldo the story of her lover's treachery, she repeatedly emphasizes her complete and total lack of knowledge about his true motives or desires. When she describes her masquerade as Ginevra, she emphasizes how "[a]ll unawares I stood in all their sight" (5.47). The repetition of "all" contrasts her ignorance with Polynesso's, Ariodante's, and Lurcanio's sight and knowledge. At the same time, as Dalinda recounts her tale, she suggests that her ignorance may have been willful:

> I might have found by certaine strange delayes
> That he but little lov'd and much did faine,
> For all his sleights were not so closely covered
> But that they might full easly be discovered. (5.11)

Dalinda's refusal to see what subsequently becomes evident is quite remarkable given Polynesso's own explicit deployment of a logic of self-deception. When he attempts to convince her to masquerade as Ginevra, he argues that disguise is necessary in order to satisfy a frustrated and deceptive desire:

> Ne do I deeme so deare the great delight
> As I disdain I should be so reject,
> And lest this griefe should overcome me quight
> Because I faile to bring it to effect,
> To please my fond conceipt this verie night
> I pray thee, deare, to do as I direct ... (5.24)
>
> . . . . .
> Thus I may passe my fancies foolish fit,
> And thus (quoth he) my selfe I would deceave,
> And I that had no reason nor no wit
> His shamefull drift (though open) to perceave
> Did weare my mistresse robes that serv'd me fit
> And stood at window there him to receave,
> And of the fraud I was no whit aware
> Till that fell out that caused all my care. (5.26)

Polynesso presents himself to Dalinda as divided between a self dominated by a "fond conceipt," a desire which has thus far been frustrated, and an "I" that would

---

different sorts of hierarchical social arrangements. See Fernand Braudel, *The Wheels of Commerce*, trans. Siân Reynolds., vol. 2 of *Civilization and Capitalism, 15th–18th Century*, 3 vols. (New York, 1982), 464–66. Moreover, it raises an important methodological issue regarding the use of psychoanalytic concepts to read other subjective modalities or social identities. If class is rendered a product of the conscious mind, psychoanalytic theory's pertinence to analyses of class is denied.

organize the satisfaction of this other self's desire. He then proposes to project this division onto Dalinda's body; the clothing that will render her "like" Ginevra signifies a desire that he knows cannot be satisfied. He thus represents himself as consciously split, in a manner similar to her retroactive construction of herself as divided between a subsequent awareness of the signs, and her initial refusal to read them.

Whereas Polynesso would subordinate his desire to his knowledge by manufacturing the object of desire, Dalinda's knowledge and lack thereof is determined by her desire. Why would Dalinda accede to Polynesso's request? Is this a sign of masochism or abjection, as Finucci has suggested? The key, perhaps, lies in the second stanza quoted above, and the floating "I" in lines 1–4 of 5.26. Not until line 4, and the third-person pronoun "his," is the reader assured that the antecedent of the "I" has changed from Polynesso to Dalinda. This confusion is also highlighted by the "deceave"/ "perceave" rhyme, which links his proposed self-deception to her refusal of perception. It is this refusal of knowledge that we might label "unconscious." In the story she tells Renaldo, she splits her representation of herself into a past self, one unknowing, and the self telling the story. The latter assumes the primary narrative function, and therefore appears omniscient at times (as in her accounts of other characters' conversations). The division between knowledge and refusal of knowledge, conscious and unconscious, is projected onto a narrative axis, such that the unconscious refusal of knowledge is ultimately subordinated to the demand for revelation and reward or punishment. Thus, while Dalinda's story represents her subjectivity as a disjointed series of identifications, the act of telling the story offers a consolidation of that subjectivity, marked by Dalinda's realization of Polynesso's unworthiness, as well as the full extent of her own participation in his plot. But this consolidation, if indeed it is such, is costly: Dalinda vows "To live her life in prayre and penitent" (6.16), and retreats to a convent in Denmark. Her fate is punctuated by Ariodante's. Though both occupy similar social positions, and have similar erotic ambitions, Ariodante is rewarded with Polynesso's dukedom, and marries Ginevra; the conflict between feudal status and courtly merit is resolved by his absorption into a feudal nobility relegitimated by the Scottish king. Dalinda's masquerade ends up conserving Ginevra as an icon of inherent worth that confirms the possessor's value. But she herself remains isolated from this general comedic renewal: her ambition is frustrated, and her only recourse is a removal from the world.

Finally, even her story becomes subordinated to Ginevra's, especially given Harington's interpretive framework. Though the tale concludes with Dalinda's fate, Harington's marginal comment reads, "Heere ends the tale of Genevra" (6.16). When Dalinda tells Renaldo of Polynesso's love for Ginevra, Harington notes, "A pollicie used sometime to woo the maid to win the mistres" (5.12), thereby collapsing Dalinda's identity into that of Ginevra. Whereas Harington uses the other principal characters to illustrate various morals (e.g., "in *Ariodant*, the hurt of a credulous jealousie ..." [69]), Dalinda's only mention is in relation to Polynesso: "In *Polynessos* entent to kill *Dalinda* you may observe how wicked men often bewray their owne misdeeds with seeking to hide them" (69). Dalinda therefore becomes one of Polynesso's misdeeds; her love for Polynesso and betrayal of Ginevra apparently offer no worthy moral, perhaps because Harington would deny that Dalinda could function as a model for the reader. For in the end, Harington's moralizing glosses to Ariosto's epic would attempt to renovate the reader's subjective position vis-à-vis virtue. Dalinda's subjectivity, however, remains too disjointed, her story too ambivalent, for any easy moralizing. She becomes a hermeneutic throwaway.

Harington's simplistic erasure of Dalinda's story forecasts the fate of the maidservant in two of the most noteworthy retellings of Ariosto's tale, Spenser's *Faerie Queene* and Shakespeare's *Much Ado About Nothing*, both of which subordinate the maidservant's voice(s) and ultimately leave her unintegrated into the narrative resolution. Certainly, one of the primary difficulties in transporting Ariosto's story from early sixteenth-century Catholic Italy to later sixteenth-century Protestant England is Dalinda's retreat to a convent. In Spenser and Shakespeare's retellings, the maidservant cannot retreat to the singular (and single) existence of the convent. She becomes something of an embarrassment, a figure that does not fit into the tale's end.

Spenser's version of Ariosto's story appears in Book 2 of *The Faerie Queene*, the book of temperance. But Spenser's version is very different from Ariosto's: whereas the latter is dominated by the maidservant's story, the former is recounted by the deceived suitor, Phedon. Guyon and his companion, the Palmer, encounter Phedon as he is being dragged by Furor, an allegorical personification of anger, followed by his mother Occasion, a classic scold. After Guyon succeeds in locking Occasion's mouth and enchaining Furor, Phedon narrates his story, which resembles its "source," though no last-minute revelation saves Claribell, Phedon's fiancée. After killing her, Phedon poisons his friend Philemon, and tries to kills Pryene (Claribell's maid); but when she runs away, he is captured by Furor and Occasion, until freed by Guyon.

Despite these differences, Spenser remains concerned with a similar complex of thematic elements in the story, including the problem of woman's honesty, the anxieties over status differentiation, the problem of masculine rivalry, and finally (when the storyteller fails to mediate these antagonisms) the disturbance of subjectivity. If Book 1 gives us certain expectations about the typical Spenserian hero and a narrative form in which that hero comes to embody his or her virtue, Book 2 completely undermines those expectations, giving us a hero who seems insufficiently heroic and/or intemperate, as well as a narrative whose explicit moral *sententiae* seem at odds with the tragedies depicted.[34] Several critics have brilliantly demonstrated Guyon's inability to deal with his and others' passions, rendering the Aristotelian virtue of temperance inoperative within a fallen world.[35] However, what I would like to focus on is less the challenge passion poses to the virtue of temperance than the material inequities that Book 2 so often encodes as passion.[36] Several

---

[34] See Harry Berger, *The Allegorical Temper: Vision and Reality in Book 2 of Spenser's Faerie Queene* (New Haven, 1957); Stephen Greenblatt, *Renaissance Self-Fashioning: From More to Shakespeare* (Chicago, 1980), 169–92.

[35] Madelon S. Gohlke, "Embattled Allegory: Book II of *The Faerie Queene*," *English Literary Renaissance* 8 (1978): 123–40; Lauren Silberman, "*The Faerie Queene*, Book II and the Limitations of Temperance," *Modern Language Studies* 17 (1987): 9–22; Harry Berger, Jr., "Narrative as Rhetoric in *The Faerie Queene*," *English Literary Renaissance* 21 (1991): 3–48.

[36] Several recent readers of Spenser have argued that the poem's project of developing a moral philosophy which would accord with Renaissance humanism and Protestant theology fails when

episodes in Book 2, including Guyon's descent into hell, suggest that class/status is a displaced (or suppressed) aspect of bodily life that he finds uncomfortable. The Phedon episode reveals how class and status differences rupture the ideality that becomes increasingly associated with an aristocratic, courtly ethos. In other words, those phenomena treated by contemporary materialism are situated within the categories of matter and body, with the result that subjectivities other than those of aristocratic men have been suppressed. Not surprisingly, the maidservant becomes the ultimate objectification of this problem.

Canto 4 opens with a theme to be found throughout Phedon's story: the problem of status difference ("There is I know not what great difference / Betweene the vulgar and the noble seed ..."[37]) and its conflicts with sexual difference, neither of which assume priority in the determination of political authority. Repeatedly, Phedon projects his anxiety over his own social status onto the various women in his life. Phedon and Philemon became friends because they shared the "tender dug of commune nourse" (2.4.18). As Harry Berger, Jr. has noted, Phedon's use of the word "commune" suggests not only a meaning of "communal," but also "base."[38] The nurse supports the two squires' friendship, their "common-ality," but as Phedon's story continues, it becomes evident that she has also produced a rivalrous confusion that can only be resolved through the extinction of commonality. Significantly, a woman of lower status mediates and troubles their homosocial relation.

As in Ariosto's *Orlando Furioso*, rivalry between men is also projected onto a woman of higher social status. Not surprisingly, therefore, anxiety over social status intrudes when Phedon becomes convinced of Claribell's betrayal. As Phedon paraphrases Philemon,

> how he vnderstood
> That Ladie whom I had to me assynd,
> Had both distaind her honorable blood,
> And eke the faith, which she to me did bynd. ... (2.4.22)

Claribell's supposed betrayal of Phedon with a "groome of base degree" (2.4.24) reveals Phedon's anxiety over his own comparatively lower status. Because Phedon disavows status difference via idealist fantasies of friendship and true love, the impact of these material differences emerges within the "primal scene" set up by Philemon. At this moment, Claribell's handmaid makes her brief, if significant, appearance. Whereas the "Tale of Ginevra" never dispels the impression of Polynesso and Dalinda's emotional involvement, Phedon's version emphasizes that Philemon

---

the poem takes as its most immediate context England's incipient colonial domination of Ireland. See Elizabeth Fowler, "The Failure of Moral Philosophy in the Work of Edmund Spenser," *Representations* 51 (1995): 47–76.

[37] Edmund Spenser, *The Faerie Queene*, ed. Thomas P. Roche (Harmondsworth, 1978), 2.4.1; hereafter cited in the text by book, canto, and stanza.

[38] Berger, "Narrative as Rhetoric," 20–21 n. 19.

uses Pryene, Claribell's maid, to further his own ends. Moreover, Pryene's only motive is "social climbing." Philemon convinces her to participate in his plot by appealing to what Sheila Cavanagh has called "the importance of being fairest."[39] Social differences, such as those of status or race, are converted into differences of beauty:

> He woo'd her thus: *Pryene* (so she hight)
> What great despight doth fortune to thee beare,
> Thus lowly to abase thy beautie bright,
> That it should not deface all others lesser light?
>
> But if she had her least helpe to thee lent,
> T'adorne thy forme according thy desart,
> Their blazing pride thou wouldest soone haue blent,
> And staynd their prayses with thy least good part;
> Ne should faire *Claribell* with all her art,
> Though she thy Lady be, approch thee neare:
> For proofe thereof, this euening, as thou art,
> Aray thy selfe in her most gorgeous geare,
> That I may more delight in thy embracement deare. (2.4.25–26)

In order to seduce Pryene, Philemon convinces her that her beauty lacks the adornment that should ideally supplement it. In so doing, he notes the social disparity between her and Claribell, but displaces the "fault" for that disparity onto fortune, which has "abased" Pryene's own beauty. Because Pryene's "unabased" beauty (beauty paradoxically supplemented with adornment) would "deface" all others' beauty, the conversion of social antagonism into beauty differences deploys the logic of status hierarchy against any sense of women's community. When Philemon focuses on how Pryene's beauty would overwhelm Claribell's, "[t]hough she [her] Lady be," he reduces the issue of status differences between women to a beauty competition between Pryene and Claribell. Since a social ontology mandates a permanent disparity between Pryene's desert and Claribell's better birth, Philemon suggests a masquerade tailored to his sexual enjoyment. At this point, it is important to note an elision also apparent in *Much Ado About Nothing*: though Phedon tells us that Philemon disguised himself like the "groome of base degree," he never tells us why Pryene would have agreed to engage in such a spectacle. In fact, unlike Ariosto's version, Pryene never speaks in this episode, and vanishes before its end. However, drawing on Philemon's own arguments to convince her, we can hypothesize that, for Pryene, social ambition requires a pornographic masquerade. And though Phedon interprets Pryene as "proud through prayse and mad through loue" (2.4.27), for Pryene, the masquerade attests to and temporarily resolves the injustice

---

[39] Sheila Cavanagh, *Wanton Eyes and Chaste Desires: Female Sexuality in The Faerie Queene* (Bloomington, 1994), 75.

of a social system organized according to birth and blood.[40] Philemon therefore manufactures Pryene's misrecognition of her own position in a manner similar to Phedon's efforts to encode as moral failures the social tensions that run throughout his narrative.

Phedon's moralizing and narcissistic interpretation of the "primal scene" suggests why he misrecognizes his own role in the tragedy, as well as why Guyon's temperance remains insufficient to account for the events. By labeling himself "[t]he sad spectatour of my Tragedie" (2.4.27), Phedon explicitly removes himself from the events and sets up the allegorical means by which he projects his own psychic states onto external personifications that are then assigned responsibility for his excessive passions.[41] His evasion of responsibility is evident in the confused syntax of 2.4.29, which recounts his murder of Claribell: "I slew her innocent" (2.4.29). But it is unclear whether "innocent" modifies "I" or "her." Moreover, despite his hatred of "false faytour *Philemon*" (2.4.30), he blames Pryene, "Her faultie Handmayd, which that bale did breede . . ." (2.4.29), for his tragedy: "my woes beginner . . . she did first offend, / She last should smart . . ." (2.4.31). He therefore pursues her with his sword, until he meets Furor: "me met in middle space, / As I her, so he me pursewd apace . . ." (2.4.32). As Phedon pursues Pryene, so Furor pursues Phedon.

But this tableau also raises some interesting generic possibilities. As Silberman characterizes it, personification externalizes an "internal" disposition, and therefore allows the subject to reject his or her proprietary interest in that disposition. Though Silberman presumes a model of subjectivity that can clearly differentiate between the internal and the external, I think her analysis of personification and subjectivity important. As recent critics have demonstrated, within *The Faerie Queene* personification persists both as the limit to and the extinction of a subjectivity that seems always to straddle the divide between interior and exterior.[42] In Phedon's case, Furor objectifies the rage and "fowle despight" which led him to murder Claribell; Occasion is a witness to Phedon's inability to "connect passions to their occasion," his inability to construe the events which actually produced his anger.[43] But what this analysis misses is the manner in which Furor replaces Pryene while also reversing the pursuit. Initially, Furor chases Phedon as Phedon chases Pryene, but she then drops out of the narrative, leaving Phedon alone with his objectified passions. We might characterize Pryene, then, as a vanishing mediator in the transfer of responsibility for passion from Phedon's psyche to the personifications who have captured him. Ultimately, the socio-political antagonisms generated by Philemon and Phedon's rivalry and Claribell's rarified social status give way to a concern with Phedon's inability to control his passions. Pryene thus comes

---

[40] Moreover, given his later description of Philemon's erotic activity with the seeming Claribell as "playing" ("with whom he playd" [2.4.28]), it appears that Phedon conflates eroticism and theatricality.

[41] See Silberman, "Limitations of Temperance," 15; Berger, "Narrative as Rhetoric," 13.

[42] David Lee Miller, *The Poem's Two Bodies: The Poetics of the 1590 Faerie Queene* (Princeton, 1988), 115.

[43] Silberman, "Limitations of Temperance," 15.

to figure in the process by which material (i.e., socio-political) inequities are equated with and replaced by a concern with the matter, the material support, or the body of aristocratic masculinity. As in the *Orlando Furioso*, the ambitions of lower-status men are disguised and displaced onto the social ambitions of working girls.

In the *Orlando Furioso*, theatricality provides a space for the maidservant to articulate a desire that (though not her "own") splits apart the homogenous image of "woman." Spenser's account of the theatrical moment (and the force of theatricality) remains ambiguous, however, insofar as his account emphasizes not the maidservant's agency but the spectator's passivity. Since Phedon merely watches rather than directs his tragedy, his own responsibility for these murderous events is extinguished. Given the interpretive needs of Book 2, the maid's theatricality is replaced by allegorical personification. Such personification, especially as it is deployed within this episode, requires an interpreter: in this case, Guyon and the Palmer, who do not shrink from their interpretive duty. Once they have glossed the events as the result of intemperate emotion ("wrath, gealosie, griefe, loue" [2.4.35]), Phedon's entrapment by personification terminates, as signified by the first mention of his name:

> *Phedon* I hight (quoth he) and do aduaunce
> Mine aunceſtry from famous *Coradin*,
> Who first to rayse our house to honour did begin. (2.4.36)

It is as if the narration and moralization of his story undo the process of subsumption.[44] Only then can Phedon assume his "proper" name and his placement within a genealogy defined largely by its social mobility, though one contained by a traditional gentlemanly emphasis on honor. But the passage into personification has disguised the material social antagonisms which threaten to undo the neo-Platonic social relations of love and friendship which Phedon wishes to enforce. The entire episode therefore witnesses a transfer of affective and interpretive authority from the theatricality of Pryene's masquerade to the personifications that are the privileged trope of allegorical narrative. Spenser thus completes the process begun by Harington's moralizing of *Orlando Furioso*.

Ariosto's *Orlando Furioso* and Spenser's *Faerie Queene* remain concerned with a narrative consolidation of subjectivity, particularly in relation to material differences of class/status and sexual difference; each reveals how the legitimation of a man's social ambition, encoded as the love for a woman of superior social status, apparently requires the delegitimation of a maidservant's social ambition. Such desire, both erotic and social, is both articulated by and concealed within a masquerade, which registers social differences between women while attempting to adumbrate them via a representation of a pre-political woman (i.e., the exceptional and/or beautiful woman). Similar problems disturb Shakespeare's *Much Ado About Nothing*, though the generic differences ultimately render such a consolidation of subjectivity

---

[44] See the description of this process as it affects Malbecco in Book 3, in Linda Gregerson, *The Reformation of the Subject: Spenser, Milton, and the English Protestant Epic* (Cambridge, 1995), 48–79.

(in earlier critical parlance, the production of character) a dicier proposition. Character has long been one of the more significant critical concepts to be deployed in readings of Shakespeare. But *Much Ado*'s emphasis on fashion tends to empty out interiority or redeploys that which was interior as exterior. Even the climactic moment when Beatrice and Benedick's love is revealed is less about the revelation of hidden feeling (the "heart") than how a conventional and public poetic form such as the sonnet testifies against the heart:

> *Claudio*: And I'll be sworn upon't that he loves her,
> For here's a paper written in his own hand,
> A halting sonnet of his own pure brain,
> Fashioned to Beatrice.
> *Hero*: And here's another,
> Writ in my cousin's hand, stol'n from her pocket,
> Containing her affection unto Benedick.
> *Benedick*: A miracle! Here's our own hands against our hearts.[45]

This articulation of the ostensible interior as that which is at odds with and finally overcome by the exterior is especially evident in the character of Margaret, the character whose fashion sense ultimately leaves her with no character whatsoever.

In contradistinction to Spenser's *Faerie Queene*, *Much Ado About Nothing* takes theatricality, especially the theatricality of clothing, as an explicit thematic focus. *Much Ado* is a play obsessed with fashion and erotic love, with (we might say) erotic love as fashion: when men love, Benedick notes (to his dismay), they lie awake at nights "carving the fashion of a new doublet" (2.3.16). *Much Ado*'s concern with fashion, its relentless visibility, and Messina's reduction of the social world to its appearances, have been viewed with critical ambivalence. Many critics have opposed to *Much Ado*'s relentless specularity a transcendent space, usually embodied in a relationship (such as that of Beatrice and Benedick) based on faith or trust.[46] Still others have derided what they see as ideological mystification and have instead focused on those characters, including Don John, Dogberry, Beatrice, and Hero, who seem excluded from the oppressive power relations that the narrative confirms.[47] Perhaps the most powerful essays have explored how *Much Ado* takes as its project the production of a sexual relation that supports women's visibility as women. This visibility is grounded in a virtuous nature that produces women's essential homo-

---

[45] William Shakespeare, "Much Ado About Nothing," in *The Norton Shakespeare*, ed. Stephen Greenblatt (New York, 1997), 5.4.85–91; hereafter cited in the text by act, scene, and line numbers.

[46] See David Ormerod, "Faith and Fashion in *Much Ado About Nothing*," *Shakespeare Survey* 25 (1972): 93–105; Elliot Krieger, "Social Relations and the Social Order in *Much Ado About Nothing*," *Shakespeare Survey* 32 (1979): 49–61.

[47] John Drakakis, "Trust and Transgression: The Discursive Practices of *Much Ado About Nothing*," in *Post-structuralist Readings of English Poetry*, ed. Richard Machin and Christopher Norris (Cambridge, 1982), 59–84.

geneity, erasing their social differences and their agency. The emphasis on visibility suggests that a theatricality associated with women will disturb patriarchal authority and patrilineal succession.[48]

Though Hero's silence troubles but does not subvert patriarchal ideology,[49] for the majority of feminist critics Beatrice has offered the best possible challenge to Messina's aristocratic patrilineal society. But I would argue that Beatrice is not a locus of real subversion. It is not so much that Beatrice's wit makes her "manlike," nor that she expresses a desire to be a man (after Claudio has shamed Hero): either one of these actions could constitute a legitimate subversion of patriarchy. Rather, Beatrice offers no substantial challenge to Messinian patriarchy because she is exceptional: though her fatherless status might underwrite her own freedom, she offers nothing to women *in toto*. By definition, the exceptional woman is inimitable; she occupies a position that (by circumstance or prescription) forbids imitation or identification. Moreover, as an ideological construct, the exceptional woman blocks the historical emergence of "women" as a socially recognized and politically salient collective. In Beatrice's case, the exceptional woman appears to articulate the possibility of "women's" resistance to the patrilineal social institutions that have subdued Hero.[50] But as Margaret's example demonstrates, the exceptional woman's effect is limited, given the very real material disparities between Beatrice's and Margaret's situations. In other words, Margaret's efforts to imitate Beatrice (as when she attempts to prove witty in 3.4 or requests a sonnet from Benedick in honor of her beauty in 5.2) are restricted by her very different social situation and prospects. Margaret's position vis-à-vis the aristocratic Hero and Beatrice therefore troubles a feminist criticism that critiques patriarchy's construction and subsequent oppression of "women," insofar as this criticism remains caught up within "women" as a totality that tends to erase those differences working against the similarity of women's social positions and experience.

But it is difficult to extricate Margaret's representation from the play's general representation of women. After all, she is a character who appears onstage infrequently, and who apparently lacks consistency.[51] Moreover, the scene that prompts

---

[48] Jean Howard, "Renaissance Antitheatricality and the Politics of Gender and Rank in *Much Ado About Nothing*," in *Shakespeare Reproduced: The Text in History and Ideology*, ed. Jean E. Howard and Marion F. O'Connor (New York, 1987), 163–87.

[49] See Carol Cook, "'The Sign and Semblance of Her Honor': Reading Gender Difference in *Much Ado About Nothing*," in *Shakespeare and Gender: A History*, ed. Deborah E. Barker and Ivo Kamps (London, 1995), 75–103.

[50] Harry Berger has suggested that Hero, though subdued, is also somewhat resentful of her position, and envious of her cousin's apparent freedom. Hence her desire to participate in the scheme which produces Beatrice's submission to Benedick (through marriage). See Harry Berger, Jr., "Against the Sink-a-Pace: Sexual and Family Politics in *Much Ado About Nothing*," *Shakespeare Quarterly* 33 (1982): 302–13; repr. in idem, *Making Trifles of Terrors: Redistributing Complicities in Shakespeare*, ed. Peter Erickson (Stanford, 1997), 10–24, here 13–15.

[51] In one case a critic has concluded that her character is fundamentally incoherent due to faulty composition. See Allan Gilbert, "Two Margarets: The Composition of *Much Ado About Nothing*," *Philological Quarterly* 41 (1962): 61–71.

so much of the play's later action — Margaret's masquerade as Hero — is never represented onstage in *Much Ado*. In marked contrast to its source material, the masquerade scene is dispersed throughout the play: we see its planning stages in 2.2, John's setup of Claudio in 3.2, Claudio's account in 4.1, and Borachio's confessions in 3.3 and 5.1. Only in 5.1 is the audience given the information that Margaret wore Hero's clothing. The play repeatedly revisits this scene, the ground of its existence, and yet it remains, in a sense, unrepresentable, as if its explicit diegetic logic — the logic of *Much Ado*'s fictional world — could not recognize what the scene reveals.

Margaret's actions and desires make the "much ado about nothing," and yet we never see her perspective on these events. She is paradoxically both central and marginal to the play's action, and she eludes the interpretive paradigms that other characters and critics use to resolve the problems generated by her inconsistent portrayal and problematic virtue. Internally, the problem of Margaret's character arises in relation to virtue. The play offers a hegemonic representation of "woman," in which woman is reduced to a visually verifiable "simple virtue." For example, in the first scene, Imogen's chastity is guaranteed by Hero's resemblance to Leonato. Later, when Claudio accuses Hero —

> Would you not swear,
> All you that see her, that she were a maid,
> By these exterior shows? But she is none. (4.1.37–39)

— he suggests that women are either defined through a chastity which unites interior and exterior, or a whoredom which is defined by and as negation ("But she is none"). In a play that equates Hero's talking to Borachio/Claudio with illicit sexuality, it is difficult to construe how Margaret's own actions fit into the male characters' efforts to police Hero's sexuality. Initially, of course, the restoration of Hero's virtue requires that Margaret's virtue be placed into question, largely because of her association with the "lewd" Borachio. Certainly, in the general rush to achieve closure (and happy closure), Margaret's virtue is reaffirmed; as Borachio tells Don Pedro, Leonato, et al., she "knew not what she did when she spoke to me, / But always hath been just and virtuous . . ." (5.1.285–86). And in Leonato's eyes, Margaret's restored virtue is well worth the loss of her imprisoned suitor.

But for Margaret, her suitor represents potentially an escape from life belowstairs. In an exchange with Benedick, she asks, "To have no man come over me — why, shall I always keep below stairs?" (5.2.7–8). Sex or service: these are Margaret's options. And what precedes this lament suggests how crucial identification with aristocratic women is to Margaret's instrumentalizing of her own sexuality. When Benedick asks her to help him write a sonnet in praise of Beatrice's beauty, she in return asks him to write a sonnet to her own beauty. Benedick's response ("In so high a style, Margaret, that no man living shall come over it, for in most comely truth, thou deservest it" [5.2.5–6]) jokingly translates her proposed beauty competition (i.e., "the importance of being fairest") into a competition between male sonneteers. Even when Margaret clearly articulates a rivalry with Beatrice, as well as a desire to escape her social position, Benedick remains incapable of recognizing

Margaret's desire for social advancement: working girls (or "maids") are not supposed to desire at all, since "[swords] are dangerous weapons for maids" (5.2.18).

Why Margaret would agree to the masquerade might be found in Borachio's later admission to Don Pedro that he courted her in Hero's dress (5.1.221–22). From Margaret's perspective, clothing and fashion serve to overcome status differences between women; as she remarks to Hero before the latter's first and failed wedding, Hero's gown surpasses that of the Duchess of Milan, and therefore challenges the latter's superior social status (3.4.12–20). In Messina, fashion is the terrain on which women stage their social ambitions. We might then read Margaret's masquerade as Hero in the light of this exchange. But Margaret's ambition, a sign of her social agency, ends up inscribed within a standard discourse of female virtue. In order that the romantic comedy have the required ending, Margaret's social ambition and agency are sacrificed or displaced onto Borachio and Don John, so that her virtue can be maintained. At the same time, she remains single, unincorporated into the play's general festivities, with the man who offered her sole possibility for social advancement (Borachio) in disgrace. In a sense, Claudio's and Don John's error in taking Margaret for Hero — their inability to acknowledge women's differences because they claim to know woman's nature — is recapitulated in the play's inscription of Margaret within the traditional discourse of female virtue.

In this reading, Margaret's desire is the key to a fully rounded characterization that, though excluded from much of the play, is nevertheless available for critical reconstruction according to the standard ideology of character. Richard A. Levin has argued that Margaret actively betrays Hero because she resents her "social betters"; focusing on the dressing scene before the wedding, he observes that her interactions with Hero reveal profound dislike and resentment.[52] It is therefore difficult not to conclude that she sacrifices her loyalty to Hero to her love for Borachio. Levin thus explains away the one interpretive difficulty (why does Margaret apparently allow Claudio to denounce Hero?) that remains for those critics who would render Margaret coherent and consistent.

Kenneth Branagh's film adaptation of *Much Ado* attempted to remedy this crux in two ways. First, Borachio and Margaret have explicit sex; second, he includes a close-up of Margaret's horrified expression when she realizes her own role in the plot against Hero. Branagh's close-up highlights, however, Margaret's own silence in the text. Though both Borachio and Leonato attempt to explain away Margaret's actions, she herself never remarks on her participation. I would like to postpone the moment in which Margaret is "restored" and read this not as a failure in composition, but as a symptomatic failure to incorporate the working girl's desire into the diegetic space. If we too quickly restore Margaret's character, we overlook how the

---

[52] Richard A. Levin, *Love and Society in Shakespearean Comedy: A Study in Dramatic Form and Content* (Newark, DE, 1985), 113–15. Levin concludes, "Whether or not Margaret did indeed conspire with Don John and Borachio the play does not demonstrate. Instead, Shakespeare uses Margaret to help develop the dark background against which Messina moves toward marriage. Margaret makes it harder to think of Don John's evil as singular; he emerges more clearly as part of a social context that includes characters in the mainstream of society" (115).

determinants of character are fundamentally hostile to the representation of working women. One moment in particular suggests the impossibility of the restorative project. I refer to the textual crux of 2.2, when Borachio plans his staged scene of seduction: "Offer them instances, which shall bear no less likelihood than to see me at her chamber window, hear me call Margaret Hero, hear Margaret term me Claudio . . ." (2.2.33–36). Many editors change "Claudio" to "Borachio," which assumes that the scene must make sense from Claudio's perspective: for Claudio to believe that Hero is unfaithful, she must be entertaining another man. In part, this would help to justify Claudio's virulent rejection of Hero at their wedding, since she has apparently chosen to replace him with his rival's servant. But this solution is predicated on Margaret's masochism (as Finucci suggested in regards to Dalinda), insofar as she is willing to assume the role of Hero for Borachio's desire: the working woman playacts so as to maintain masculine desire for what she is not (an aristocratic woman), even though she apparently desires what her partner is. In some measure this reading forces Margaret to participate in her own elision, while maintaining Borachio's identity. Margaret would therefore assent to the discursive elaboration of differences between men and the suppression of such differences between women. On the other hand, if we were to preserve the original "Claudio," we could read Margaret's assent to Borachio's request as (from her perspective) a reciprocal social fantasy on the part of two servants, one which does not use the fellow servant to symbolize an aristocratic woman's debasement. And this reading does not render Claudio's position nonsensical: given that John accuses Hero of being "Leonato's Hero, your Hero, every man's Hero" (3.2.88–89), that Margaret would call Borachio "Claudio" could refer to Claudio's fear that from a woman's perspective, all men are alike, that female sexuality extinguishes class and status differences between men.

The point here, of course, is not which reading is correct, but rather, what an editor's choice reveals about the perspective that he or she privileges. Moreover, the crux and its various solutions suggest that the scene makes "realistic" sense only from either Claudio's or Margaret's perspective. What this editorial problem tells us is that the perspectives of the aristocratic man and the working woman cannot be brought together; they are differends, in that they cannot be rendered congruent according to some prior ground, even the ground of character. In the working woman's desire, the ideology of character finds its limit. For in *Much Ado*, the theatrical logic of character (in which presumably interior dispositions are made visible to the spectators) is pushed to its claustrophobic extreme. All desire, even the apparently "authentic" desires of Beatrice and Benedick, are revealed to be social productions; as the final lines reveal, one's "hand" (handwriting) speaks against and supersedes one's heart. But Margaret's desire is fundamentally dissimulating, since in some measure its more "authentic" expression requires her disguise as another, more privileged, woman. Margaret's disguise articulates her desire, but only at the cost of her own identity: her subsumption through identification with aristocratic women (Hero and Beatrice). Like Dalinda in *Orlando Furioso* and Pryene in *The Faerie Queene*, Margaret's desire reveals how the maid remains a point of unintelligibility within a representational field that naturalizes sexual difference as sexual hierarchy, while also maintaining the priority of birth and blood. The disguise plot is evidence of the pressure that status differences between women brought to bear on efforts to naturalize sexual difference, as well as efforts to disguise such differences as differences of marital state and morality.

Though the story of Ariodante and Ginevra originated in Italy, it is clear that it resonated in England, particularly in the 1590s. But its various translations and adaptations also bespeak a certain level of discomfort with the original autonomy granted to the maid. Whereas Dalinda is the primary narrator for much of Ariosto's version, Spenser and Shakespeare greatly restrict the maid's contribution. In large part, this may be because, in the larger culture, the maid, as both servant and single woman, evidences the overwhelming importance of marriage (ideologically, if not practically) for early modern English women, especially after the Protestant Reformation. Whereas Dalinda can retreat to a convent, Pryene and Margaret cannot be offered such a tidy resolution; as a consequence, they either vanish without comment (Spenser) or remain onstage, unincorporated into the general festive resolution (Shakespeare). In both cases, the prevailing understanding of character dominant in the text seems unable to incorporate the troubling figure of the maidservant into its imaginary. Finally, this story contains, I think, an important lesson for feminist critics and historians, and our efforts to restore the hitherto silent and invisible to historical representation. For the maidservant's masquerade as her mistress sets up a relation between the visible and invisible that suggests that visibility is not always an unqualified good. Visibility is always implicated within hegemonic discourses that do not necessarily serve the "interests" of the invisible; the purchase of visibility often requires that one surrender desires and goals that cannot be articulated within available forms. Disguise indicates that the feminist projects of historical recovery should be suspicious of the rhetoric of visibility, and the assumptions regarding agency, representation, and power that often accompany it. Moreover, it remains imperative that we approach our most important category of analysis ("women") with some caution, since such categorization can ultimately silence those whom we would most wish to speak.

Tracey Sedinger
University of Northern Colorado

10

"NEWS FROM THE DEAD":

The Strange Story of a Woman Who Gave Birth, Was Executed, and Was Resurrected as a Virgin

On 14 December 1650 Anne Greene, unmarried servant to Thomas Read in Oxfordshire, was hanged for the murder of her newborn son. As she dangled from the scaffold, her friends, eager to lessen her pain, thumped her breasts and pulled on her legs with all their weight in an effort to hasten her death. At length, when everyone presumed she was dead, she was taken down, placed in a coffin, and carried to the private house of the town apothecary, where several local physicians were gathered to perform a dissection. Much to their amazement, however, when they opened the coffin they observed that she seemed to be breathing:

> They perceiving some life in her, as well as for humanity as their Profession-sake, fell presently to act in order to her recovery. First, having caused her to be held up in the Coffin, they wrenched open her teeth, which were fast set, and powred into her mouth some hot and cordiall spirits: whereupon she ratled more then before, and seemed obscurely to cough: then they opened her hands (her fingers also being stifly bent) and ordered some to rub and chafe the extreme parts of her body, which they continued for about a quarter of an houre; oft, in the mean time powring in a spoonfull or two of the cordial water; and besides tickling her throat with a feather, at which she opened her eyes. ...[1]

---

[1] A portion of this paper was published as "'A Wench Re-Woman'd': The Miraculous Recovery of Anne Greene," *Renaissance Papers* (1997): 100–12 and is reprinted by permission of the Southeastern Renaissance Conference. For the source, see Richard Watkins, *Newes from the Dead or a True and Exact Narration of the Miraculous Delivery of Anne Greene*, Second Impression with Additions (Oxford, 1651), 2.

There are at least five versions of this story, one told by William Petty in his private writings and four accounts in the popular press: two brief news accounts in the *Mercurius Politicus;* the anonymous *Declaration from Oxford, of Anne Greene;* William Burdet's *A Wonder of Wonders;* and Richard Watkins's *Newes from the Dead.*[2] These last four were published as newsbooks, cheap pamphlets issued shortly after an execution in order to capitalize on the public's appetite for the sensational. Such pamphlets served as more than seventeenth-century tabloids; they also played a vital role in spreading official ideas about crime and punishment, and at least ostensibly, they sought to inculcate proper values and behavior. In this case, however, because the criminal survives her execution, the writers must find a way to explain why law and providence fail to coincide. In so doing, these pamphlets reveal more about the contradictions inherent in early modern ideas about female behavior and sexuality than they do about morality or the power of the state.

Anne Greene was one of many unmarried women prosecuted for killing their newborn infants in early modern England. The history of infanticide in the seventeenth century is a dark one and illustrates the way law was often used to regulate female sexuality. Before 1560 cases of infanticide rarely appear in the assize records.[3] Infanticide was newly criminalized during this period; in the Middle Ages such cases were commonly considered the province of the church courts and were usually punishable by penance rather than death. Under Elizabeth's reign, as the regulation of personal conduct shifted from the church to the secular courts, infanticide came under heightened scrutiny. By some scholars' accounts there was as much as a 225 percent increase in the number of women indicted for this crime between 1576 and 1650.[4] This is not to say that infanticide was commonplace during the sixteenth and seventeenth centuries. Despite the pressures placed on unwed mothers, the records indicate that deliberately neglecting or killing children was

---

[2] *Mercurius Politicus,* no. 28, 12–19 December 1650 and no. 32, 9–16 January 1651. Joad Raymond includes these in *Making the News: An Anthology of the Newsbooks of Revolutionary England, 1641–1660* (New York, 1993), 182–84. Petty's account appears in "History of the Magdalen (or The Raising of Anne Greene)" in *The Petty Papers, Some Unpublished Writings of Sir William Petty,* ed. from the Bowood Papers by the Marquis of Lansdowne (New York, 1967), 157–67. *A Declaration from Oxford, of Anne Greene, that was lately hanged but since Recovered* (London, 1651) is basically the same as Burdet's version but adds a brief description of a visitation from the angels that Anne experienced while she was dead. This version also includes the story of a woman who gave birth after she had been buried. Twenty-five years later, Greene's case was still notorious. John Evelyn mentions the event in his diary where he describes his friend Petty, "Doctor of Physick, . . . growne famous as for his Learning, so for his recovering a poore wench that had ben hanged for felonie, the body being beged (as costome is) for the Anatomie lecture, he let bloud, put to bed a warme woman, and with spirits and other meanes recovered her to life; The Young Scholars joyn'd and made her a little portion, married her to a Man who had severall children by her, living 15 yeares after, as I have ben assured": *The Diary of John Evelyn,* ed. John Bowle (New York, 1983), 252–53.

[3] J. A. Sharpe, "The History of Crime in Late Medieval and Early Modern England: A Review of the Field," *Social History* 7 (1982): 200.

[4] Peter C. Hoffer and N. E. H. Hull, *Murdering Mothers: Infanticide in England and New England, 1558–1803* (New York, 1981), 8.

A Wonder of Wonders.

BEING

A faithful *Narrative* and true *Relation*, of one *Anne Green*, Servant to Sir *Tho. Reed* in *Oxfordshire*, who being got with Child by a Gentleman, her Child falling from her in the house or Office, being but a span long, and dead born, was condemned on the 14. of *December* last, and hanged in the Castle-yard in *Oxford*, for the space of half an hour, receiving many great and heavy blowes on the brests, by the but end of the Souldiers Muskets, and being pul'd down by the leggs, and was afterwards beg'd for an Anatomy, by the Physicians, and carried to Mr. *Clarkes* house, an Apothecary, where in the presence of many learned Chyturgions, she breathed, and began to stir; insomuch, that Dr. *Petty* caused a warm bed to be prepared for her, let her blood, and applyed Oyls to her, so that in 14 hours she recovered, and the first words she spake were these; *Behold Gods Providence* l *Behold his miraculous and loving kindness* l VVith the manner of her Tryal, her Speech and Confession at the Gallowes; and a Declaration of the Souldiery touching her recovery. *Witnessed by Dr. Petty, and Licensed according to Order.*

Title page from William Burdet's *A Wonder of Wonders, Being a Faithful Narrative and True Relation, of one Anne Greene* (London, 1651). Reprinted by permission of the British Library: Shelfmark E 621(11).

rare.[5] Nonetheless, infanticide seems to have been sufficiently widespread (or at least feared) to warrant special legislation. In 1624 "An Acte to Prevent the Murthering of Bastard Children" was passed, specifically targeting unmarried women who attempted to conceal the deaths of their illegitimate infants.[6] Reversing the normal rules of evidence, the statute presumed the mother's guilt in the death of an infant unless she could prove otherwise. Although the law made *concealment* of the death of a bastard child the judicable crime, hiding the pregnancy itself was viewed as substantiating evidence that the mother intended to do away with her infant.

The case of Ann Price illustrates the law at work: a servant in the house of a gentlewoman, Price was impregnated by one of her fellow servants. She managed to hide her pregnancy so that "no Person in the house did in the least suspect her till after she was delivered." After the baby was born, she wrapped it in her apron and locked it in a box. When the child was inevitably discovered, Price claimed that, "finding her pains come fast upon her," she knocked on the floor with her shoe to call for help. Since she was three flights of stairs away, no one heard her. She was found guilty of murder, "the concealing of the Child being a material Point of Evidence against her."[7] Prior to the passage of "An Acte to Prevent the Murthering of Bastard Children," the courts had to prove the child had been born alive before convicting the mother of murder. After 1624, however, the law made concealment the crime and referred specifically to unmarried women because it covered only illegitimate children. Thus infanticide was legally a gendered crime and, like witchcraft, it was one of the few crimes where the accused was presumed guilty unless she could prove her innocence.

Given the often precarious situation of the unwed mother, evidence of innocence was frequently difficult to find. In the absence of witnesses to a live birth, any indication that the mother had prepared for the birth — the hiring of a midwife or the purchase of linens, for instance — served as proof that she had not

---

[5] See Keith Wrightson, "Infanticide in European History," *Criminal Justice History* 3 (1982): 8–9.

[6] "Many *lewd* Women that have been delivered of *Bastard* children, to avoyd their shame and to escape punishment, doe secretlie bury or conceale the Death of their Children and after if the Child be found dead the said Women do Alleadge that the said Childe was borne dead; whereas it falleth out sometimes (although hardlie is it to be proved) that the said child or children were murthered by the said Women their *lewd* Mothers or by their assent or procurement: For the preventing therefore of this great mischief, be it enacted by the authority of the present parliament, That if any woman be delivered of any issue of her body, male or female, which being born alive, should by the laws of this realm be a *bastard*, and that she endeavor privately, . . . either by herself or the procuring of others, so to conceal the death thereof, as that it may not come to light, whether it were born alive or not, but be concealed: in every such case the said mother so offending shall suffer death as in the case of murther, except such mother can make proof by one witness at least, that the child (whose death was by her so intended to be concealed) was born dead" (emphasis added): *Statutes of England* 21 James I, c. 27. This act remained on the books until 1803. According to Hoffer and Hull, "Bastard neonaticides constituted over 70 percent of all murders of infants under nine years of age in the records. Concealment of pregnancy is mentioned in 55 percent of these cases" (*Murdering Mothers*, 18).

[7] *Proceedings at the Sessions-House in the Old-Bayly*, April 13–14, London, 1676.

"intended to conceal" and was grounds for acquittal.[8] A married woman accused in the death of her infant was not bound by the same rules of evidence; in her case, a conviction could be obtained only if there were unequivocal proof that the child had been born alive and that she had deliberately killed it.

It is unclear whether the law actually saved children or had the reverse effect because of the way that it affirmed negative attitudes about unmarried mothers. While court records suggest that at least until the mid-seventeenth century an increased number of women were prosecuted for the murder of their newborns, the law did not seem primarily intended to protect the lives of bastard children.[9] The repetition of such words as "lewd" and "bastard" indicates that this statute was more concerned with the initial crime of fornication and with illegitimacy rather than with the actual death of the child. And given the spate of legislation passed in the decades prior to 1624, we can conjecture that economic concerns played at least as large a role as morality. For example, a 1576 statute allowed the courts to sentence parents who failed to maintain their illegitimate children to the county gaol. Further legislation enacted in 1610 granted authorities the right to commit to the House of Correction "every Lewd Woman" who bore a chargeable bastard.[10] While begetting an illegitimate child was not a crime under English law, bearing a child that was chargeable to the parish was. Since this particular statute provided only for the punishment of women, it too served to intensify the social prejudices already pressuring unmarried mothers, stigmatizing them both for their lack of chastity and for their poverty.[11] Because of the shame associated with poverty, some scholars conjecture that while infanticide was never condoned, it was sometimes seen as preferable to charging the child to the parish. Thus, the study of infanticide "uncovers a perplexing relativity in popular attitudes towards the value of infant life which contrasts markedly with the clear prescriptions of contemporary official morality."[12] As Mark Jackson explains, "Contemporary preoccupations with unmarried women and with the fate of their illegitimate children stemmed from a variety of factors, notably from anxieties about the appropriate behaviour of single women and about the role of women in the family, from concerns about the concealment

---

[8] For further discussion of this statute, see Mark Jackson, "Suspicious Infant Deaths: The Statute of 1624 and Medical Evidence at Coroners' Inquests," in *Legal Medicine in History*, ed. Michael Clark and Catherine Crawford (Cambridge, 1994), 66–67.

[9] By the end of the century, the courts became more lenient and most women were acquitted, despite the fact that the 1624 law made conviction easier. See Susan Dwyer Amussen, *An Ordered Society: Gender and Class in Early Modern England* (Oxford, 1988), 115.

[10] 7 James, cap. 4: "every lewd woman which shall have any bastard which may be chargeable to the parish, the justices shall commit such woman to the house of correction, to be punished and set on work, during the term of one whole year." Earlier statutes also sought to control unmarried women. The Statute of Artificers (1563), for example, allowed town authorities to order unmarried women between the ages of twelve and forty into service; those refusing could be sentenced to jail until they acquiesced.

[11] Mark Jackson, *New-Born Child Murder: Women, Illegitimacy and the Courts in Eighteenth-Century England* (New York, 1996), 30.

[12] Keith Wrightson, "Infanticide in Earlier Seventeenth-Century England," *Local Population Studies* 15 (1975): 10. Amussen makes a similar argument: *An Ordered Society*, 113–14.

of illicit sex, and, perhaps most importantly, from fears about the financial burden of increasing numbers of illegitimate children."[13]

Since in early modern thought a woman was "understood either married or to be married,"[14] single women, whether spinsters or widows, were often treated with suspicion and hostility. The situation for a single *mother* was even more dire. Unwed mothers overstepped the marital order by having children out of wedlock and received some of the most scathing attacks in legal and religious treatises. Concerns about primogeniture, paternity, and purity of bloodlines as well as fears about the social drain illegitimacy placed on the parish stigmatized these women. Pregnancy and childbirth outside of marriage imposed a heavy burden not just on the young woman left with the child but on society as well because the county in which the child was born was often considered responsible for its support should the mother be unable to care for it. Further, producing illegitimate children betrayed a sexuality, a life outside of marriage and presumably beyond patriarchal control, that needed to be contained before it laid waste to the social order. As the authors of *Half Humankind* point out, "The Renaissance viewed women as possessed of a powerful, potentially disruptive sexuality requiring control through rigid social institutions and carefully nurtured inhibitions within the woman herself."[15] In the opinion of Joseph Swetnam, in fact, any sign of sexuality outside of marriage deprived women of a legitimate place in society. Spurning such women as "wanton harlots," Swetnam argues,

> you have thus unluckily made your selves neither maidens, widowes, nor wives, but more vile than filthy channell durt fit to be swept out of the heart and suburbes of your Countrey, oh then suffer not this worldes pleasure to take from you the good thoughts of an honest life: But downe downe uppon your knees you earthly Serpents, and wash away your black sinne with the cristall teares of true sorrow and repentance, so that when you wander from this enticing world, you may be washed and cleansed from this foul leprosie of nature.[16]

The rhetoric of monstrosity and shame becomes even more vehement in descriptions of unmarried infanticides. Women accused of causing their children's deaths, whether through abandonment or outright murder, are described as "matchlesse monsters of the female sex," "vipers," "savages," and "bloody dogs." And as is the case with other unmarried mothers, their sexuality makes them particularly suspect. The word "lewd" occurs in virtually all the commentary on the subject: the tags "harlot," "strumpet," and "whore" are equally prevalent. One of the more famous

---

[13] Jackson, *New-Born Child Murder*, 29.

[14] T. E., *The Lawes Resolution of Women's Rights* (London, 1632), 6.

[15] Katherine Usher Henderson and Barbara F. McManus, *Half Humankind: Contexts and Texts of the Controversy about Women in England, 1540–1640* (Urbana, 1985), 55.

[16] Joseph Swetnam, *The Araignment of Lewde, Idle, Froward and Unconstant Women* (London, 1615), 27.

examples, cited repeatedly in legal definitions of infanticide from the period, provides a good instance of this phrasing: "A Harlot delivered of a childe, hidde it in an Orchard (it being alive) and covered it with leaves, and a Kite stroke at it, and the childe dyed therof, and the mother was arraigned and executed for Murder."[17] This focus on sexuality is largely limited to *unmarried* infanticidal mothers. In the late sixteenth and early seventeenth centuries, both legally and in popular culture, infanticide came to be associated almost exclusively with unmarried, sexually active women — the "looser sort" in Percival Willughby's words.[18]

The street literature detailing infanticide echoes the judgmental and moralistic tone of the polemical literature, and though it invariably describes the perpetrators as "whores," the women it deals with are not always prostitutes. The term "whore" seems a free-floating signifier,[19] attached to any woman who fails to fit the model of chaste wife.[20] *Deedes Against Nature and Monsters by Kinde* (1614), for example, tells the story of Martha Scrambler ("a lascivious, lewd and close strumpet"), an unmarried mother who kills her baby by throwing it in the privy and is discovered only when a yelping dog leads her neighbors to "the sweet Babe lying all besmeared with the filth of that loathsome place."[21] Although Scrambler's story was written before the "Acte to Prevent the Murthering of Bastard Children," it provides a representative example of the way popular literature treated unmarried women suspected of killing their illegitimate infants.

Like legal accounts of infanticide, *Deedes Against Nature* depicts the crime as unnatural and monstrous. That monstrousness is almost exclusively the result of Scrambler's unrestrained sexuality, a sexuality that, according to the pamphlet writer, deprives her of her identity not just as a mother but also as a woman. The author explains that her delivery was all the easier because of "her lusty body, strong nature, and fear of shame." (The word "shame" is used nine times in the course of the narrative.) He depicts her as a "Caterpillar of nature, a creature more savage than a shee wolfe, more unnatural than either bird or beast, for every creature hath a tender feeling of love to their young, except some few murtherous-

---

[17] Michael Dalton, *The Countrey Justice* (London, 1619), 218.

[18] Willughby, *Observations in Midwifery*, quoted in Wrightson, "Infanticide in Earlier Seventeenth-Century England," 11.

[19] Peter Lake's term: "Deeds Against Nature: Cheap Print, Protestantism and Murder in Early Seventeenth-Century England," in *Culture and Politics in Early Stuart England*, ed. Kevin Sharpe and idem (Stanford, 1993), 257–83, here 264.

[20] In fact, virtually all female faults were sexualized. Gossip was "a kind of incontinence of the mind"; curiosity was "a deflowering of the mind"; a woman who drank was "a prostitute to wine." See Mary Fissell, "Gender and Generation: Representing Reproduction in Early Modern England," *Gender & History* 7 (1995): 433–56, here 442; Fissell quotes from Richard Allestree's *The Ladies Calling* (At the Theatre, Oxford, 1673), 11, 148, 14. Linda Woodbridge explains that assigning the "label 'whore' to any unmarried non-virgin ... was a way of assimilating the puzzling maid/not maid into a recognizable category: to categorize [is] to understand. The unchaste never-married woman was a special sort of monster; her crime was heinous because it disrupted the schematic order of the world ...": *Women and the English Renaissance: Literature and the Nature of Womankind, 1540–1620* (Urbana, 1984), 84.

[21] *Deedes Against Nature and Monsters by Kind* (London, 1614), n.p.

minded strumpets, *woemen* I cannot call them. . . ." Since she is not a married woman, a *feme covert* (the legal definition of the wife, literally, a covered woman),[22] Scrambler has "no husband to cover her act of shame." As such, the pamphlet places her in counterdistinction to the good, married mother, who "esteems the fruit of her own womb, the precious and dearest Jewel of the world, and for the cherishing of the same will (as it were) spend her life's purest blood, where, contrariwise the harlot (delighting in shame and sin) makes no conscience to be the butcher of her own seed. . . ." Such women must be punished, as much for their uncontrolled sexuality as for the murder of their babies.

The story of Anne Greene differs from the typical account of the unmarried infanticide because she survives her execution. Her case is anomalous, too, because once she recovers, no attempt is made to execute her again, contrary to British law. According to Blackstone, "It is clear that if, upon judgment to be hanged by the neck till he is dead, the criminal be not thoroughly killed, but revives, the sheriff must hang him again; for the former hanging was no execution of the sentence, and if a false tenderness were to be indulged in such cases, a multitude of collusions might ensue."[23] There is no indication in any of the accounts why Greene was not hanged again. But, as I will show, she seemed to have greater symbolic (and monetary) value alive than she did executed. Given the enormous stigma attached to unmarried mothers, how, then, do early modern writers explain Anne Greene?

Because public execution constituted the principal method by which the power of the state was confirmed, an "imposing demonstration of the state's might and authority,"[24] we would expect the pamphlet literature chronicling executions to serve the same purpose and warn would-be wantons of the dangers of promiscuity. In this case at least, it does not. The pamphlets' apparent purpose of illustrating the repercussions of crime and of reestablishing order seem thwarted by Anne's resurrection. Confronted with a criminal whose execution offers no lesson about proper female behavior because she survives that execution, these writers attempt to recon-

---

[22] As T. E. explains it, wives "be by intent and wise fiction of the Law, one person" with their husbands (*Lawes Resolution*, 4). And according to Blackstone, "By marriage the husband and wife are one person in law: that is, the very being or legal existence of the woman is suspended during the marriage, or at least is incorporated and consolidated into that of the husband; under whose wing, protection, and cover, she performs everything": *Ehrlich's Blackstone*, ed. J. W. Ehrlich, 2 vols. (New York, 1959), 1: 83.

[23] *Ehrlich's Blackstone*, 2: 524.

[24] J. A. Sharpe, "'Last Dying Speeches': Religion, Ideology and Public Execution in Seventeenth-Century England," *Past and Present* 107 (1985): 144–67, here 166. Several recent scholars have questioned this view of the public execution "as a theatre of punishment, in which the power of the centralising state was ritually inscribed in the flesh of the victim, a public demonstration of the power of the prince and the awful majesty of the law," seeing it instead as a subversion of that authority: Lake, "Deeds Against Nature," 275. For a discussion of the public execution as a carnivalesque subversion of state authority, see Thomas Laqueur, "Crowds, Carnival and the State in English Executions, 1604–1868," in *The First Modern Society*, ed. A. L. Beier, David Cannadine, and James M. Rosenheim (Cambridge, 1989), 305–55.

struct her into a socially acceptable version of proper womanhood. They rewrite woman good, to paraphrase Sheila Delany.[25]

The earliest account of Anne Greene's botched execution is probably that told in two issues of the *Mercurius Politicus,* a weekly Interregnum newsbook edited by Marchamont Nedham. Published less than a week after the incident in December 1650, this account provides only a cursory treatment. Like the lengthier pamphlets describing the event, this version relates the incident as "a remarkable act of providence," but begins with the birth of the infant rather than the miraculous recovery. This account lacks most of the moralism of the typical crime pamphlet, and attempts to present the story in a matter-of-fact, straightforward way, thus only hinting at the complexities and contradictions that make this tale so fascinating. Nonetheless, it carefully emphasizes Anne's innocence (at least of murder) from the start, and looks forward to a more thorough account of the event "to the end that this great work of God may be fully and truly known, as becommeth so great a matter."[26] Never attempting to explain the miracle of Anne's survival, the writer nevertheless assures the reader of God's infinite wisdom and the order of the universe.

Two other versions in the popular press, William Burdet's *A Wonder of Wonders* and Richard Watkins's *Newes from the Dead,* develop the narrative much more fully and provide a vivid example of the way the same event could be invested with different meanings.[27] Confronted with a woman who fails to fulfill the stereotype of the good woman — the woman who is "chaste, silent, and obedient" — the writers must find ways to explain God's apparent beneficence toward her. They accomplish this in two very different ways: Burdet by virtually ignoring Anne's sexuality and focusing on the injustice of her execution, and Watkins by denying her sexuality and reinscribing her into culture as a scientific and literary text.

Although it is clear from the beginning of both Burdet's and Watkins's accounts that Anne did not murder her baby but that it was stillborn, so great is the transgression represented by her pregnancy that she is condemned to die anyway. The explicit sexuality revealed by her pregnancy suggests that she is potentially disruptive. But both writers emphasize the injustice of this sentence. Burdet admits: "She was carried before a Justice, who upon examination, confessed, that she was guilty of the Act, in committing of the sin, but clear and innocent of the crime for murdering of it, for that it was born dead; ... but after a short tryal, she was convicted for her life, and received sentence to be hanged on *Oxford* Gallowes."[28]

In many ways, Burdet's version of the story is typical of other crime pamphlets from the period and follows their pattern fairly closely in its rendition of crime, confession, repentance, and punishment. Burdet begins with a brief summary of the

---

[25] Sheila Delany, *Writing Woman: Women Writers and Women in Literature, Medieval to Modern* (New York, 1983), 188.

[26] I first quote no. 28, 12–19 December 1650, then no. 32, 9–16 January 1651, in Raymond, *Making the News,* 182–84.

[27] Yet another account, *A Declaration of Anne Greene,* differs only slightly from *A Wonder of Wonders* and, although published anonymously, was apparently the first version of Burdet's pamphlet.

[28] Burdet, *A Wonder of Wonders,* 2.

crime: Anne, very busy at work turning malt, suddenly feels ill and retires to "the house of office." There "a Child, about a span[29] long sprung from her, but abortive, which much impair'd her health and strength" (1). Soon one of her fellow servants finds her uttering that she is "undone, undone, undone" (2).

From the start of the pamphlet Anne is portrayed as hardworking, a detail that immediately sets this narrative apart from other accounts of infanticide which seek to erase the everyday lives of their subjects. Rarely is mention made of work, family, or friends, a characteristic that further isolates the already marginalized woman. Here, on the other hand, Anne is clearly part of a community of servants who immediately respond to her cries for help. Coupled with the fact that there is no question here that she miscarried, these details help to make her more sympathetic. Still, while there is no doubt that Anne is not guilty of murdering her baby, there is also no doubt that she is aware of the birth. Being fearful that a discovery will be made, she lays the baby in a corner and covers it with dirt and rubbish. But Burdet minimizes her guilt in this action by emphasizing the impossible situation she finds herself in: "Alas, alas! Mary, that ever I was born to live and die in shame and scorn," he portrays her as moaning. And he implies the injustice of her trial by pointing out that she was impregnated by "a Gentleman of good birth, and kinsman to the justice of the Peace" (2). Later, after telling of her resuscitation, he denounces her sentence, arguing that she was convicted without due and legal process by a corrupt and partial jury.

Burdet continues his narrative by offering the obligatory confession, but here he presents not so much a confession as a statement of contrition and innocence. Christlike, Anne meets her death asking God to forgive her prosecutors. Fixing her eyes on her executioner, she prays, "God forgive my false accusers, as I freely forgive thee." And her last words, according to Burdet, are "Sweet Jesus, receive my soul" (4). The pamphlet thus transforms her into a saint with at least some power and majesty. Yet even as she meets her death, Anne refuses to play her prescribed role completely and legitimate her punishment with the standard statement of wrongdoing. At the moment of her execution, the woman who has been cowed by the circumstances of her class and gender displays a glimmer of resistance. Of course, the designated purpose of the confession was often thwarted. The criminal might refuse to confess, meeting his/her death with curses and shouts, or even show up at the execution drunk. And not incidentally, the confession postpones the moment of death so the convicted might hold forth for much longer than intended in hopes of a pardon or simply to delay the execution.[30] The confession also grants a kind of authority to the criminal on the scaffold, giving her a voice and an audience to hear that voice. As Catherine Belsey explains, "To speak is to possess meaning, to have access to the language which defines, delimits and locates power.

---

[29] "The distance from the tip of the thumb to the tip of the little finger, or sometimes to the tip of the forefinger, when the hand is fully extended; the space equivalent to this taken as a measure of length, averaging nine inches": *OED*.

[30] Laqueur discusses the various subversions of the scaffold in "Crowds, Carnival and the State."

To speak is to become a subject."[31] Although she does not admit her guilt in murdering her baby, Anne does repent her misspent youth and calls upon God to forgive her. Burdet could hardly create a more sympathetic heroine; thus the chastening spectacle of the scaffold is at least partially subverted.

Burdet spends little time on the resurrection, using it only to reaffirm "the poor Creature's" innocence and to illustrate the "great hand of God in this business." While Watkins's Anne is basically silent after she revives, Burdet depicts her extolling God, saying as she awakens, "Behold God's providence, and his wonder of wonders" (5). Unlike the justice who convicts Anne, Burdet is concerned not with policing sexuality but with showing how a good woman was unjustly prosecuted. Perhaps his pamphlet represents the popular press's reaction to what was clearly an unjust law. There is evidence that commentators from the period recognized the severity and potential injustice of the courts in cases of infant murder. For example, in his *Observations in Midwifery*, Percival Willughby discusses the case of a woman indicted for infanticide who was so mentally incompetent that she was unable to defend herself. The coroner spoke for her, using the size of the baby to argue her innocence. But to no avail: "the whole Bench saw that shee was a foole. It was in the Protector's dayes, and I feared that shee would have summum jus. The judg shewed the statute-Book to the jury. Neither judg, nor jury regarded her simplicity. They found her guilty, the judg condemned her, and shee was, afterwards, hanged for not having a woman by her, at her delivery."[32] By the eighteenth century even the courts seemed to recognize the potential injustice of the 1624 statute. Although unmarried women continued to be prosecuted under the law, they were treated more leniently, and most were acquitted. In some counties the conviction rate between 1620 and 1680 was as much as 53 percent, higher than the conviction rates for other kinds of homicide in the period;[33] in the eighteenth century conviction rates dropped to 20 percent for women tried at the Old Bailey and were even lower in other parts of England. By the beginning of the nineteenth century, the injustice of the law was more widely recognized. Thomas Percival, for one, pointed out that the statute making "concealment of the birth of a bastard child full proof of murder, confounds all distinctions of innocence and guilt, as such concealment, whenever practicable, would be the wish and act of all mothers, virtuous or vicious, under the same unhappy predicament."[34] The law was finally repealed in 1803. Burdet, too, seems uneasy with the statute. The crime pamphlet here, then, uses the repentance and confession of its wrongdoer not to set right a perverted

---

[31] Catherine Belsey, *The Subject of Tragedy: Identity and Difference in Renaissance Drama* (London, 1985), 190–91.

[32] Willughby, quoted in Jackson, "Suspicious Infant Deaths," 70.

[33] Amussen notes a conviction rate of 53 percent in Sussex from 1600 to 1640 (*An Ordered Society*, 115). Other scholars posit different rates. J. A. Sharpe, for instance, found that conviction rates in Essex tended to fluctuate, from a maximum of 55 percent between 1630 and 1634 to a minimum of 10 percent from 1655 to 1659: *Crime in Seventeenth-Century England: A County Study* (Cambridge, 1983), 134.

[34] Thomas Percival, *Medical Ethics* (Manchester, 1803), 84: quoted in Jackson, "Suspicious Infant Deaths," 73.

social order, but rather to comment upon a perverted legal system. Ultimately, Anne's resurrection provides a vivid example of a victim's justified refusal to follow the script dictated by the authorities, even if that refusal was not consciously her own. In this case, as Burdet presents it, the intentions of divine providence supersede those of the state.

Far more interesting and complex is Watkins's version, *Newes from the Dead, or a True and Exact Narration of the Miraculous Deliverance of Anne Greene*. Arguing that this "rare and remarkable accident" had been "variously and falsely reported amongst the vulgar," Watkins seeks to provide a faithful record of the event. Unlike Burdet, Watkins spends the bulk of his text relating Anne's recovery. As he does so, the narrative speculates on menstruation, pregnancy, and the viability of the fetus. Thus *Newes from the Dead* seems consciously different from other popular accounts of crime and wondrous events. Its serious, analytical tone and its focus on the scientific aspect of the miracle suggest a more learned audience than that of the typical crime pamphlet. Its overt purpose is neither to titillate nor to explicate providential justice, though it does both. Nonetheless, in its obsession with Anne's body and its reconstruction of her into a good woman, it reveals many of the same cultural anxieties and concerns of the other pamphlets.

With William Petty, the anatomist, as his obvious source, Watkins offers an extremely detailed account of the treatment of Anne's body and its reactions to the doctors' varied ministrations. The doctors examine and manipulate every part of Anne's body, tickling her throat, letting her blood, chafing her "extreme parts," and anointing her neck, her temples, and the bottoms of her feet with oils and spirits. And they note her every reaction: her sweat, pulse, and bowels; her bruises and blisters; her fever and swelling. Watkins also records everything she eats and drinks, from the julep and cold beer that she drank on the 15th of December to the "part of a chick" that she ate on the 19th. The amount of detail here is remarkable for a news pamphlet, its pseudoscientific tone only thinly masking a prurient interest in the female body. Frances Dolan has argued that executions of women "downplayed the female body in order to highlight the divine comedy of the soul's release. Thus, the erasure of the condemned women's bodies becomes a means of avoiding the festive, unruly, carnivalesque possibilities of public executions ... and instead represents these women as authoritative and virtuous in spite of their bodies, which are always already disorderly because they are female."[35] Just the opposite seems the case here. The focus is almost completely on Anne's body, and her authority derives in large part from that body. While she may have averted a literal dissection by coming back to life, she seems figuratively dissected in Watkins's text.

The dissection of criminals in the name of scientific knowledge was becoming an increasing practice during the period, and the female body was all the more desirable because it was so rare. By following an execution with a public autopsy, legal authorities hoped to find an additional method of disciplining the body. The autopsy was conceived both as a deterrent to crime and as a way to reinstitute the

---

[35] Frances Dolan, " 'Gentlemen, I have one more thing to say': Women on Scaffolds in England, 1563–1680," *Modern Philology* 92 (1994): 157–78, here 166.

recalcitrant body back into society once a crime had been committed. In death, at least, the body could serve the public good by imparting scientific knowledge.[36] (There was also some belief that the criminal body differed from that of ordinary people. An autopsy might reveal literal signs of that difference — a hairy heart, for instance — that would help explain criminality and make it less threatening.) By the eighteenth century the selling of dead bodies was to become a profitable business.[37] Anne's body seems similarly commodified and disciplined here. As Watkins himself remarks, "in the same Room where her Body was to have been dissected for the satisfaction of a few, she became a greater wonder, being revived, to the satisfaction of multitudes that flocked thither daily to see her" (6). Once the doctors realize what a potential source of fame and profit Anne is, they decide to charge admission to those who want to see her: "they thought it a seasonable opportunity, for the maid's behalf, to invite them either to exercise their Charity, or at least to pay for their Curiosity. And therefore (themselves first leading the way) they commended it to those that came in, to give every one what they pleas'd, her Father being there ready to receive it" (6). And later, after the pamphlet is published, Anne's body will be displayed for an even broader audience and will provide income for its author.

Only after the miracle is fully related and valued does Watkins turn to the crime: "And now, having done with the Sufferings, and the Cure, it will not be amiss to look back, and take a Review of the Cause of them" (6). In this portion of the narrative the pamphlet writer takes great pains to restore Anne to proper womanhood not just by diminishing her guilt in the murder but even in the fact of having a baby out of wedlock, arguing that she may not have known she was pregnant. It is likely, Watkins argues, that Anne was unaware that she was pregnant because she had "continual Issues which lasted for a Moneth together: which long and great Evacuation might make her judge, that it was nothing else but a flux of those humors which for ten weeks before had been suppressed; and that the childe which then fell from her unawares, was nothing but a lump of the same matter coagulated" (7). To relieve her of culpability, Watkins must take away her will and con-

---

[36] Jonathan Sawday describes anatomy as a kind of social/sexual control: the "science of *seeing*, and thus knowing and controlling the body, in order to harness its appetites and desires," in *The Body Emblazoned: Dissection and the Human Body in Renaissance Culture* (New York, 1995), 219; but given the fascination with the female body revealed in cases such as this one, it seems just as likely that anatomy might also foster those appetites and desires.

[37] Scholars have noted the remarkable change in attitudes toward the body that increased scientific knowledge brought about: "With the advance in understanding of anatomy and the corresponding development of private trade in corpses, we can find in the early eighteenth century a significant change in attitude towards the dead human body. The corpse becomes a commodity with all the attributes of a property. It could be owned privately. It could be bought and sold. A value not measured by the grace of heaven nor the fires of hell but quantifiably expressed in the magic of the price list was placed upon the corpse. As a factor in the production of scientific knowledge, the accumulated rituals and habits of centuries of religion and superstition were swept aside": Peter Linebaugh, "The Tyburn Riot Against the Surgeons," in *Albion's Fatal Tree: Crime and Society in Eighteenth-Century England*, ed. Douglas Hay et al. (London, 1975), 72.

sciousness. Furthermore, he argues, the child was stillborn and not capable of being murdered.

Examining the fetus for viability, he finds that it was not a span in length, and its sex was hardly distinguishable; it had no hair and surely had never had life. In fact, Watkins conjectures, it rather seemed a "lump of flesh" than a "well and duly formed infant." Lacking direct witnesses to the birth, one of the primary ways for a woman to escape punishment according to the 1624 statute was to prove that the fetus was not viable. Court records throughout the seventeenth and eighteenth centuries provide examples of acquittals using pseudo-medical evidence to prove the premature birth of the child. For example, in the trial of a woman named Jane Todd, evidence of imperfect finger- and toenails and lack of hair forced an acquittal: "she did not go her full Time, the Child's Nails not being in their full Proportion, and she having made Provision for its Birth, it was the Opinion of the Court, from the strict Examination of the Evidences, that it was Still-born, (as she affirm'd) and that she flattered herself with concealing her Shame, by carrying it off with so much Privacy: Upon the whole the Jury acquitted her."[38] Likewise, using her midwife and fellow servants to support his argument, Watkins posits that Greene's child was not viable, the miscarriage occurring not more than seventeen weeks after conception.

While Burdet speculates that the father was a gentleman and kinsman to the Justice of the Peace, Watkins actually names the baby's father: young Jeffrey Read, the grandson of Anne's employer. In naming her partner, Watkins hints at the sexual exploitation that was frequent between masters (or masters' sons) and their female servants during this period. As further evidence of Anne's innocence, Watkins gives one additional fact only to dismiss it: "her Grand Prosecutor Sir Thomas Read died within three daies after her Execution; even almost as soon as the probability of her reviving could be well confirmed to him. But because he was an old man, and such Events are not too rashly to be commented on, I shall not make use of that observation" (7). It was her employer, Thomas Read, who initially brought the accusation of murder against her. God seems totally on Anne's side, smiting her false accuser dead while preserving Anne. But given his rational and scientific intent, Watkins seeks to minimize this point.

Unlike most crime pamphlets of the day, Watkins offers no confession. The lengthy speech presented by Burdet is recounted in only the most general terms here: "after singing of a Psalm, and something said in justification of herself, as to the fact for which she was to suffer, and touching the lewdness of the Family wherein she lately lived, she was turned off the Ladder" (1–2). If, as I have suggested earlier, the confession serves the dual purpose of manifesting state authority and conferring limited agency and power on the criminal (what Foucault calls "two-sided discourses")[39] that power seems deliberately suppressed here. Although

---

[38] "Jane Todd," *Old Bailey Session Papers*, July 1727, 2; quoted in Jackson, "Suspicious Infant Deaths," 68.

[39] Michel Foucault, *Discipline and Punish: The Birth of the Prison*, trans. Alan Sheridan (New York, 1995), 68.

Anne is acquiescent and does offer the requisite gallows speech, there is no attempt in this account to record her actual words. We are told that after she revives, Anne sighs and talks to herself, and that she "fell into like speeches as she had used in prison before the execution" (6), but we never hear her speak. Anne's voice completely disappears in this account, a strategy that seems consistent with Watkins's reconstruction of her. A good woman is a silent woman. In this representation, her hanging thus becomes a kind of purgation of her soiled body, and she is reborn as a maid. But in order for this transformation to take place, she must be totally ignorant of what has happened to her before, during, and after her execution. As Frances E. Dolan phrases it, she is "an automaton, a machine that was temporarily turned off rather than a human agent struggling for life."[40]

Even more remarkable than Watkins's manipulation of his story in an effort to rewrite Anne's life are the dedicatory poems written by the students at Oxford that are appended to the narrative. (Actually, in the first edition of *Newes from the Dead*, the poems precede the narrative. But because the number of poems nearly doubles in the second edition — from fourteen pages to twenty-four — I shall use this edition.) That this eight-page narrative is overwhelmed with poetry seems significant. Anne becomes a conduit for the male poetic voice. Where the narrative presents Anne as a scientific text to be examined and understood, now she becomes a literary text. Earlier, her revival suggests male power and creativity; godlike, the scientists at the autopsy are credited with her resurrection. The poems, on the other hand, suggest another form of creativity and power as they resurrect her into art. As one overconfident student phrases it,

> ... For by this Historie
> The Author doth a Third Life to her Give,
> And makes her Innocence and Fame to Live.
> Her Life is writt here to the life: she fell
> At a cheap rate, when 'tis describ'd so well.
> For, th' Author's Pen's so good, that one would Die
> To be Reviv'd by such a History.
> (21, misnumbered page 11 in text)

Ironically, as Anne is silenced, the young student poets of Oxford find their voices.

The poetry is even more extreme in its reconstruction of Anne, making her into a kind of regenerate Eve or even a Christ-figure: "Now may the nine-liv'd Sex speak high and say / That here they fought with Death, and won the day. / The *fatall Tree*, which first began the strife, / Sided with them, and prov'd a *Tree of life*" (20, misnumbered page 10). In other places it rewrites her as a martyr, depicting her as a virgin who, phoenix-like, rises "out of the ashes": "All's purg'd by Sacrifice: / The Parent slain, doth not a Virgin Rise?" (12) and "Rare Innocence! a Wench re-woman'd!" (14). Her restored maidenhood seems a greater miracle than

---

[40] Frances E. Dolan, *Dangerous Familiars: Representations of Domestic Crime in England, 1550–1700* (Ithaca, NY, 1994), 138.

her restored life: "Mother, or Maid, I pray you whether? / One, or both, or am I neither? / The Mother died: may't not be said / That the Survivor is a Maid?" (16, misnumbered page 6) And, "Shee's a maid twice, and yet is not *dis-maid*. / O Paradoxe! if truth in thee can lye, / No wonder if the maid could live and dye" (32, misnumbered page 22). Given the extent to which Anne is sanctified in the course of the pamphlet, we might be tempted to read her pregnancy as comparable to that of the medieval female mystics described by Caroline Walker Bynum who endured bizarre bodily experiences: strange bleeding and lactations, mystical pregnancies, and even an incorruptible body in death.[41] She might even be compared to the Virgin Mary. Like Mary, she seems to have experienced a kind of manless conception, her virginity remaining intact even after having given birth.

Anne's reconstruction as a kind of saint simply exaggerates the paradoxical status of the criminal both on the scaffold and in the pamphlet literature. Since both the saint and the criminal were exemplary figures — one a figure of all that should be emulated, the other of all that should be shunned — the two sometimes coalesce in this literature.[42] In fact, the process that identified the criminal with Christ and the saints reconciled the criminal with his executioners in a final act of atonement that served to legitimate the actions of the state by associating them with Christ and the saints and thereby with the will of God.[43] The association between the saint and the criminal is even more acute here; Anne's resuscitation recreates her as a resurrected Christ. Yet the cultural process of atonement seems diverted precisely because the execution is unsuccessful. The incident actually disaffirms the power of the state, and explains the reason why this case must be examined so carefully by the pamphlet writer.

Not all poems included are poems of praise; the period's characteristic ambivalence toward women is evident here as well. As one of the student poets explains it, Anne Greene's story simply serves to exemplify the cunning and manipulative nature so characteristic of women:

---

[41] Caroline Walker Bynum, *Fragmentation and Redemption: Essays on Gender and the Human Body in Medieval Religion* (New York, 1991), 86–94.

[42] The reconstruction of the criminal as saint occurs several times in this literature. See, for example, Gilbert Dugdale, *A True Discourse of the Practices of Elizabeth Caldwell* (London, 1604), in which the female criminal becomes the epitome of piety and rectitude even after she is found guilty of adultery and attempted murder. The connection between the women criminals in the popular literature and female saints does not seem strange at all if we agree with Stephen Nichols's argument that "hagiography is a mediated, scripted genre controlled by the institution of the Church, designed to marginalize unauthorized prophetic voices" that would subvert central institutionalized authority, most specifically the voices of women. "The only body that speaks in a hagiographical text is a dead body; it speaks, moreover, by having been turned into a text": Maureen Quilligan, *The Allegory of Female Authority: Christine de Pizan's Cité des Dames* (Ithaca, NY, 1991), 243. The crime literature also seeks to contain the subversive voices of women through the institutionalized authority of the state, though not always successfully.

[43] Katharine Park, "The Criminal and the Saintly Body: Autopsy and Dissection in Renaissance Italy," *Renaissance Quarterly* 47 (1994): 1–33, here 23.

> Admire not, 'tis no newes, nere think it strange,
> Twere wonder if a Woman should not change.
> They have mysterious wayes, and their designes
> Must be read backward still, like Hebrew lines.
> See, these with Death dissemble, and can cheat
> Charon himself to make a faire retreat.
> Well, for this trick Ile never so be led
> As to beleive a Woman, though shee's dead.
>   (18, misnumbered page 8)

Another poet seeks to show his wit as he puns on "morally light" and "light in weight": "I'le prophecy, Shee'l Lovers soone insnare / Without a Trope ther's Halters in her hayre. / Of the same cause here the effects doe fight, / One thing both hang'd and sav'd her, shee was *Light*" (26, misnumbered page 16). But these negative verses are the exception. Most of the poetry seems to anatomize Anne in order to reconstitute her as whole again: as a virgin. What is important here is the way that Anne's body provides an occasion for verse. As we have seen, this reconstruction is possible at least partially because of Anne's economic value. A shame to her household and community before her execution, she becomes a source of pride and an economic boon afterwards. Furthermore, she is a source of fame, both to the doctors who revived her and to the pamphleteers and poets who wrote about her.

And so, both writers would have us believe, she lived happily ever after. Indeed, a handwritten note in the Bodleian copy of *Newes from the Dead* suggests as much: "Anne Greene was portioned by the Students, married, had several children and lived about fifteen years after her Execution." With marriage and motherhood, she is completely reintegrated into the patriarchal structure. Thus Anne Greene is fully remade — and re*maid* — into a more socially acceptable version of womanhood.

The stories of Anne Greene provide a vivid illustration of the various ways the popular press invested criminal accounts with different meanings. It is precisely because these texts are so ephemeral in nature that they can reflect the multiple anxieties and varying interests of early modern culture. In Anne Greene's miracle "the same story [is] two stories, with quite different cultural resonances and different implications for understanding the world."[44] And in this particular case the cultural implications of the narratives are especially evident, not just because this story was told so many times, but even more interestingly, also because virtually the same story was told in several French *occasionnels* of the sixteenth century.[45] These French pamphlets relate an almost identical story of concealed pregnancy, unjust execution, and miraculous survival.

---

[44] Raymond, *Making the News*, 172.

[45] Raymond notes the French versions: *Making the News*, 172–73. For the translated texts themselves and a fuller discussion of them, see Roger Chartier, "The Hanged Woman Miraculously Saved: An *occasionnel*," in *The Culture of Print: Power and the Uses of Print in Early Modern Europe*, ed. Roger Chartier, trans. Lydia G. Cochrane (Princeton, 1989), 59–91.

The *occasionnels* concern a young servant, also named Anne (even more remarkably, Anne des Grez, in one version), who is falsely accused of infanticide but who survives her hanging through the intervention of the Virgin Mary. The injustice of the sentence is more blatant in this case than in the English versions because this Anne is not pregnant at all. The daughter of Anne's master gives birth, kills her baby, and implicates Anne in the crime. Further, the association with Christ is even more striking: Anne remains on the gallows three days and three nights before she is taken down and discovered to be alive. Roger Chartier argues that these narratives "came to be put to the service of Church authority at a time of bitter tensions and struggles" and function as anti-Reformation propaganda.[46] Likewise, the English accounts of Anne Greene can be read as serving authority. To those who might question the potential injustice of infanticide persecutions, the narrative provides assurance that God will intervene, but only on the rare occasions when the law blunders. In any event, the story of the hanged woman miraculously revived struck a cultural chord in both early modern England and France. Most importantly, the various versions of this event illustrate the way that female bodies provided important sites for re-negotiating ideas about society and culture.

Susan C. Staub
Appalachian State University

---

[46] Chartier, "Hanged Woman," 82.

11

FRANCES HOWARD AND MIDDLETON AND ROWLEY'S *THE CHANGELING*:

Trials, Tests, and the Legibility of the Virgin Body

In May 1613 the court of James I was presented with a petition, or libel as it was often called, from Lady Frances Howard, stating "that the Earl her Husband was incapable of consummating their Marriage, and praying a Commission to examine, if her Complaint was well founded. . . ."[1] The petition listed the relevant facts: she and Robert Devereux, Earl of Essex, had been married in January 1603 when she was thirteen and he was fourteen; both had been in good health since the marriage; and, within the space of the last three years, the couple had lived together "after the fashion of other married folks" (*ST*, 786).[2] Also noted was the fact that Frances "in hope of lawful issue, and desirous to be made a mother, lived together with the said Robert at bed and board, and lay both naked and alone in the same bed, as married folks use: and desirous to be made a mother, from time to time, again and again yielded herself to his power, and as much as lay in her offered herself and her body to be known; and earnestly desired conjunction and copulation" (*ST*, 786). Despite these earnest desires on her part, conjunction proved unattainable, copulation impossible, and consummation unachievable.

---

[1] *Cobbett's Complete Collection of State Trials* . . . , compiled by T. B. Howell, vol. 2 (London, 1809), 785. Subsequent citations are given parenthetically as *ST*. The ease and frequency with which King James I bestowed titles makes tracking historical figures difficult. Frances Howard became Countess of Essex in 1606 and then Countess of Somerset upon her remarriage in 1613; her first husband, Robert Devereux, was Earl of Essex; her second husband, Robert Carr, became Viscount Rochester in 1611 and Earl of Somerset in 1613. To avoid confusion, I will refer to Frances Howard as Frances, to Robert Devereux as Devereux, and to Robert Carr as Carr.

[2] While the libel states that Frances and Devereux were married in 1603, all other evidence points to the fact that the actual ceremony took place on 5 January 1606.

While Frances's annulment petition was not the most controversial in early modern England — King Henry VIII's would surely win this title — her libel does provide us a window through which we can examine a number of concerns extending beyond the legal and marital realm, namely the anxiety circulating around the legibility of the virginal body. We can see Frances's vexed role — she claims to occupy the seemingly contradictory positions of wife and virgin and requests a legal return to her role of single woman — as raising questions about the relationship between maidenhood and marriage, between the signs of virginity and its social significance. That Frances could be examined and tested, that her body could be semi-publicly probed and prodded to verify her alleged virginal status, indicates the ideological importance of such a confirmation. That this verification can exist only in the negative — the production of bloodied sheets on the morning following a wedding serves as just one vivid example of this confirmation — speaks to the manner by which an early modern woman was visually and symbolically seen to make the transition from maid to wife and mother, and the circumstances under which she would be allowed to do so.

Despite the multitude of dramatic and theatrical moments wherein a woman's sexual status is questioned, investigated, and incorrectly determined, there still existed a belief in the apparent ease with which the female — rather than the male — body was rendered sexually legible. This conviction assumed that virginity could be read through bodily behavior, that the appearance of purity was a truthful indicator of sexual inexperience. This "ease," which proved to be anything but easy, manifested itself in a number of different discourses — medical, courtesy, and legal — which sought to claim a position of privileged knowledge regarding female sexuality. Yet, as we can see from the public doubt generated by Frances's annulment petition, while the sexual status of the female body could be neither confirmed nor disproved as virginal, the body was able to perform the role of the virgin adequately and believably. As demonstrated by the events which occupied the court during the summer of 1613, proclaiming oneself a virgin was far from an easy task. How, we can ask, did the hearing come to focus in such a public manner on the most private of body parts, allowing Frances's virginity to be upheld in the legal arena but challenged in the realm of gossip, poetry, and letters? And, we might also ask, what was it that permitted the investigation of Frances's body to adopt the trappings of a staged performance?

The union of Frances and Devereux had been originally lauded as a successful match when it was first arranged by the well-connected Howard family; it was praised in Ben Jonson's wedding-night masque *Hymenaei* as "that blest *Estate* / Which all good *minds* should celebrate."[3] Whether intended to be romantic or pragmatic, the match, it quickly became apparent, was far from ideal; the fairy-tale glow attached to the marriage by Jonson's impressive spectacle faded. The couple,

---

[3] *Hymenaei*, lines 107–108 in *Ben Jonson*, ed. C. H. Herford and Percy and Evelyn Simpson, vol. 7 (Oxford, 1941). In the 1616 Folio Jonson deleted all references to the original performance and removed the names of Frances and Devereux from the title page, apparently hoping to distance his work from the scandal that surrounded the ill-fated marriage.

separated directly after their marriage, were reunited in 1609. But by 1613 plans for an annulment were underway.

While the historical record surrounding the annulment case relies as much on rumor and gossip as on more reputable "facts," it seems accurate to accept the speculation that much of the impetus behind the desire for marital dissolution resulted from the entrance of Robert Carr, one of James I's favorites and a useful political ally, into the lives of the Howards. It was believed that, soon after their initial meeting, Frances and Carr began a clandestine affair. Whether it was Frances's desire to remarry or her family's, the situation that the Howards found themselves in was the same: how to extricate Frances from her first marriage and remarry her to Carr. Divorce was not a viable option; according to the 1604 *Constitutions and Canons Ecclesiastical*, a couple granted a divorce could not "contract Matrimony with any other person" while both remained living.[4] The only solution lay, therefore, in securing an annulment.

Marriages were most often annulled because of a failure on the couple's part to consummate their relationship. This failure generally stemmed from the husband's impotence — be it because of "lack of sexual organs, natural frigidity, 'quasi-natural' frigidity, [or] impotence caused by *maleficium* or *sortilegium*."[5] The petitions in these cases, like that of Frances's 1613 libel, obeyed a rather strict format: the wife alleged a legitimate marriage, subsequent cohabitation (usually for a three-year period), her desire to be a mother, and her husband's inability to satisfy that desire. Necessary in this declaration, however, was the husband's acquiescence in open court to declare himself impotent; such a declaration would necessarily damage his intentions, if not completely disqualify him, for any future remarriage. Devereux's refusal to admit any impotence required a series of linguistic additions to the formulaic script. Inserted after the requisite paragraph regarding Frances's desire for "conjunction and copulation" was the following: "Yet before the said pretended Marriage, and since, the said Earl hath had, and hath power and ability of body to deal with other women, and to know them carnally, and sometimes have felt the motion and pricks of the flesh carnally, and tending to carnal copulation, as he saith and believeth ..." (*ST*, 786). Devereux's declaration of his multiple infidelities required that the nullity commission believe that he was sexually active with all women but Frances — a difficult charge to accept, one assumes.

Despite Devereux's claim that he was sexually experienced, neither his former nor present lovers, if indeed there were any, were called to testify to his prowess along with the dozens of witnesses who spoke of "see[ing] them [Frances and Robert] in naked bed together as man and wife for divers nights ..." (*ST*, 790).[6]

---

[4] Quoted in David Lindley, *The Trials of Frances Howard: Fact and Fiction at the Court of King James* (London, 1993), 86.

[5] R. H. Helmholz, *Marriage Litigation in Medieval England* (Cambridge, 1974), 87.

[6] A parade of eleven witnesses commented that, while they had seen the couple acting as man and wife, they believed the marriage had not been consummated. See *ST*, 788–94.
The notes of the commission's chair, George Abbot, Archbishop of Canterbury, appended to the trial transcript, belie the easy acceptance of Devereux's sexual prowess. Abbot notes the Lord Chamberlain's belief that "the earl had no ink in his pen" (*ST*, 806). Interestingly, Devereux, like

Rather than examine his body to verify his intermittent sexual abilities, the court decided to turn to the object of his disaffection and prove that Frances herself was sexually pure. While it was important for Devereux's reputation that he claim virility, it was seen as essential that Frances prove the opposite: she was not now, nor had ever been, sexually active. If she were not a virgin, it would be assumed that the marriage had indeed been consummated or that the rumors circulating around her relationship with Carr were accurate. In either case, the court would be forced to deny her suit. The decision to overlook Devereux's body indicates that the jurists believed that it was impossible to read his sexual virility (or lack thereof) on his own body; rather, his selective impotence could be displaced, located, and easily read on Frances's body.

The court, therefore, refocused its gaze away from his body onto hers. The trial transcript notes the decision to examine her body: "[T]he Court thought it necessary to satisfy themselves of the truth by the inspection of midwives and matrons. Whereupon it was decreed by the Court, that six midwives of the best note, and ten other noble matrons ... should inspect the Countess, the Entry whereof is as follows ..." (*ST*, 802). The "Entry," interestingly enough, is in Latin, a notable change from the vernacular English used to record the major portions of the trial. The finding, however, was plainly stated: "That she is a virgin uncorrupted" (*ST*, 803).

The findings of the inspection took much of London by surprise, as we find from the number of non-institutional records — letters, pamphlets, and poems — that dwell upon the subject. Through the waves of London rumor and gossip we can see how the results of the medical test and Frances's own character were interpreted, both being considered flexible enough to be reshaped and remolded. Indeed, this profusion of written commentary seems to highlight the fact that the physical examination became something less than an anatomical endeavor and more akin to an "exercise in the construction of reputation."[7] John Chamberlain, whose letters provide a running commentary on both historical events and court gossip from 1597 to 1626, captures this transformation when he explains that "[Frances] hath ben visited and searcht by some auncient Ladies and midwifes expert in those matters, who both by inspection and otherwise find her upon theyre oath a pure virgin: which some Doctors thincke a straunge asseveration. ..."[8] Chamberlain's missive in its very vagueness brings to the forefront the friction uncovered by the panel's findings. What exactly is it that the doctors "thincke a straunge asseveration": Frances's virginity, the matrons' oath, or the test itself?

Indeed, the early modern impulse to consider the female body more easily legible was complicated by the cloud of ambiguity and contestation which circulated around the determination of Frances's virginity. One summation of the virginity

---

Frances, did remarry, but his second marriage collapsed amid rumors that the child his wife Elizabeth bore him after six years of marriage was not his own (Lindley, *Trials*, 95–96).

[7] Katharine Eisaman Maus, *Inwardness and Theater in the English Renaissance* (Chicago, 1995), 139.

[8] Norman Egbert McClure, ed., *The Letters of John Chamberlain*, vol. 12, pt. 1 (Philadelphia, 1939), 461, letter dated 23 June 1613.

test, written by Sir Anthony Weldon, touches upon both Frances's cloudy sexual reputation — "she was (*intacta virgo*) which was thought very strange, for the world took notice that her way, was very near beaten so plain, as if (*regis via*) and in truth, was a common way before [Carr] did over travel that way" — and the circumstances surrounding the test itself. Frances had requested, for modesty's sake, that she be allowed to cover her face during the examination; the request was approved. Weldon, however, saw this maneuver — a real-life version of the theater's "bedtrick" — as designed to allow a sexually inexperienced girl, rather than Frances herself, to enter the examination room. One year after Weldon made public his exclusive "discovery," another writer broadened the scope by including the name of the alleged chaste replacement: "whereupon some saies this, and some saies that, and most that the *Countesse* was not searched, but that one of Sir *Thomas Monsons daughters* was brought in to bee searched in her place, and so both *Jury* and *Judges deceived*, but how true this is, is not credible. . . ." Despite this author's careful challenge to the legitimacy of the rumor, his choice to publish a name indicates his acceptance of the rumor's credibility. An anonymous poem about the examination echoes these findings: "This Dame was inspected but Fraude interjected / A maide of more perfection."[9] Fraud or not, the annulment, granted some three months after it first appeared before the court, concluded that the marriage was not consummated but that Frances's body was fit for procreation.

The ultimate success of the suit, however, did not silence the critical reverberations. Not only did the petition confuse the boundaries between which bodies were available for scrutiny and by whom, but it did so by literally opening the bedroom door and inviting everyone inside to look around. Even more troublesome than the opening of closed doors, as noted in the various excerpts which describe the virginity test, was the fact that a woman who was characterized as a "lewde woman for soe shee was" (*ST*, 916) — and around whom existed rumors regarding her extramarital affair with Carr — had been legally declared a virgin. The finding raised disturbing questions regarding not only virginity tests and their ability to discover the "truth" but also the ability of a woman to perform an acceptable sexual status. What had begun as a legal petition to annul an unconsummated marriage was transformed into an indictment of Frances's sexual morality, an inquiry into the possibilities of deciphering the overt signs of female sexual knowledge, and an investigation of the interchangeable performativity of female bodies.

Frances Howard's libel and the court-mandated virginity test provide a material backdrop upon which we can place the competing discourses which surrounded the virginity of unmarried women. Virginity or chastity, for those influenced by the medieval Catholic Church, was seen as the epitome of spiritual devotion and

---

[9] *The Court and Character of King James written and taken by Sir A.W., being an eye and eare witnesse* (London, 1650) sig. E, 25; repr. G. Smeeton, 1817. Weldon, a rabid Parliamentarian, attacks Frances and her family as a means of highlighting the corruption emanating from the royal family. Anon., *Truth Brought to light and discovered by Time, or A Discourse and Historicall Narration of the first XIIII yeares of King James Reigne* (London, 1651), 31–32; Chester City Record Office MS CR 63.2.19, fol. 14.

worldly sacrifice, the ideal state of uncorrupted sexual and spiritual purity. The female body, considered by the patristic writers to be sensual and polluted, could be transformed through virginity into a sacred vessel to be cherished and guarded so that it would remain intact for the woman's "marriage" to Christ.[10] However, by the time of Frances Howard's trial, the iconography associated with religious virginity had changed sufficiently, owing in part to Henry VIII's concerted efforts financially and ritualistically to bankrupt the Catholic Church in England. Thanks to him, monasteries and convents had been sold, their lands being delivered to the Crown, and the spiritual sanctity accorded to the virgin brides of Christ had diminished in importance. Although he was not completely successful — as witnessed, for example, by the sixteenth-century Northern rebellions, the outpouring of recusant literature, and the seventeenth-century Gunpowder Plot — the covert existence of Catholics and Catholic sympathizers did not mean that the virginal woman occupied the same space she had previously.[11] This is not to say that she had faded from sight; rather, it seems more appropriate to argue that her symbolic weight had shifted.[12] While still useful in the dramatization of moral and theological lessons, the meanings ascribed to the virgin expanded with regard to both her individual family and the larger communal circles in which she was situated. Lawrence Stone notes that female virginity gained value "in the marriage market of a hierarchical and propertied society [assuring] that there should be no legal doubts about the legitimacy of the heirs to property and title,"[13] and often becoming the equivalent

---

[10] For an overview of biblical and medieval Christian views of virginity as the epitome of spiritual perfection, see John M. Bugge, *Virginitas: An Essay in the History of a Medieval Ideal* (The Hague, 1975).

[11] Examples of the ways in which the Protestant advocacy of marital chastity co-existed with the Catholic emphasis on virginity can be found in Heather Dubrow, *A Happier Eden: The Politics of Marriage in the Stuart Epithalamium* (Ithaca, NY, 1990), esp. 13–27. Similarly, John Rogers provocatively explores this commingling in Revolutionary texts — "How are we to explain the inconsistent and incompatible affirmations of the life of sustained virginity in a text seemingly devoted to the affirmations of the state of marriage?" (236) — in "The Enclosure of Virginity: The Poetics of Sexual Abstinence in the English Revolution," in *Enclosure Acts: Sexuality, Property, and Culture in Early Modern England*, ed. Richard Burt and John Michael Archer (Ithaca, NY, 1994), 229–50.

[12] The transition of virginity from a primarily religious ideal to one with a broader cultural reach is perhaps best marked by the literary and artistic iconography which surrounded the most prominent virgin of this time, Queen Elizabeth I. On the cult of the Virgin Queen, see, among others, Frances A. Yates, *Astraea: The Imperial Theme in the Sixteenth Century* (London, 1975); and Roy Strong, *The Cult of Elizabeth: Elizabethan Portraiture and Pageantry* (London, 1977). On Elizabeth's own deployment of her virginity, see Susan Frye, *Elizabeth I: The Competition for Representation* (New York, 1993). On the ways in which dramatists and poets made use of her virginity, see Philippa Berry, *Of Chastity and Power: Elizabethan Literature and the Unmarried Queen* (London, 1989); and Louis Montrose, *The Purpose of Playing: Shakespeare and the Cultural Politics of the Elizabethan Theatre* (Chicago, 1996), chap. 10, "The Imperial Votaress," 151–78; and Jacqueline Vanhoutte, "A Strange Hatred of Marriage: John Lyly, Elizabeth I, and the Ends of Comedy," in this volume.

[13] Lawrence Stone, *The Family, Sex and Marriage in England, 1500–1800* (New York, 1977), 502.

of property itself. In addition to securing and preserving actual economic interests such as patrilineal inheritance and the avoidance of bastardy, female chastity also functioned symbolically as a more generalized guarantor of social order and cohesion.[14]

If it strikes us as somehow ironic that the absence of one act — sexual intercourse — was indicative of the presence of a series of social markers — family honor and paternal certainty — there are signs that it might have struck the early modern interpreters of the female body as similarly problematic. For when there is no way to tell if a body is, indeed, virginal — the very nature of virginity leaves the body marked by absence, which is to say, unmarked — how can the woman's purity and the attendant attributes of familial honor and communal pride be confirmed? How, one might ask, could the virgin's un-written-upon body be accurately read by those surrounding her, including potential suitors and protective fathers? As the Howard libel and the subsequent examination of Frances's body proved, accepting a woman's word was not considered a viable option. There had to be some more reliable manner to verify her sexual status, some more certain means by which to locate a concrete mark which could be used for the purpose of classification and categorization.

Both medical texts and courtesy manuals proposed methods for confirming the status of the virginal body, the former focusing on reading the interior of the body and the latter on reading the exterior. While these discourses appear to be generically opposed, one relying on "scientific" proofs, the other on examples of socially condoned behaviors, they share a desire to write and read a legible female body whose sexuality is considered to be easily discernible through a series of identifiable signs. What these texts have in common is not only their attempt to locate virginity somewhere on the woman's body but also their desire to ensure that what the female body seems to be saying is a true reflection of what it has — or has not, as the case may be — done. Ironically, the methods described by these multiple discourses seem to provide young women with a blueprint for performing their virginity; that is to say, the texts voice a series of moments wherein instructions for appearing virginal are subtly imparted to the discerning reader. As such, the very impossibility of locating the desired sign becomes abundantly clear despite the best efforts of the writers, just as the possibilities for falsifying virginity become equally obvious. For, as the spate of pamphlets and poems produced in the wake of Frances's virginity test demonstrate in their apparent contrast to the official court record, there always exists the possibility that even the certainty gained from reading the body may be uncertain.

In his wedding masque *Hymenaei*, Ben Jonson writes that the wedding night "hath other treasures / Then these (though long conceal'd) / Ere day, to be reveal'd."[15] While the "other treasures" he refers to are most certainly those asso-

---

[14] Montrose, *The Purpose of Playing*, 128. See also Keith Thomas, "The Double Standard," *Journal of the History of Ideas* 20 (1959): 211–12; Susan Dwyer Amussen, *An Ordered Society: Gender and Class in Early Modern England* (Oxford, 1988); and Mark Breitenberg, *Anxious Masculinity in Early Modern England* (Cambridge, 1996), 24.

[15] Jonson, *Hymenaei*, lines 394–396.

ciated with the pleasures of the wedding night, namely the deflowering and sexual initiation of the virgin bride, it is Jonson's assumption that there are "conceal'd" secrets which will be "reveal'd" on this night which complicates the discovery of the bride's "treasures." His poetry indicates not only that the secrets of the woman's body can be intimately known at some time, but also that, like all such "treasures," these too have been purposefully hidden by the possessor. Jonson's lyrical conclusion is echoed by Tassie Gwilliam, who, in her study of eighteenth-century counterfeit virginity cases, notes the existence of the "powerful desire to be able to read traces on the female body — in particular the desire of men to discern the presence of other men on 'their' women's bodies — and women's reciprocal impulse to erase those markings or render them unreadable."[16] The key to successful discovery, then, lies in perfecting a method of reading which is immune to the woman's "impulse to erase" or conceal her "treasure."

The early modern desire to discover the secrets of the female body coincided with larger trends in the medical superstructure which made use of the discourse of the burgeoning colonial project in its attempts to map, name, and exhibit the body under surveillance. These discourses, different though they were in both the sites from which they emanated and the materiality of the bodies being explored, do make use of similar language and iconography to create legible maps. At the same time that the territory in question — be it the New World across the Atlantic, or north of England in Ireland — was being observed, exploited, and conquered, so too were the body's boundaries being fixed, measured, and charted. As Peter Stallybrass notes, the female body was considered ripe for ideological manipulation through such geographical mappings. Queen Elizabeth I's virgin body, for example, was used to represent both her "impermeable [physical] container, and hence a map of the integrity of the state" in such paintings as a 1598 Dutch engraving where her "body encloses all Europe: her breasts are France and the Low Countries, her left arm is England and Scotland, her right arm is Italy."[17] Like the cartographers and artists, the bridegroom's privilege in gaining access to the female body's secrets mirrors the anatomist's interest and proficiency in uncovering what remained "conceal'd."

In many ways we can read Jonson's tribute to the wedding night's pleasures as an anthem for the early modern anatomy theaters and investigations which took hold of both courtly and popular imaginations in Western Europe.[18] "The vogue for

---

[16] Tassie Gwilliam, "Female Fraud: Counterfeit Maidenheads in the Eighteenth Century," *Journal of the History of Sexuality* 6 (1996): 520.

[17] Peter Stallybrass, "Patriarchal Territories: The Body Enclosed," in *Rewriting the Renaissance: The Discourses of Sexual Difference in Early Modern Europe*, ed. Margaret W. Ferguson, Maureen Quilligan, and Nancy J. Vickers (Chicago, 1986), 129. See also John Donne's Elegie XIX, "To his Mistris Going to Bed," where the poet praises his beloved as "my America! my new-found-land" in *The Complete English Poems of John Donne*, ed. C. A. Patrides (London, 1985), line 27.

[18] Jonathan Sawday notes that that by the late sixteenth century the very use of the word "anatomy" in the title of a text seemed to be a mark of the text's modernity. See *The Body Emblazoned: Dissection and the Human Body in Renaissance Culture* (London, 1995), 44. For a more general discussion of the anatomy genre, see Devon L. Hodges, *Renaissance Fictions of Anatomy* (Amherst, MA, 1985).

anatomy ... involved a fascination with the ocular, with exposing what lay hidden to the scrutiny of the ... gaze."[19] While Jonson advocates for such discovery on an individual level, the bridegroom's exposure of a bridal body, the anatomists and medical specialists pressed for the more general uncovering of the universalized female body through their examinations. Medical treatises investigated virtually every part of the body, often arriving at the Galenic conclusion (derived from Aristotle) that the female body existed as an inversion of the male body; the "one-sex model," as Thomas Laqueur calls it, imagines the difference between male and female bodies as one of degree, not kind. Weaker though it was, the female body was still explained and measured by the male body. As Laqueur writes, "There was in both texts and images a quality of obsessive insistence, a constant circling around, always back to the male as standard."[20] What seems especially telling in this world which conceived of women as inverted men — with each organ in the female body paralleling a comparable male organ, the ovaries being female testes, the uterus a female scrotum — is the complete absence of the corresponding male equivalent for the female hymen.[21] It is the one part of the sexualized body which does not invertedly mirror the male body model. Why, we must ask, is the one difference in the otherwise perfectly corresponding bodies related to the proof and diagnosis of virginity? Does the existence of the uniquely female hymen provide women with a physical component that allows their bodies to be interpreted as legible in a way that men's bodies cannot?

If we think of Mary Douglas's theory that the body stands "for any bounded system [whose boundaries represent any] which are threatened or precarious," we can consider the hymen as the representational boundary for the female virgin body.[22] The hymen, described most often as a sinewy membrane, becomes for the early modern anatomists the single physical indicator of a woman's virginity and becomes

---

[19] Patricia Parker, "*Othello* and *Hamlet*: Dilation, Spying, and the 'Secret Place' of Woman," *Representations* 44 (1993): 60–95, here 66.

[20] Thomas Laqueur, *Making Sex: Body and Gender from the Greeks to Freud* (Cambridge, MA, 1990), 98. For a detailed and persuasive critique of Laqueur's argument, see Janet Adelman, "Making Defect Perfection: Shakespeare and the One-Sex Model," in *Enacting Gender on the English Renaissance Stage*, ed. Viviana Comensoli and Anne Russell (Urbana, 1999), 23–52. Adelman not only specifically sees the "one-sex" model as questionable in its hegemonic historicity, but she also envisions its modern use as reinforcing and reinscribing the absence of women in medical models. For a general overview of these debates, see Winfried Schleiner, "Early Modern Controversies in the One-Sex Model," *Renaissance Quarterly* 53 (2000): 180–91.

[21] It also strikes me as interesting that neither Laqueur's *Making Sex* nor Audrey Eccles's study of early modern gynecology and obstetrics contains an index entry for "hymen." Eccles also refrains from broaching any topic dealing with the medical issues surrounding chastity or virginity; see eadem, *Obstetrics and Gynaecology in Tudor and Stuart England* (Kent, OH, 1982). William C. Carroll similarly notes that the premier reference work in the early modern period, Galen's *De usu partium*, never mentions the hymen; see his "The Virgin Not: Language and Sexuality in Shakespeare," in *Shakespeare and Gender: A History*, ed. Deborah E. Barker and Ivo Kamps (London, 1995), 294.

[22] Mary Douglas, *Purity and Danger: An Analysis of the Concepts of Pollution and Taboo* (London, 1966), 115.

metonymically the material equivalent and defining characteristic of her sexual state.[23] Extending Douglas's paradigm, we can also conceive of the hymen as a liminal structure, the barrier which separates and marks the woman's transition from maiden to wife, from "conceal'd" to "reveal'd," from the Bakhtinian closed, classical body to the openly grotesque body, from pure to corrupt. Ironically, while the hymen itself represents a transitional state — a body whose ultimate goal is geared toward marriage and sexual intercourse and, therefore, the destruction of the membrane itself — the search for the hymen seeks to create a fixed body that can be defined in absolute terms as virginal.[24] The hymeneal presence paradoxically intends to provide the guarantee which allows for its destruction: proof of a woman's virginity will allow her to safely and legitimately become sexually active.

The search for the hymen became part of an anatomist's repertoire, with his findings included in chapters which focused on the womb and other reproductive organs. While the majority of anatomists agree on what the hymen is — "a thin and sinewy Skin or *Membrana*, interlaced with many smal Veins, which hath a hole in the midst, through which the Menstrual Blood passeth, about the bigness of ones little finger" — and while they agree, in theory, on its significance — "it were the entrance, the piller, or locke, or flower of virginity" — there is little agreement with regard to its use as a reliable proof of virginity.[25] It is possible to divide the anatomists into categories: those who adamantly support the hymen's material existence, and those who question not only its purpose but also its presence. Marie H. Loughlin places, among others, Helkiah Crooke in the former group and Ambrose Paré in the latter.[26] It seems to me, however, that the findings of both of these anatomists, whether praising or doubting the hymen's existence and purpose, include contradictory and conflicting assertions which, in many ways, undermine the very nature of their individual projects.

Crooke, in his *Microcosmographia*, describes the hymen as hiding "the orifice of the Maiden's bosome of modesty," writing that it is "the onely sure note of unsteyned virginity . . . for when the yarde entreth into the necke of the wombe, then the fleshy membranes which are among the caruncles, are torn up even to their rootes." It is the effusion of blood which marks the breaking of the virgin's "seal," providing a clear and obvious sign that the virgin has been successfully deflowered.

---

[23] Indeed, Hymen is the name given to the mythological figure who graces dramatic and poetic weddings, marking the woman's entrance into sexuality. The 1933 *OED* defines "hymen" as both "The god of marriage, represented as a young man carrying a torch and veil . . . marriage . . . A wedding-hymn" and "The virginal membrane, a fold of mucous membrane stretched across and partially closing the external orifice of the vagina." For the second usage, the *OED* lists Helkiah Crooke's 1615 *Microcosmographia* as the first English reference.

[24] Marie H. Loughlin, *Hymeneutics: Interpreting Virginity on the Early Modern Stage* (Lewisburg, PA, 1997), 29–30.

[25] Nicholas Culpeper, *A directory for midwives: or a guide for women in their conception, bearing and suckling their children*, 2nd ed. (London, 1656), 23; Helkiah Crooke, *Microcosmographia: A Description of the Body of Man* (London, 1615), 223 [sic, erroneous pagination].

[26] Loughlin, *Hymeneutics*, 30. Loughlin also creates a third category — those who are ambivalent about the hymen's representational quality — and places Nicholas Culpeper in this group.

The decisiveness of Crooke's findings, however, weakens as he explains that not all virgins bleed heavily. He admits that if the virgin has menstruated within the past four days before intercourse or if she is extremely relaxed during intercourse, she may be "dilated with little or no paine." This lack of pain, and lack of blood, "hath beene the cause why some have unworthily suspected the uncorrupted chastity of their wives." Crooke advises that in these specific cases, so as to avoid such unfair scrutiny, the mother or friends of the bride should advise the groom of the "Brides purgations" so that he will know what to expect — or not expect — upon defloration.[27]

Crooke extends his commentary on the hymen in his section on anatomical controversies. He begins by noting that the question of whether there are "certaine markes or notes of virginity in women and what they are" is a common one, generating much interest. He cites a number of physicians, both those who claim to have seen the hymen and those who claim they have not, and concludes that if the hymen does not exist, then "[w]ee must therefore finde out some other locke of Virginite."[28] His use of the insistent "must" conveys worry or, at the least, concern. If he is so certain that the hymen provides the necessary "locke," why "must" we search elsewhere? Similarly, it is worth considering how Crooke's opening assertion — that the hymen is the "onely sure note" of a woman's virginity — segues into his advice about the lack of bridal pain or blood upon sexual initiation. Does his cautionary warning to potential grooms indicate that this "sure note" is less than sure? Can his admonition to publicize the "purgations" serve as a method whereby an unchaste bride conceals her previous sexual experience?

While Crooke shunts his concerns about the questionable hymen to an appendix of controversies, others are far more forthright about their doubts. Indeed, Ambrose Paré, in his medical writings, not only denies that the hymen is the marker of virginity, but he also questions whether such a membrane even exists. "But it is worth observation, that in all this passage there is no such membrane found, as that they called *Hymen*, which they feigned to be broken at the first coition." Paré claims that the confusion is an ancient mistake which was made because of the appearance of blood after a woman's first sexual encounter. This blood, he asserts, is caused by the "violent attrition of certaine vessels lying in the inward *Superficies* of the necke of the wombe," not as a result of the tearing of the hymeneal membrane.[29] Paré's writings seemingly contradict Crooke's with regard to the hymen's status. The conflicting conclusions of these authors not only raise the question of the reliability of any single medical treatise but, perhaps more importantly, allude to the reasons why proving or disproving the existence of the hymen seems so imperative to these anatomists.

It is possible to claim that these contradictory assertions speak to a persistent debate between anatomists, a long-standing "controversie betwixt the famous Writers ... concerning the Anatomical notes or tokens of Virginity," to quote one

---

[27] Crooke, *Microcosmographia*, 223 [sic]–36.

[28] Crooke, *Microcosmographia*, 255–56.

[29] Ambrose Paré, *The Collected Works of Ambrose Paré*, trans. Thomas Johnson (London, 1634; repr. New York, 1968), 130.

Restoration scientist looking back at the earlier texts.[30] Nevertheless, there exists under the surface of these reports a concern that the power of the anatomists and their theaters with their ability to examine beneath the surface of the skin, to see farther into the body than had ever been seen before, has failed with regard to the female virginal body. As we can see from the faultlines found in Crooke's investigation, the secret that the female body holds inside of it remains hidden from the trained observer's eye.[31]

Much in the same way the rhetoric of the blazon performed a fantastical partitioning of the female body, separating it into its constituent parts which could then be described and praised by the male poet, the anatomist's theater similarly reenacted the literal division of the female body by a male specialist. While there are obvious generic differences, it should not be overlooked that both the rhetorical and the physical dissections disclosed the fetishistic desire to "discover," to literally uncover and expose, the female body and to consume, construct, and circulate it according to the needs of the specific "writer" and "reader," be it an audience member in the anatomy theater or a purveyor of a printed text. Jonathan Sawday summarizes what is at stake in both kinds of discoveries: "If a poetic reputation could be constructed, in the court, via the fantasy reduction of the female body into its constituent parts, then a scientific reputation could also be built at the expense (this time) of real as opposed to literary bodies."[32] In both cases, the female body performed a ritualized role, her part overdetermined by those who had designed and deconstructed it. For the blazoned body to escape from the pen of the courtier seems an impossibility; for the dissected body to elude the eye of the anatomist seemed, as the hymeneal writings of Crooke and Paré demonstrate, not only possible but often disturbingly probable.

The twists and turns that the anatomists' treatises take demonstrate the difficulty of either definitively locating the hymen or proving its role as guarantor of virginity. These moments of friction within the texts — the desperate need to locate the "locke" of virginity, for example — can be seen as highlighting the shortcomings of the burgeoning field of dissection when it was applied to the virgin body; at the same time, these faultlines also point toward the problematics of reading the female body through a purely physical investigation. If medical treatises fall short in their attempts to read the interior of the female body, equally vexed were those efforts to decipher her exterior. Unlike the anatomical discourses which sought to uncover the truth of a woman's body from the inside out, conduct books and courtesy manuals represented the alternative: by reading the exterior surface of a woman, one could write her inner sexual character. Richard Brathwait, in a work whose very

---

[30] Robert Boyle, *Certain Physiological Essays* . . . (London, 1661), 87.

[31] We may think here of Othello's plea: "Make me to see't; or (at the least) so prove it / That the probation bear no hinge nor loop / To hang a doubt on . . ." (*The Riverside Shakespeare*, ed. G. Blakemore Evans [Boston, 1974], 3.3.364–66). Othello's desire that Iago provide the "ocular proof" (l. 360) necessary to prove Desdemona's infidelity is invertedly mirrored in the anatomists' attempts to provide the ocular proof guaranteeing a woman's virginal state.

[32] Sawday, *The Body Emblazoned*, 212.

title, *The English gentlewoman, drawn out to the full Body,* underscores the authorial metaphors, neatly encapsulates this premise of external legibility when he warns women against behaving wantonly: "How cautelous shee is, lest suspition should tax her? Outwardly, therefore, shee expresseth what she inwardly professeth."[33] Brathwait's message is clear: if the female body projects the appearance of virginity, it can be assumed that this outer reflection is the perfect mirror of its inner reality.

The discourses of conduct and courtesy assume a multitude of forms, encompassing certain homilies, prayers, and sermons along with educational and how-to tracts. They contrast in their notions of unstable female sexuality with the philosophical, theological, and legal languages intended to represent female character and status as fixed givens: givens founded on nature, Scripture, and precedent. Conduct literature, as such, was a fluid genre, embracing texts which might otherwise seem to be at odds with one another. What these discourses share in common is an exhortative quality which stresses the importance of behavior and appearance as forming the basis of one's character. Rather than accept character as an absolute, conduct and courtesy writers, such as Juan Luis Vives, Brathwait, and Baldesar Castiglione, base their conclusions on the assumption that male and female character is malleable and easily subject to manipulation. As Ann Rosalind Jones has pointed out, men and women, these writers might claim, are capable of being trained for their social roles through the knowledge and imitation of external actions. This process is, in many ways, a "self-fashioning" of sorts.[34] The very fluidity and flexibility of one's exterior might allow for the creation of a spectrum of correct postures or for the change in these postures over time, but it also created an ideological mechanism whereby imitation of a form was considered as acceptable as, if not more so than, the actual embodiment of the form's characteristics. Despite Brathwait's belief, exterior and interior did not necessarily need to match one another if the exterior obeyed the social rules expounded in the conduct literature and dutifully played the correct part assigned to it.

That the body could be molded and altered by changing behaviors and manners followed from taking the advice of those who cast themselves in the position of instructors and authors. "I will speak of this excellent Lady as I would wish her to be," declares Magnifico in Castiglione's *Book of the Courtier*, "and when I have fashioned her to my taste," Magnifico claims that he will take her as his own; he will be Pygmalion to her Galatea. Of course, Magnifico's verbal fashioning of the Lady

---

[33] Richard Brathwait, *The English gentlewoman, drawn out to the full Body* (London, 1631), 203–4.

[34] See Ann Rosalind Jones, "Nets and Bridles: Early Modern Conduct Books and Sixteenth-Century Women's Lyrics," in *The Ideology of Conduct: Essays on Literature and the History of Sexuality*, ed. Nancy Armstrong and Leonard Tennenhouse (New York, 1987), 40–41. My thinking about conduct literature is greatly indebted to Jones's formulations. Although she emphasizes the class tensions which manifest themselves in courtesy manuals, seeing the attacks on "unnatural women" as the result of a displaced anxiety about "the artifices of the class-climbing man" (41), I interpret these efforts at legibility to be equally gender-based. See also Suzanne Hull, *Chaste, Silent, & Obedient: English Books for Women 1475–1640* (San Marino, CA, 1982); and Stephen Greenblatt, *Renaissance Self-Fashioning: From More to Shakespeare* (Chicago, 1980).

is accomplished through Castiglione's writing of her. Similarly, Vives writes in his preface to Catherine of Aragon, the patroness of his *Instruction of a Christen Woman*, that she will see her picture fashioned through his words: "as if a peynter wold brynge unto you your owne visage and image, most counnyngly peynted. For lyke as in that purtrature you myght se your bodily similitude: so in these bokes shall you se the resemblaunce of your mynde and goodnes."[35] Almost unanimously the "taste" to which the "excellent Lady" — the mythical female courtier or the Queen of England — was "fashioned" deemed her primary outward sign to be chastity.

Vives advises his reader, firmly and simply, "that chastyte is the principall vertue of a woman, and countrepeyseth with all the reste: if she have that, no man wyll loke for any other: and if she lacke that, no man wyll regarde other." Not content with this rather general statement about the requisite attributes which grace the virginal woman — be she a chaste faithful wife or an unmarried maiden — Vives specifies what is lost and gained along with one's chastity: "Take from a woman her beautie, take from her kyndrede, riches, comelynes, eloquence, sharpenes of wytte, counnynge in her craft, gyve her chastite, and thu hast gyven her all thynges. And on that other syde, gyve her all these thynges, and calle her a noughty packe, with that one worde thou hast taken all from her."[36] Though Vives seems to have intended his text clearly to articulate a set of definitive boundaries for acceptable female behavior, as indicated by the listing of the consequences which follow the loss of chastity, his cautionary advice brings into play the complexity that he seeks to deny, opening the system of blurred behaviors that he would prefer to close.[37] Intended to convey a straightforward and uncontestable series of truisms, *Instruction* becomes a text which complicates its own message.

Commissioned for Mary Tudor by her mother, *Instruction* was designed as an educational tract for the young princess, but is more often grouped with conduct or courtesy manuals, as only two of its thirty-eight chapters are devoted to what a woman should study and read.[38] Given its generic duplicity, it is difficult to categorize who its desired audience was: parents who supported the humanist interest in female learning, those who wished to teach their daughters about proper social behavior, the daughters themselves, or, more likely given the success of the 1529

---

[35] Baldesar Castiglione, *The Book of the Courtier*, trans. Charles S. Singleton (Garden City, NY, 1959), 205; Juan Luis Vives, *A very frutefull and pleasant boke Called the Instruction of a Christen Woman* (1523), trans. Richard Hyrde (London, 1540), sig. B4.

[36] Vives, *Instruction*, sigs. L4v, G4v. While Vives does not prescribe a punishment for such a loss, the illustration found on the first page of text in the 1541 edition — the figure of Lucrece pointing a dagger toward herself — seems self-explanatory.

[37] Janis Butler Holm, "Struggling with the Letter: Vives's Preface to *The Instruction of a Christen Woman*," in *Contending Kingdoms: Historical, Psychological, and Feminist Approaches to the Literature of Sixteenth-Century England and France*, ed. Marie-Rose Logan and Peter L. Rudnytsky (Detroit, 1991), 265–97, esp. 272–73.

[38] Valerie Wayne, "Some Sad Sentence: Vives' *Instruction of a Christian Woman*," in *Silent but for the Word: Tudor Women as Patrons, Translators, and Writers of Religious Works*, ed. Margaret Patterson Hannay (Kent, OH, 1985), 16.

Hyrde translation, some combination of readers.[39] No matter who the audience was, a frictional faultline in Vives's comments cannot be ignored: he notes that chastity can be "gyven" and removed just as arbitrarily by "one worde." Who is the "thu" who "take[s] ... gyve[s] ..." and "calle[s]"? The virgin's parents? Her supposed lover? The subject of the action, the "thu" who has such power, certainly is not the woman whose fortunes can change with little advance warning and even less agency on her part. Rather, the actor in this drama of fallen chastity seems to be one who is able either to impart all qualities to a woman or to leave her with nothing. Even more important, and more troubling for the woman in question, is that the judgment the "thu" metes out to her is accomplished through the reading of her body, not through the act of sexual intercourse.

Even if we consider "thu" to be social opinion or the community's voice, we are left wondering how this marker of public note is able to "gyve" our subject something which, according to anatomists, already exists as a physical part of her body. What marks of virginity can be "gyven," apart from confirmation of an unruptured hymen? Similarly, we must question how the sexual status of the virgin can be so easily erased with just "one worde."[40] Given the emphasis Crooke places on the amount of blood present at defloration, it would seem to follow that a single word was not nearly forceful enough to rupture such a strong, yet sinewy, sign of virginity. For all that Vives contends that a woman, or her parents as is more often the case, is the agent in control of her own chastity — "Therfore must we speke somethyng of the ordryng of the body of a virgin" — he writes about a virgin who can be deflowered without ever engaging in intercourse, whose chastity seems to be beyond the limits of any type of "ordryng." What Vives is obviously arguing is that it is the appearance of virginity — the "*Maiden-Blush*" which "argues a spotlesse soule," as Brathwait describes it — which is of greater importance than the actual truth of the virgin's sexuality. As Thomas Tuke notes in his *A Treatise Against Painting*, "It is not enough to be good, but she that is good, must seeme good; she that is chast, must seeme chast." Paraphrasing Jeremiah 3:3, Vives notes, "Our lorde curseth an unchaste woman sayeng: Thou haste the face of an harlotte."[41] This curse, it seems, locates itself in the fact that this woman's outer

---

[39] The massive popularity of Vives's volume is evidenced by the thirty-six editions published in England and the Continent throughout the sixteenth century.

[40] Despite my contention that this "one worde" cannot convert a woman from chaste to sexually active, we cannot ignore the power of such sexually charged language. As Desdemona's inability to say the word "whore" — Am I that name, Iago?" (*Othello*, 4.2.118) — reminds us, the link between women and sexual slander is especially strong in the early modern period. See, among others, Laura Gowing, "Language, Power, and the Law: Women's Slander Litigation in Early Modern London," in *Women, Crime and the Courts in Early Modern England*, ed. Jennifer Kermode and Garthine Walker (Chapel Hill, NC, 1994), 26–47; and Lisa Jardine, " 'Why Should He Call Her Whore'? Defamation and Desdemona's Case," in *Reading Shakespeare Historically* (London, 1996), 19–34.

[41] Vives, *Instruction*, sig. G4ᵛ; Brathwait, *English Gentlewoman*, 217; Thomas Tuke, *A Treatise Against Painting* (London, 1616), sig. D1ᵛ; Vives, *Instruction*, sig. M1ʳ. Erasmus would seem to agree, noting, "The gaye costly apparayalle, the peynted face, the pleasant and mery endityngs of

visage alerts her community to her inner sexual sin. If, as Valeria Finucci writes, "Conduct books for women have the purpose of regulating feminine desire by proposing, and thus promoting, the image of an acceptable desirable woman,"[42] then *Instruction*'s subject need not necessarily be a virgin but must be able to be read as one by those around her.

Unlike the anatomists who asserted that virginity could be found within a woman's body, Vives, as well as Tuke and Brathwait, seems to ignore this concern to concentrate solely on the appearance of virginity. If certain actions, specifically those which contradict the ideal feminine attributes of silence and obedience, will make one appear to be unchaste, we must question whether the opposite can be similarly argued: can certain behavior make an unchaste woman appear to be chaste? Can virginity be assumed, worn as if it were a mask composed of specific movements and speeches? Is this what Thomas Becon is referring to in his "Catechism" when he lists a number of activities young maids should "avoid, if they tender their good name"?[43] As such, the donning of virginity might be seen as somehow akin to the act of courtly *sprezzatura*. If *sprezzatura* relies on the appearance of ease to belie the actual effort necessary to achieve that appearance, the conduct of virginity similarly depends more on upholding the superficial appearance of chastity than on adhering to the physical restrictions which render a woman truly a virgin.

Teaching women how to create a readable chaste body, rather than advising them how actually to remain chaste, seems to be the principal, though unacknowledged, goal of such conduct literature. It is a goal, however, which appears to undermine the idea professed by Vives that "a woman hath no charge to se to but her honestie and chastyte. Wherfore whan she is enfurmed of that she is sufficiently appoynted."[44] While Vives might claim that chastity alone leaves a woman "sufficiently appoynted," his treatise seems far more concerned that the "thu" who notes her appearance is able to easily read her as marked by the outward signs of "honestie" and "chastyte." Similarly, as Tuke and Brathwait underscore, the act of "seeming" virginal — the performance of the outward signs of virginity — takes precedence over the reality of "being" a virgin.

The libel initiated by Frances Howard, the anatomists' debates regarding the existence of the hymen, and the conduct writers' emphasis on maintaining the appearance of virginity exist as separate discourses which surround a similar set of concerns. How can the virgin be successfully and accurately recognized? How can her body best be represented, whether through the anatomical sketches in a medical text or "drawn out" in a courtesy manual, so as to most easily be read? How can

---

yonge men, the propre knackes and gyftes sente to and fro, are playne tokens and sygnes that virginitie dieth"; see Desiderius Erasmus, *The Comparation of A Vyrgin and a Martyr* (1523), trans. Thomas Paynell (London, 1537; facs. repr. Gainesville, 1970), 58.

[42] Valeria Finucci, *The Lady Vanishes: Subjectivity and Representation in Castiglione and Ariosto* (Stanford, 1992), 49.

[43] Thomas Becon, "Catechism" (1564), quoted in Kate Aughterson, ed., *Renaissance Woman: A Sourcebook: Constructions of Feminity [sic] in England* (London, 1995), 27.

[44] Vives, *Instruction*, sig. B2r.

one guard against the possibility of misreading her body and her sexuality? The moments of friction found in these works point to the difficulty inherent in achieving these goals, in determining the equation whereby a body part or a bodily action reflects and guarantees the virginal state. As if to pose a possible answer to this quandary, Ambrose Paré related a story about the "faking" of virginity. William C. Carroll notes that in Paré's example, "Virginity is ... reduced to one of the performing 'arts', constituted by nothing more than a set of manipulable signs."[45] Given Paré's emphasis on the representational performativity of virginity, we might best turn to the theater to examine the ways these rival languages — legal, medical, and courtesy — meet and merge in the dramatic. As such, we can look at the way these questions are addressed in Thomas Middleton and William Rowley's *The Changeling*, a play which places the dilemma of locating the virgin body on center stage.

First licensed for performance in 1622, *The Changeling* — and its main plot — was based on one of the luridly moralistic tales included in John Reynolds's 1621 *The Triumph of God's Revenge against the Crying and Execrable Sin of Willful and Premeditated Murder*. While most of the elements of Reynolds's story remain — romantic intrigue, marital infidelity, jealousy and murder — Middleton and Rowley's drama also includes a number of references to local scandals. Both directly and subtly, the play takes notice of the annulment trial of Frances Howard. Despite the fact that the trial itself had taken place almost a decade before the play was produced, the torrid event was still a part of public memory, having been recently revived as Frances and Carr were released that very year from their six-year imprisonment in the Tower for their roles in the murder of Sir Thomas Overbury.[46]

A close reading of *The Changeling* provides a number of indirect correlations between the troubles haunting the dramatic world of Alicant and those similar tribulations which were uncovered during Frances's most recent trial. A particularly textured link between the play and the Howard scandals can be found in Middleton and Rowley's emphasis on the virginal body.[47] Such a connection seems especially notable in those scenes which focus on the virginity tests administered to both Beatrice-Joanna and her maid Diaphanta. Indeed, Diaphanta's fear that Beatrice-Joanna will "search me, will she, / Like the forewoman of a female jury" echoes the task undertaken by the panel of matrons who examined Frances.[48] In addition,

---

[45] Quoted in Carroll, "The Virgin Not," 296.

[46] For more on this part of Frances's life, see Anne Somerset, *Unnatural Murder: Poison at the Court of James I* (London, 1997).

[47] A. A. Bromham and Zara Bruzzi, in *"The Changeling" and the Years of Crisis, 1619–1624: A Hieroglyph of Britain* (London, 1990), entitle their first chapter "A Contemporary Changeling: Frances Howard," but they place little emphasis on the virginity tests or the substitution of female bodies. For more on the connection between the Howard trials and *The Changeling*, see J. L. Simmons, "Diabolical Realism in Middleton and Rowley's *The Changeling*," *Renaissance Drama* 11 (1980): 135–70, esp.154–63; and Lisa Hopkins, "An Echo of *Hymenaei* in *The Changeling*," *Notes and Queries* 241, n.s. 43 (1996): 184.

[48] Thomas Middleton and William Rowley, *The Changeling*, in *Drama of the English Renaissance 2: The Stuart Period*, ed. Russell A. Fraser and Norman Rabkin (New York, 1976), 4.1.99–100. Subsequent citations are given parenthetically.

the questionable manner by which Beatrice-Joanna "passes" the test — first noting the symptoms exhibited by the virginal Diaphanta, then imitating them for Alsemero, and finally placing Diaphanta in her wedding-night bed — echoes the rumors which circulated around the substitution of another woman for the veiled Frances. While Margot Heinemann, in her political study of Thomas Middleton, claims that the facts of the "notorious Countess of Essex" case could "hardly be staged," the virginity trials in Act 4, scenes 1 and 2 of *The Changeling* disprove such a conclusion.[49] The "reading" of the virgin's body which was enacted in the trial transcripts, encoded in Latin, is here dramatically and vernacularly represented in the theater with Middleton and Rowley's staging of a series of examinations: Beatrice-Joanna's testing of Diaphanta's sexual status, and Alsemero's similar subsequent testing of Beatrice-Joanna.

Though her criticism of the Howard examination is, unfortunately, not specific, Heinemann is clearer about the dramatic rendition of the test, in part agreeing with those critics who have considered *The Changeling*'s virginity-trial scenes "ludicrous, unrealistic and a blemish on the play."[50] However, to disregard these scenes, or to read the centrality of virginity in the play solely as a means to investigate "a religious ideal,"[51] ignores the energy and effort that the playwrights put forth not only in adding these incidents to Reynolds's source material but also in enhancing the detail and texture as they developed the idea. Indeed, Dale B. J. Randall takes to task those critics who would read these tests as absurd, arguing that "The testing which ensues in *The Changeling* is not a blemish, not a strangely unaccountable lapse of taste or decorum on the playwrights' part, but an attempt to give serious, persuasive, interesting, and effective dramatic form — stageable form — to the theme of chastity."[52] Just as the anatomists and conduct writers found themselves genuinely concerned with and perplexed by the task of determining the legibility of the virgin body, we can assume that the dramatists similarly considered the issue to be of legitimate importance. Interestingly, the conclusions that Middleton and Rowley arrive at by the play's close seem as fraught with frictional faultlines as the writings with which their drama intersects.

Having been unfaithful to her new husband with the murderer of her former fiancé, Beatrice-Joanna stumbles upon a vast array of medical paraphernalia in Alsemero's "physician's closet" (4.1.20). Included with the manuscripts and pregnancy tests is a glass labeled "M" and "A merry sleight, but true experiment," designed by

---

[49] Margot Heinemann, *Puritanism and Theatre: Thomas Middleton and Opposition Drama under the Early Stuarts* (Cambridge, 1980), 178. It is unclear whether it is the test itself or the results that Heinemann finds unstageable.

[50] Heinemann, *Puritanism and Theatre*, 178. Heinemann reads the virginity trial scenes as "grotesque . . . Such grotesque indignities are what the wicked bring upon themselves, rather than the lifetime of romantic love they hope for" (178). Such moral indignation at Beatrice-Joanna's behavior seems to match, in many ways, the feelings expressed by seventeenth-century writers like Weldon toward Frances's behavior.

[51] Douglas Duncan, "Virginity in *The Changeling*," *English Studies in Canada* 9 (1983): 26.

[52] Dale B. J. Randall, "Some Observations on the Theme of Chastity in *The Changeling*," *English Literary Renaissance* 14 (1984): 347–66, here 361.

Antoine Mizauld, "to know whether a woman be a maid or not" (4.1.41–45). The combination of the words "merry" and "true" may seem contradictory and fanciful; nevertheless, the reference to Mizauld, a sixteenth-century French scholar and doctor who had written about, among other things, virginity tests, lends scientific certainty and authority to Alsemero's medical experiments. It is not only the name-dropping of Mizauld that serves this legitimizing purpose, however; the medical description of the symptoms is also made explicit. If the party under suspicion is chaste, after drinking a spoonful of the water from Glass M she will "incontinently gape, then fall into a sudden sneezing, last into a violent laughing; else dull, heavy, and lumpish" (4.1.49–51). Beatrice-Joanna, acting perhaps as the proxy for the incredulous audience, initially doubts the validity of such a test; under the guise of testing Diaphanta's virginity, she tests the validity of the Glass M potion itself.[53] Both Beatrice-Joanna and Diaphanta drink from Glass M and, as would be expected if the test were accurate, only Diaphanta is affected. Beatrice-Joanna observes that, as Diaphanta exhibits all the expected symptoms while she remains unmoved:

> Most admirable secret! On the contrary,
> It stirs me not a whit, which most concerns it.
> ... Just in all things and in order
> As if 'twere circumscribed. (4.1.109–12)

Interestingly, the Glass M test seems to combine both the anatomical and courtesy discourses through a performative discourse: it seeks medically to open up on the theatrical stage the inner secrets of the female body through the display of a series of outward signs. If Beatrice-Joanna comes to accept the truth behind the test through her own failure to display any of its effects, we too are led to believe that Glass M, within the world of the play (like the biblical ordeal potion prescribed in Numbers 5:11–31), can accurately determine a woman's sexual status.

Middleton and Rowley's test is designed specifically for the theatrical venue. Unlike the majority of virginity tests, which focus on the color or consistency of a woman's urine or rely on the passage of hours for any visible indications, all the symptoms induced by the Glass M mixture can be visibly enacted on stage in an obvious and pronounced manner. While the specific effects of the Glass M test are original to the play, *The Changeling*'s reliance on this examination belongs to a larger discourse which surrounded such investigations. Laurent Joubert, a sixteenth-century French physician, provides examples of these tests in his 1578 medical treatise, *Erreurs populaires*: "Give her a little powdered lignum aloe to drink or to eat; if she is a virgin she will piss immediately. Item: put on hot coals some broken patience dock leaves, and have the maiden smell the smoke; if she does not bepiss herself she is not a virgin; likewise if she does not become pale from patience dock flowers." While Joubert proceeds to discount such tests as "ill-founded," the tests he does praise — those which seek to probe the vaginal opening in order to dis-

---

[53] Lois E. Bueler, "The Rhetoric of Change in *The Changeling*," *English Literary Renaissance* 14 (1984): 95–113, here 110.

cover if the hymen is ruptured — are also subject to a similar scrutiny. By inserting a candle or other such probe into the woman, Joubert claims that the test itself acts to divorce the woman from her virginity. "And if, upon probing her, the conduit is found to be very narrow, such that the candle will go in only with great difficulty, what will be said? That she is a virgin? Certainly, but she will not be one any longer, after the candle has been inserted."[54] The ultimate conclusion raised by Joubert is that there is no single test that can accurately determine a woman's virginity. As Joubert notes, simply by submitting to the test itself, a woman already compromises her virginity; in the process of proving its existence, she most likely guarantees its destruction.

Raised in Joubert's analysis of these tests is the question of what exactly a virgin is. If one's virginity can be erased with a candle probe, what exactly is the nature of the relationship of virginity to the act of sexual intercourse? Is it the rupturing of the hymen — by whatever means possible — that marks the loss of virginity? Is it merely the appearance of virginity that is satisfactory evidence of its presence? Beatrice-Joanna's performance, as she imitates the true virgin Diaphanta, can be read as raising these same questions: what exactly does a virginity test indicate if a non-virgin can successfully pass herself off as virginal? Marjorie Garber has noted that the symptoms predicted by Glass M are akin to the signs of female orgasm as noted by Freud: gasping, sneezing, laughing, and melancholy.[55] While the forging of such a link is slightly anachronistic, Garber's impulse to consider the faking of an orgasm as comparable to the faking of virginity is worth considering. Indeed, in both cases, the woman in question is performing her own sexuality, be it active and interested or innocent and unknowing, for a specified spectator, according to a script of someone's choosing.

That both types of sexuality can be performed becomes even clearer when we note Alsemero's recounting of Diaphanta's pre-wedding night message from Beatrice-Joanna:

> Her woman came pleading her lady's fears,
> Delivered her for the most timorous virgin
> That ever shrunk at man's name, and so modest
> She charged her weep out her request to me
> That she might come obscurely to my bosom. (4.2.117–21)

As audience members, we are privy to the knowledge that Beatrice-Joanna is far from a "timorous virgin" by this time, but Alsemero believes in the portrait of her

---

[54] Laurent Joubert, *Popular Errors*, trans. and annotated by Gregory David de Rocher (Tuscaloosa, AL, 1989), 210–11, 216. The tests cited by Joubert belong to a long line of similar examinations which predate the early modern period. For examples from the late thirteenth and early fourteenth centuries, see Helen Rodnite Lemay, *Women's Secrets: A Translation of Pseudo-Albertus Magnus's "De Secretis Mulierum" with Commentaries* (Albany, 1992), 126–29; Kathleen Coyne Kelly, *Performing Virginity and Testing Chastity in the Middle Ages* (London, 2000), 28–32.

[55] Marjorie Garber, "The Insincerity of Women," in *Desire in the Renaissance*, ed. Valeria Finucci and Regina Schwartz (Princeton, 1994), 23–26, esp. 25.

that her maid has painted. "Push, modesty's shrine is set in yonder forehead" (4.2.126), he notes when Beatrice-Joanna enters the room, underscoring his belief that he can accurately read her sexual status in her face and reminding us of the words of the conduct book writers. Nevertheless, despite his reliance on his eyes for proof, he does decide to perform the experiments of the anatomists and administer Mizauld's test to her; "I cannot be too sure though," he muses (4.2.127). Just as Beatrice-Joanna appeared virginal to the onlookers, so too can she manipulate her own bodily motions to mimic the actions she had previously noted in Diaphanta. She utters in an aside, "I'm put now to my cunning; th' effects I know, / If I can now but feign 'em handsomely" (4.2.137–38).

"Feign 'em handsomely" she does: Beatrice-Joanna gapes, sneezes, laughs maniacally, and falls into melancholy, and Alsemero's belief in her virginity is guaranteed, at least for the time being. She has, for all purposes, allowed him to read her body as he — and she — wishes to, producing the simulacra of the virginal, for Garber "orgasmic," response.[56] In addition to altering the text of her body so as to satisfy Alsemero's desires, she has also reversed the authorial power dynamic by using her readerly knowledge of Diaphanta's body to produce the illusion that her own body is still under the control of her husband. The question remains, though: does the test actually work? Beatrice-Joanna's feigning of the symptoms demonstrates that, while the test may be medically accurate as demonstrated by Diaphanta's reaction, it collapses with regard to its claim to truly prove a woman a virgin. "Through logic [a set of syllogisms whereby if a woman is a virgin, she will experience a number of reactions] the dramatists undercut the whole notion of a virginity test" which they have encouraged the audience to trust.[57] That is to say, if Glass M is an accurate reader of virginity, Beatrice-Joanna's defloration by the aptly named DeFlores should be uncovered. Alsemero's dependence on his medicine ultimately fails because it relies on the female body to speak its sexuality honestly. The play, as such, asserts what the anatomists and conduct writers must have already suspected: women can counterfeit their reactions or "mask the signs that their bodies should offer as clear signals for men to read."[58]

It is only, in fact, at the close of *The Changeling*, when Beatrice-Joanna's bloodied body is dragged out of the closet by DeFlores, that the violation her body has suffered can be accurately read; not only does her bloodstained body provide for legibility, but it also serves as a tangible reminder of the displayed post-wedding night sheets present in myth and community ritual. Her presence on stage is a dramatic reenactment of the transformation Crooke depicts: the rupturing of the

---

[56] Garber, "Insincerity of Women," 27.

[57] Bueler, "Rhetoric of Change," 111 n. 23.

[58] Deborah Burks, "'I'll Want my Will Else': *The Changeling* and Women's Complicity with their Rapists," *ELH* 62 (1995): 759–90, here 779. Burks, like many critics of *The Changeling*, positions herself in the place of Alsemero, expressing the fear that she too has been duped by Beatrice-Joanna. She writes, "The audience is as desperate that the truth be known as the characters are to discover that truth" (778).

virgin seal which produces "paine and effusion of blood."[59] The lifeless, unchanging body — the body being examined under the gaze of an anatomy theater or being painted by the author of a conduct book — is the only one which is legible; although, as we have seen, even this static body can elude the desire for legibility. Alsemero's moan upon uncovering Beatrice-Joanna's duplicity — "oh cunning devils! / How should blind men know you from fair-faced saints?" (5.3.108–9) — only reiterates both the futility of reading the female body successfully and the ability of those "cunning devils" to mask themselves and perform as "fair-faced saints."

By placing *The Changeling* in dialogue with the anatomists' treatises, the courtesy manuals, and the Howard annulment transcripts, poetry, and letters, we are left with the knowledge that reading a woman's virginity is a task which seems far to surpass the extensive array of available tools which have been assembled. Virginity, as noted from Beatrice-Joanna's re-enactment of it, is less a state of sexual innocence than a performing art whose outward signs can be gleaned from and imitated through astute and intelligent observation. For the single woman — or the historical and fictional married women, like Frances Howard or Beatrice-Joanna, who seek to still occupy the role of virgin despite having physically forfeited that position — the importance of being, or seeming to be, a virgin cannot be overstated. As Juan Luis Vives has noted, a woman who maintains her virginity retains all familial and personal graces and gifts; the woman who fails to preserve it — or, equally important, cannot adequately perform the role — loses not only the hymeneal membrane but suffers as well the loss of the potential social, economic, and political benefits afforded the virginal single woman. The magnitude of the project of making female virginity identifiable and verifiable — the multitude of attempts to define it, to dissect it, to describe it — falls short of its intended goal, providing contradictory conclusions about the ambiguity of a body whose very being is supposed to be pure, whole, and ultimately legible.

Mara Amster
Randolph-Macon Women's College

---

[59] Crooke, *Microcosmographia*, 223 [sic].

INDEX

"Acte to Prevent the Murthering of Bastard Children," 196, 199
An Account of Marriage, 82
adultery, 68–69, 121
Aethelthyth. *See* Etheldreda
Aethelwold, St., 11, 13
Agatha, St., 24, 27, 28
Agnes, St., 26, 27, 28, 29, 30, 37, 150
Alençon courtship, 105
Ambrose, St., 26, 27
Anastasia, St., 27
Anatomy of Mortality, 160
anchoresses, 36–37
androgyny, xvii, 112, 113, 114, 133, 135–36, 139
Andromeda myth, 105
Anglo-Norman England
　Norman abbots, 1–4
　Norman conquest, 1, 2
　Norman ecclesiastics, 1, 23
　pre-Conquest Saxon women, 1
　saints' lives, 1
Anglo-Saxons, 1, 3, 5, 6, 11
Anne, St., 35
annulment, 211–12, 213, 215, 227, 232
antifeminist tradition, 127
Ariosto, Ludovico, 170
　Orlando Furioso, xviii, 174, 175–81, 182, 185, 190
Aristotle, 219
Armesworde (wall at), 13

Arthur, King, legends, xii, xv, 41–61, 140–41. *See also* Malory, Thomas
astrology, 135, 139
Audree, St., 11–14, 18
Augustine of Hippo, St., 31, 34
Aylmer, John, *Harborowe for Faithfull and Trewe Subjectes*, 103–4, 107

Bacon, Francis, "Of Marriage And Single Life," 83
Bakhtin, Mikhail, 220
ballads, 66–67
Bandello, 174
Barker, Jane, "A Virgin Life," 83
Barthes, Roland, xii
The Batchelor's Delight, 82
The Batchelor's Directory, 66
Baudrillard, Jean, x
Becon, Thomas, "Catechism," 226
Bede, Venerable, Life of Aethelthryth, 4, 5, 12. *See also* hagiography
Behn, Aphra, 83
Belsey, Catherine, 202–3
Benedictine monasticism, 2, 11. *See also* monastic houses
Benson, Larry D., 138
bereavement. *See* mourning
Berger, Harry Jr., 182
Bible, xii, 18, 103, 127, 136–37, 223, 225, 229
birth. *See* childbirth
bishops, role of, 2, 6, 9, 14, 17, 73

Boccaccio, Giovanni, 130–31
bodies, 121, 223
   bride's, 219
   criminal, 205
   dead, 205, 208
   and early modern anatomy theaters, 218–22
   in early modern science, 204
   female, x, xi–xii, xiv, 13, 14, 15–16, 17, 25–26, 43, 101, 119, 121, 122, 125, 128, 132, 150, 158, 183, 204, 207, 209–10, 212, 214–19, 222, 226–27, 229, 231
   male, 212, 214, 219
   marital, 122, 124
   as means of self-regeneration, 16
   spiritually perfected, 16
   virginal, 121, 212, 217–28, 222–23, 225–28, 232
   widow's, 121–22, 125, 128–29
Bokenham, Osbern, 23, 33–34, 38
   Legendys of Hooly Wummen, 23, 34
Book of the Courtier, 158, 223–24
Bourdieu, Pierre, 121, 122, 128
Bouwsma, William J., 156
Branagh, Kenneth, *Much Ado about Nothing*, 189–91
Brathwaite, Richard, 222–23, 225, 226
   The English Gentlewoman, 156
Breitenberg, Mark, 150, 152
Bride, St. *See* Brigid, St.
The Bride, 67
Bride of Christ, ix, xiii, 22, 26–30, 38, 216
bridegroom (heavenly), 10, 26, 27, 30
brides, 218, 221
   as trope, 26, 37
Brigid, St., 16, 17
Brown, Wendy, 170
Bullinger, Henry, 71
Bullough, Geoffrey, 174
Burdet, William
   A Wonder of Wonders, 194, 201–4
   title page, 195
Butler, Judith, 44–45, 46, 97, 112
Bynum, Caroline Walker, 208

Camden, William, 106, 108
Capellanus, Andreas, *Art of Courtly Love*, 141
Capgrave, John, xv, 23, 28, 30–33, 34–35, 38–39
   Abbreuiacion of Chronicles, 31
   Life of St. Katherine of Alexandria, 23, 30–33
   Solace of Pilgrims, 31
Carr, Robert, xix, 213, 214, 215, 227
Carroll, William C., 227
Cartwright, Jane, 149, 164
   "Jane Cartwright," 148 fig. 1
   See also A Young Woman
Cartwright, William, 149, 150, 163 fig. 5, 164
Castiglione, Baldassare, *Book of the Courtier*, 158, 162, 223–24
Catherine de' Medici. *See* de' Medici, Catherine
Catherine of Aragon, 224
Catholic Church, 215–16. *See also* virginity
Cavanagh, Sheila, 183
Cavendish, Margaret, 83
Caxton, *Golden Legend*, 23
Cecilia, St., 7, 27, 37
celibacy, xv, xvi, 65–66
   as choice, 81, 82, 94
   in marriage, 11
   opposition to, 68
   as Protestant ideal, 83, 95
   recommended, 70
   in relationship to money-lending, 92
Certain Sermons or Homilies, 170–71
Chamberlain, John, 214
charitable bequests, 73
charity, xiii, 35, 72, 73–74, 76, 89, 95
Chartier, Roger, 210
Chaucer, Geoffrey, xvii, 35, 119–32, 133–46

Canterbury Tales, 122, 123, 126–28
  Friar's Tale, xvii, 121, 123, 126
  Knight's Tale, 123
  Legend of Good Women, 122, 123, 124–26, 128
  Nun's Priest Tale, 123
  Parson's Tale, 121
  Troilus and Criseyde, 32, 122, 123, 126–32, 133–46
  Wife of Bath's Prologue and Tale, xvii, 122–23, 126–28, 132–46
childbirth, 120, 193, 196–98, 201, 208
  premature, 206
  procreative behavior (decline in), 66
  out of wedlock, ix, xiv, xviii–xix, 194–96, 197–99, 202, 203
  See also illegitimacy; miscarriage
children, 197
  illegitimate, 196–99
  stillborn, 206
  See also infanticide; paternity
chivalry, 42, 54
  ideal of, 60
  chivalric career, 53, 55
  chivalric identity, xv, 49, 53, 54, 56, 61
  chivalric society, 42–44, 50, 60
  knight–lady relationship, 43, 44, 61
  See also knighthood
Christ, 37, 208, 210, 216
Christine, St., 27
church, role of, ix, xiv–xv, 1–19, 21–39, 135, 137, 140. *See also* Protestantism
Clark, Alice, 173
class, 5, 36, 49–53, 84–85, 143, 170–72, 174, 178, 182. *See also* social status
classical mythology, xvi, 105, 111, 112, 124–26, 141–42, 223
Cleopatra, xvii, 122–26
Clifford, Lady Anne, 158–64
  family of, 160
Coldingham, 11

Conchubranus, hagiographer, 5, 15
conduct books, for women, 66, 83, 129, 156–57, 160, 217, 222–26, 227, 229, 231, 232. *See also* Vives, Juan Luis
Conquerer, the. *See* William I
Constitutions and Canons Ecclesiastical, 213
Cooke, Elisabeth, 149
courtly culture, 42, 130, 131, 141, 182. *See also* knighthood; romance
courtly love, 42
courtship, 175
crafts, 86, 90, 133, 173
Cressy, David, 150
crime, by women, 193–210. *See also* infanticide
Criseyde, xvii, 32, 122, 123, 126–32
Crooke, Helkiah, 220–22, 225, 231–32
cross-dressing, ix, 112, 113

Danes, in England, 13
  grave robbers, 14
  pagans and raiders, 1, 6, 11, 14, 15
  pirates, 6
Daniel, Samuel, 160
Darerca, St. *See* Modwenna
de Silva, Guzman, 100–1
de' Medici, Catherine, 155
death rituals, 149–50, 164
  performance of, 152–56
  See also widows
debt, 85–96
Declaration of Oxford, of Anne Greene, 194
deconstruction, 128, 135
Deedes Against Nature and Monsters by Kinde, 199–200
Dekker, Thomas, 79
  The Roaring Girl, 115
Delany, Sheila, 201
desire
  feminine, 169, 175, 177, 185, 189–90, 226

masculine, 130m 178–80, 190, 218
  performance of, 190
  See also homosociality
Desmond, Marilyn, 125
Devereux, Robert, earl of Essex, 211, 212–14, 211–14
Dido, xvii, 122–26, 128
Dinshaw, Carolyn, 128
A Discourse Concerning the Celibacy of the Clergy, 83
A Discourse of Marriage and Wiving, 155
A Discourse of the Married and the Single Life, 82
divine retribution, 4
divorce, 213. *See also* annulment
Dolan, Frances E., 204, 207
Dolce, Lodovico, 155
Douglas, Mary, x, 121–22, 219–20
dowry, xiii, 72–74, 89, 90–91, 95, 120
Dudley, Robert, earl of Leicester, 105, 106, 110, 111, 112
Dulwich Picture Gallery, 147, 149

Edgar, King, 11–12, 14
educational endowments, by women, 36
Edward the Confessor, 2
Edward I, 3
Edward III, 34
Ehrlich's Blackstone, 200
Elisabeth Cartwright, 148 fig. 1, 149
Elizabeth I, xii, xiv, xvi, 82, 97, 100–15, 167, 172, 194, 218
  as virgin goddess, 106
  queenship debate, 103
Elizabethan comedy, 97, 99, 102
Ely, see of, 4, 11, 12, 13, 14. *See also* monastic houses
embodiment, 121, 129–31, 135, 138, 223
  of marriage, 124
  of widowed voice, 127
emigration, 68, 76, 77, 78, 80–81, 93, 95

The English Gentlewoman, 156–58, 222
  title page, 159 fig. 3
English religious houses. *See* monastic houses
English royal abbesses, 5
Epistola Adversus Jovinianum, 136
Etheldreda (Aethelthryth, Audrey), St., 1, 3, 4, 11–15, 18
Euphemia, St., 28
execution, 193, 200–1, 203, 204, 208

Fair Unknown motif, 49
female bonding, 98, 107, 111–13, 114, 168, 169, 170
Ferster, Judith, 138
feudalism, 176, 180
fin' amours. *See* courtly love
Finucci, Valeria, 177–78, 226
The First Blast of the Trumpet Against the Monstrous Regiment of Women, 103
fore-destination, 24, 25, 30
Foucault, Michel, 45, 206
Freud, Sigmund, 230
Frye, Northrop, 97, 99

Galen, 219
Garber, Marjorie, 230, 231
Gascoigne, George, 105
gender, concept, 44–45, 113, 121, 161–62
Geoffrey of Burton, 5, 15
Gilbert, St., 31, 34
Gilte Legende, 23, 35
Gittings, Claire, 156
Goldburch peak, 11
Gorboduc, 105
Gottfried, Barbara, 137
Gower, John, 140
Graunt, John, 79
Greene, Anne, xviii, 193–210
  Anne des Grez, 210
Greenhill, John, 149
guilds, women's membership of, xiv, 173

Gwilliam, Tassie, 218

hagiography, xiv, xv, xix, 1–19, 21–39
 Anglo-Saxon, 5
 female, 6
 Norman, 11
 hagiographic corpus (texts), 31, 34, 36
 renunciation, 7
Half Humankind, 198
An Harborowe for Faithfull and Trewe Subjectes, 103–4
Harling, Anne, 35–36, 38
Harrington, John, 170, 174–76, 180–81
Heinemann, Margot, 228
Henry I, 4, 11
Henry VIII, 212, 216
Henryson, Robert, 132
Hereward rebellion, 4
Hering, Francis, 79
Hervey, Bishop, 11
heterosexuality, xvi, 45, 97, 99, 111, 113
Hobbes, Thomas, 81, 96
Hodges, Thomas, 68
Hogdson, Jane, 150
An Homily on the State of Matrimony, 101
homosocial relationships
 male, 51, 54
 female, 59, 107, 111, 114
 homosociality, 170, 182
Howard, Lady Frances, xviii, xix, 211–32
husband, 120, 123, 149, 213, 231
 death of, 154
 widow's role as, 122
hymen, as marker of virginity, 219–22, 225, 230
Hymenaei, 212, 217–18

Ignatius of Antioch, St., 24
illegitimacy, 196–200

incest taboo, 47
infanticide, 194–97, 203, 210
inheritance, xvi, 72, 73, 84, 86, 91–92, 120
Instruction of a Christen Woman, 224–26, 232

Jackson, Mark, 197
jacobean usury statute of 1624, 92
Jacobus de Voragine, *Golden Legend*, 22–24, 27
James I, xix, 211, 213
Jerome, St., 136–37
Jones, Ann Rosalind, 168–69, 223
Jonson, Ben, *Hymenaei*, 212, 217–18, 219
Joubert, Laurent, 229–30
Juliana, St., 27, 36, 37
Justina, St., 28

Karras, Ruth Mazo, 168–69
Katherine of Alexandria, St., xv, 1, 7, 21–39
 Katerine, 37
 Katherine Wheel, 22
kept women, ix, xi, 69
Klapisch-Zuber, Christiane, 155
knighthood, xv, xvii, 41–61, 140–41, 143, 175, 177
Knox, John, 107
 The First Blast of the Trumpet Against the Monstrous Regiment of Women, 103
Kowaleski, Maryanne, 167

labor, agricultural, ix, xvi, 90
ladies' clause, 44, 46, 58
Laqueur, Thomas, 219
Late Middle English Prose Katherine, 21–23, 28–30, 32, 35
Laud Charity, 73
Laud, William, Archbishop of Canterbury, 73
The Law's Resolutions of Women's Rights, 66, 167

lay status, xv, 33, 36
lesbians, ix, xi
A Letter Sent by the Maydens of London, 168
Levin, Richard A., 189
Liber Eliensis, 4, 11, 12
Life of St. Aethelthryth, 4
Lincoln, see of, 4
Llewellyn, Nigel, 149
London, see of, 2, 4, 7
Lotman, Jurij, xii
Loughlin, Mary H., 220
Lucy, St., 26, 27, 37
Lumiansky, R. M., 138
Lydgate, John, 34
Lyly, John, xvi, 97–115
   Campaspe, 99, 107, 108, 110–11, 114
   Endymion, 99, 109, 113
   Gallathea, 98, 99, 104, 110, 111–14
   Sappho and Phao, 99, 108, 110, 113–14

Macherey, Pierre, xii, xix
maidenhood. See virginity
Maids and Mistresses, 168
The Maids Complaint Against the Batchelors, 69
maidservants, 168, 174, 181–82, 185, 191
   masquerading as mistresses, 174–75m 183–85, 187–90
male bonding, 42, 45, 54–55, 114, 182
Malory, Sir Thomas, xv, 41–61
   Arthuriad, 41–43, 46, 48, 54, 56, 57
   "Tale of Sir Gareth of Orkney," xv, 49–55
Map of Mortality, 160
Margaret, St., 1, 27, 34, 36, 37
marriage, ix, xv, xvi, 3, 5, 41, 42, 43, 46, 48, 55, 56, 57, 60, 65–96, 97–115, 119–20, 122–25, 127, 133–38, 140–46, 156, 160, 167–68, 171, 172, 173, 175, 191, 197–98, 200, 205, 209, 212, 232
   annulment of, 212–13, 215, 227
   consummation of, 211, 213, 218, 220
   deferred, xiii, 55, 67, 69, 71, 74, 76, 82, 84, 93, 94–95, 100–1, 103, 106, 113, 114
   divorce, 213
   female sovereignty in, 134, 138, 142, 144–45
   impediments to, 70 (financial), 71 (migration), 75, 77 (disease), 79 (individualism), 82
   marital obligations, 11
   marital-type bond, 26, 27
   medieval concepts of, 122
   as monogamous, 66
   as necessary, 99, 103
   opportunities, 68, 74, 77
   prevention of, 74, 75
   Protestant marital ideal, 83, 95
   remarriage, 120, 123, 127, 130, 155, 213
   as sacrifice, 112
   shifts in, 65
   as social institution, 66
   and social status, 171, 174–75
   spiritual, xv, 22, 25, 28, 29, 30, 32, 37–38
   as unfavorable to men, 56
   wedding proliferation, 48
   withholding, 55
Marriage Duty Act, 69
marriage portion, 72–74, 95
Marriage Promoted, 73–74
martyrdom, xiv, xv, 6, 12, 22, 23–26, 28, 207
   as alchemy, 24
   martyr-to-be (-in-waiting), 24, 25, 32
   martyrological corpus (text), 25–27, 29
   as traditional, 38
Mary, Queen of Scots, 102
Mary, Virgin, 29, 208

Mary Magdalen, St., 34
Mary I Tudor, 102–3, 224
Maurice, bishop, 6
medicine, 212, 214, 217, 218–22, 226, 228–30, 232
men
 feminization of, 144, 145
 masculine memory, 149–50, 152, 158, 161
 masculine moral authority, 15
 masculine power, 138
 masculine rivalry, 177, 181–82, 188
 sexuality, 213–14
 single, 122
menstruation, 204, 220–21
Mercurius Politicus, 194
Microcosmographia, 220–22, 225, 231
Middleton, Thomas, 65
 The Changeling (with Rowley), xix, 211, 227–32
 The Roaring Girl (with Dekker), 65, 115
midwifery, 206, 214
miracles
 conventional, 6
 corpse (incorrupt body), 13–14
 health-giving spring, 14
 indivisible sarcophagus, 14
 liberation of Brihstan, 4
 posthumous, 13–14
 resurrection (of pig), 18
 severed head, 6
 silver cup, 16–17
 transformations (Modwenna), 15
 vengeance, 4, 5, 12
miscarriage, 202, 206
misogyny. *See* patriarchy
Mizauld, Antoine, 229, 231
Modwenna, St., 1, 3, 4–5, 7, 15–18
 cult of, 15
monastic houses, 1–4, 7, 11
monasticism, 2, 10, 11, 14, 35–37, 83, 180, 181, 216. *See also* nuns; virginity
Monenna, St. *See* Modwenna, St.

money-lending, xii, xiv, xvi, 65–96
 formal, 87, 93
 as income-generating, 89, 90
 for individual gain, 93, 96
 as obligatory, 91, 94, 96
monks, 3
More, Henry
 Map of Mortality, 160
mortality, 78–81
mothers, 66, 156, 196–97, 200, 209, 211–13, 221
 as mourners, 154
 sexuality of, 198–201
 single, 194–210
mourning, xvii–xviii, 130, 147–64
 auto-mourning, 150, 158, 164
 pre-posthumous, 149–50, 164
 See also death rituals; gender; widows
Mrs. Jane Cartwright, 148, fig. 1, 149, 164

Nedham, Marchamont, 201
never married, status, ix, xi, xii, 65–66, 75, 84, 93, 96, 167
Newes From the Dead, or a True and Exact Narration of the Miraculous Deliverance of Anne Greene, 194, 201, 204–7
Niccholes, Alexander, 155
Norman Conquest, 1, 2, 3, 4, 11
nuns, ix, xiv, 3, 6, 10, 11, 13, 14, 16, 18, 19, 33, 36, 180, 181, 216; *see also* virginity

Observations in Midwifery, 203
Ortner, Sherry, 172
Osbert of Clare, 2
Osith, St., 1, 3, 4, 6–10, 18
 cult of, 7
Ovid, *Metamorphoses*, 158

Paré, Ambrose, 220, 221, 222, 227
Parker, Patricia, 219
passio, 21–25, 27, 30

paternity, 198, 217
patriarchy, xi, xii, 6, 30, 46, 48, 101, 110, 120, 127, 152, 161–62, 187, 198
patrilineage, 217
Paul, St., xii, 6, 136
Pentecostal Oath, 44–46, 54, 58
Percival, Florence, 124
Percival, Thomas, 203
Perry, Blanche, 82
Peter, St., 2, 6
Petrarch, 107
Petrarchan motifs, 107
Petty, William, 194, 204
Philip II of Spain, 100–1
Pinney, Hester, 85–86
plague, 11, 68, 77, 79–80, 93, 95
Pointon, Marcia, 160–61
portraiture, xii, xvii–xviii, xix, 147–64
poverty, 71, 72, 73, 74–75, 76, 120, 121, 123, 197
    Elizabethan Poor Law, 74
    Overseers of the Poor, 74
    See also social status
predestination. See fore-destination
pregnancy, 198, 201, 204, 205–6, 208
    at marriage, xiii
    concealed, 196, 209
    mystical, 208
    testing of, 228
    unmarried, 76, 196, 198, 201. See also illegitimacy
    See also miscarriage
Price, Ann, 196
primogeniture, 198
Prior, Mary, 173
property, ecclesiastical, 2–3, 7
    women and, xiii, xiv, xix, 6, 10, 12, 13, 14, 35, 71–72, 92, 120–21, 143, 155, 216–17
    See also dowry
Prose Lancelot (French), 58
prostitutes, ix, xi, xii, xiii, 102, 199
prostitution, 199
Protestant Reformation, 167, 191, 210

Protestantism, 67, 68, 69, 70, 83, 95, 101, 167, 181, 191
Prouty, Charles, 174

Randall, Dale B. J., 228
rape, xvii, 25, 46, 105, 107, 110, 111, 140–41
    sexual aggression, 12
    symbolic, 14
Read, Thomas, 206
reading, by women, 16, 33–39, 83, 127, 129–30, 156, 158, 160
relics, 6, 11, 14
remarriage, xii, xiii, xvii, 120–21, 123, 127, 130, 155, 156, 160. See also widowhood, widows
Restoration period, 66, 75
Richard, Bishop of London, 4, 6
Ridyard, S. J., 1
Robbins, Andria, 150
Roman de la Rose, 138
romance, 49
Rowlands, Samuel, 67
Rowley, William
    The Changeling, xix, 227–32

Sackville, Thomas and Thomas Norton, *Gorboduc*, 105
saints
    Anglo-Saxon virgin saints, 3, 4
    saint's revenge, 6
    saint's passion, 21–25, 27, 30. See also passio
    See also under individual saints
sanctity
    female, 17, 25
    of queens, 5
Sawday, Jonathan, 222
Schiesari, Juliana, 153–54
Schofield, Roger, 65, 80, 93
Scrambler, Martha, 199
Sedgwick, Eve, 44
servants, ix, xiii, xiv, xvi, xviii, xix, 72, 73, 76, 78, 82, 84, 86, 90, 168, 170, 173–75, 177, 181,

185, 190, 191, 196, 202, 206, 210. *See also* maidservants
sex ratio, 68, 76–81
sexual promiscuity
 of men, 69
 in the royal court, 68
Sexburgh, St., 13
Shakespeare, William, 67, 99, 102, 107, 114
 All's Well That Ends Well, xvi
 Antony and Cleopatra, 98
 As You Like It, 97–98, 107, 108, 113
 Comedy of Errors, xvi
 Henry VI, 98
 Love's Labor's Lost, xvi
 Macbeth, 98
 Measure For Measure, xvi, 102, 110
 Much Ado About Nothing, xviii, xix, 170, 174, 181, 185–91
 Othello, 114
 Taming of the Shrew, xiii
 Twelfth Night, 114
Silberman, Lauren, 181, 184
social status, 182, 202
 of males, 177, 181–82
 transcendence of, 144
Sowernam, Esther, 167–68
Spenser, Edmund, 170, 174
 Faerie Queene, xviii, 181–85, 186, 190
spinsters, ix, xiii, 198
 satirical attacks on, 69
 as wealthy money-lenders, 86
Sponsa Christi. *See* Bride of Christ
Stallybrass, Peter, 218
Staten, Henry, 150, 158
Statius, *Thebaid*, 130
Stone, Lawrence, 216
Strocchia, Sharon, 152
Strode, George
 Anatomy of Mortality, 160
Stuart period. *See* Tudor/Stuart period
subject, female, x, 3, 6, 12, 18, 26, 30, 109, 132, 135, 169, 170, 203

Swetnam, Joseph, 102, 198

Tale of Florent, 140
Tale of Ginevra, 175–80
taxation, 69
Taylor, Ann, 160
Thorton, Alice, 84
'Tis Merrie When Gossips Meete, 67
Todd, Jane, 206
A Treatise of Marriage, 68
Triptych Picture of Lady Anne Clifford, 158, 159 fig. 4, 161–62, 164
Trojan War, legends, 1, 126–32, 133–46
Tudor/Stuart period
 migration patterns, 76, 80
 social system, 66
 women's work in, 85
Tuke, Thomas, 225, 226

Ursula, St., 27

van Belcamp, Jan, 158
Vie Seinte Audree, 4, 11
Vie Seinte Modwenna, 4, 15, 17
Vie Seinte Osith, 4, 6
vill of Chich, 6
Virgil, 125
Virgin Mary, 208, 210
virginity, xiii, xiv, xv, 1, 3, 5–6, 7, 11, 12–14, 25–26, 27, 121, 207–8, 212, 214–17, 219, 220–22, 224–26, 228, 230
 tests of, xiv, xviii, xix, 121, 188, 211–32
 virgin martyrs, xiv, 3, 5, 6, 12, 21, 25–28, 30
 vocational, 27, 28, 37
 See also body; celibacy; hymen
Vita beati Eadwardi, 2
Vives, Juan Luis, *Instruction of a Christian Woman*, 153, 223, 224–26, 232
Vulgate Bible, 137

wage earning, ix, 72, 74, 77–78, 84, 85, 90, 173
Wandesford, Alice. *See* Thornton, Alice
war, and marriage, 68, 77, 78, 80–81, 93, 95
Watkins, Richard
  Newes from the Dead, 194, 204–7
Webster, John, *Duchess of Malfi*, 114
Weldon, Sir Anthony, 215
Westminster, see of, 2
widowhood, widows, ix, xi, xii–xiii, xiv, xvii–xviii, xix, 119–32, 133–34, 135, 147–64, 173
  identity of, 133–34
  as mourners, 129, 147–64. *See also* mourning
  sexuality of, 124–25
  social status of, 120–24, 127, 155–56, 164

  percentage of, 154
Wilfrid, bishop, 11, 14
William I, 2–4
Willughby, Percival, 199, 203
witchcraft, 196
wives, 66, 98, 101–2, 125, 133–34, 142, 144, 156, 199, 212–13
  as mourners, 154
  See also widows
women, exchange of, 47–48, 112
A Wonder of Wonders, Being a Faithful Narrative and True Relation of one Anne Greene, 194–95, 201–4
  title page, 195
writing, by women, 11, 33, 168
Wrightson, Keith, 171
Wycliffe, 137

A Young Woman, called Mrs. Cartwright, 151 fig. 2